When Death Do Us Part

Understanding and Interpreting the Probate Records of Early Modern England

When Death Do Us Part

Understanding and Interpreting the Probate Records of Early Modern England

Edited by

TOM ARKELL
NESTA EVANS
and
NIGEL GOOSE

A LOCAL POPULATION STUDIES SUPPLEMENT

Published in 2000 by
LEOPARD'S HEAD PRESS LIMITED
1–5 Broad Street, Oxford, OX1 3AW

© Local Population Studies
Department of Humanities, University of Hertfordshire, Hertfordshire WD2 8AT

ISBN 0 904920 42 9

*The publication of this volume has been
assisted by an award from the
Marc Fitch Fund,
which is gratefully acknowledged.*

Typeset by Cambrian Typesetters, Frimley, Surrey
Printed in Great Britain

Contents

List of Contributors

TOM ARKELL, member of the Editorial Board of *Local Population Studies* and former Senior Lecturer, Warwick University

JEFF COX, Senior Lecturer in Inorganic Chemistry, University of Wolverhampton

NANCY COX, Honorary Research Fellow in History, University of Wolverhampton

AMY ERICKSON, Kerstin Hesselgren Visiting Research Professor, Uppsala University

NESTA EVANS, Honarary Senior Research Fellow, University of Surrey Roehampton and Associate Lecturer, Open University

NIGEL GOOSE, Professor of Social and Economic History and Director of the Centre for Regional and Local History, University of Hertfordshire

MARY HODGES, former Principal Lecturer, Oxford Brookes University

BERNARD JENNINGS, Emeritus Professor of Adult Education, University of Hull

CHRISTOPHER MARSH, Reader in the School of Modern History, Queen's University Belfast

CHRISTINE NORTH, County Archivist, Cornwall

MARK OVERTON, Professor of Economic and Social History, University of Exeter

ANN TARVER, former Leverhulme Research Associate, Warwick University, and part-time Tutor, University of Keele

BARRY TRINDER, Senior Lecturer in Industrial Archaeology, University College Northampton

MARGARET SPUFFORD, Research Professor of Local and Social History, University of Surrey Roehampton

PETER SPUFFORD, Reader in Economic History, University of Cambridge, and Chairman of the British Record Society

EDMUND WEINER, Principal Philologist, Oxford English Dictionary.

List of Tables

List of Figures

Preface

This book springs from a proposal by Margaret and Peter Spufford for a companion volume to *Surveying the People* on probate records, but as often happens in such cases, its final format is quite unlike the original conception and it has taken much longer to emerge than was initially anticipated. In the end, the lack of a comprehensive volume providing guidance for either professional or amateur researchers on the possibilities and problems involved in using probate records encouraged us to extend the scope of this book.

When death do us part is now divided into three sections. The first introduces the legal context that produced our surviving probate records and discusses the uses and potential for historical study of the three principal sources—wills, inventories and accounts—and the reliability of the prices encountered in the two latter. It is extended by the appendices of selected extracts concerning probate from various ecclesiastical Canons and Acts of Parliament and of sample probate documents. The second part contains four very different approaches to studying wills and two explorations of the potential of probate accounts. Where the latter have survived in significant numbers, they remain a greatly underused source which we hope that this volume will help rectify by encouraging their study in combination with other records. The third section is devoted to probate inventories, but not in isolation, since three chapters demonstrate some of the benefits awaiting those who tackle them with other sources, while two others explore a relatively novel approach to studying inventories that concentrates on their language.

Despite the wide coverage of these chapters, the editors remain conscious of their incompleteness, in particular concerning those topics that were discussed and drafted by potential authors but never came to fruition. In addition, we have not managed to provide a coherent discussion of the main opportunities and pitfalls of the large-scale computerisation of probate records, even though two contributions derive from it.

Most chapters have been written specially for this volume, but the four that stem in varying degrees from earlier versions deserve their wider exposure. Margaret Spufford's chapter comes from a *Local Population Studies* article published in 1971, which was incorporated three years later into her *Contrasting communities*, but remains as relevant here as it was on its first appearance nearly 30 years ago. Chapter 8 by

Christopher Marsh is condensed from a longer one published in 1990 in *The records of the nation*, a book that also included another chapter which Amy Erickson has incorporated in part into her current contribution. The parentage of Peter Spufford's chapter can be traced back to 1994 when it appeared in French in *Annales HSS*, but it has been greatly modified since. We are grateful to the holders of the copyright of the original versions of these chapters for permission to print them in revised versions here.

We also wish to thank Joan Thirsk and Keith Wrightson for their support and encouragement at an early stage, Anne Tarver for supplying our map of the dioceses, Roger Penhallurick for drawing the map of Cornwall, the staff of Cornwall Record Office for helping with Latin transcriptions and translations and The National Portrait Gallery for permission to reproduce the painting used for our cover. Crown copyright material is reproduced by permission of the controller of HMSO. In addition, we are grateful to Cornwall Record Office, Gloucestershire Record Office, Hampshire Record Office, Hertfordshire Archives and Local Studies, Lichfield Record Office, Nottinghamshire Archives, Suffolk Record Office, West Sussex Record Office and Worcester Record Office for permission to reproduce the texts of documents in their care.

A book of this nature inevitably acquires a mounting list of indebtedness during its development. For a start we thank sincerely all our authors for offering us their contributions so willingly and for their patience when we suggested that they might be altered; the close proximity of content between so many chapters posed numerous time-consuming editorial problems which, without their forebearance, would have generated more frustration and delay. We are equally grateful to the other members of the editorial board of *Local Population Studies* for supporting this publication from its inception and for commenting very helpfully on earlier drafts of many chapters, particularly Andrew Hinde and Matthew Woollard. Matthew also provided invaluable help in collating the bibliography and standarduising both textual and footnoting conventions. We owe Kevin Schürer special thanks for his prominent role in our initial discussions, which established the book's framework and stiffened our resolve to complete it. Finally, our gratitude is perennial to Roy Stephens of the Leopard's Head Press for his unfailing support and to the Marc Fitch Fund for a very generous award towards the printing costs of *When death do us part*.

PART I

Probate Records

1

The Probate Process

TOM ARKELL

Church courts

To understand the probate process in early modern England and Wales and the documents which have survived from it, we need to know something about the church courts that were responsible for it. They were established separately from the secular courts during William the Conqueror's reign and appear to have reached their zenith by the early-sixteenth century.

The church courts operated under canon law, working in a loose form of partnership and sporadic rivalry with the secular civil and common law courts. They were concerned mainly with ensuring that the church was administered efficiently and that sound moral behaviour was maintained among its adherents. Their responsibility ranged from the discipline of the clergy, the fabric of church buildings and their seating, licensing teachers and preachers, containing recusancy, the non-payment of tithes and other church dues to defamation, matrimonial disputes, sexual misconduct among the laity and testamentary business.[1] The main powers of the church courts derived from their moral sanctions of excommunicating wrong-doers or shaming them with humiliating public penances.[2] The secular courts normally tried the more serious moral offences, such as rape, because they alone could imprison or execute the guilty.

The major religious and political developments of the Tudor and Stuart period affected significantly the operation of the church courts, but scarcely reduced their influence before the later seventeenth century. The Henrician Reformation of the 1530s broke with Rome, of course, and established the monarch as Supreme Head of the new

---

[1] Helmholtz, *Roman canon law*, pp.1–3; Tarver, *Church court records*, p.32.
[2] Carlson, *Marriage*, pp.148–9; Houlbrooke, *Church courts*, pp.46–50; Tarver, *Church court records*, pp.27–30.

Church of England. Somewhat surprisingly, the jurisdiction and structure of the church courts survived virtually unchanged, as their medieval laws were only modified gradually by parliament and never revised thoroughly.[3] At the same time the courts' authority was enhanced by being brought directly under royal control and their lawyers were trained in civil, and not canon, law.[4]

The Reformation also made the church courts much more active as they strove to impose the religious changes on each parish and enforce church attendance on everyone. A sizeable rump, however, remained obstinately hostile or indifferent to the new established church, which was weakened eventually by this collapse of religious uniformity.[5] In the early-seventeenth century attacks by the ardent Puritans or extreme Protestants on the church authorities, civil lawyers and eventually the monarchy triggered off a fight back in the 1630s before they all fell victims of the Civil War.[6] The church courts were then abolished temporarily in the 1640s and 1650s, but without an adequate substitute to take over their duties.[7] Therefore the church courts were restored along with the King in 1660, when they became more receptive to the principles of common law and continued to persecute Dissenters and other sectaries for another generation until the Revolution Settlement of William and Mary.[8]

The irremediable decline of the English church courts began only after 1689, not as the result of any deliberate attack by the secular authorities, but as an unintended side-effect of the grant of toleration to the Dissenters. Church attendance was no longer enforceable, but sex offences were still reported and tried in large numbers until the second quarter of the eighteenth century; in theory the church courts' powers to discipline the laity then survived for another hundred years until they were taken away finally in the mid-nineteenth century.[9]

Although a uniform national pattern of church courts existed in theory, it did not operate in practice, mainly because of the differences in the ways in which bishops and archdeacons shared out their work.[10] The new Church of England preserved the administrative structure of

---

[3] Helmholz, *Roman canon law*, pp.36–7; Carlson, *Marriage*, p.142.

[4] Marchant, *Church under law*, p.2; Helmholz, *Roman canon law*, p.14.

[5] Houlbrooke, *Church courts*, pp.1, 15.

[6] Marchant, *Church under law*, p.8.

[7] For example, the new Court for Probate was not created until 1653, when it was based only in London and had a brief to help track down concealed royalist estates by scrutinising the wills; see Kitching, 'Probate during the Civil War', part 1, pp.283–4 and part 2, pp.346–56.

[8] Erickson, *Women and property*, p.29; Marchant, *Church under law*, p.240.

[9] Hair, *Before the bawdy court*, p.23; Marchant, *Church under law*, p.238.

[10] Marchant, *Church under law*, p.14.

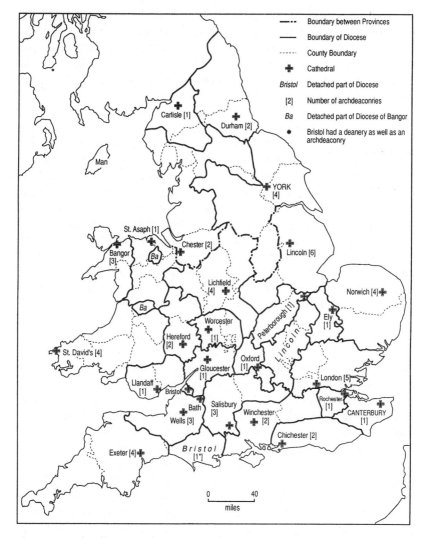

Figure 1.1 The dioceses of England and Wales

the pre-Reformation church virtually unaltered. It functioned at five main levels: parish, rural deanery, archdeaconry, diocese or bishopric and finally the archbishops' provinces of Canterbury and York. Only these last three or top tiers normally supported church courts. Appeals, together with some of the most important cases, were reserved for the courts of the archbishops, with most going to Canterbury as the senior and much larger of the two provinces, covering 44 of the 52 counties of England and Wales. The consistory courts, which operated at diocesan level usually from their cathedral, transacted most business. In 1540 Henry VIII increased the number of dioceses in England and Wales by five to a total of 22 in the province of Canterbury and a mere four under York.[11]

The lowest level of ecclesiastical court was normally the archdeacon's, with jurisdictions approximately the size of counties, but not always with matching boundaries. Some, such as Berkshire and Surrey, operated much more independently than others. In part this was because the dioceses varied greatly in size; Lincoln contained six archdeaconries and London five, while ten smaller dioceses had no more than one archdeacon each, often with restricted authority. In some larger dioceses, bishops appointed their own officials as commissaries to particular archdeaconry courts. This demoted the legal status of their archdeacons, but raised the status of their courts with extra powers delegated to them from the bishops. The archdeaconries of Nottingham and Richmond were also consistory courts and so operated more independently, while some rural deans in the province of York exercised some of their archdeacon's powers.[12] In addition, some archdeacons were restored after 1660 with somewhat diminished powers.[13] Another major complication was created nationwide by the existence of many parishes or areas, known as peculiars, which were exempt for historical reasons from the authority of their local archdeacon, and sometimes also from their bishop. These either held their own courts or were subjected to a different outside authority.[14]

Consistory and archdeaconry courts normally conducted their business in frequent regular sessions. In Essex during the Elizabethan period, for example, nearly all routine sessions of the archdeacon's court were held in the parish church of different market towns at about three-weekly intervals with additional *ad hoc* meetings, when required, in inns or the archdeacon's own residence.[15] Other archdeaconries, such as Oxford, Berkshire and Sudbury, appear to have functioned similarly and

---

[11] These totals exclude the dioceses of Westminster, which was abolished in 1550, and Sodor and Man, which came under York but covered the Hebrides in Scotland.

[12] Marchant, *Church under law*, pp.173, 14, 111.

[13] Bray, *Anglican canons*, p.908; Tarver, *Church court records*, p.2.

[14] Most peculiars are listed in Gibson, *Probate jurisdictions* and mapped in Humphery-Smith, *Phillimore atlas*. Locating the probate records of some peculiars can prove quite elusive.

[15] Emmison, *Elizabethan life*, pp.x–xii.

to have met almost as frequently, although maybe less peripatetically.[16] Those which met regularly in one place, such as Winchester and Lewes, proved to be more costly and much more inconvenient.[17] The authority of the higher levels of church administration was strengthened by regular visitations from their officials to the outlying parts of the dioceses, about every three or four years, and annually in the archdeaconries.[18]

Probate

During the middle ages, the church gradually acquired the right to prove wills and grant administrations of the estates of the dead in all but a few places in England and Wales. At the time the church's administrative structure and range of courts and offices were better suited to conducting probate business than those of any other organisation, especially since its peripatetic courts could often attend to probate matters.[19] However, this arrangement generated one serious complication. The church courts were directly responsible for overseeing the disposal of deceased persons' personal estates only, that is their moveable goods, credits and leasehold property, but not of their real estate, which comprised freehold and copyhold land and buildings.[20]

Issues concerning the inheritance of freehold or copyhold land were determined initially by manorial courts and were settled by local customs or usage or, in other words, common law. Originally, dying property-owners expressed their wishes about the disposal of their real estate in a last will and of their moveable goods in an earlier testament, but by the sixteenth century the two documents were commonly merged into one 'last will and testament'. This reflected the fact that the church authorities had become responsible for establishing testators' genuine wishes regarding the disposal of all their property, but not for resolving any disputes about their real estate. The church was always eager to prevent corrosive arguments among families and neighbours over the division of deceased people's property or the non-payment of their debts and so usually sought to discourage intestacy. However,

---

[16] Brinkworth, 'Study and use', p.103; personal communication from Nesta Evans.
[17] Lander, 'Church courts', p.234.
[18] However, in Winchester diocese they took place every year and in Norwich every seven years; see Houlbrooke, *Church courts*, p.29.
[19] Marchant, *Church under law*, p.23.
[20] Houlbrooke, *Church courts*, p.90; Helmholz, *Roman canon law*, pp.81–2.

writing a will was never essential for anyone who wanted to dispose of their real estate according to local custom.[21]

The gradual decline of the manorial courts during the early modern period steadily eroded the influence of local customs over the inheritance of real estate. Parliament also promoted this trend by passing a number of acts from 1540 onwards which encouraged landowners to use written wills to bequeath their property and favoured eventually more uniform inheritance practices that gave greater discretion to testators throughout the country. These affected those areas, such as Wales, Yorkshire, Kent and London, where the practices of partible inheritance and reasonable parts, which prevented a man from leaving most of his moveables to persons outside the family, were most firmly established.[22] However, we must not assume that when testators disposed of real estate by will that it included all that they possessed, especially if their property was entailed or subject to a strict settlement.

Initially the executor(s) or administrator(s) had to pay for all funeral and administrative costs, all outstanding debts, most legacies and sometimes even the upbringing of young children from the proceeds of the deceased's personal estate. Opportunities for disputes over these issues were curtailed by a well-established practice whereby several relatives, creditors and/or reputable neighbours drew up inventories of all the moveable goods and chattels of the deceased as soon as possible after the death of those with personal estates of any value. They were costed according to their secondhand or selling prices and their total formed the assets available to the executor(s) for distribution.

The church courts charged fees for validating and preserving wills and probate inventories and were frequently accused of exorbitant overcharging. Two of the first measures attacking the clergy passed in 1529 by Henry VIII's Reformation Parliament were acts that limited the fees paid by executors of deceased laymen both for processing the probate of their wills and inventories and also for mortuaries.[23] Two earlier attempts by parliament in 1357 and 1415 had failed to curb the fees charged for proving wills, especially in the higher courts, but the maximum fees established by the Act of 1529 remained in force for over a century, despite subsequent inflation. Even so, the fees that the church courts were entitled to charge for handling probate cases made up a very

---

[21] Burn, *Ecclesiastical law* (1775), 4, pp.41, 176–235; Tarver, *Church court records*, pp.56–81.

[22] 31 Hen. VIII, c.3 (1539); 32 Hen. VIII, c.1 (1540); 4 Wm. & M., c.2 (1692); 7 & 8 Wm. III, c.38 (1696); 2 & 3 An., c.5 (1703). Fuller details of these acts are given in Appendix 2.

[23] 21 Hen. VIII, c.5 (1529); 21 Hen. VIII, c.6 (1529).

substantial proportion of their income.[24] This stemmed in part from the steady rise in the standard of living among the middle orders of society, which created an increasing number of people with sufficiently valuable personal estates to involve the probate process.

The process

It has been established already that there was no single uniform pattern of church administration throughout all 26 dioceses. Considerable differences existed in particular between the provinces of Canterbury and York, but, in the words of Helmholz, 'the history of probate jurisdiction in England has been too little studied for a complete picture of its operation to have emerged'.[25] Therefore a brief summary of the probate process provides only an approximate account of many people's experiences that was applicable more or less to different dioceses.

A grant of probate began the process, when the executor(s) and witnesses swore an oath that the will which was being proved was definitely the testator's last one. In return the executor(s) received permission to administer the deceased's estate, with the decision being legally confirmed by an entry written in the act book of the relevant probate court. This was required to start within four months of the testator's death, but often it began much sooner.[26] When the executor(s) named in the will could not or would not act, the church authorities were posed with a problem similar to that which arose when a person of sufficient means died intestate, without making a will. Both situations were resolved by appointing administrators to carry out the required duties. Most administrators were either the widow or the next of kin, but a few were major creditors or even reputable neighbours. The probate courts appointed these administrators by letters of administration, which normally required them to reinforce their oath to administer the deceased's estate faithfully by entering into a bond, with perhaps two other sureties, for about double the estimated value of the personal estate. In addition, they might guarantee to complete their work in about a year, by which time they had to provide the court with both an inventory of the deceased's goods and credits and an account of their own administration. Parliament prescribed how these administration bonds should be worded from 1671 onwards.[27]

---

[24] Marchant, *Church under law*, pp.15–30.
[25] Helmholz, *Roman canon law*, p.79.
[26] Tarver, *Church court records*, p.56.
[27] 22 & 23 Ch. II, c.10 (1670).

Some intestates had already indicated their intentions so clearly during their last illness to several witnesses that after their deaths their wishes could be written down briefly as a substitute for a will. These nuncupative wills could be as much a source of potential conflict among the surviving family as no will at all. However, the courts normally preferred to endorse some form of will if at all possible so that parliament helped regularise nuncupative wills from 1677 onwards by applying strict limits to what was acceptable and the timescale involved.[28]

Receiving the grant of probate was only the start of the process, although a small or middling estate with a clear and uncontested will, accompanied by an inventory or sometimes even without one, could often be wound up very quickly.[29] Complications, which might delay the completion of the probate process for a lengthy period, were often triggered by family quarrels or suspicions and arose for various reasons. These included challenges to the will's validity or to specific clauses, the need to provide for young orphaned children, contested debts owed by or to the deceased and a refusal or inability to pay certain legacies from the sale of the personal estate.[30] Although there was a well-established sequence for settling different kinds of debts, the administration of insolvent estates was complicated by the fact that cases concerning debts came under the civil, rather than spiritual, courts.[31]

Before such non-standard probate cases could be settled, the administrator had to present detailed accounts to the court for a judge to confirm that all legitimate debts owed by the deceased had been paid as well as all possible legacies. The intention was that this would prevent subsequent quarrels or litigation. From 1685 onwards, parliament restricted the need for these probate accounts to be made to the occasions when estates were in dispute.[32] Legal challenges by disgruntled relatives or creditors could be expensive and long-drawn out and may have taken as much as 18 months on average at Norwich in the 1630s.[33] In addition, the church had a duty to unearth concealed wills and illegally-administered estates, but prosecutions on these grounds were rare.[34] Disputes concerning land or real estate could not be referred to

---

[28] 29 Ch. II, c.3, ss 19–24 (1676).

[29] Houlbrooke, *Church courts*, p.115.

[30] Willis, *Church life*, p.45; Houlbrooke, *Church courts*, pp.97–113.

[31] Helmholz, *Roman canon law*, pp.82–5; Burn, *Ecclesiastical law* (1775), 4, pp.286–93.

[32] 1 Ja. II, c.17, ss 5–8 (1685).

[33] Tarver, *Church court records*, pp.76–81; Marchant, *Church under law*, p.17.

[34] Houlbrooke, *Church courts*, pp.94–5.

the church courts. Most other serious probate disputes were heard in the consistory courts, with a few being resolved in the archbishops' courts.

These higher courts could also make the initial grant of probate when the deceased had held a personal estate worth five pounds, or perhaps more, in an ecclesiastical jurisdiction different from where he or she had resided. Thus the consistory and archbishops' courts normally took responsibility for the probate of the better-off gentry as well as of the clergy and others with sufficient possessions. Probate for most minor gentry and below was processed at the archdeaconry level or its equivalent. The existence of many peculiars and detached portions of archdeaconries and dioceses led to more wills being proved at the consistory courts of most dioceses than one might anticipate. The boundaries of the different authorities in the Diocese of Ely provide a good example of how complex they could be, even though at first it appears to cover, with just one archdeaconry, all but a fraction of the single county of Cambridgeshire. In practice, however, most of the county, about 110 parishes, lay in the Bishop of Ely's peculiar and so was administered directly by his consistory court. The Archdeaconry of Ely contained only the town of Cambridge and some 38 parishes in three detached portions, mainly in the south-west of the county, while the University of Cambridge also had its own Vice-Chancellor's Court for probate purposes. Thus a diverse patchwork of ecclesiastical jurisdictions covered this one county.[35]

Information about access to the probate courts is scarce and elusive. By the late-seventeenth century, for example, they were held twice a year in two different towns in each of the four archdeaconries of Lichfield diocese.[36] But when required, executors and administrators had more informal contact with some court officials who could also delegate their powers to reliable local clergymen. The physical registering, storing and indexing of wills with any relevant inventories, administration bonds and accounts entailed considerable office work. Normally the registry retained the original will while the executor was given a transcript certifying that it had been proved and another copy was made in a register or large bound volume where interested parties could consult it.[37] Conversely, the executors or administrators were responsible for making two copies of each inventory and providing the probate authority with one.[38] The survival of these probate documents has varied

---

[35] See Chapter 9, below.

[36] Tarver, *Church court records*, p.56.

[37] Burn, *Ecclesiastical law* (1775), 4, p.205; Marchant, *Church under law*, p.24.

[38] Burn, *Ecclesiastical law* (1775), 4, p.236.

enormously by place and over time. The Canons of 1604 claimed that
until then the archdeacons' and peculiar jurisdictions had been much
more inefficient than the consistory courts, because many had 'no
known nor certain registrars nor public place to keep their records in'.[39]

The fees for probate that were established from 1530 onwards by the
Act of 1529 were based solely on the value of the deceased's personal
estate.[40] They appear to have been respected widely for at least a century,
certainly at York and Norwich, but were increased eventually because of
inflation.[41] Personal estates were grouped into three different bands for
purposes of charging. Those worth five pounds or less were exempt from
any charges, apart from a fee of 6d. to the registrar for copying the will
and another 6d. when letters of administration were required because of
intestacy. For goods valued between £5 and £40 the set charge was 3s.
6d. and for personal estates over £40 it was 5s. These prescribed fees
were all maxima and some courts charged less, at least for a time. The act
made it clear that these differential fees depended simply on the value of
the 'goods of the testator', that is their gross rather than net value, but
the wording of the next act, limiting the mortuary fees that could be
charged on the estates of the dead, spelled out that, unlike probate fees,
they were determined by the value of the deceased's moveable goods
after their debts had been deducted and not before.[42]

Sometimes it is stated quite wrongly that the law obliged people to
make a will when their goods were worth over five pounds. In fact it
was the fee structure which determined future policy. Because the
church authorities could only charge for grants of probate when the
personal estate was valued at over five pounds, they encouraged, but
could not compel, those above this limit to apply. Conversely, they
merely discouraged those below the cut-off point of five pounds, since
by the Act of 1529 they could not refuse to process free of charge those
presented correctly to them whatever their value. It must also be stressed
that the same act did not initiate the taking of inventories, but rather
elaborated the instructions of Archbishop Stratford's Canons of 1342.[43]

Caution

This account of the vagaries of the probate process should encourage us
to take great care in interpreting the surviving probate records. Like all

[39] Bray, *Anglican canons*, p.427, Canon 126 (1604).
[40] 21 Hen. VIII, c.5 (1529).
[41] Marchant, *Church under law*, p.25; Burn, *Ecclesiastical law* (1775), 4, p.212.
[42] 21 Hen. VIII, c.6 (1529).
[43] Burn, *Ecclesiastical law* (1775), 4, p.236.

non-standard historical documents, they yield up their secrets reluctantly. On first encounter with a collection of these papers, it is natural to assume that all are equally reliable. However, a close inspection of their layout or handwriting may reveal that some were created much more conscientiously than others. Many may appear to be quite superficial, but the most detailed ones are potential mines of information, with fascinating and instructive detail about so many different aspects of life in the early modern period that sometimes historians of other periods must look enviously upon them.

Nonetheless, we must remain constantly cautious about taking at face value all the data contained within these probate documents for a variety of reasons. For example, it would be misleading simply to equate a man's financial standing before death with his debts and credits after it because, as Hufton explained, 'when the male head of a household died, his creditors moved immediately to demand payment of all outstanding bills'.[44] Thus, these documents' limitations must be understood as well as their strengths together with a proper appreciation of the process and laws or conventions which moulded them. The succeeding chapters in this section are directed towards this end, exploring in some detail the legal system, the influences on the format and content of wills, probate inventories and accounts, the reliability of their prices and the many different ways in which historians have studied them all.

[44] Hufton, *Prospect before her*, p.239.

2

Probate 1500–1800: a System in Transition

JEFF AND NANCY COX

Introduction

This chapter is concerned with the process of probate, the official mechanism for the orderly transmission of property at death. Strictly the term referred to the transmission of property through the last will and testament of the deceased, but in practice probate was extended to cover the administration of intestate estates for which there was no will. It is in this wider sense that we use the term here in outlining the system of jurisdiction and discussing the diverse documents it generated. The whole body of probate documents, probably totalling several millions, cries out for interpretation. It offers unrivalled insight, not only into private life and family relationships, but also into developments in agriculture, industry and trade during early modern times.

The standard format of some probate documents, particularly the probate inventory, may tempt us to use the source without fully understanding it, but its air of simplicity cloaks a complex of laws and customs and an often tenuous link between precept and practice.[1] William Holdsworth, the eminent legal historian, was one of the first to draw attention to the discrepancies between what a fifteenth-century commentator on ecclesiastical law had said and what was done in the courts. 'It might be necessary, for the sake of completeness, to set down such rules if one were writing a book about these matters; they could be comfortably ignored when it came to actual practice.'[2] If

---

[1] The difference between precept and practice is a recurring theme in Erickson, *Women and property*. For a specific example see p.107. For other examples see Steer, *Farm and cottage inventories*, p.5; Priestley and Corfield 'Rooms and room use' p.95; Overton, 'English probate inventories', pp.205–15.

[2] Holdsworth, *History of English law*, 3, p.541, on the difference between William Lyndwood's exposition in the fifteenth century on those incapacitated from writing a will and actual practice.

contemporary lawyers felt unsure, at our remove in time we may well struggle after certainty.

Probate did not operate in isolation; it was embedded in a much broader and less well-defined system of transmission and in a web of principles concerning duties, rights and obligations. Consequently aspects of probate became the concern of virtually every English public institution from parliament to the church and the manor and to all the courts whether based on canon law, common law, equity or custom. This chapter is divided into three sections: the legal system, the transmission of property at death, and checks on personal representatives. Four themes recur throughout the chapter: the gap between precept and practice; the struggle for supremacy between competing jurisdictions; a change in attitude to possessions and to their disposal after death; and the pressures of new ideologies, new technologies and new commodities.

The legal system

Until 1858 probate was granted by ecclesiastical courts. Apart from local anomalies, there were three tiers of jurisdiction. Most probates were granted at the archdiaconal court, under the archdeacon.[3] Originally he had deputised for his bishop, but he had long since acquired customary jurisdiction. An appeal lay from the archdeacon's court to the bishop's consistory court.[4] This was usually presided over by his chancellor or 'official', who had been since the twelfth century the ordinary (that is, the official authorised to grant probate) competent to exercise all the bishop's jurisdiction, although the bishop retained the right to act himself. The chancellor was assisted by a registrar who was responsible for the writing out of court documents, including testaments, and by apparitors who executed court mandates and who seem to have sought out those who failed to act on behalf of the deceased. From the consistory court appeal lay to the archbishops' courts.[5]

At the provincial (or archdiocesan) level, for Canterbury there was the court of the 'official principal' or Court of Arches. This was a court of appeal from the diocesan courts, but also a court of first instance in all ecclesiastical causes. It seems not to have been the main court

---

[3] Not all dioceses were divided into archdeaconries and in others the archdeaconries appear to have been subdivided for the purposes of probate. Particularly in the north there were the lower rural deans' courts: see Houlbrooke, *Church courts*, pp.30–4.

[4] This was confirmed by 24 Hen. VIII, c.12, see Blackstone, *Commentaries*, III, p.64.

[5] Holdsworth, *History of English law*, 1, pp.599–600.

involved in testamentary disputes, except from the peculiar courts.[6] Probate was primarily the concern of the prerogative court sitting at the Doctors' Commons and presided over either by the official principal, or by a special commissary. By the canons of 1604, this court had jurisdiction over all cases where *bona notabilia* (literally noteworthy goods) were left in more than one diocese. The term *bona notabilia* was ill-defined. Swinburne, 'sometime judge of the Prerogative Court of York', averred that it probably meant goods worth over £10,[7] whereas Richard Burn, an eighteenth-century authority on ecclesiastical law, gave £5 as the general rule, but quoted 29 Ch. II, c.3 s.24 to show that local anomalies could still apply.[8] The probate documents themselves illustrate some of the difficulties. For example, Francis Taylor of Uffculme (1624) had goods worth only £2 7s. in his house, but a chattel lease worth £10 for land lying in a different jurisdiction. In this case the clerk of the Prerogative Court declared that his court had no claim since the goods in Uffculme were worth less than £5. Eighty years later, William Gingell, yeoman of Stoke Gifford (1708), had leasehold property worth £25 in Westerleigh, Gloucester diocese, and nearly £150 in Stoke Gifford, Bristol diocese, where probate was granted rather than at Canterbury.[9] The complexities did not end with property in two dioceses. If a man died in one diocese, with *bona notabilia* in another, the archdiocese had the administration, but if a man died on a journey the goods with him did not count as *bona notabilia*—an exception of particular relevance at a time of many travelling salesmen such as chapmen and pedlars, not to mention bargemen, drovers and carriers.[10] Similar courts and jurisdictions were to be found in the archdiocese of York, but it will emerge below that practice in the northern province differed from that in the southern.

Various bodies both ecclesiastical and lay, had 'peculiar' jurisdiction over particular areas.[11] Some had originated from conflict between bishops and their chapters, leading to the apportionment of land and the jurisdictions that went with it. The greater abbeys had been exempted from episcopal jurisdiction and their rights passed into lay hands at the

---

[6] 25 Hen. VIII, c.19, see Blackstone, *Commentaries*, III, p.65.

[7] Swinburne, *Briefe treatise* (1635), p.63; Holdsworth, *History of English law*, 1, p.602.

[8] Burn, *Ecclesiastical law* (1775), 4, p.179. He gave £10 as the sum in London.

[9] Wyatt, *Uffculme wills*, pp.xv & 46; Moore, *Goods and chattels*, p.186. More work is needed on *bona notabilia* to establish under what circumstances Canterbury and York were able to enforce their claim to such cases.

[10] Burn, *Ecclesiastical law* (1775), 4, p.179.

[11] Holdsworth, *History of English law*, 1, p.601.

Reformation. Some manorial courts were also exempt. Such peculiar courts could be found at almost every level; for example, the parish of Sevenoaks, Kent, was in the peculiar of Shoreham in the deaneries of Shoreham and Croydon.[12] From peculiars outside episcopal or archiepiscopal control, right of appeal lay to the rather unsatisfactory high court of delegates, which had acquired the jurisdiction formerly exercised by the pope.[13] The practice of peculiars varied; some differed substantially from the surrounding diocese, others hardly at all. By different usage, recording items not usually recorded or continuing to require an inventory long after the practice had ceased elsewhere, peculiars at times illuminate aspects of probate.

The chancellor of the University of Oxford had acquired an independent jurisdiction over ecclesiastical matters, including probate, which by 1479 was beyond even archiepiscopal authority. His jurisdiction extended to the whole of England, so long as a member of the university was involved, a unique privilege. His court retained its jurisdiction throughout the early modern period and it was only attenuated, in some areas by disuse and in others by act of parliament, during the nineteenth century.[14] The University of Cambridge was slower to establish its jurisdiction, but had succeeded by the early modern period.

Certain large towns had acquired control over estates devolving on the orphans of citizens. The most notable example was the City of London, but Bristol, Exeter and others had similar rights. Surviving documents reflect the problems the authorities had in seeing that orphans inherited estates with the same value they had when left, possibly several years before. Consequently the accounting throughout tended to be fuller and more exacting.

Ecclesiastical courts had, with the exceptions mentioned, exclusive jurisdiction to grant probate and administration, but by the early modern period they had largely lost jurisdiction over debt, a fruitful source of testamentary dispute.[15] Executors and administrators,[16] otherwise known as personal representatives, heirs, creditors and legatees, could sue and be

---

[12] Lansberry, *Sevenoaks wills*, p.vii.

[13] Holdsworth, *History of English law*, 1, pp.600, 603–5.

[14] Holdsworth, *History of English law*, 1, pp.166–74.

[15] Helmholz, 'Debt claims', pp.68–82. He argues that the change had largely happened before *c*.1530, but subsequently occasional cases still appeared in the ecclesiastical courts; see, for example, *English Reports*, 161, Ecclesiastical, 440 (1726), Lloyd v Beatniffe alias Smith. (Hereafter cases from *English Reports* will be given in the conventional mode 161 *ER*, Ecc. (1726), 440.)

[16] Women could and frequently did act as executrices and administratrices, but for the sake of convenience, the male term has been used throughout when it is not appropriate to use the inclusive term 'personal representative'.

sued in the courts of common law, particularly the King's Bench. These courts became increasingly aggressive during the sixteenth century. They challenged the right of ecclesiastical courts to enquire into the truth of inventories and to examine the executors' accounts. They were all too willing to prevent effective action through writs of prohibition and by invoking the Statute of Praemunire (1392/3).[17] It was probably a changing perception of the church's role in secular affairs which caused the ecclesiastical courts to mount little resistance,[18] perhaps fostered by the sustained attack on the church by the crown in the early-sixteenth century.[19] Nevertheless, the ecclesiastical courts continued to attract business. They were relatively cheap and expeditious, and they offered compromise and arbitration so most cases were settled out of court.[20]

The adversarial approach of the common law rendered the courts unfit to dispense justice where testamentary disputes involved many parties. They could challenge but not displace the ecclesiastical courts. Chancery, and to a degree other equity courts, filled the gap. Chancery could take a comprehensive view of the rights, assets and liabilities of estates, examine the conduct of personal representatives and settle all claims in one proceeding.[21] Furthermore, Chancery developed equitable principles for the law of trusts. This area was expanding, particularly after the Statute of Uses (1535)[22] encouraged the setting up of trusts and marriage settlements to make long-term provision for widows and children leading inevitably to disputes after death.[23] During the seventeenth century Chancery attracted clients mainly from the home counties and mainly from the upper, if not the highest, ranks of society. The number of cases increased tenfold, partly from tradesmen and merchants, but mostly from women. They used Chancery to settle disputes over property, particularly after the disappearance during the Commonwealth of other equity courts like the Court of Requests. The system became overloaded and Chancery became notorious for delay.[24]

[17] The Statutes of Praemunire (1353 and 1393) forbade the prosecution of law suits in foreign courts of law, notably the papal courts.

[18] 16 Rich. II, c.5.

[19] Holdsworth, *History of English law*, 1, pp.625–9; Holdsworth, *History of English law*, 3, p.594; Helmholtz, 'Debt claims', pp.78–9; Houlbrooke, *Church courts*, pp.9–15, 39.

[20] Houlbrooke, *Church courts*, pp.40–4.

[21] A useful summary of the *modus operandi* of Chancery is contained in Erickson, *Women and property*, p.31.

[22] 27 Hen. VIII, c.10.

[23] Holdsworth, *History of English law*, 7, pp.288, 303–4.

[24] Erickson, *Women and property*, pp.31, 77, 118. No comparable analysis has been made for the eighteenth century.

By 1500 the palatinates of Chester, Lancaster and Durham had also acquired equity courts which competed to some extent with Chancery. These courts were largely used for smaller suits and by people of lower status and/or wealth, probably because they avoided long journeys and were cheaper. However, their business declined rapidly during the seventeenth century, and they were of little importance after 1700.[25]

By 1800 the jurisdiction of the competing courts had stabilised. Common law courts had jurisdiction over debts, over wills involving land and over the interpretation and validity of devises,[26] while ecclesiastical courts granted probate or administration. They could also hear disputes, although many suits concerning legacies and the distribution of the residue after creditors had been paid were heard in Chancery.[27]

The transmission of property at death

The transmission of property at death was not straightforward. Just as there were several competing jurisdictions, so a variety of ideas circulated about transmission. Interests of state or of landlord could conflict with those of the deceased and of his widow and children, relatives and creditors. Each jurisdiction developed its case law based on a distinctive philosophy of duties and rights. Additionally, the validity of customary law was recognised, though it might vary from place to place. Above all parliament imposed new requirements overriding established practice, while those preparing for death exercised great ingenuity to circumvent unacceptable restrictions. We focus on some of the main ideas concerned with the transmission of property at death and the way they were implemented by the several jurisdictions and on the practical implications for those approaching death.

The ancient Germanic method of transmitting property was by intestate succession (that is, with no will) according to fixed rules.[28] Dying out in the south, the custom of intestate succession remained in the north the dominant method of transmitting personal property into the early modern period. This custom required a man, even when he made a will, to leave one-third of his moveable property divided equally among his children, and another third to his widow. Only after 1692

---

[25] Erickson, *Women and property*, pp.31, 117.
[26] In modern times, this term is applied to any gift by will of freehold land or rights arising out of or connected with land, whereas a bequest relates to personal property. The distinction was not always so clear.
[27] Holdsworth, *History of English law*, 7, p.652.
[28] Brundage, *Mediaeval canon law*, p.87.

were testators living in the province of York free to leave their estates as they chose so that widows and/or children could no longer claim their 'reasonable part', 'any law, Statute or Usage to the contrary . . . notwithstanding';[29] the same privileges were extended later to the city of York,[30] to Wales,[31] and to London.[32] Thus by the end of the seventeenth century, the influence of custom had been much reduced in that those not incapacitated had the right to make a will leaving their disposable property as they pleased. However, for those dying intestate, the customary provisions for children and widows continued to apply. Canon law gave two-thirds of the residual goods to be divided equally among the children,[33] and one-third to the widow.[34] The estates of the unmarried went equally to all siblings. Advanced payments to children such as marriage portions or outlays for apprenticeships, plus bequests from other sources or grants of land, were taken into account in the apportionment. On the presumption that the eldest son was likely to have inherited the land, the ecclesiastical courts were inclined to interpret liberally the rules concerning moveable goods in favour of the younger children.[35]

Since 1357 the ecclesiastical courts had been obliged to appoint administrators 'from the next and most lawful friends of the deceased person intestate' to act as executors.[36] This was interpreted as those with the greatest interest in the estate,[37] generally the widow.[38] The courts also appointed administrators when a will was defective, or when executors declined to act, had died or were in some way incapacitated. In the sixteenth century the appointment of an administrator was usually recorded on the inventory, but after 1600 there was often a separate document, a bond appointing the administrator and setting out his obligation. This bond was actually required by an act of 1670 which appears to have formalised existing good practice.[39] The administrator

---

[29] 4 Wm. & M., c.2.
[30] 2 & 3 An., c.5.
[31] 7 & 8 Wm. III, c.38.
[32] 11 Geo. I, c.18, s.17.
[33] All when there was no widow.
[34] Erickson, *Women and property*, p.178, suggests ecclesiastical courts usually allocated more than the legal minimum to widows.
[35] Erickson, *Women and property*, pp.72–3.
[36] 31 Ed. III, st.1, c.11.
[37] 161 *ER*, Ecc. (1728), 444, Elmes v Elmes.
[38] The claims of the widow were outlined in 21 Hen. VIII, c.5 and 161 *ER*, Ecc. (1752), 13, Stretch formerly Pynn v Pynn confirms this was accepted as the general rule by the courts.
[39] 22 & 23 Ch. II, c.10.

usually had two bondsmen. The bond gave occupation and abode for each individual named and yields useful information on kinship and occupation. Usually at least the first bondsman was a relative or a working associate; by the eighteenth century the second was often a court servant or even the fictional John Doe. A slightly different bond was sometimes issued, a tuition bond binding a guardian to care for the estate and for the children until they were of age. A surprisingly liberal aspect of the law entitled children over seven to choose their guardians. Documents recording their choice are occasionally found.[40] Administrators were bound by custom and by canon law until parliament standardised distribution in 1670, allowing the widow one-third of the residue, half if there were no children, and the children, including the heir at law, two-thirds divided equally, though making allowance for portions already given. The brothers and sisters of the deceased gained rights for the first time, receiving half the estate divided equally when there were no children.[41] Unlike the old canon law, the act seems to have been applied rigorously.[42] It improved the prospects of the heir at law and of some relatives, but worsened those of the widow, although at least one childless widow attempted unsuccessfully to claim half of the estate under the act and half as her customary portion.[43]

Letters of administration with inventory were apparently used occasionally for a purpose other than settling an intestate estate immediately after death. On this legal commentators are silent, perhaps because no modification of the process was involved. They concerned estates not formerly submitted to probate, either testate or intestate, which included either bonds payable some years ahead or leases, particularly those granted for three lives or for long terms. A later claimant, even two or three generations removed from the deceased, might find himself without documentary evidence. The solution was to apply for letters of administration and to exhibit an inventory listing the bond or lease in question.[44] Such inventories were in standard form but the list of assets was obviously defective, even if an entry such as 'wearing apparel' was included as a fig leaf of respectability. Whether these processes were used in other ways has not been studied.

---

[40] For example, Thomas Bryan, being above the age of seven, after his mother died chose his uncle as guardian; see Lichfield Joint Record Office, (hereafter LJRO) Anne Bryan, Atcham, 1725.

[41] 22 & 23 Ch II, c.10.

[42] Erickson, *Women and property*, p.178.

[43] 21 *ER*, Chanc. (1682/3), 672, Stapleton v Dom. Sherwood.

[44] For example, Hereford Record Office, John Adams of Broseley, Salop (1671); Cox and Cox, 'Probate inventories', 2, pp.221–2.

The transmission of land followed different principles. There were three main possibilities practised at some time in some parts of England: gavelkind, equal partition among all sons as practised in Kent and in some manors elsewhere; ultimogeniture, the inheritance by the youngest son; and primogeniture or inheritance by the eldest. In England the laws governing the devolution of land increasingly expected the heir to be one male, generally the eldest son. By contrast, in the absence of sons, all daughters were co-parceners or equal co-heirs.[45]

In the middle ages the freedom to leave land as the holder chose was limited. It depended upon whether the land was freehold or not, and, if not, the nature of tenure. Virtually all land was transmitted by intestate succession except that leased for a term of years, which could be devised by will. However, the Statute of Wills of 1540 made it lawful to devise in a will land held by socage,[46] (the commonest form of tenure), but land held under other tenures continued to descend automatically to the heir until 1660 when all were turned into 'free and common socage'.[47] Even then many landowners seem to have adhered to intestate succession for their land, perhaps because ecclesiastical courts had virtually no jurisdiction over the execution of wills devising land.[48]

Technically, copyhold land was held at the will of the lord, but increasingly the courts had come to accept that it should descend according to the custom of the manor, and the lord had little more to do than endorse the work of the manor court. The king's courts, while recognising the customs of the manor, in other respects regarded copyhold land the same as freehold and thus covered by the same rules of transmission.[49]

Wives and widows occupied a distinctive place in the transmission of property. A woman on marriage was deemed under *coverture* or under the cover of and as one with her husband. All her property became his on marriage and in her widowhood she depended upon his kindness towards her, or upon the provisions of law and custom. This arrangement was unique to England and her colonies. Elsewhere in Europe, husband and wife held property equally and jointly. Natural justice suggested that a woman who had made a substantial contribution towards the household through her dowry should retain what she had brought to the marriage when it ended at the death of her husband.

---

[45] Holdsworth, *History of English law*, 3, pp.171ff.

[46] 32 Hen. VIII, c.1.

[47] 12 Ch. II, c.24; Holdsworth, *History of English law*, 3, pp.36ff.

[48] Houlbrooke, *Church courts*, p.90.

[49] Holdsworth, *History of English law*, 3, pp.198–212.

Society also held the view, expressed in law and custom, that a husband should provide so far as possible for his widow so that she did not become a liability on others. The widow had two rights, freebench and dower. The former gave her one-third of her husband's manorial lands either during widowhood or for life, depending on the custom of the manor. The latter under common law entitled her to one-third of all her husband's real estate for life.[50]

Through a last will and testament the testator laid down how his non-inheritable estate was to be distributed after his death. Lawyers agreed that anyone could make a will unless disabled by a special rule of law. Disagreement revolved around who this covered. Lyndwood, the fifteenth-century expert on canon law, recognised five classes of disabled persons, several of these taken straight from Roman Law and inapplicable to any English system. Apart from the mentally incapable, the two most contentious groups were married women and infants. The incapacity of the former was qualified,[51] but for the latter it was absolute before majority, which for making a will a boy attained at 14, and a girl at 12.[52]

Technically the will and the testament were distinct; the former, according to Burn, was limited to land and the latter to chattels. Only the testament required an executor. Burn followed the practice of his predecessors and made no such distinction, and we do not here.[53] A sufficient will and testament required three elements; the date, the testator's signature or mark duly witnessed, and a nominated executor or executors. These could be male or female, and did not have to be of age. A will lacking one or more of these elements was invalid, though the ordinary might accept it as a true statement of the deceased's intentions and grant probate in the same way as for a nuncupative will (that is, spoken before witnesses), attaching to it letters of administration. Other elements, not essential but virtually always present, were how and to whom the estate was left, and a residual legatee. An overseer was sometimes appointed to take the executor to court if he failed in his duties. Overseers were more common in some

---

[50] Erickson, *Women and property*, p.238.

[51] For example, 161 *ER*, Ecc. (1728), 441, Keller v Bevoir, interpreted the wife's marriage articles to grant her the right to make a will even though it was not made explicit. See also Erickson, *Women and property*, Tables 12.1 and 12.2 for women making wills.

[52] Holdsworth, *History of English law*, 3, pp.541–5. *ER*, Chanc. 21 (n.d.), 1047, Chamberlain v Chamberlain is less definite than Holdsworth indicating 17 years as the accepted majority but down to 14 if the boy were proved 'to be of discretion'.

[53] Burn, *Ecclesiastical law* (1775), 4, p.41.

areas than others and generally became less common during the seventeenth century.[54]

Custom and common sense must have guided many testators in constructing their wills, but the preamble of an act of 1529 laid four principal obligations upon testators. They should see to the 'payment of their debts', the 'necessary and convenient finding of their wives', the 'virtuous bringing up and Advancement of their children to marriage', and 'charitable Deeds . . . for the Health of their Souls'.[55] This last was probably why the medieval church had encouraged the Roman practice of making wills over the ancient Germanic custom of intestate succession. The continued support of the Church for testate succession is reflected in the order of service for the Visitation of the Sick. From 1552 to this century, the rubric required the clergy to remind the dying of their duty to make a will and to declare their debts.[56]

The ecclesiastical courts generally viewed defective wills kindly so long as the intentions of the deceased were explicit. A nuncupative will, given by word of mouth before at least two credible witnesses and subsequently written down (though never signed), was invariably acceptable, the named executor being granted administration *cum testamento annexo*. Less orthodox testamentary documents were also accepted, such as a letter to his wife written by a man on his way home from India.[57]

Men increasingly chose to tie up their property through marriage settlements, entails and heirlooms, so curtailing the freedom of their descendants to leave property as they chose. Dower involved losing the use of part of the hereditament to the widow, which could affect an estate adversely. Landowners therefore used the Statute of Uses to create marriage settlements granting a jointure to the widow and depriving her of dower. This gave the husband and his heir flexibility while still providing for the widow. Landowners exploited the same statute to create entails defining how the estate was to pass from one generation to another. In effect the heir and his successors held the land in trust and could not dispose of it during their lives. Thus they could only provide for their daughters and younger sons by purchasing real estate or by marrying heiresses. Both were used effectively and increasingly, although it was not unknown for lawyers to find loopholes which allowed entails to be broken.

[54] Erickson, *Women and property*, pp.159–61 and Table 9.2. The proportion of male testators appointing overseers varied from 75 per cent in Sussex 1579–1682 down to 5 per cent in rural Yorkshire 1640–90.

[55] 21 Hen. VIII, c.4.

[56] *Book of Common Prayer.*

[57] 161 *ER*, Ecc. (1755), 280, Repington v Holland and Repington.

Whereas entails and marriage settlements affected hereditaments, creating heirlooms restricted the executors' rights to personal property, since heirlooms were regarded as attached to the freehold as if a fixture and therefore not devisable. A testator could leave articles to his heir, declaring them to be heirlooms, and the new status was recognised by the courts which could decree a conveyance to that effect. There seems to have been no restriction on what could be declared an heirloom: furniture, hangings, dairy equipment have each been noted, but the practice seems to have been used sparingly. Burn discussed heirlooms briefly,[58] but not how far the practice could be taken. Presumably the courts would not have accepted wholesale designations of heirlooms, but one 'gent' left tables, forms and beds, a maltmill and weeting mit, a cooking pot, all grates, the clock, two presses and six chairs 'to be kept and continued in the house as heirlooms'.[59] It is not possible to ascribe inventories to this house among subsequent inventories for members of the family but each showed a much smaller personal estate.

Checks on personal representatives

The freedom of personal representatives to act was not only constrained through action in court by aggrieved parties. The ordinary could require them to prove they had discharged their duties properly by demanding a full inventory of all the personal goods and chattels belonging to the deceased at death, and an account of the winding up and the distribution of the estate. We deal with each in turn.

For probate to be granted, the personal representative had to take an inventory of all the deceased's personal possessions, properly valued by competent persons, and to exhibit it before the ordinary.[60] The inventory was intended as a check on the personal representative and as a protection for creditors and legatees. Perhaps as a result, over the years a format acceptable in the courts had become standardised.[61]

Many historians have accepted that taking inventories dates only

[58] Burn, *Ecclesiastical Law* (1775), 4, pp.64, 144, 242.
[59] William Chettoe of Horton in Wem, Salop, (1681), LJRO.
[60] Much illustrative material is contained in Cox and Cox, 'Probate inventories'; Cox and Cox, 'Valuations'. One of the best expositions of the probate system in so far as it relates to inventories is Overton, 'English probate inventories'. However, this by no means covers the whole spectrum and we disagree with him on a few points. For a bibliography see Overton, *Bibliography*.
[61] 161 *ER*, Ecc. (1754), 228, Plunkey formerly Sharpe v Sharpe in which the judge ruled on the necessity of a particular format, though he gave no guidance on the goods and chattels to be included. The inventories themselves show this had been common practice at least since the sixteenth century.

from an act of 1529.[62] Earlier survivals suggest otherwise.[63] The purpose of the act was primarily to prevent the ecclesiastical authorities overcharging for probate.[64] With this intent it enunciated a scale of fees, but it also defined who should have administration and who should make an inventory and how. Whether this was new or confirmed established practice is unclear. The latter seems more likely.

The act appears to have expected an inventory for a personal estate, testate or intestate, whatever its value, and only distinguished between estates in the matter of charges.[65] If the act only implied a requirement to make an inventory, the legal authorities certainly made it explicit. Swinburne stated categorically 'an Inventory is necessary to bee made by an Executor Testamentary, [as] is evident as well by the lawes Ecclesiasticall of this Realm, confirmed by continuall use; as also by the statutes of the same'.[66] Burn, writing over a century later, was no less definite.[67]

The act does not seem to have led to inventories being taken universally, but it does seem to have increased either the taking and/or exhibiting of inventories by personal representatives or their retention by the ecclesiastical courts. Many more inventories survive from the latter part of the sixteenth century, with a peak during the seventeenth. Incidence varies from diocese to diocese. Overton found that in the late-seventeenth century the estates of 58 per cent of adult males and widows in Kirkby Lonsdale were appraised. For Gloucester the figure was 30 per cent, for Norfolk and Suffolk 20 per cent, but for the Vale of Evesham a mere 10 per cent.[68]

---

[62] 21 Hen. VIII, c.5.

[63] For example, the earliest surviving inventory in Southampton is dated 1447, and two others predate the 1529 act. (Roberts and Parker, *Southampton probate inventories*, pp.2–13). See also Cox and Cox, 'Probate inventories', p.133 for earlier regulations.

[64] Previous attempts had been made in 31 Ed. III, st.1, c.4 and 3 Hen. V, c.8.

[65] Another widely held misconception is that there was no obligation to make an inventory on estates valued at less than £5. We can find no evidence for this. 21 Hen. VIII, c.5, which is often cited as evidence, makes it clear that its terms covered all estates, though certain documents relating to those under £5 were to be processed free if correctly presented. See Chapter 1, p.12.

[66] Swinburne, *Briefe treatise* (1635) p.50. Swinburne specifically excluded from his treatise intestacy and an inventory. The obligation was spelled out in the bond entered into by all administrators, legally required from 1670 but common before that date.

[67] Burn, *Ecclesiastical law* (1775), 4, p.235.

[68] Overton, 'English probate inventories', p.209, does not make clear how he derives these figures. They are taken from various sources, not necessarily comparable, though it is probably safe to assume they are based on burial records.

During the eighteenth century the practice of taking, or at least of exhibiting, inventories virtually died out. The different rates of decay suggest diocesan decisions rather than a central ruling. At Winchester inventories had almost disappeared from diocesan records by 1720, whereas Lichfield continued to exhibit them until about 1750.[69] Peculiars like Ellesmere in Shropshire and Richmond in Yorkshire exhibited inventories into the 1790s. These late inventories are often especially detailed.[70]

We must distinguish between making an inventory, for there is evidence this continued, and exhibiting it before the courts, which became less common. Thomas Turner, the diarist of East Hoathly, Sussex, more than once helped take an inventory at death, although by his time they were rare among the probate documents of his diocese, Chichester.[71] In one instance Turner described two appraisers being appointed, one to represent each of the parties concerned. If this were regular practice by the 1760s, an inventory made and acknowledged by competing interests may have been accepted as a true record in the common law courts without recourse to the ecclesiastical court.[72] Such documents may survive in the files of an estate or of a solicitor, like that of Thomas Baylis, yeoman of Mayshill, Gloucestershire (1744).[73]

In passing judgement in Phillips v Bignell and others (1811), where the executor had refused to exhibit, Sir John Nicholl affirmed that 'the canons require an inventory to be exhibited even before probate is granted; and this was the practice in this court and indeed is still the practice in some county jurisdictions'. He added that current practice was less strict and since 1792 it had been generally accepted that a personal representative was not obliged to exhibit an inventory unless an interested party demanded it. Nicholl assumed that, even though no inventory had been exhibited, one had been made at the time of the testator's death in 1796. The case involved minors and he ruled the inventory should now be exhibited, granting costs against the

---

[69] The method of storing documents at Lichfield is revealing. Increasingly the terms *nulla* or *sine* are written in a contemporary hand on the outside of each package of documents confirming there was no inventory inside. If there was, the value was written instead.

[70] For example, those for Richmond give full lists of clothing, a practice that had died out elsewhere in England during the early-seventeenth century.

[71] Vaisey, *Diary of Thomas Turner*, pp.224, 247.

[72] Vaisey, *Diary of Thomas Turner*, pp.306–7. The inventory concerned was taken for bankruptcy but Turner described it in similar terms to the several probates he helped to wind up. It was because the disputing appraisers made settlement difficult that Turner detailed their activities.

[73] Bristol Record Office AC/AS 91.

executor.[74] Other cases show the courts generally ordered an inventory be exhibited if requested by an interested party.[75]

A weakness of the 1529 act was that it provided no proceedings to force the personal representatives to carry out its provisions.[76] With the common law courts only too ready to challenge the ecclesiastical courts by writs of prohibition and other blocking devices, we have to ask why so many personal representatives voluntarily undertook this often onerous and costly task when there was apparently no mechanism to force them to do so. The answer may lie in the threat to their own pocket. If no inventory were taken, the common law courts assumed the estate of the deceased covered all debts and legacies and obliged the personal representatives to make up any shortfall.[77]

The high proportion of tradesmen appraised suggests it was self-interest rather than the law that moved personal representatives to take and to exhibit inventories. Debts owed to tradesmen sometimes represented a substantial proportion of their estate and the debts they owed often came to a similar sum. Margaret Justice, widow, had set up as a milliner in Wellington, Shropshire. At her death in 1687 her personal estate was valued at £83, but she owed £62. When her household goods at £19 were deducted, her business assets and her debts cancelled almost exactly. It was no wonder her executrix was anxious to see a good inventory made. Her contemporary Joseph Grafton of Shrewsbury, apparently a clothier, left an estate similarly encumbered and with similarly few assets once the debts were paid.[78] These are two of a small group whose inventories listed debts both owed and owing, but many other tradesmen's inventories suggest that debts at death were an important but uncertain factor in the estate. For example, John Beare of Ludham, Norfolk, died in 1589 with a shopful of mercery wares and £31 of shop debts owing to him out of a total estate of £78.[79] James Walker, drysalter of Leeds, died two centuries later in 1781 with debts an even greater proportion of his assets. His estate excluding debts came to £543; his shop book showed 114 people

---

[74] 161 *ER*, Ecc. (1811), 972, Phillips v Bignell and others. We thank Mrs D. Davies (University of Wolverhampton Library) for this reference. Nicholl was referring to Slater v Sladen (Prerogative Court, Michaelmas 1792).

[75] For example 161 *ER*, Ecc. (1752), 7, Taylor v Newton.

[76] 161 *ER*, Ecc. (1811), 972, Phillips v Bignell and others.

[77] As for example in 161 *ER*, Ecc. (1754), 211, Elliot formerly Holwell, v Holwell.

[78] Margaret Justice probate 1687; Joseph Grafton, St Mary's peculiar, probate 1685, both LJRO.

[79] Norwich Record Office, INV 5.139.

owed him £590.[80] In neither case is it known how much the deceased owed but the careful listing of debts suggests anxiety about the settlement.

In the taking of inventories precept and practice seem to have corresponded more closely than with other aspects of probate. The act of 1529 gave the personal representative some choice in whom to enlist to help draw up the inventory, but essentially they were those with an interest in the estate, creditors, legatees, or next of kin. Only when all these failed was he to choose 'two honest men'. They were to draw up a list of 'all the Goods, Chattels, Wares, Merchandize as well moveable as not moveable', a list somewhat expanded by Burn to include 'all . . . cattle as bulls, cows, oxen, sheep, horses, swine, and all poultry, household stuff, money, plate, jewels, corn, hay, wood severed from the ground, and such like moveables'.[81] Valuation was not mentioned in the act, as Swinburne noted. He regarded the two processes as distinct and not necessarily conducted by the same people. Whereas the inventory was to be made by individuals with an interest in the estate, it was to be valued by 'some honest and skilfull persons' who were to declare 'the just value [of the goods] in their judgements and consciences, that is to say, at such a price as the same may be sold at that time'.[82] Burn implied this practice had a long history. Quoting the constitution of Othobon (1236) he declared that those who 'competently understand the value of the deceased goods' should value them.[83] Occasionally documents surface that support Swinburne and Burn, such as the illuminating depositions in Tarleton v Taylor in 1692.[84] The appraisers used a scribe to write down their inventory, something Swinburne did not mention, and several specialists to value parts of the estate. The deponents made quite clear the duties of each participant.[85]

[80] Borthwick Institute, York, TEST CP 1781/7.

[81] Burn, *Ecclesiastical law* (1775) 4, p.238. On page 415 Burn gave a *pro forma* inventory with more detail. His list here consisted of 'purse and apparel, horses and furniture, horned cattle, sheep, swine, poultry, plate and the household goods, leases, rents in arrears, corn growing, hay and corn, ploughs and other implements of husbandry, debts, total, other debts supposed to be desperate', and 'debts owing by the deceased'. This was apparently not intended as a summary format, but as guidelines under which individual items could be listed. This *pro forma* inventory in parts accords neither with the law nor with the practice in most areas and during most of the period, as we shall demonstrate.

[82] Swinburne, *Briefe treatise* (1635), pp.56–7.

[83] Burn, *Ecclesiastical law* (1775) 4, p.250.

[84] Public Record Office, E134; 4 Wm. & M., Mich. 39 and Hil. 22.

[85] Cox and Cox, 'Probate inventories', pp.135–6.

Although Swinburne distinguished carefully between appraiser and valuer in their selection and duties, inventories show that for many estates the same people did both. This does not reflect slackness or inefficiency. Indeed, the evidence is overwhelming that inventories were usually made carefully and the goods valued appropriately,[86] though this may be less true by the mid-eighteenth century.[87] For most estates, those the act of 1529 deemed suitable to be appraisers were also likely to be capable of proper valuations. Creditors, legatees, and kinsmen would have known the market prices of stock and of produce since almost everyone was involved in agriculture to some degree. Equally, tradesmen's creditors would have known prices within the trade, and virtually everyone would have taken part in or attended sales of goods after funerals or after bankruptcies.

Personal representatives had to ensure that the deceased's goods were accurately listed and properly valued, but the guidelines were few and far between. Disputes were resolved in countless actions in the courts but, in spite of this enormous body of case law, locating a clear exposition of the law at a given moment is well nigh impossible. Legal authorities such as Swinburne and Burn touched on but did not resolve the uncertainties; the inventories themselves are often the best guide to what was to be included. The law regarding four types of property is particularly difficult to interpret; goods with little or no resale value in the market, debts, leases, and attachments to the freehold.

During the middle ages only stored foods like dried and salt fish and meat, flour and grains, butter and cheese, and possibly onions were recorded in domestic inventories. All else was apparently deemed for day to day use and without value. In the early modern period newly or more widely available commodities like tobacco, tea, spices, and potatoes did not fit into the traditional categories, although their exclusion from domestic inventories appears not to have been challenged, possibly because (except for potatoes) they were all shop goods with no potential for resale in the market. Thus we find tea cups but no tea, cake tins but no dried fruits to make cakes, stoves to dry

---

[86] Cox and Cox, 'Valuations in probate'. Valuations are generally slightly lower than prices of apparently equivalent goods in the market. However, there was a hiatus between the home and the market, (the cost of transport for example or bringing an animal into sale condition) which probably accounts for the difference. See Chapter 5, below, for the efforts of the ecclesiastical courts to ensure proper valuation and Chapter 6 for a more detailed discussion of valuations.

[87] Vaisey, *Diary of Thomas Turner*, p.247, 'And I dare say we valued it [a fellow tradesman's estate] at £50 under the real worth, were it to be sold'.

sweetmeats but no sweetmeats, sugar nippers but no sugar, tobacco boxes but neither tobacco nor pipes. By contrast, in tradesmen's inventories these goods were listed and may be taken as diagnostic of trading activity. The same is true of haberdashery and of smallwares; not listed in domestic inventories, their presence in retail shops, in quantity and in variety, reveals their widespread use. Furthermore, while the stock in shops suggests that women could increasingly afford kerchiefs at their necks and aprons about their waists, the appraisers increasingly gave only a global value for clothes even though there was a vigorous second-hand market.[88]

Debts owed by the deceased should not have been recorded since they were not assets, but debts owing to the deceased were not necessarily recorded either. Debts of specialty, those acknowledged in a properly signed and witnessed document like a bond, presented no problem once the document was in the personal representative's hands. The debtor could then be forced to pay up through the courts. Just as common were debts agreed verbally or recorded in contentious ways. Since these were irrecoverable in the courts, according to Lyndwood, they should not have been recorded until they became cash in hand.[89] Of these dubious debts those in the shop book presented particular problems, since the customer had not signed for them, and the other party to the deal was dead. In the sixteenth century the shop book does not appear to have loomed large in retail trade, and few appraisers listed the shop book separately from other debts. However, as it became integral to trading practice, it became too valuable an asset for creditors to ignore. As early as 1609 parliament recognised the shop book as a record of debts for one year from the date of entry.[90] Those debts not collected within that time had little legal validity and probably account for many of the 'desperate debts' in inventories. There is a tendency, no more, for debts to be recorded less frequently in the eighteenth century, which is at present unexplained.

There were three main ways of leasing land; *pur autre vie* (that is, for life or for lives), for a term of years, and at will. English law on property attaches far more importance to seissin, that is occupation, than to claims of ownership. As a consequence and after much argument during the

---

[88] Lemire, 'Peddling Fashion'.
[89] Quoted in Burn, *Ecclesiastical law*, 4, p.238. Although Burn endorsed Lyndwood on this point, he added 'But unless they be bad debts, it seemed best to insert them, and even if they be bad debts, or desperate, yet they may be inserted, specifying them as such'. He further added that they would not count as a part of the goods unless recovered.
[90] 7 Ja. I, c.12.

middle ages, a lease for lives came to be regarded as a form of real estate and its transmission at death followed the same rules as those for freehold land.[91] On the other hand, a lease for years, even if the term were to 'one and the heirs for 500 years', was regarded as part of the personal estate, though the personal representative had to have the document in hand.[92] The injustice of this distinction was rectified partly in 1676 when leases for life could be used to settle debt, and entirely in 1741 when they were to be distributed as if personal estate.[93] Since a tenancy at will could be terminated at any time, its value was indefinable. Probably such tenancies should not have been put on inventories, though the legal commentaries implied rights for that growing season by saying that a tenant at will could enter and take off crops he had sowed.

Over the years the courts had established clear principles on the boundary between real property (including attachments to the freehold) and personal, but developments in several spheres during the early modern period challenged the orthodoxy on which the law was based.

The early modern period saw dramatic changes in the domestic environment and the way people exploited it. Innovatory aids to comfort like glass in the windows, wainscoting on the walls, and internal doors became commonplace well down the social scale. These had belonged to the executor as moveables, but Swinburne declared them fixtures, as did Burn.[94] Innovation challenged appraisers of trade inventories too. During the early modern period agriculture, industry and trade increasingly used heavy plant, by its nature fixed to the premises. Objects which had been free standing when activity was conducted on a small scale became fixtures, such as cheese and cider presses, anvils and bellows, presses and stamps, spinning machines and calendars,[95] tobacco engines and malt mills, and shop fronts, counters and display cabinets. The money involved was considerable. For example, an inventory of Coalbrookdale iron works taken in 1718 valued two pairs of bellows at £80 each, and the forge hammer at £10, while the total value was estimated at over

---

[91] The same is true of advowsons, and some other so-called 'incorporeal' assets.

[92] Burn, *Ecclesiastical law* (1775), 4, p.239.

[93] 29 Ch. II, c.3 and 14 Geo. II, c.20. Burn, who asserted that leases for life should be included, was writing after this act when this would have been common practice. However, the inventories in some parts of the country, such as in Devon and Cornwall, suggest the practice was common before the act.

[94] Swinburne, *Briefe treatise* (1635), p.51; Burn, *Ecclesiastical law* (1775) 4, pp.240–2.

[95] Calendar, a machine used to press cloth so that it has a glazed surface.

£3,000.[96] The most dramatic newcomer was the steam engine. This was built into the engine house and clearly fixed, yet it could be worth as much as £350. The obvious injustice of such assets being unavailable to pay debts and legacies eventually caused the law's inflexibility to crumple. In Lawton v Lawton (1743) it was confirmed that the courts 'will do . . . to the utmost they can in favour of creditors'. The judge conceded that the strict rule requiring all to go to the heir had increasingly been relaxed for two forms of property: the one 'between landlord and tenant as marble chimney pieces and things necessary for trade', the other 'between tenant for life and the remainderman' since the former 'will not erect such things [as fire engines] unless they go to the executor'.[97] These issues continued to exercise the courts, but mainly after the period when inventories are an important source.

Changes in agricultural practice provoked similar disputes between heir and personal representative. In the middle ages a distinction had been drawn between personal assets created or improved by man and real assets that were part of nature's bounty.[98] Some depended on the stage in production, so that growing grass and trees went to the heir, while hay and felled timber went to the executor.[99] A further distinction had developed between crops planted or sown by man in ploughed land and harvested by cutting (personal assets), and those that were not (real assets). From the sixteenth century, if not earlier, some crops did not fit this pattern—flax and hemp were pulled and not cut, root crops were dug, clover and improved grasses were sown but were regarded as grass, and orchards were planted and pruned but viewed as trees provided by nature. By Burn's time only some of these issues seem to have been resolved. Quoting Wentworth, Burn opined that roots growing in the garden 'as carrots, parsnips, turneps, skirrets, and such like, shall go . . . to the heir, because they cannot be taken without digging and breaking the soil', although he also pointed out that, according to Lord Coke, the executors should have the year's crop from roots set. Possibly this was most pertinent regarding potatoes. But for other crops such as 'clover, sain foin and the like' all he could say was that 'no case hath occurred, wherein these matters have come to question; this kind of husbandry having been in use only of late years'.[100]

[96] Shropshire Records and Research, Shrewsbury, Coalbrookdale Company stock book 1718–1727, MS330. This inventory was not made for probate and included some fixtures.

[97] 26 *ER*, Chan. (1743), 811; Cox and Cox, 'Probate inventories', pp.139–43.

[98] Cox and Cox, 'Probate inventories, pp.219–20.

[99] Burn, *Ecclesiastical law* (1775), 4, p.238.

[100] Burn, *Ecclesiastical law* (1775), 4, p.240.

The increase in fixtures was accompanied, coincidentally or otherwise, by what appears to have been a change in how people used their houses. Weatherill writes of public and private areas; others of greater specialisation in the use of rooms.[101] This change in attitude is reflected in the documents. Sixteenth-century inventories are frequently just lists of possessions, those of the seventeenth century are more commonly lists taken room by room, and by 1750 they are often just lists of rooms, each valued but with no information on the contents.[102]

This change in perception by appraisers must reflect a change in the way people viewed possessions. The arrangement of the house and the value of each room had become more important than the individual items. It reflects too a change from payment of creditors and legatees in kind to payments in cash, because for this purpose global valuations agreed by all parties were all that were needed. The simplified inventory had the added advantage that it reduced disputes over what was a fixture. So long as all parties agreed on the total the detail could be omitted.

Another factor drove the appraisers towards a simplified inventory: the sheer plethora of possessions of ordinary people. At the start of the early modern period the stark bareness of most houses is striking to modern eyes. The domestic possessions of a well-to-do yeoman or tradesman in the sixteenth century might have numbered less than a hundred items with most of the investment tied up in the patriarchal bed and the major cooking utensils. In a full eighteenth-century inventory, there could be easily as many articles in a single room.

Probate accounts[103]

The dishonest executor was a stock medieval villain, as in the poem 'Winner and Waster'.[104] The sixteenth-century lawyer William Perkins advised testators to give their property away during their lifetime, advice taken by a friend of the Josselins of Earls Colne.[105] The executor,

---

[101] Weatherill, *Consumer behaviour and material culture*; Priestley and Corfield, 'Rooms and room use'.

[102] The change came earlier for the rich and in the south-east and more slowly for the poor and in the north.

[103] This section was written in collaboration with Dr. Erickson, and we gratefully acknowledge her help. It is brief, as the subject is dealt with fully by her in Chapter 5, pp.103–19 below.

[104] Gollanz, *Winner and waster*, quoted in Dyer, *Standards of living*, p.87.

[105] McFarlane, *Diary of Ralph Josselin*, p.352; 21 August 1655: 'Mrs. Church gave my wife a faire table cloth and six napkins all diaper which shee gave her formerly by will, and now shee would bee her own executor and deliver them to her'.

Perkins believed, 'may use such deceit that the legacies should never be assigned, delivered or paid, notwithstanding that they have goods in their hands of the testator's of the value of one thousand pounds over and above the debts and legacies of the devisor etc.'[106] For this reason after probate was granted the personal representative had to present an account to the ecclesiastical court, usually about one year after probate. The account, like the inventory, was in standard format. Starting with the inventory total, it then listed other assets now in the hands of the personal representatives, set out all outgoings and ended with a sum available for distribution.[107] Some accounts, but not all, specified how this residue was to be distributed.

Accounts survive from the 1520s onwards, but not in great numbers compared with other probate documents.[108] Spufford suggests a mere 27,000 survive, perhaps one for every 100 inventories,[109] though more recent research reveals nearly double that number.[110] Survival varies greatly from area to area. None survive for Westmorland, but over 13,000 for Kent.[111] At Lichfield there are about 1,300, stored not in the individual bundles of probate papers, but among the papers of the consistory court, suggesting they resulted from court action and not from the ordinary process of probate. This procedure is not typical of other parts of the country. Accounts remained a check on the personal representative into the eighteenth century and beyond, but their usefulness was steadily eroded during the period.

The ecclesiastical courts must have acquired the power to make executors accountable some time before an act of 1357 made administrators 'accountable to the Ordinaries as the Executors be . . .'.[112] Precisely what this meant remains obscure. Lyndwood averred that an

---

[106] Perkins, *Profitable booke*, quoted in Holdsworth, *History of English law,* 3, p.556.

[107] Most of the so-called orphans' inventories produced for probate in the City of London include three totals; the 'whole sum' of the goods and chattels, the 'total sum' including the debts not yet collected, and a third apparently consisting of the sum available for distribution as in a conventional account. The three could vary considerably.

[108] The number of accounts and their survival is discussed more fully by Erickson, Chapter 5, below. Here only a brief outline is given to make sense of the subsequent section on the development of accounts.

[109] Spufford, 'Limitations of the probate inventory', p.154.

[110] British Record Society Probate Accounts Index Project.

[111] British Record Society Probate Accounts Index Project, but Garrard, 'English probate inventories', p.62, gives a higher figure for Kent.

[112] 31 Ed. III, st.1, c.11. For the origins of ecclesiastical testamentary jurisdiction, see Holdsworth, *History of English law*, I, pp.625–9.

account was only required if demanded,[113] while Swinburne declared
that its purpose was to avoid 'the utter undoing and spoyling of many
fatherlesse, and friendlesse children', implying it was only to be rendered
when minors were involved. He defended the practice declaring 'no
man with safe conscience, speake against the rendering of an account',
implying that some were doing just that.[114] Subsequent events suggest
that many viewed the inventory as sufficient check on personal
representatives, backed by the right to take them to court.

The 1529 act formalising how inventories were to be made implied a
requirement to render account.[115] Only in the 1670 act was the procedure
clarified, and then only to some extent.[116] Firstly, an administrator was
required to 'make or cause to be made a true and just account of his said
Administration'. Secondly, it laid down that ordinaries 'shall and may, and
are enabled to . . . call such Administrators to account'. Whether the
'shall' was intended to make the practice universal or the 'may' took
priority so that the act was only permissive and enabling is not clear.
Certainly the act did not signal a marked increase in the number of
accounts. Either the practice of the ecclesiastical courts was already
reasonably effective, or they were unable to exploit their new powers.

Fifteen years later an act made permanent that of 1670 but with an
important amendment, that:

> 'No administrator shall . . . be cited . . . to render an Account . . .
> (otherwise than by an Inventory . . . thereof) unless it be . . . in behalf
> of a Minor . . . or as a Creditor or next of Kin, nor be compelled to
> account before any of the Ordinaries . . . anything in the said last Acts
> contained to the contrary notwithstanding'.[117]

The act restricted the power of the ordinary to require an account unless
requested by specific parties, and suggests inventories alone were
thought to make personal representatives sufficiently accountable in
most circumstances. The 1685 act thus seems to introduce new
practices, rather than to formalise existing ones, unlike the previous acts.
Its effect was marked. The number of accounts went down, sharply in
some counties like Lincolnshire, Northamptonshire, West Sussex and
Hampshire, more gradually in others like Kent and Somerset.[118]

---

[113] Lyndwood, *Provinciale* (1929), pp.174, 176–7, quoted in Houlbrooke, *Church
courts*, pp.91–2.
[114] Swinburne, *Briefe treatise* (1635), pp.85–6.
[115] 21 Hen. VIII, c.5.
[116] 22 & 23 Ch. II, c.10.
[117] 1 Ja. II, c.17.
[118] The pattern is clear in the British Record Society's results.

Conclusion

Probate is a challenging study for historians, and an understanding of its many facets a prerequisite to extracting valid data from its many diverse documents. Those operating the system—parliament, the church, the courts, and not least those personally interested in the estates of the deceased—each had their own agenda, their own assumptions and their own rules of operation. Like any document, those for probate were produced for a particular purpose under a particular set of customs, laws and regulations. They were produced for posterity only in the sense that many were documents of record to be produced in a court of law if demanded, but they were not written for the historian. Holdsworth's *History of English law* comprises 17 volumes; much of the first 12 relates to the early modern period. Perhaps half the contents of these bear upon probate. We cannot easily become expert in all aspects of law, custom and practice impinging on probate. This chapter provides a guide and some ideas to stimulate debate about the system. The rest of the book considers particular aspects of the system and how effectively they can be used by historians.

3

Wills as an Historical Source

NIGEL GOOSE AND NESTA EVANS

The survival of wills

Wills are undoubtedly a remarkably rich historical source, but they survive for only a proportion of the early modern population and this survival is strongly biased by age, social class and gender. There are chronological and geographical variations too, neither as yet fully explored, although it is clear that few wills survive before the late-fourteenth century. This does not, however, necessarily imply that few were made, for most courts only began to register wills in the later fifteenth century, significantly increasing their chances of survival. Occasionally, early wills survive due to the intervention of an unusual jurisdiction, such as that of the Court of Orphans in Bristol.[1] But generally, relatively few are to be found before the fifteenth century, or even before the middle of that century, as in the archdeaconry court jurisdictions of East Anglia.[2]

Even when it is known that wills were made in considerable numbers, their survival is far from guaranteed. In the diocese of Hereford, for example, thousands of probates were registered in the fifteenth century but only a few wills survive.[3] It is possible that in some jurisdictions only disputed wills were registered, whilst selective record keeping may also explain why many wills produced in manor courts to prove inheritance rights to copyhold property have been lost. It is also likely that some wills never went to probate. But survival varied geographically too, often for no obvious reason: the archdeaconry courts in fifteenth-century Suffolk provide a fuller record than those of Norfolk and Norwich, whilst St Albans archdeaconry excels with over 1,300 wills surviving for 1430–80, and 303 for the small town of St Albans alone between 1471 and 1500.[4]

---

[1] Wadley, *Notes on the wills.*
[2] Gottfried, *Epidemic disease*, p.14.
[3] Faraday and Cole, *Calendar of probate.*
[4] Gottfried, *Epidemic disease*, p.21; Flood, *St Albans wills.*

Table 3.1 Number of currently indexed wills, 1400–1700

Date	Number	Cumulative Total
Pre-1400	6,103	6,103
1401–1500	35,995	42,098
1501–1600	291,009	333,107
1601–1700	463,306	796,413

The general increase in record keeping from the mid-sixteenth century is reflected in the preservation of more wills as originals and register copies, although it remains impossible to tell how many were made but never proved or not preserved. Regionally, only the north-west and the south-west of England are distinctly poorly served, the latter due both to lack of care and wartime destruction.[5] Some northern counties may, however, have higher ratios of wills to population than some southerly counties, and it has been suggested that north Essex is particularly unfavoured.[6] The total number of wills that survive remains unknown, but a minimum figure has been established by Takahashi, who has counted all those indexed to date for the Province of Canterbury in the Index Library series, which includes the majority of its courts. Not all courts are fully represented. The earliest in date is the index to Prerogative Court of Canterbury wills starting in 1383; many courts are fully covered up to 1700, whereafter the indexes are far fewer in number.[7]

The number of wills included in the Index Library volumes are presented in Table 3.1. From the above figures, at least 42,000 wills survive for late-medieval England, whilst early modern historians working in the southern half of England have readily available to them a minimum of three-quarters of a million wills between 1501 and 1700. The true figure is certainly far higher as some important courts are unrepresented, including the Consistory Court of Canterbury, and that of Norwich after 1603, and Erickson estimates that as many as two million wills survive between the mid-sixteenth and mid-eighteenth centuries.[8] The coverage by archdiaconal and consistory court varies

---

[5] Moore, '"Jack Fisher's 'flu": a virus revisited', pp.283–4.

[6] Macfarlane, *Reconstructing historical communities*, p.69.

[7] Had Dr Takahashi used printed indexes other than those of the Index Library, he would have considerably increased the number of wills he found. Additionally, virtually all county record offices have card indexes to their holdings of probate records: see Camp, *Wills and their whereabouts* and Gibson, *Wills and where to find them*.

[8] Erickson, *Women and property*, p.204.

regionally, while there are also local variations in survival that do not
always correlate with the size of the population at risk.[9] Nevertheless,
the data in Figure 3.1, representing indexed wills from 19 counties
proved 1401–1646, indicate a steady and continuous rise in the number
of wills proved in the provincial courts included in this sample from the
1510s to the 1610s, whereafter the number levels out.[10] Comparing the
rate of increase of will survival with estimated national population
growth, many more wills *per capita* survive for the early-seventeenth
century compared to the early-sixteenth, but much of this proportional
growth was achieved early in the period, and from the 1570s the
number roughly keeps pace with population growth.[11]

   The trends shown in Figure 3.2 for the Prerogative Court of
Canterbury (PCC) are particularly interesting. Here numbers increase
considerably from the mid-1480s, only to fall back once again from the
1510s to the 1530s, a feature that has yet to be noticed, let alone
explained, by economic historians. Thereafter their number again
increases, with a particularly sharp upward curve during the final third
of the sixteenth century, and sustained growth through to the 1620s.
The business of the PCC increased markedly during the later 1640s and
early 1650s due to the impact of the Civil Wars and Interregnum upon
provincial ecclesiastical courts, and from 1653–60 the new Court for
Probate had sole testamentary jurisdiction throughout England and
Wales, which explains the high annual totals shown in Figure 3.3.[12] This
is evident too for the provincial towns considered in Chapter 10 below,
whilst in Reading the habit of using the central court (the restored
PCC) was sustained after the Restoration, even though many of the
testators concerned were not notably wealthy.[13] While, therefore, the
Prerogative Courts were supposedly reserved for those owning property
in more than one diocese, and were generally the province of relatively
wealthy testators owning property in at least two counties, in practice
there could be considerable flexibility. Part of the attraction of these
courts was the superior skills of the lawyers working there, while there

---

[9] See Chapter 10, below, pp.193–4.
[10] A detailed list of the courts included in this sample is provided in Appendix 3.
    We are very grateful to Dr Takahashi for providing us with this unpublished
    data.
[11] See also Takahashi, 'Number of wills', pp.205–6.
[12] Kitching, 'Probate during the Civil War', part II, pp.346–56. There is a gap in
    the Index Library series of PCC wills, from which these figures have been
    drawn, between 1630 and 1653. This is because a similar index, compiled from
    Probate Act Books but performing the same function, was already available:
    Mathews and Mathews, *Years books*.
[13] See Table 10.2, p.194.

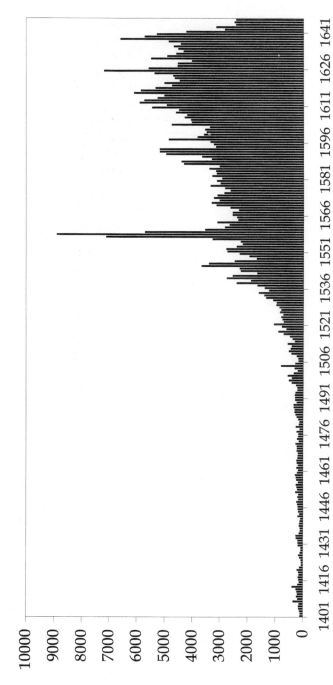

Figure 3.1 Wills from provincial courts, 1401–1646

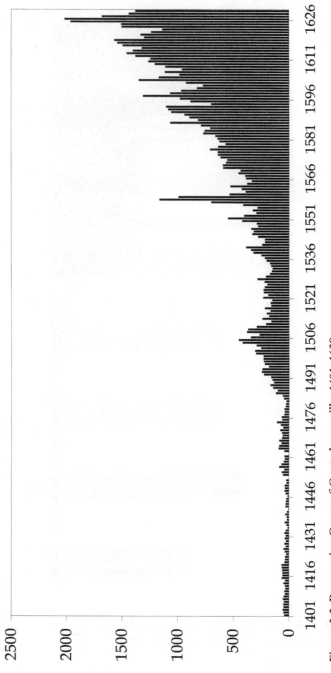

Figure 3.2 Prerogative Court of Canterbury wills, 1401–1629

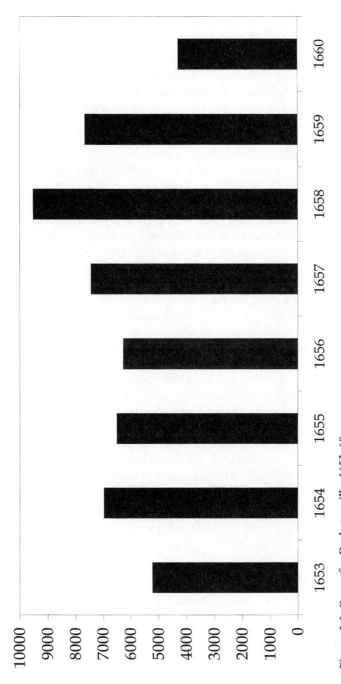

Figure 3.3 Court for Probate wills, 1653–60

was also greater kudos attached to the use of the highest ecclesiastical probate courts in the land.[14]

Will-writing was clearly far more common amongst the wealthier social groups in early modern England, those with significant personal goods or property to bequeath. Land ownership in particular rendered will making advisable and the devising of lands by will was encouraged by the Statute of Wills of 1540 and subsequent legislation.[15] It did not, however, make it absolutely necessary, for both lands and tenements could be devised by common law or manorial custom. Personal goods could also be allocated or distributed prior to death, as no doubt they were for many of those towards the bottom of the social scale. The precise sector of the population for whom wills survive is difficult to establish. For the small town of Grantham, Coppel found that it was largely the 'middling rich' who made wills in the sixteenth century, although will-making reached a little further down the social scale by 1600, whilst for Staplehurst in Kent (1566–1601) Zell discovered that the sample was dominated by those described as 'householders', and the poor were clearly under-represented.[16] For the Fenland village of Willingham, however, Spufford found that the poorer tenants produced most wills, and that it was family responsibilities rather than wealth which increased the likelihood of will-making.[17] Certainly, men with under-age children or no obvious heir occur frequently among testators in the Archdeaconry of Sudbury. Of the wills proved in this court in the six years 1630–5, 18.5 per cent are those of men with under-age children, although 22 per cent were made by childless persons, perhaps also suggesting the need to clarify inheritance where there was no obvious heir.[18] For Whickham in the Durham coalfield, Levine and Wrightson suggest that only 'a small minority' made wills, though examples can be found at 'all social levels from cottager to substantial yeoman', but this industrial community is unlikely to be typical.[19]

Accordingly, quantitative estimates of will survival vary. For rural Flixton, Evans' calculation from a small sample for 1560–1600 shows that 25 per cent of adult males buried left a will.[20] For Elizabethan

[14] Stephens, *Sources*, pp.36–7.
[15] 32 Hen. VIII, c.1, 34 & 35 Hen. VIII, c.5; and see above, Chapter 1.
[16] Coppel, 'Wills and the community', pp.78–9, which employs archdeaconry and PCC wills; Zell, 'Social parameters', pp.107–13.
[17] Spufford, 'Peasant inheritance customs', pp.170–1.
[18] Evans, *Wills of the Archdeaconry of Sudbury, 1630–1635*, p.xi.
[19] Levine and Wrightson, *Making of an industrial society*, p.283. No precise quantitative estimate of the proportion who made wills is given.
[20] Evans, 'Inheritance', p.55.

Staplehurst in Kent, Zell found that only half of adult males who died were noticed in any way by the probate courts, and only about one-third left a will.[21] For one Nottinghamshire parish just over one-quarter of those dying between 1572 and 1600 left a will, but this calculation includes all deaths, and the proportion would have been higher had adult males been considered alone.[22] A similarly high proportion, one-third, of adults buried in one chapelry in Kirkby Lonsdale in Cumbria in the early-seventeenth century left a will, but the Quaker influence is in evidence here, while in Earls Colne in Essex at the same period the proportion was as low as 8 per cent.[23] The market town of Grantham (1581–1610) also exhibits a low proportion, just 10 per cent of potential testators leaving a will.[24] In larger towns numbers also appear to have been relatively low, no doubt partly because a higher proportion of urban populations were poor. In Cambridge and Reading approximately 12 per cent and 10 per cent of adults left wills in the early-seventeenth century, or 19 and 17 per cent of adult males.[25] Furthermore, while labourers accounted for 4 per cent of a sample of 936 wills in Cambridge 1580–1640, as many as 27 per cent were designated as labourer in five parishes in a census of the 1620s.[26] Other studies also show that labourers are not wholly unrepresented in probate evidence and that the majority of testators were probably of middling rank, although this latter fact may merely reflect their numerical prominence in early modern society.[27] The situation found in the Consistory of Ely in the 1620s and 1630s, where 22 per cent of identifiable testators declared themselves to be labourers, is probably exceptional.[28] Thus while social coverage is anything but narrowly restricted, there can be little doubt that surviving wills are socially biased, and largely fail to reflect the experiences of either the rural or urban poor.

Given that wills could not be written by minors, and were commonly drawn up as death approached, they will also be biased by

---

[21] Zell, 'Social parameters', pp.110–12.

[22] Palliser, *Age of Elizabeth*, p.98.

[23] Unpublished research by Sarah Harrison, cited in Coppel, 'Wills and the community', p.78

[24] Coppel, 'Wills and the community', p.78.

[25] See Chapter 10, below, pp.193–5.

[26] The census is, however, biased towards the poorer parishes, so the discrepancy might be somewhat less stark for the town as a whole: Goose, 'Economic and social aspects', pp.99–100.

[27] Moore, '"Jack fisher's 'flu": a virus revisited', pp.287–90; Palliser, *Age of Elizabeth*, p.98

[28] Takahashi, 'Number of wills', p.209; Spufford, *World of rural dissenters*, p.170.

age, and as such may relate largely to those either at the height of their achievements or to those already past their peak. Relatively few testators wrote their wills whilst in good health, although it was not unknown for a will to be written in advance and then signed on or near the deathbed, sometimes with the addition of a codicil modifying the bequests made.[29] Those who did this often held positions of spiritual or political authority, and may thus have wished to set an example, although Benjamin Trott of All Saints, Cambridge, took no chances by writing his will in August 1665 'in regard of the danger of these infectious times': in the event it was not proved until 1668.[30]

What is quite clear is that women are severely under-represented. Married women could only write a will with their husband's approval, as granted by Zachary Soones of Colchester to his wife Judith in 1662, probably because she had been married before and owned a number of say looms that she wished to bequeath, but few such wills survive.[31] Evidence from York suggests that the general exclusion of married women from will-making may have been a fifteenth century phenomenon, although in London few married women made wills at the turn of the fourteenth century, indicating that here at least common law had already prevailed over canon law.[32] By the sixteenth century female testators are largely spinsters or widows. Prior's analysis of PCC wills 1558–1700 shows that married women never accounted for as much as one per cent of the total, despite a slight increase after the Interregnum, while in the lower courts in Gloucestershire the numbers are tiny.[33] Widows' wills are far more numerous, reflecting the enhanced possibility of both independence and prosperity that widowhood could bring, for the fortunate minority of widows at least.[34] Widows could thus form a sizeable proportion of all testators, and as a result women normally constituted between 14 and 18.5 per cent of testators in the Diocese of Ely in the decades between 1540 and 1770, rising from roughly 11 per cent in the 1540s to a peak of just over 20 per cent in the 1630s and falling back thereafter.[35] In Gloucester

---

[29] Coppel, 'Will-making on the deathbed', pp.37–45.

[30] Public Record Office (hereafter PRO) PCC wills, Year Books of Probate, 1668, f. 55, will of Benjamin Trott, All Saints, Cambridge.

[31] Essex Country Record Office, D/A BR 8/77, will of Zachary Soones, proved 1667.

[32] Goldberg, 'Women in fifteenth-century town life', p.115; for London and a useful discussion of the differences between canon and common law see Lacey, 'Women and work', pp.29–40.

[33] Prior, 'Wives and wills', pp.208–10.

[34] Holderness, 'Widows in pre-industrial society'; see also Chapter 16, below.

[35] Carlson, 'Historical value'.

Consistory Court 1541–80, women's wills accounted for almost 18 per cent of a sample of over 7,000.[36] In the market towns of Woodstock and Thame in the seventeenth century widows accounted for 24 per cent of all surviving probate documents and constituted 22 per cent of all testators, whilst 20 per cent of testators were widows or spinsters in the small town of Hertford 1660–1725.[37] In the larger towns of Cambridge, Colchester and Reading the proportion of wills left by women, the great majority of them widows, rose steadily from 16 per cent 1500–49, to 19 per cent 1550–99, 22 per cent 1600–49 and 26 per cent 1650–99.[38] Moving northwards, a similar proportion of testators were women in Leeds and Hull 1520–1650, at just under 19 per cent; just one in eight of these were spinsters, and a mere six out of a total of 407 were married.[39] These figures tally quite closely with those presented in Erickson's general survey, which found that women constituted 12–17 per cent of will-makers in the sixteenth century, around 20 per cent in the seventeenth, and 25 per cent by the early-eighteenth, the vast majority being widows.[40] Wills thus provide a perhaps surprising degree of insight into the affairs of the widowed female population of early modern England, in both town and countryside and in geographically disparate regions. The proportion of wills left by women appears to increase slightly in the seventeenth century but more markedly in the larger towns, possibly because of the characteristic skew in their sex ratios towards women.

The format of wills[41]

Wills were usually dictated on the deathbed to a scribe, although nuncupative wills, made by word of mouth before witnesses, had been recognised as perfectly valid and legal since at least the eighth century, the statute of 1540 making it clear that they could only be used for transmission of moveable goods and not for lands.[42] Nuncupative wills, although usually very brief and lacking detailed bequests, often have a

---

[36] Litzenberger, 'Local responses', p.418.

[37] See Chapter 16, below; Adams, *Lifestyle and culture*, p.xv.

[38] Calculations from 6,195 wills proved in prerogative, consistory, archdeaconry and peculiar courts: the overall figure for 1500–1699 is 22 per cent.

[39] Cross, 'Northern women', pp.83, 85.

[40] Erickson, *Women and property*, pp.204–5.

[41] For a more extended and valuable discussion of the process of will-making and the institutional and personal ties that it reflects in a local context see Levine and Wrightson, *Making of an industrial society*, pp.288–94.

[42] 32 Hen. VIII, c.1.

special interest as they purport to record verbatim the words of the dying person. A typical reason for making such a will was given by William Stofforde of Gislingham in Suffolk in 1575. This testator 'for wante of a clarke or scrivener to wright, was enforced by reason of greate payne in the presence of [witnesses names] to declare to them his minde & to make a will nuncupative'.[43] Of 576 wills proved in the Archdeaconry Court of Sudbury 1636–38, 11.2 per cent were nuncupative.[44]

Wills commence with the date of their dictation, the testator's name and, usually, also their occupation or status and place of residence. Many testators proceed to mention their state of health and almost invariably describe themselves as 'sick in body', but also 'whole in mind and in good and perfect remembrance', or some similar phrase. There are, however, exceptions. Everard Wright of St Albans, innholder, had particular difficulty in 1613, being 'deprived then and long before of the use of his speech yet of perfect mind and memory' he made his will 'by sufficient figures and evident demonstrations of his meaning' in the presence of several witnesses.[45] Until the late-seventeenth century, the first bequest is almost invariably of the testator's soul to God, or prior to the Reformation 'to our Lady Saint Mary and to all the company of heaven', or to both. This is followed by disposal of the body to a chosen burial place. In pre-Reformation wills, bequests to the parish church and other religious institutions usually follow, ranging from the financing of pilgrimages through to more common bequests to the church 'for tithes forgotten', church reparations, the endowment of chantry priests or to the four orders of friars.[46] Although these by no means ceased after the mid-sixteenth century they declined significantly in both town and countryside, a higher proportion of charitable bequests being directed to secular ends.[47]

The remaining content of wills varies according to what individuals had to leave. Land, buildings, livestock, trade goods and tools, furniture and household utensils, and articles of clothing, are all commonly found, besides gifts of money in cash or bonds. Real estate is often problematic, however, for inheritance of land could also be ensured by other means, such as manorial custom, as Jennings shows below.[48] In some cases the will

---

[43] Suffolk Record Office, 1C500/1/34/23.

[44] Evans, *Wills of the Archdeaconry of Sudbury, 1636–1638.*

[45] St Albans Archdeaconry wills, Everard Wright, St Albans, proved 1614.

[46] Some valuable examples are to be found in Owen, *Making of King's Lynn*, pp.251–6.

[47] Jordan, *Charities of London*, p.69; Jordan, *Charities of rural England*, pp.25, 93, 220, and see below, pp.50–1.

[48] See below, pp.66–8 and Chapter 17.

of a man, known from other sources to own property, includes no real estate, simply because his children had already been established with land and houses. Hence the will of John Goosy of Old in Northamptonshire of 1613 left nothing to his eldest son Robert because he had already received the lease of 'a quartern of land in Naseby, and a great brass pot'.[49] Nearly half the resources given to his children by the seventeenth-century clergyman Ralph Josselin, in goods, lands, and portions for apprenticeship, education and marriage, had already been bestowed before he made his will.[50] The appointment of executors, supervisors or overseers and the naming of witnesses comes at the end of the document, together with the testator's signature or mark. The grant of probate, in Latin until 1733, is found on both register copies and original wills.

The majority of early modern wills were not written by lawyers, although testators who used the Prerogative Court of Canterbury were more likely to employ them. Very occasionally they were written by the testator himself, as in the case of John Hill, a shopkeeper of Hertford, who in 1705 was sufficiently proud of the fact to note that his will was made 'with my owne handwriting'.[51] Most were written by parish clergy and other educated men with considerable experience in drawing up a will. Townspeople were more likely to use scriveners or public notaries, if only because of their availability. In smaller market towns will writers were less likely to be professionals, and a study of wills over a period of at least 20 years should reveal several regular amateur scribes. In the small Suffolk town of Bungay 127 wills were proved 1550–1600, 40 per cent of which were written by five men—three clergymen and two laymen.[52] Litzenberger identified as many as 11 scribes in Tewkesbury 1541–80 though only four in Cirencester, while in the larger town of Reading eight professional scriveners were identified 1580–1619, 13 1620–59 and 11 1660–99.[53] Marsh has noted that 'there is very little to indicate that public notaries were widely operative in rural England during the reign of Elizabeth'.[54] The same is largely true for the seventeenth century, though by now they were regularly found in the larger towns, Reading producing two examples, while in the university town of Cambridge, perhaps unsurprisingly, they feature throughout the sixteenth and seventeenth centuries, as many as 17

[49] Quoted in Everitt, 'Farm labourers', p.456.
[50] Macfarlane, *Family life*, pp.54, 64–7.
[51] Adams, *Lifestyle and culture*, p.131.
[52] Evans, 'Inheritance', p.59.
[53] Litzenberger, 'Local responses', pp.422–3; unpublished research based on all extant Reading wills.
[54] Marsh, 'In the name of God?', p.233.

active in 1620–59, and ten 1660–99. Across seventeenth-century East
Anglia both scriveners and notaries were almost wholly restricted to the
five large towns of Norwich, King's Lynn, Ipswich, Great Yarmouth
and Bury St Edmunds, just one scrivener featuring in the smaller town
of Sudbury and a single notary in Beccles.[55]

The use of wills

As recently as 1974 Spufford could write that 'wills are largely unused
by local historians'; three years later Macfarlane also noted that they
'were little used by historians until a few years ago'.[56] The situation has
changed out of all recognition in the last 20 years, for wills have since
been exploited for a multitude of purposes, even if their full scope is yet
to be realised. In the process there has been considerable debate about
their value as historical evidence, either in themselves or in comparison
with other extant documentation, and these debates have helped shed
new light on the nature of the probate process and the wills it generated.

Charity

One of the oldest uses to which wills have been put significantly pre-
dates the remarks of Spufford and Macfarlane, and this is to establish
levels of charitable giving, most comprehensively examined in Jordan's
monumental trilogy.[57] Through examination of charitable bequests
from wills proved in all levels of ecclesiastical court in addition to
bequests made in donors' lifetimes from ten English counties, Jordan
concluded that during his chosen period:

> a veritable revolution had occurred during which private donors,
> men who held in view a vision of the future, had repaired the damage
> society had sustained from the slow ruin of the Middle Ages . . . a
> revolution too in which men's aspirations for their own generation
> and those to come had undergone an almost complete
> metamorphosis, as the essentially religious interests of the later
> Middle Ages yielded to social aspirations which were most
> aggressively secular. . . .[58]

[55] Patten, *English towns*, Figures 16 and 20, pp.273, 283.
[56] Spufford, *Contrasting communities*, p.56; Macfarlane, *Reconstructing historical communities*, p.67.
[57] Jordan, *Philanthropy*; Jordan, *Charities of London*; Jordan, *Charities of rural England*.
[58] Jordan, *Philanthropy*, p.240. The city of Bristol is included as one of Jordan's 10 'counties'.

A total of £3.1 million was devoted to charitable causes between 1480 and 1660 in these ten counties, almost £1.5 million of this to either the relief or social rehabilitation of the poor, while religious bequests declined from 53 per cent of the total in 1480–1540 to just 7 per cent by 1561–1600, and only recovered to 12 per cent by the mid-seventeenth century.[59] Jordan's figures show a trough in the 1540s followed by a great outpouring in the 1550s, steady growth in the Elizabethan period, and a further surge in the early-seventeenth century climaxing in the 'incredible generosity which marks the years 1611–1640'.[60]

A veritable industry has grown up dedicated to criticism of Jordan's methods and conclusions, within which there is both justice and injustice. Above all he failed to allow for inflation, although to be fair he was by no means unaware of this problem but felt that the construction of an accurate price index, and identification of regional price differences, was impossible.[61] On both points he was wrong, for the general level of inflation revealed by the Phelps Brown/Hopkins index has regularly been confirmed by other series, while regional prices moved at least roughly in line. Crude deflation of his figures does indeed produce a somewhat different trend, in particular a sharp fall in total donations through from the 1560s to 1590s, now followed by a more modest recovery, but nevertheless one that produces a net real increase of 83 per cent when the decadal averages for secular bequests 1611–40 are compared with 1480–1540.[62] But philanthropy, in many of its guises, is cumulative, and it is particularly important to remember that 82 per cent of benefactions took the form of endowments, with little variation between counties.[63] Hadwin's further re-working of the data to allow for this, for all of its methodological uncertainties, produces a more accurate picture of the total available to the poor: while the situation pre-1540 defies estimation, between the mid-sixteenth and mid-seventeenth centuries the value of privately provided poor relief expanded by more than a factor of four.[64] Moreover, further deflation to allow for population growth still reveals a *per capita* expansion well in excess of a factor of two.[65]

---

[59] Calculated from Jordan, *Philanthropy*, Table 1, p.368.

[60] Jordan, *Philanthropy*, pp.243–5.

[61] Jordan, *Philanthropy*, pp.34–7.

[62] Bittle and Lane, 'Inflation and philanthropy', pp.203–10, calculations from Table 3, p.209; Hadwin, 'Deflating philanthropy', pp.105–17.

[63] Jordan, *Philanthropy*, p.24.

[64] Hadwin, 'Deflating philanthropy', pp.112–13.

[65] Hadwin, 'Deflating philanthropy', .p.113, and see Wrigley and Schofield, *Population history*, pp.531–3.

Methodological difficulties remain, however, though again we must appreciate that Jordan was himself aware of the 'frailties' of his data, suggesting a minimum error range of 10–15 per cent.[66] One particularly worrying problem is that charitable endowments may have failed through mismanagement or misappropriation, but despite some urban examples of this its extent is impossible to calculate, and Jordan does appear to have conducted checks that would have identified this problem for the larger endowments at least.[67] His data must also under-estimate informal philanthropy, particularly that offered on a day-to-day basis, and there is considerable literary evidence to suggest that this was declining during the second half of the sixteenth century. Furthermore, substantial charitable bequests may have had an adverse impact upon willingness to establish formal poor rates.[68] Estimates of 'generosity' must also take account, not only of the sums given, but also of the ability of the donor, and although Jordan did make efforts to estimate the wealth of a sample of donors and the percentages of that wealth the different classes gave to charity, he did not identify changes over time.[69] For Worcester, Dyer has compared charitable bequests with inventory totals, to conclude that not only were total charitable bequests lower in 1600–19 than 1550–69, but they were lower still as a proportion of the total wealth available.[70] How typical Worcester was in this respect remains to be seen.[71] Finally, the impact of giving, and the degree of generosity behind it, must be related to the magnitude of the problem itself, and there can be little doubt that poverty was more acute by the early-seventeenth century than it had been in the early-sixteenth.

Two further problems must be noted, as well as some possibilities. Wills do not record the sum total of charitable donations. Jordan also used a range of other archival sources, and will bequests accounted for only 63 per cent of the aggregate total, rising to 78 per cent in Bristol

---

[66] Jordan, *Philanthropy*, pp.31–40.

[67] Slack, *Poverty and policy*, pp.169–70; Jordan, *Philanthropy*, p.33; but see MacCaffrey, *Exeter*, pp.109–10, who finds that loan funds remained largely intact through from the later sixteenth to the mid-seventeenth century.

[68] Wales, 'Poverty', p.359.

[69] Jordan, *Philanthropy*, pp.330–7 and Table VII, pp.376–7. He did, however, provide the raw data for calculation of the changing proportion of various charitable donations made by the different socio-economic groups: Table XI, pp.386–7.

[70] Dyer, *City of Worcester*, pp.241–2.

[71] Dyer's methodology might itself be questioned, for he compared total recorded charitable giving with total inventory values for different periods, regardless of the changing numbers of individuals concerned, rather than matching individual bequests with wealth.

but falling as low as 28 per cent in Buckinghamshire.[72] Second, wills held locally and proved in consistory or archdiaconal courts will also convey an inadequate impression, for in Jordan's sample 94 per cent of the total benefactions made by will were found in the Prerogative Courts of Canterbury and York.[73] Notwithstanding these problems, the value of wills has been far from exhausted, and Jordan's work points up further possibilities. Rarely is any serious attention paid to the geographical distribution of giving, apart from reiteration of Jordan's key conclusion about the overwhelming importance of the contribution of London merchants in particular, and urban philanthropy in general.[74] Both regional and local differences deserve fuller exploration, and these could be substantial. Within the small county of Buckinghamshire, while 85 per cent of its parishes benefited from donations in excess of 10s., less than one in five possessed endowments 'sufficient to serve as social catalysts'.[75] Donations by social and occupational class and by gender, again topics on which Jordan is far from silent, could be further explored too. Women were by no means insignificant in this regard, although they contributed more as a proportion of the total in rural areas than they did in London.[76] Their charitable interests differed somewhat from those of men, in Buckinghamshire, Yorkshire and in London showing more wholly secular concerns.[77] In Retford in Nottinghamshire 1600–42, 44 per cent of testators gave to the poor, the percentage making gifts declining with social status: 78 per cent of gentlemen made charitable bequests, 45 per cent of yeomen, 37 per cent of tradesmen and 33 per cent of husbandmen and labourers. Legacies of real estate were most commonly made by gentlemen, yeomen and tradesmen, while women were predominant in gifts of household moveables.[78] Finally, rather than endlessly debating the relative importance of public and private charity in the early modern period, we

---

[72] Jordan, *Philanthropy*, pp.23–4.

[73] Jordan, *Philanthropy*, p.23.

[74] London provided £1.9 million, 61 per cent of the aggregate total for 1480–1660: Jordan, *Philanthropy*, p.241 and see Jordan, *Charities of London*, *passim*.

[75] Jordan, *Charities of rural England*, p.73.

[76] In Buckinghamshire women formed 13.5 per cent of all donors, and provided 13.0 per cent of the county total; in Yorkshire they formed 13.0 per cent of donors, providing 12.55 per cent of benefactions; and in London 14.9 per cent providing 9.1 per cent: Jordan, *Charities of rural England*, pp.27, 224; Jordan, *Charities of London*, pp.28–9.

[77] Jordan, *Charities of rural England*, pp.27–33, 96–8, 224–5; Jordan, *Charities of London*, p.30.

[78] Marcombe, *English small town life*, pp.115, 274–6.

need a fuller appreciation of the great range of strategies that were adopted to deal with poverty, by the poor themselves as well as through the political and administrative mechanisms available, within which wider context the evidence from wills should be set.

Religious preambles

It was once regarded as a straightforward procedure to infer religious persuasion from will preambles and hence determine the speed and extent of religious change, particularly in the aftermath of the Reformation. The work of Dickens on Nottinghamshire and Yorkshire, distinguishing 'traditional' from 'non-traditional' wills 1538–51, provides an early example, subsequently followed by historians of both rural and urban society, often with the additional employment of a 'neutral' category.[79] In 1971 Spufford published the important article reproduced below, discussing the possibility that will formularies reflect the opinion of the scribe as much as the testator, which might render them questionable as evidence of true religious belief.[80] Her conclusion, based upon Orwell and Willingham in Cambridgeshire, was that while standard formulations can indeed be found and associated with particular scribes, there was a sufficient range of choice of scribes for a testator to choose a man with at least the same general beliefs as himself, while when an individual held particularly forceful religious opinions these come through clearly in the terminology employed in his will, a point soon endorsed in a study of late-seventeenth century Matlock.[81]

Since then standard formularies for religious preambles to wills have been identified, the first in *Fly. An Almanacke*, published in 1657, followed rapidly by West's *Simboleography* (*Symbolaeographia*) which dates from 1590, although Spufford cast doubt upon the circulation and influence of the latter.[82] More recently, a much earlier formula has been identified in the will of William Tracy of Gloucestershire, written in 1530, which was probably disseminated in manuscript before it was printed in Antwerp in 1535. Although only a few individuals used this preamble, it was employed in areas as widespread as Sussex, Gloucestershire, Suffolk, London and Yorkshire.[83] In a sample of 3,000

---

[79] Dickens, *Lollards and Protestants*, pp.171–2, 215–18; Palliser, *Reformation in York*, pp.28–9, 32.

[80] See Chapter 7, below; also Chapter 8, pp.167–75.

[81] Matlock Population Studies Group, 'Wills and their scribes', pp.55–7.

[82] Capp, 'Will formularies', pp.49–50; Poole, 'Will formularies', pp.42–3; Spufford, 'Will formularies', pp.35–6.

[83] Craig and Litzenberger, 'Wills as religious propaganda', pp.423–30.

Gloucestershire wills made between 1541 and 1580, 350 different preamble formulas were used, but 325 of these were used by just 20 per cent of the sample, scribes tending to provide neutral statements in the absence of any strong expression of preference by the testator.[84]

Will preambles have been described as 'an idiosyncratic mixture of formula and personal expression',[85] and there has been further debate concerning the significance of the use of particular forms of words, as well as of the significance or otherwise of neutral forms. Some historians go so far as to deny they possess any meaning at all, though most give them at least qualified credence.[86] Recent work has emphasised the need carefully to examine the full range of preambles, in all of their complexity, and hence Litzenberger groups them into 17 preliminary categories before reducing these to the conventional 'traditional', 'neutral' and 'Protestant' classifications.[87] These debates must be borne in mind when assessing the conclusions drawn from wills. What studies to date appear to indicate, however, is considerable regional variation in the speed with which Protestantism was embraced. Testators in the city of York remained remarkably conservative through to the brief reign of Mary, whereafter the majority adopted a neutral formulation. Clearly Protestant wills accounted for roughly one-third of the total 1560–90, rising to 45 per cent in the last decade of the century, and only then did traditional formulations disappear completely.[88] This contrasts with the counties of Nottinghamshire and Yorkshire more generally, for here non-traditional wills began to appear in the late-1530s, becoming increasingly significant until they formed a clear majority by the early-1550s.[89] In Gloucestershire, there was a pronounced swing away from traditional preambles in Edward's reign, although the close attentions of the radical Protestant Bishop Hooper may have had a decisive influence here. Traditional forms revived under Mary but declined rapidly thereafter, neutral wills accounting for over 85 per cent through the first 20 years of Elizabeth's reign, and clearly Protestant formulations only reaching 7 per cent of the total in the 1570s. Here, therefore, the new religion was embraced only slowly.[90] For Retford in Nottinghamshire

---

[84] Litzenberger, 'Local responses', pp.434–5.

[85] Craig and Litzenberger, 'Wills as religious propaganda', p.431.

[86] Levine and Wrightson are at the former end of the spectrum in arguing that 'they tell us little of the personal faith of the individual man or woman': *Making of an industrial society*, p.291.

[87] Litzenberger, 'Local responses', pp.420–1.

[88] Palliser, *Tudor York*, pp.248–54.

[89] Dickens, *Lollards and Protestants*, p.172.

[90] Litzenberger, 'Local responses', pp.417–18, 427–8.

Marcombe has traced the trend through to the later sixteenth century, revealing a collapse in Catholic preambles during the reign of Edward VI and a revival in the Marian interlude, with Protestant preambles gaining ascendancy from the 1580s.[91] Duffy also identified a Marian reaction in the wills of the parish of Otley in Wharfedale, reflected in the use of a revised Catholic formula, a tendency that he regards as widespread and found also in towns such as Leeds.[92]

Some of the best studies use wills together with other sources to trace the gradual acceptance of the reformed church. Two examples are Litzenberger on the diocese of Gloucester 1541–80, and Whiting's work on popular religion in the Diocese of Exeter. Litzenberger analysed 8,000 wills, besides the records of ecclesiastical courts, bishops' papers and parish and borough records, and these additional sources confirm the evidence of will preambles, showing considerable resistance to religious change extending well beyond 1559, and little indication that the new religion was making clear headway until the 1580s.[93] Whiting combines the evidence of churchwardens' accounts with wills to suggest that the conventional view of the south-west as 'remote, conservative and change-resistant' is false, for popular support for Catholicism was waning by 1547, and collapsed in most places during Edward's reign, more noticeably in the east of the region than in the west.[94] However, positive support for Protestantism remained a minority activity throughout the Reformation decades, though more apparent in town than countryside, and wills containing possibly Protestant preambles constituted only some 12 per cent of the total in the diocese of Exeter as late as the 1560s.[95] Catholic devotion may have been largely suppressed, but it was most usually replaced by 'conformism, passivity, or even indifference'.[96] The combined work of Mayhew and Goring, setting will preambles and bequests alongside other evidence, has shown that the process of religious change was particularly slow in Sussex, though more rapid in the east than the west, in the Weald than in the Downs and in urban and industrial areas than in agricultural ones.[97]

Turning to the early-seventeenth century, from his study of some 70

---

[91] Marcombe, *English small town life*, pp.222–5, 254–5, 279.
[92] Duffy, *Stripping of the altars*, pp.517–23.
[93] Litzenberger, 'Responses of the laity'.
[94] Whiting, *Blind devotion*, p.145.
[95] Whiting, *Blind devotion*, pp.155–71 and graph H, p.278.
[96] Whiting, *Blind devotion*, p.171.
[97] Mayhew, 'Progress of the Reformation', pp.46–8; Goring, 'Reformation and reaction', pp.141–54.

Sussex gentry wills made between 1620 and 1670, Fletcher found 'that the doctrine of justification by faith was universally accepted in gentry circles'.[98] More recently, Duffin has analysed 366 Cornish gentry wills between 1600 and 1660. Like Fletcher she took three features of preambles as indicative of likely Puritanism: a 'demonstrable confidence in predestination', 'a stated belief in physical resurrection' and 'emphasis on personal sin'. She found that 24 per cent mentioned predestination, 8 per cent a belief in physical resurrection, and many of these two previous categories also emphasised personal sin; 7.4 per cent included all three indicators, 25.1 per cent included at least one.[99] In the Diocese of Ely, however, mention of election was rare. Working from the premise that 'idiosyncratic and strongly flavoured dedicatory clauses give an absolute minimum of testators with strong convictions', Spufford has sampled the Ely diocesan wills, finding the first mention of election in 1590, and just 31 further examples from 1,600 wills over the next 40 years. But while ardent Calvinists might have despaired at their small number, it is notable that the social composition of this 31 covered the complete spectrum, including servants, labourers, a cross-section of petty craftsmen and yeomen.[100]

As indicators of religious belief wills must clearly be used with great care. Duffy's scepticism as to their value as an index of the growth of popular Protestantism, as opposed to a reflection of the resilience of Catholicism, may be overstated, but he is surely right to warn against oversimplified interpretations of preambles, the placing of excessive emphasis upon omission rather than commission and the influence that a prudential response to external constraints and ministrations might have had.[101] For this reason, the increasingly sophisticated analyses of will preambles by Litzenberger and others are to be welcomed, and, particularly when employed in conjunction with other sources, can assist in mapping out not only the geography and chronology but also the social incidence of religious belief in early modern England.

Occupational structure and economy

For economic historians wills are often less useful than inventories, but they have been used for both small and large scale surveys of

---

[98] Fletcher, *County community*, p.63.

[99] Duffin, *Faction and faith*, pp.43–5.

[100] Spufford, *World of rural dissenters*, pp.17–18. In itself this is an interesting restatement of Spufford's views on the value of preambles which might be compared with Chapter 7, below.

[101] Duffy, *Stripping of the altars*, pp.5, 504–23.

occupations and status. The attraction of wills is that they are among the most numerous of personal documents to survive, and although by no means all testators gave their occupation or status, it is usually possible to build up a viable sample from the number that do, while the body of many wills also mentions the names and occupation or status of other local inhabitants.

Patten's study of occupations from wills in Norfolk and Suffolk 1500–1700 is the largest regional survey of its kind, employing a total of over 150,000 wills, though focused specifically upon the urban system.[102] For the majority of the smaller towns in his survey, wills form the only consistently available source. The scalograms drawn by Patten from this impressive dataset indicate increasing sophistication and specialisation within urban economies as the heights of the urban hierarchy are approached and towns grew in size. Furthermore, despite a high degree of overall stability in the East Anglian urban hierarchy, the larger towns were not only growing more rapidly between 1603 and the 1670s than they had in the previous 80 years, but they were becoming much more economically advanced: towns in general had 'become more modern', but it was 'the larger ones that had become most modern'.[103] Nevertheless, across the seventeenth century the presence of distributive retailers became almost universal, even in the smaller East Anglian towns.[104]

Patten's survey employs occupational ranking as its key analytical tool, whilst other urban studies have generally attempted to identify occupational structure. A pioneering example is Dyer's study of Worcester 1540–1620, which revealed a highly industrialised town with 40 per cent employed in the cloth industry prior to 1590, and 50 per cent thereafter.[105] Goose also relied heavily upon wills in his comparative study of occupations in Cambridge, Colchester and Reading 1500–1700, identifying the trades of 4,594 individuals, sufficient to elucidate their changing structures despite the relative paucity of information for the earlier sixteenth century.[106] The close relationship between the economic and demographic fortunes of these towns and the prosperity or otherwise of their leading economic sectors led Goose to question the notion that pre-industrial towns are best

---

[102] Patten, *English towns*, Chapter 6.
[103] Patten, *English towns*, pp.294–6.
[104] Shammas, *Pre-industrial consumer*, pp.227–8.
[105] Dyer, *City of Worcester*, pp.81–3.
[106] Goose, 'Economic and social aspects', Chapter 3; Goose, 'Decay and regeneration', pp.53–74; Goose and Cooper, *Tudor and Stuart Colchester*, pp.76–87.

characterised as 'unspecialised' or 'variegated' economies, suggesting instead that it is more appropriate to focus upon their key economic functions, rather than upon those features which represent the lowest denominator common to them all.[107] Like Patten, he also emphasised the growing sophistication and specialisation of the larger towns and the growing range of occupations they exhibited, already evident by the mid-seventeenth century and not purely a late-seventeenth century phenomenon.[108]

For Cambridge, Colchester and Reading, comparison of these 4,594 occupations from wills with a larger sample of 8,490 occupations from a wide range of borough documentation produced a close match, suggesting that if wills are clearly socially biased this is true of most sources. The question of the relative merits of freemen's lists and wills has, however, engendered debate, Pound insisting upon the superiority of the Elizabethan Norwich freemen's lists over probate evidence from his comparison of both sources with an occupational census of 1589, despite the fact that Patten's tests of will data against Norwich freemen's records produced highly significant correlations between the ranking of occupations from the two sources.[109] But freemen's lists and apprenticeship indentures possess their own bias, being heavily skewed towards the more carefully restricted and regulated trades, omitting those that did not require apprenticeship, excluding individuals who were either not required or unable to take up the freedom, and fluctuating in coverage according to the ability of individual corporations to regulate their economies—a growing problem for many by the early-seventeenth century. Comparison between 991 apprenticeship indentures for Colchester 1580–1629 and 917 occupations drawn from wills for a similar period reveals expected discrepancies: indentures give somewhat higher figures for the textile and clothing trades, and lower figures for service, transport and miscellaneous occupations, while the food and drink trades are also slightly better represented amongst the indentures. Unsurprisingly, trades most highly regulated by local and national governments figure more prominently in indentures than in wills. Fortunately, the *orders of magnitude* are similar, except for the service and transport categories where numbers are anyway relatively small, and each set of data reveals

---

[107] Goose, 'English pre-industrial urban economies', pp.24–30, reprinted in Barry, *Tudor and Stuart town*, pp.63–73.
[108] Goose, 'In search of the urban variable', p.177.
[109] Pound, 'Validity of the freemen's lists', pp.48–59; Patten, *English towns*, pp.246–7.

clearly the major, long-term shifts in the town's economy. A similar exercise for Reading, however, comparing the town's freemen register with will evidence for the seventeenth century, presents a very different picture. Here close scrutiny of the register reveals erratic recording of many trades, and this document fails to show the decline of the town's textile industry from the second quarter of the century that is indicated by occupational evidence from wills and abundant contemporary comment.[110] It may therefore be the *quality* of the occupational data, as much as its provenance, that is the crucial consideration.

It is, perhaps, paradoxical that will evidence had been used more extensively in urban studies, where alternatives are more commonly available, than in rural surveys, but a first step towards the rectification of this is provided below by Evans' examination of occupations in Cambridgeshire from roughly 19,000 men's wills proved in the Diocese of Ely 1551–1800.[111] This clearly identifies the problem of nomenclature, for the precise activities of those described as 'yeoman', 'husbandman' or 'labourer' are difficult to determine unless wills are read in full, or used in conjunction with inventories. Nevertheless, the overwhelming dominance of agriculture in the county can be demonstrated, there is some indication of the long-term decline of smallholders in some areas, while the unusually large number of labourers' wills might indicate the persistence of smallholders in others, such as the Isle of Ely and fen-edge parishes.

Occupational evidence from wills, rural or urban, is inevitably socially biased to some degree, and does not provide comprehensive coverage. This is revealed by the rare opportunities that arise to compare will data with census returns or parish registers which give occupations. From the parish register of the small Suffolk market town of Halesworth, 77 different occupations could be identified 1653–99, only 20 of which occur amongst the wills of Halesworth testators in the same period. Even when gentlemen, yeomen, husbandmen, soldiers, servants and labourers are omitted, the Halesworth register records 25 crafts and trades excluded from Patten's list for East Anglian towns during the half century 1650–99.[112] For early-seventeenth-century Cambridge, we have already noted that the number of labourers recorded in wills is far smaller than the proportion revealed by a census of the town's poorer parishes in the 1620s.[113] The bias to

---

[110] Unpublished Colchester research; Goose, 'Decay and regeneration', pp.57–61.
[111] See Chapter 9, below, pp.176–88.
[112] Evans, 'Occupations in parish registers', p.361.
[113] See above, p.45.

be found in wills is, however, at least predictable, and probably less likely to be affected by changing demographic, social and financial pressures than is the case with freemen and apprenticeship records. But for many historians the key consideration will be availability, for relatively few long series of apprenticeship indentures or freemen's admissions survive, particularly for unincorporated towns: wills can be found for most towns, and indeed most villages, covering the entire pre-industrial period. For comparative purposes, therefore, particularly over long time spans, the use of wills is not simply preferable, but is essential.

A careful reading of wills can often provide much more than a bare indication of the range and structure of occupations. Wills have been used successfully to gain at least an impression of the relative wealth of different occupational or ethnic groups, either alone or in conjunction with inventories.[114] They can also, however, offer additional insights into the organisation of particular industries and occupations. From Worcester wills Dyer was able to deduce that independent producers were far more common than were weavers employed by putting-out clothiers, while the regular use of spinners working in their own homes only became common towards the end of the sixteenth century.[115] Retained employees were also found in the Colchester cloth trade by the later seventeenth century: John Winnock, baymaker, left £1 per loom to 'all my weavers that work for me', whilst Solomon Fromanteel left the same sum to 'all my weavers that are masters of families and have my tackling to work in'.[116] The extent of diversification into investment in lands and tenements can also be established, as Reed has shown for seventeenth-century Ipswich.[117] In Hallamshire in Yorkshire, wills show that local cutlers commonly farmed a smallholding, and also indicate the crucial importance of water power to the trade.[118] Cambridge wills reveal a diverse array of trade and craftsmen holding booths in Stourbridge Fair, investment ranging from the one-eighth of a booth bequeathed by John Munnes in 1586 to the 40 left by Robert Chapman, alderman, in 1563; others reveal the

---

[114] Dyer, *City of Worcester*, pp.85, 89, 113, 120, 234; Palliser, *Tudor York*, pp.141–4; Goose, 'Decay and regeneration', pp.64–5; Goose and Cooper, *Tudor and Stuart Colchester*, pp.99–100.

[115] Dyer, *City of Worcester*, pp.97, 100.

[116] PRO, PCC wills, Cann, f.50, John Winnock, baymaker, St Peters, Colchester, 1685; Essex Record Office, Bishop of London Commissary Court wills, Solomon Fromanteel, baymaker, St Nicholas, Colchester, 1694.

[117] Reed, 'Economic structure', pp.100, 117.

[118] Hey, 'Origins and early growth', pp.353, 357–8.

complexity of the fair.[119] For ports, wills help reveal the structure of investment in shipping. Hence in Colchester, while mariners and merchants were the most prominent owners of ships, other occupations include glovers, clothiers, doctors and clockmakers, four of the 48 identified being women, with vessels most commonly held in fractions, occasionally as small as one thirty-second.[120]

Wills are particularly valuable for what they reveal about women's work. The evidence is often oblique, taking the form of specific bequests of either property or tools to a widow, from which it might be inferred that she was to carry on her late husband's trade.[121] For Salisbury, Wright suggests that, as much production was based in the home, the descent of the family dwelling *may* also indicate descent of the business, although this could have been a strictly temporary arrangement.[122] Wright also found examples of specific bequests of tools to wives, but they were few in number, and the low proportion of females who retained servants or apprentices is taken to confirm that 'comparatively few women took over their spouse's business'.[123] This may be unduly pessimistic: in Cambridge, Colchester and Reading, specific bequests of tools to wives, or of widows themselves bequeathing 'the tools of my trade', indicate that some women at least were active as butchers, brewers, bakers, innholders, vintners, barbers, weavers and clothiers, tallowchandlers, pinmakers, braziers and armourers, suggesting that the economic activities of women far exceeded their traditional roles in marketing, brewing or as spinners for the cloth trade.[124] In sixteenth-century Sheffield, similar bequests of cutlers' tools were made to wives and daughters.[125] More quantifiable evidence, such as the Oxford apprenticeship records, indicates that the participation of widows was low when trade was booming, only increasing in depressed

---

[119] Cambridge University Library, Archdeaconry of Ely wills, Thomas Hobson, carrier, St Benedict, Cambridge, 1568; John Munnes, St Clement, Cambridge 1586; Alice Bradley, widow, Holy Sepulchre, Cambridge, 1616; John Johnson, locksmith, 1666. PRO, PCC wills, Chayre, f.9, Robert Chapman, Holy Trinity, Cambridge, alderman, 1563; Sadler, f.2, John Badcock, alderman, 1635.

[120] From analysis of all Colchester wills proved in the PCC, consistory, archdeaconry and peculiar courts, 1500–1700. PRO, PCC wills, Berkeley, f.3, Robert Morphee, St Peters, Colchester, dyer, 1656.

[121] Transmission of property to widows in rural areas is discussed below under *Inheritance*.

[122] Wright, '"Churmaids"', p.112.

[123] Wright, '"Churmaids"', pp.113–14; see also Chapter 16, below, p.318.

[124] Goose, 'Economic and social aspects', pp.101–2.

[125] Hey, 'Origins and early growth', p.347.

periods, while in early-eighteenth-century London only some 5–10 per cent of businesses were run by women, and most of these were 'feminine businesses'.[126] On the other hand, wills clearly indicate that women, particularly widows, not only played their part in a range of occupations, but also participated in economic life as property owners, shipowners, owners of booths in major English fairs, as leaseholders of woolmarkets, owners of fulling mills, as moneylenders and could enter into partnerships with male counterparts.[127] They also provide rare glimpses of true familial partnerships, such as in the will of Robert Reeve of Reading, clothier, written in 1620, which gives full recognition to his wife Alice, who 'hath laboured hard with me through all her youth in the getting of all mine estate'.[128]

Population

Given the availability of parish registers from 1538, it is perhaps unsurprising that the use of wills for demographic purposes has generally been marginal or supplementary, usually restricted to the study of mortality.[129] Their use as a potential index of both mortality and fertility is discussed at more length in Chapter 10 below, so will be introduced only briefly here. Despite their social bias, the number of wills proved does provide a useful indication of the major epidemic outbreaks in early modern England, even for diseases which particularly affected the poor, such as plague. They therefore form a useful supplement to parish register data, filling gaps in registration and providing vital information on the earlier sixteenth century, as well as for the mid-sixteenth century when few registers survive. As an index of fertility, the numbers of children mentioned in wills can only stand as a weak surrogate, for there are too many unknowns, particularly the age profile of the will-leaving population which may itself have been affected by prevailing death rates. Nevertheless, the urban evidence presented below does indicate a distinct upward shift in replacement rates after the mid-sixteenth century, and a stabilisation in the seventeenth, suggesting the possibility that a rise in urban fertility may have contributed to their late-sixteenth and early-seventeenth century expansion.

[126] Prior, *Women in English society*, pp.105–10; Earle, *Making of the English middle class*, p.173.

[127] From Cambridge, Colchester and Reading wills 1500–1700; Cross, 'Northern women', p.89.

[128] Berkshire County Record Office, Archdeaconry of Berkshire wills, Robert Reeve, the elder, clothier, Reading, 1620.

[129] The one major study for the early modern period is Slack, *Impact of plague*, especially Chapter 3.

Wills can, however, be used for other demographic purposes, and hence for seventeenth-century Colchester they have been employed to gauge the extent of integration of the immigrant 'Dutch' community through the patterns of intermarriage that they reveal.[130] Another interesting recent suggestion by Razzell is to use wills as a check upon standards of burial registration.[131] Early analysis indicates that up to 43 per cent of testators could not be traced in burial registers for the later sixteenth and early-seventeenth centuries, the proportion decreasing substantially to roughly 17 per cent by the early-nineteenth century. The evidence to date is, however, narrowly based, and the will-leaving population is by no means a cross section of early modern society. If a key reason for these results is that testators were often buried outside their parish of residence, it is probable that the wealthier will-leavers would be more likely than the poor to be able to make such arrangements, and thus registers may more accurately reflect burials of the lower social classes. In this regard, an analysis of the proportion who left instructions to be buried outside of their parish of residence, broken down by period and social class, might prove informative.

Family and kinship

One topic that has particularly benefited from use of wills is the study of family and kinship. The range of kin named as beneficiaries is a powerful index of the depth and range of kinship bonds in early modern society, but such bonds can also be assessed through analysis of the role of kin as witnesses, overseers, executors or guardians of children. Precise quantification of bequests is often impossible, the strength of the bond they indicate difficult to interpret, and the life-cycle stage of the testator and its effect obscure, but it would be perverse to argue that the patterns they show indicate nothing at all. The seminal contribution is Wrightson and Levine's study of Terling in Essex, which appeared in 1979, the same year in which Vann explored family structure in Banbury from will evidence.[132] These studies, and others conducted since, have led Wrightson and Levine recently to conclude that 'statistical studies of the relatives recognised in the wills of the inhabitants of a now quite substantial number of English parishes are unanimous in showing that the range of kin mentioned . . . was

[130] Goose, '"Dutch"', p.272.
[131] Razzell, 'Conundrum', pp.477–8.
[132] Wrightson and Levine, *Poverty and piety*; Vann, 'Wills and the family', pp.346–67.

genealogically both narrow and shallow'.[133] Despite a degree of variation between communities, few individuals were included in wills beyond the range of the immediate nuclear family, siblings, sons- and daughters-in-law, grandchildren, brothers- and sisters-in-law and nephews and nieces. This was as much if not more true of the northern industrial community of Whickham in Durham as it was of more southerly agricultural villages, for here, although 70–80 per cent of testators recognised kin beyond their immediate family, the range was similarly restricted, whilst kinship links between householders were in fact considerably less dense than in Terling.[134]

The strength of both social and family relationships has recently been emphasised by Spufford and Takahashi, who argue from the evidence of will witnessing in Chippenham and Willingham that both family and friendship networks continued to operate across any economic divisions one might attempt to impose.[135] But another recent study, of eight Lincolnshire parishes 1567–1800, from counts of 10,763 bequests made in 1,442 wills, firmly concludes that testators increasingly focused upon the nuclear family at the expense of unrelated individuals and the community at large, and identifies key periods of change as the decades around 1600 and the mid-later eighteenth century.[136]

Despite its formal nature, a will can occasionally reveal much about the quality of early modern relationships. Stone's thesis that there was little affection between spouses in the early modern period, for example, can be countered by the expressions of trust and love between married couples found in wills.[137] Most men with under-age or no children clearly expected their wives to be capable of managing the family farm or business, and a high proportion made their wives sole or joint executrices.[138] Wills proved in the Archdeaconry of Sudbury 1636–9 bear this out, 55.1 per cent of men who mentioned a wife appointing her as sole executrix and another 15.2 per cent making their wives joint executrices.[139] The figures for Thame and Woodstock are very similar,

---

[133] Wrightson and Levine, *Poverty and piety*, p.192.

[134] Levine and Wrightson, *Making of an industrial society*, pp.330–3.

[135] Spufford and Takahashi, 'Families', pp.379–414.

[136] Johnston, 'Family, kin and community', pp.176–92.

[137] Stone, *Family, sex and marriage*, pp.70, 81–2; Erickson, *Women and property*, pp.156–7; Marcombe, *English small town life*, p.148.

[138] Todd, 'Freebench and free enterprise', pp.181–8. Wills from a diversity of regions and community types 1414–1710 reveal that between 63 and 89 per cent of husbands named their wives as sole or joint executor: Erickson, *Women and property*, pp.156–8

[139] Evans, *Wills of the archdeaconry of Sudbury, 1636–1638*, p.viii.

although here it seems to have been unusual for widows to inherit their husbands' business. Marriages that were both loving and companionate thus appear to have been the rule in early modern England, at least for the majority of the population. But there is also evidence in wills of affection for children, either in the manner in which legacies are carefully divided between heirs, or in provision for education and guardianship, and perhaps most powerfully in the way in which provision is often made even for as yet unborn children. On the other hand tensions can be revealed too, providing frequent evidence of resentment towards step-parents, and occasional indications of attempts to control unruly children through the threat of withdrawal of legacies. In London, however, by the late-seventeenth century parents rarely went this far, the majority of fathers providing no sanction even against daughters marrying without consent.[140]

Inheritance

There is no doubt that the nuclear family was of central concern to will-makers at all levels of English society, and this is particularly evident in the arrangements made for the transmission of lands and tenements. Freehold land was readily devisable by will, arranged by feoffments to use prior to 1536, and the Statute of Wills of 1540 and subsequent legislation encouraged the practice, although for lands held by knight service of the crown only two-thirds could be bequeathed freely, protecting crown wardship rights. Women were expressly forbidden to devise freehold land by will in 1542–3, although examples have been found of wives doing just that despite statutory prohibition.[141] The situation with copyhold land was more complex. Freedom of alienation of land for copyholders by inheritance was established by 1500, despite legal restrictions on devising such land by will, and as early as the thirteenth century there is some evidence that copyhold land could be sold despite customary restrictions upon descent.[142] By the sixteenth century, however, practice varied widely: in some parts of the country copyhold land by inheritance (as opposed to years or lives) could be freely devised by will, while in others, such as Swaledale in Yorkshire discussed by Jennings below, it could not. Similarly, at Long Wittenham, Oxfordshire, copyholds for lives were never devised by

---

[140] Houlbrooke, *English family*, p.215; Earle, *Making of the English middle class*, p.188.

[141] 34 & 35 Hen. VIII, c.5; Prior, 'Wives and wills', pp.202–3.

[142] Macfarlane, *Origins of English individualism*, pp.106–8; Houlbrooke, *English family*, p.231; Wrightson and Levine, *Making of an industrial society*, p.281.

will, but transferred by surrender in the manorial court.[143] One mechanism often used to avoid customary restrictions was for a tenant to surrender lands to the use of his will. Hence in 1671 Timothy Lane of St Stephens in Hertfordshire, 'one of the customary tenants of the manor of Park', bequeathed his lands as he desired, 'being empowered by a surrender taken the 7th day of May 1669 by Mr William Ellis, gentleman, steward of the manor aforesaid to the use of my last will and testament'.[144]

Even where it was legally possible to devise land by will the opportunity was not always taken and manorial custom relied upon instead, as at Ombersley in Worcestershire where customs relating to copyhold by inheritance were particularly strong.[145] On the other hand, land was sometimes devised by will in a manner completely at odds with manorial custom.[146] But although practice was inconsistent, there are many instances where wills can be employed to indicate inheritance practices. Even where manorial custom was clear, as at Kibworth Harcourt in the south Midlands, wills provide essential information to complete the picture of inheritance. Here, Howell has shown that while peasant landholdings were kept intact by the sixteenth century, passing in most instances to the widow alone when all the children were minors but more commonly to a son if over the age of 21, every effort was made to accommodate other family members. Hence, inheriting sons were usually given responsibility for the maintenance of the widow on the family property, while younger children were frequently given the stock and the gear, often returned to the use of the heir in exchange for maintenance.[147] Much the same procedure was adopted in the west Midlands villages studied by Dyer, an earlier tendency to divide holdings being superseded by bequeathing them intact by the early-sixteenth century, other children being provided with goods or cash instead.[148] A strong concern to provide for all family members was found by Spufford in Chippenham, Orwell and Willingham in Cambridgeshire. Here, however, this was sometimes achieved by division of the landholding itself, though most commonly by burdening it with onerous obligations to other close family, which in the long run had a similar effect upon the survival of smallholdings unless they were

---

[143] Todd, 'Freebench and free enterprise', pp.177–8.
[144] Hertfordshire County Record Office, Archdeaconry of Huntingdon wills, Timothy Lane, St Stephens, yeoman, 1671.
[145] Large, 'Rural society', pp.107–12.
[146] Thompson, 'Grid of inheritance', pp.342–3.
[147] Howell, 'Peasant inheritance customs', pp.139–46.
[148] Dyer, 'Changes in the size of peasant holdings', p.292.

rendered viable by the diversity of opportunities that the fenland community of Willingham provided.[149] Spufford notes, however, that wills do not provide a complete picture, for land was commonly passed to heirs as they came of age, and hence in this area the will sample is skewed towards testators with younger children to provide for.[150]

Towards the lower end of peasant society, Everitt also found that primogeniture by no means always held sway, identifying many examples of division of lands and goods, more or less equally, between all dependants.[151] Erickson's work on Lincolnshire, Sussex and Yorkshire left her in no doubt that while eldest sons tended to be favoured in the transmission of landed property, 'it was expected that both daughters and younger sons might have the equivalent value in moveables that the heir had in land', whilst Churches' study of Whitehaven 1660–1750 more than bears out these conclusions.[152]

It is not only for peasant society that wills can prove valuable in this respect. Cooper's survey of inheritance practices amongst the great landowning families employs wills alongside other sources, showing the increasing prevalence of primogeniture, more easily achieved through the strict settlement in the seventeenth century, although provision for younger sons tended to be more closely related to their number rather than anything else.[153] Furthermore, wills provide clear evidence of the persistence of provision in land for younger sons in some cases, as well as revealing a considerable increase in the size of marriage portions provided for daughters.[154] In towns, the evidence suggests that businesses tended to be precarious, rarely extending further than three generations, and it is possible that the custom of dividing money and moveable goods between the widow and children by the provision of thirds played a part in this.[155] There is, however, as yet no full-blown study of inheritance practices in provincial towns, although late-seventeenth and early-eighteenth-century London wills reveal that the middle classes generally tended towards primogeniture in the disposal of their real estate, but shared money and goods very equally between heirs.[156]

---

[149] Spufford, 'Peasant inheritance customs', pp.156–76.
[150] Spufford, 'Peasant inheritance customs', pp.169–76.
[151] Everitt, 'Farm labourers', pp.455–6.
[152] Erickson, *Women and property*, pp.61–78; Churches, 'Women and property', pp.165–80.
[153] Cooper, 'Patterns of inheritance', pp.192–233.
[154] Cooper, 'Patterns of inheritance', pp.220, 306–27.
[155] Hoskins, 'The Elizabethan merchants of Exeter', p.151; Dyer, *City of Worcester*, p.180.
[156] Earle, *Making of the English middle class*, pp.314–15.

Generally, men and women were not treated equally when it came to inheritance. Whittle's analysis of female landholding in six Norfolk parishes 1440–1580 from wills, court rolls and estate surveys revealed low numbers holding land throughout the period, a product of an inferior legal position and pervasive cultural attitudes; where they did inherit, this was often due to their precarious economic situation.[157] In late-seventeenth and early-eighteenth-century Hertford there were clear gender differences between recipients of different types of legacy, men being much more likely to receive land and tools, women to receive linen and household goods, providing a reminder of the basic division of gender roles that, despite exceptions, this society sustained.[158]

Amussen has pointed out, however, that when widows made wills they 'had very different considerations' in mind from men. They seldom had to establish their children, but, when they did have land to dispose of, they were more likely to favour daughters than sons, providing 'a subtle critique of the patriarchal assumptions of the period'.[159] Furthermore, the PCC and Oxfordshire women's wills examined by Prior indicate 'greater independence both economically and psychologically' by the end of the seventeenth century, as larger numbers of wives made wills without their husband's consent, left nothing to their spouses and showed greater independence too in provision for their children's future.[160]

Literacy

Cressy has established himself as the historian of early modern literacy, employing the evidence of signatures and marks on wills, marriage licences and depositions made in church courts 1560–1700, the majority drawn from London, Essex, East Anglia, Devon and Durham. A series of irregular fluctuations produced a long-term reduction of illiteracy, but behind this picture lies a diversity of social, gender and geographical experience. Gentlemen were almost universally literate throughout, except in Elizabethan Durham, while labourers and women were almost universally illiterate, apart from a dramatic increase in female literacy in late-seventeenth-century London.[161] Three-quarters of trade

---

[157] Whittle, 'Inheritance, marriage, widowhood and remarriage', pp.33–72.

[158] Adams, *Lifestyle and culture*, p.xxxi.

[159] Amussen, *Ordered society*, pp.91–2.

[160] Prior, 'Wives and wills', pp.219–21. It must be said, however, that the numbers upon which Prior's conclusions are based are very small indeed.

[161] Cressy, *Literacy*, pp.106–7, 142–7.

and craftsmen were illiterate in the 1560s, but only 50 per cent so by the early-seventeenth century, making just limited further improvement thereafter, although those in London and Middlesex performed better.[162] Yeomen made much greater progress than did husbandmen, the latter remaining roughly 80 per cent illiterate throughout, the former achieving a level of just 25 per cent or so, despite setbacks at the start and end of the seventeenth century.[163]

A question mark must remain over the relationship between the ability to sign a document and literacy, however. Both Cressy and Schofield have argued that the ability to sign generally indicates the ability to read, probably to read fluently, and the likelihood of an ability to write other things, a view supported by nineteenth-century English and French evidence. Moreover, the ability or inability to sign is at least standard, direct and universal, and therefore represents a valid comparative tool.[164] It does appear to be true that reading would usually be learned before writing, but while this might be taken as indicative of the literacy of those who could sign, it might also mean that others who did not get so far as to learn how to sign could also read, while some of those who could sign their names might not be able to write fluently.[165] The additional problem remains of instances where individuals signed on one occasion and made a mark on another, apparent from the wills examined for Helpston, Northamptonshire in the seventeenth and early-eighteenth centuries, a problem that cannot always be explained by incapacity or failing health.[166] But the fact that wills were so commonly made shortly before death, by individuals who were inevitably frail, probably means that they are even less reliable than other documents upon which signatures can be found, Cressy suggesting that they might exaggerate illiteracy by as much as 25 per cent.[167] Most progress is likely to be made where signatures are studied alongside other possible indicators of literacy, such as school foundations, book production and book ownership, although unfortunately wills and inventories generally provide little information on the latter topic due to the low value of most popular books.[168]

[162] Cressy, *Literacy*, pp.153–4.
[163] Cressy, *Literacy*, pp.156–7.
[164] Cressy, *Literacy*, pp.53–5; Schofield, 'Measurement of illiteracy', pp.318–25.
[165] Spufford, *Small books*, p.45; Schofield, 'Measurement of illiteracy', p.324.
[166] Moyse, 'Helpston', pp.333–43; Cressy, *Literacy*, p.58.
[167] Cressy, *Literacy*, p.108.
[168] Spufford, *Small books*, p.48.

Conclusion

The uses to which wills can and have been put by early modern historians has by no means been exhausted by the foregoing discussion: household utensils, furnishings and clothing are sometimes described in more detail than is given in inventories, they can often assist in dating the foundation of institutions such as workhouses or hospitals, rates of interest are frequently mentioned, architectural historians can learn from references to wainscot or glass windows, and wills have also been used for dating the changing fabric of churches.[169] This is clearly a source that offers vast potential for the study of a wide range of topics in the fields of economic, social and demographic history. It is a potential that remains unfulfilled, for the surface of this huge body of data has hardly been scratched, and the great majority of studies based largely upon this evidence have been very local in focus. This is perhaps unsurprising, for reading, transcribing, processing and analysing wills is a highly time-consuming task, particularly for those proved in the prerogative courts, where the wealth of most testators often led them to dictate testaments of considerable length. Furthermore, wills are only loosely systematic in their format, which renders a coherent approach to their analysis problematic. Clearly, we need more studies of particular localities in order to contextualise the conclusions drawn to date, but there is as much if not more need for broader surveys, intrinsically comparative, and drawing upon wills proved at all levels of ecclesiastical court. That said, the shortcomings of wills as historical evidence, and their inevitable bias, must not be lost sight of. Many of the better pieces of historical writing based upon them have, and will continue to, set them alongside other available evidence, allowing the insights they appear to provide to be tested, to produce a more rounded and convincing view of early modern economic and social structures and development.

---

[169] Evans, 'Inheritance', pp.53–4; Goose and Cooper, *Tudor and Stuart Colchester*, p.90; will of Thomas Robinson, blacksmith, St Runwald, Colchester, 1662; Haward, 'Medieval masons', p.168.

4

Interpreting Probate Inventories

TOM ARKELL

In Chapter 2 above the influence of changing laws and customs on the form and content of probate inventories was explained, stressing the need for students to understand fully their context and explain which possessions were normally excluded.[1] It also reinforces warnings from experienced practitioners against taking at face value all data contained in the inventories.[2] These issues will be discussed in this chapter, which concentrates on many perceptive approaches to studying inventories, often combined with other sources, which have transformed our knowledge and understanding of early modern society and economy.

Coverage

The bulk of the one million or so probate inventories that survive for England and Wales come from an extended seventeenth century (c.1580–1720), with most of the rest deriving from the half centuries before and after.[3] They do not cover all counties equally because relatively few are now available for Devon or Essex, for example, Cambridgeshire or west Kent before 1660 or most of Yorkshire before the 1680s.[4] Overall fewer inventories have survived than wills, with the ratios varying greatly by ecclesiastical court and over time.[5] This applies

---

[1] See in particular the section on checks on personal representatives in Chapter 2, above, pp.25–34.

[2] Moore, *Goods and chattels*, pp.1–4; Priestley and Corfield, 'Rooms and room use', pp.93–7; Vaisey, 'Probate inventories and provincial retailers', pp.91–103; Spufford, 'Limitations of the probate inventory', pp.142–54.

[3] Moore, 'Probate inventories', pp.16–17; Erickson, 'Introduction to probate accounts', p.285.

[4] Cash, *Devon inventories*, pp.ix–x; Steer, *Farm and cottage inventories*, pp.3–4; Evans, Chapter 9, below; Zell, 'Wealth', p.203; Hey, *Rural metalworkers*, p.22.

[5] The survival of wills is discussed in the opening section of Chapter 3 in this volume by Goose and Evans, above, pp.38–47.

especially to the Prerogative Court of Canterbury (PCC), where most researchers have discovered that inventories for their chosen area are rare before 1660, while subsequent ones are often damaged or inaccessible.[6] This is why PCC inventories account for no more than 2.3, 2.5 and 6.4 per cent of those available in three well-researched areas, with the highest occurring in a peculiar surrounded by parishes from another diocese.[7]

Attempts to calculate precise survival rates for inventories are always elusive. They depend upon the relevant burial registers' completeness, how well they identified adult men, spinsters and widows from wives and children who did not have inventories and upon the time span covered.[8] This problem is illustrated by two west Midlands parishes. In one the author reported that 10 per cent of those who died between 1676 and 1775 had extant inventories, but omitted to say that it was 18 and 1.5 per cent in the first and last quarters.[9] Because these percentages included all burials, the proportions of those eligible for probate should be increased by between two and three times. In the other parish probate inventories survive for some 25–30 per cent of adult males buried when the registers were most reliable, although the burials of a further quarter of the probated men were also not recorded.[10]

The Coxes have already reported Overton's finding that the proportion of extant inventories for adult males and widows in some late-seventeenth century studies ranged from about 10 to 60 per cent, with a norm of perhaps 20 to 30 per cent.[11] These figures appear to match Kenyon's conclusion that about half the families in the Sussex town of Petworth fell below the inventory limit.[12] There, as elsewhere, many of the better-off gentry were excluded, not all above the 'inventory limit' were covered comprehensively and a few inventories survive for those below it. Comparisons with exemption lists from the Hearth Taxes show that a few inventories are found elsewhere among

---

[6] Garrard, 'English probate inventories', pp.69–72; Reed, *Buckinghamshire*, p.x.

[7] Alcock, *People at home*, p.12; Moore, *Goods and chattels*, pp.4–8; Stanes, 'Peculiar of Uffculme', pp.1–6.

[8] These issues, of course, apply equally to calculations for the survival of wills, covered in the chapter by Goose and Evans.

[9] Johnston, 'Probate inventories and wills', p.21.

[10] Alcock, *People at home*, pp.13, 177. His proportion of untraced people in the burial registers who left wills is comparable to other samples from Devon and Staffordshire in Razzell, *Essays*, pp.209–13.

[11] Overton, 'English probate inventories', pp.209, 313 n.30.

[12] Kenyon, 'Petworth', pp.38–9.

the upper reaches of the exempt.[13] Because exempt householders ranged from some 20 to 80 per cent in different communities, with a norm around 30 to 50 per cent, care is needed when comparing the surviving inventories of one area with another.

Farming

By far the most important economic activity in Tudor and Stuart England was farming, which manifold probate inventory studies have illuminated in the last 50 years. Hoskins demonstrated their potential first with two seminal articles on agriculture in Leicestershire in the sixteenth and seventeenth centuries.[14] Then most Leicestershire villages conformed to the three open-field mixed husbandry template of the textbooks. Hoskins, however, used their probate inventories to show that the system did not rotate rigidly between spring- and winter-sown corn and fallow, as the literary evidence suggested, nor did individual farmers have to wait for the parliamentary enclosure movement of the later eighteenth century to introduce more flexible balances between pasture and arable farming.

Hoskins analysed the most detailed inventories surviving from some sample years between 1500 and 1703 to show that the two main crops grown were barley and pulses (peas and beans), both sown in the spring. Wheat and a little rye were sown in winter in no more than a quarter of the area of the barley fields, while a few acres of oats were grown in most pulse fields, and by the later seventeenth century more beans and wheat were sown than peas and barley. But the main change was the increasing conversion of arable land to pasture, when some arable strips were laid down to grass for several years in leys and large pasture closes were created when the open fields in some parishes were enclosed by agreement. It was prompted by the London market's increasing demand for cattle and sheep, which increased the number of specialist graziers whose inventories recorded herds and flocks of an unprecedented size after 1660.

Hoskins' attempt to show that the later Stuart Leicestershire farmers became richer, with larger holdings, was less convincing. According to him, the average personal estate left by Leicestershire husbandmen rose

---

[13] Arkell, 'Incidence of poverty', pp.32–5, 44; Levine and Wrightson, *Making of an industrial society*, pp.161–3, where 78.8 per cent were exempted from the Hearth Tax.

[14] Hoskins, 'Sixteenth century', pp.123–83; Hoskins, 'Seventeenth century', pp.149–69.

from £14 in 1500–31 to £67 in 1603 and a median of £74 in 1638–42. These figures make no allowance for inflation nor for the fact that some labourers' inventories were 'indistinguishable from those of middling husbandmen. Sometimes the labourer was even better off'. In addition, the median value of yeomen's estates in 1638–42 was £138, but Hoskins noted another complication as nearly a quarter had retired from active farming and, on their exclusion, the yeomen's median rose to £176.[15] Such averages or medians often disguise as much as they reveal, like the claim that until the mid-seventeenth century the 'typical' Leicestershire farmer was a small peasant with an average of some 20 sown acres, when in fact only half had between 10 and 30 acres and the rest either less or more.

Despite such limitations, Hoskins had blazed a trail which many followed in other counties. Thirsk tackled many more inventories in the much larger county of Lincolnshire, which she subdivided into four main farming regions.[16] Havinden's study of seventeenth-century Oxfordshire showed the ever-expanding London market's influence on agricultural change in the county's flexible open-field farms.[17] Comparisons between the inventories for 1580–1640 and 1660–1730 revealed a greater increase on the limestone uplands in the median sheep flock and in the proportion of wheat sown at the expense of barley, rye and oats than in the Thames Valley. Havinden's wheat calculation, however, used far fewer inventories than the one for sheep because only those made in the summer months before the harvest gave the complete acreage of the different crops.

Whetter's study of seventeenth-century Cornwall showed how the east and centre of the county responded more to the influence of market forces than the west and north coast.[18] In and near the towns there were more cows for milk, but elsewhere in the east and centre, the number of cattle bred for beef increased, with farmers in moorland areas specialising in rearing and those with better grazing in fattening. Cornish flocks of sheep were small, but the proportion with 25 or more in their inventories rose from 37 per cent in 1600–20 to 49 per cent in 1680–1700, while barley replaced wheat as the main corn crop. Later Overton compared Whetter's crop distribution analysis with similar data from other counties to highlight the absence of pulses in Cornwall.[19]

---

[15] Hoskins, 'Seventeenth century', p.155.
[16] Thirsk, *English peasant farming*.
[17] Havinden, 'Agricultural progress', pp.66–79.
[18] Whetter, *Cornwall*, pp.21–58.
[19] Overton, *Agricultural revolution*, pp.93–5.

Thirsk made heroic use of such studies to link them with soil types and provide two accounts of the farming regions for 1500–1640 and 1640–1750 in the *Agrarian History of England and Wales*.[20] The latter reflects the mushrooming of inventory studies because, when it was published 17 years later than the former, it was four times longer.

The best of these local studies usually explored several common themes, such as the balance between arable and pasture farming, the extent and nature of agrarian change and the development of regional specialisation in response to market opportunities, often concentrating on areas smaller than a county but larger than a parish. Zell demonstrated how pasture farming dominated some dozen Kentish Wealden parishes in the Elizabethan period.[21] In general, the smaller the farm, the more geared it was to subsistence, with pasture and arable more evenly divided and the cattle used more for dairying. The more prosperous farmers' inventories contrasted sharply with a much higher ratio of livestock to corn and a concentration on raising and fattening cattle to sell for beef. Attempts to estimate reliably the comparative values of arable and pasture farming were often impaired by the problem of isolating draught animals and fodder crops, such as hay, so that a simple livestock to corn value ratio was frequently the best available substitute.[22]

In five Forest of Arden parishes, Skipp showed that the land growing arable crops rose from a third in the sixteenth century to three-fifths by the later seventeenth century.[23] The average number of cattle per farm declined from 14 in 1530–69 to under 9 in 1610–49, with beasts reared for meat accounting for most of this decline, but the proportion of households making cheese expanded dramatically. This decrease in livestock numbers was replicated at the same time in nearby east Worcestershire as well as in Lincolnshire.[24] Pickles discovered an even greater decline in farming in eight parishes or chapelries in mid-Wharfedale, Yorkshire from 1686 to 1740.[25] There some 90 per cent of all farming wealth derived from pastoral activities, but the numbers of cattle and sheep both fell by one-third and the acreage of sown arable also decreased on all but a handful of the largest farms.

[20] Thirsk, 'Farming regions', pp.1–112; Thirsk, *Agrarian history, V, i.*

[21] Zell, 'Wealth', pp.212–18.

[22] Hey, *English rural community*, pp.59–60 explains clearly why simple livestock/crop ratios should not be accepted as pasture/arable ones.

[23] Skipp, *Crisis and development*, pp.42–54; Skipp, 'Economic and social change', pp.84–111.

[24] Yelling, *Common field*, pp.158–9.

[25] Pickles, 'Agrarian society', pp.63–70.

Meanwhile, Edwards examined seventeenth-century dairy farming in north Shropshire, where he detected five sub-regions.[26] Small peasant farmers practised a similar level of dairying throughout, but dairy production expanded remarkably among an increasing number of commercially-minded farmers with large herds, mainly in the extreme north-east of the county, close to Cheshire. This was disclosed by the median value of the cheese recorded in the five regions' inventories and their mean number of cows compared with other cattle at the beginning and end of the century as well as by the wealthier farmers' own inventories. By contrast, the median number of cattle from all farming inventories showed little change because many smallholders and cottagers owned one or two. Had they been omitted, as in Zell's study of the Weald, the impact of market opportunities on north Shropshire farming would have seemed greater than it actually was, as Thirsk clearly appreciated.[27] Goodacre wrestled with this problem in his study of the rural hinterland of Lutterworth, Leicestershire, where very few sixteenth-century inventories survived for smallholders or cottagers, but their number rose fourfold between the 1590s and 1630s because 'people previously concerned with supplying the household' were 'launched into market production'.[28]

Probate inventories have also been used to detect agrarian innovations. Potatoes, for instance, were first mentioned in west Cumberland in an inventory of 1665, although there were very few references there before the 1740s.[29] Havinden searched thousands of Oxfordshire inventories before locating the first reference to turnips in 1727.[30] In north Shropshire, the first mention of clover in the inventories was in 1673 with a few more in the 1690s, but it did not become widespread until later.[31] Such references, however, only record the date of the farmer's death, not his innovation, and do not indicate when the new development was consolidated, as Overton's study of the diffusion of turnips and clover in Norfolk and Suffolk exposed.[32] There the proportion of farmers growing some turnips rose from under one per cent before 1660 to 20 per cent in the 1680s and 50 per cent in the 1720s, by when 20 per cent had also sown clover. Yet neither crop was

[26] Edwards, 'Development of dairy farming', pp.175–90.
[27] Zell, 'Wealth', p.212; Zell, *Industry in the countryside*, pp.95–6.
[28] Goodacre, *Transformation*, pp.93, 125.
[29] Marshall, 'Agrarian wealth', p.513.
[30] Havinden, 'Agricultural progress', p.72.
[31] Edwards, 'Development of dairy farming', p.183.
[32] Overton, 'Diffusion', pp.205–21; Overton, *Agricultural revolution*, pp.99–101, 110.

diffused widely before 1750.[33] The four-wheeled wagon was a huge improvement on the two-wheeled cart; it was employed on farms first in the early-seventeenth century, but was not taken up generally until later. The first inventory near Lutterworth to mention a wagon came from 1634, but most wealthy farmers there did not have one until the 1680s.[34] The Oxfordshire inventories do not mention wagons before the 1660s, although by the 1690s 20 per cent of farmers possessed one.[35] Meanwhile, the farmers in the remoter parts of west Cornwall had to make do without even carts.[36]

Overton has also generated estimates of crop yields per sown acre from inventories with an approach that Allen and Glennie refined later.[37] Because very few inventories recorded both the yield and acreage for the same crop (19 out of some 5,500 farming inventories studied in Hampshire, Norfolk and Suffolk), this method infers the crops' yields from valuations for both standing and harvested grain.[38] The resulting estimates are only approximate since they depend on assumptions such as the allowances to be made for tithe, whether the stored grain was threshed or not, appraisals of the costs involved and how crops in the ground were valued. Appraisers tended to value crops soon after sowing according to the costs incurred already (such as for seed, manure and ploughing) and not to estimate their anticipated selling prices until later in the growing season, when they knew the harvest's likely quality. As a result, these estimates of crop yield per sown acre were made only for areas devoted to commercial grain farming, where sufficient inventories distinguished, quantified and valued separately specific types of grain, as well as for those farmers appraised between June and August with at least ten or even 20 arable acres. Nevertheless, when the same assumptions are applied consistently, the long-term trends which emerge are relatively reliable, unlike the actual yields. Campbell and Overton used this method to calculate rises of between 88 and 21 per cent in the yields of barley, oats, wheat and rye in Norfolk from 1584–99 to

---

[33] In theory roots, clover and grasses were part of 'nature's bounty' and so belonged to the heir and not the executors, so that some crops may have been omitted from the earlier inventories—see Chapter 2 above, p.33.

[34] Goodacre, *Transformation*, p.145.

[35] Havinden, 'Agricultural progress', p.78.

[36] Whetter, *Cornwall*, p.43.

[37] Overton, 'Estimating crop yields', pp.363–78; Allen, 'Inferring yields', p.117–25; Overton, 'Re-estimating crop yields', pp.931–5; Glennie, 'Measuring crop yields', pp.255–83.

[38] Campbell and Overton, 'New perspective', pp.67–75.

1710–39.[39] Glennie's analysis of seventeenth-century Hampshire inventories revealed increases by the 1680s of 50 per cent for barley and 42 per cent for wheat.[40]

Our understanding of agricultural developments in the early modern period owes much to how these inventory studies explored diversities in farming practice and changes over time. They are most convincing when there are sufficient inventories for selective sampling to omit the least detailed and allow for seasonal differences. Ideally, they should also allow for inflation before 1640 and identify fodder crops and draught animals when comparing the relative values of arable and pasture farming.

Trades and crafts

No other economic activity has such a wealth of probate inventory data available as farming, although for some trades and crafts enough exists for historians to tackle them in depth. For this purpose, the quality of the detail is usually as important as the quantity because the relatively few inventories that list and value the equipment and materials of a particular trade can often illuminate it with great clarity.

One recurring discovery made by most studies of better-off tradesmen and craftsmen outside the larger towns is how misleading single occupational labels can be since many were also substantial part-time farmers. Thirsk linked this phenomenon with a pastoral economy, suggesting that about half England's farmers in the seventeenth century were also part-time craftsmen.[41] Hey's study of the Sheffield region's rural metalworkers illustrated from their inventories how farming combined with the different metal crafts, such as cutler, scythesmith, grinder and nailmaker, to create large gradations of wealth and sharp variations in farming practices that stemmed in part from the different balances between farming and metalworking.[42] Hudson's comparison of two large textile townships in west Yorkshire provides another insight. The assets in the textile workers' inventories (1690s–1760s) were 'fairly equally balanced' between textile production and farming in Calverley, while in Sowerby they were of less value, with the bulk in industry and trade.[43]

---

[39] Campbell and Overton, 'New perspective', p.70.
[40] Glennie, 'Measuring crop yields', pp.272–4.
[41] Thirsk, 'Industries', p.86; Thirsk, 'Seventeenth century agriculture', p.172.
[42] Hey, *Rural metalworkers*, pp.16–41.
[43] Hudson, 'Land', pp.27–31; see also Moore, *Goods and chattels*, p.18.

Rowlands portrayed a similar picture between 1660 and 1710 among west Midlands metalworkers, who accounted for a third of the area's probate inventories.[44] Evidence of husbandry appeared in 56 per cent of these, but the balance varied from 73 to 10 per cent between the different trades. The scythesmiths had the highest proportion and the largest holdings, followed by the nailers who farmed no more than an acre or two each, with the locksmiths and lorimers concentrating more on their industrial work.[45] Scythemaking was a seasonal business in north Worcestershire, concentrated between January and April and dovetailed between farming activities, and the inventories from different seasons reflect this.[46] Zell found the distinction between families with or without farms more useful than one between farmers or craftsmen and tradesmen for the Elizabethan Weald, where 'more than half the tradesmen identified by their inventories were also farmers'.[47] However, Kussmaul has argued that inventories exaggerated the extent of dual employment because most who were not dual employed had no inventory.[48]

In the Weald woollen clothmaking was a major industry, organised on a putting-out basis and involving most households to some extent in at least one process. Probate inventories, supplemented by wills, are the best sources to trace them.[49] The woolmaking process was directed by clothiers whose servants washed, oiled, sorted and weighed the raw wool before it was put out to be carded, dyed and then spun. Some clothiers' inventories record how each process enhanced its value in the 1580s, when raw fleece wool was worth about 2s. 10d. per quarter, cleaned white wool about 3s. 6d. and dyed wool ranged from 4s. 4d. to 9s. per quarter, depending on the dyes used and the time taken.[50] Carding and spinning were undertaken mainly by outworkers, as over half the Wealden inventories from 1565 to 1599 attested. Next came weaving, done by specialists with their own looms, worth between £1 and £3, recorded in one inventory in ten. The clothiers often paid the weavers for their cloths very late so that many were still owed money when they died. Few fulling mills appear in fullers' inventories because most rented them. The shearmen who finished or dressed the woollen cloth used shears and other equipment that

---

[44] Rowlands, 'Society and industry', p.53.
[45] Rowlands, *Masters and men*, pp.41–3.
[46] Large, 'Urban growth', pp.176, 188 n.34.
[47] Rowlands, *Masters and men*, pp.44–6; Kussmaul, *Rural economy*, p.10.
[48] Zell, *Industry in the countryside*, pp.108–9.
[49] Zell, *Industry in the countryside*, p.170.
[50] Zell, *Industry in the countryside*, p.165.

together cost between £5 and £8.[51] The clothiers directed the whole business, finally delivering the cloths to London merchants, who often delayed payment for three to six months. The better-off clothiers had plenty of wool, dyestuffs, finished cloths and credit owed by cloth dealers, but their clothmaking tools were rarely worth more than £20–25.[52] In the Lake District, the Kendal shearmen were more important, controlling the production of woollen cloth from 1576 to 1636 and often owning equipment for carding, spinning or weaving as well as for dressing the cloth.[53]

The inventories indicate similar but variable patterns in other textile-producing areas. In east Shropshire, linen was produced as well as wool, with a quarter of the inventories mentioning hemp or flax between 1660 and 1710, but only one in ten from 1710 to 1750. Spinning wheels were universal, appearing in an eighth of the inventories before 1700 and a quarter after it, with five different types in use and the cheapest valued at about 1s. 6d. Here dyers treated various finished cloths rather than yarn and undertook several finishing processes such as shearing; four very detailed dyers' inventories from the market town of Wellington show how they operated.[54] Weaving remained a specialist activity, but because 'loom' also meant bucket here it could cause confusion![55] The main textile industry in and around Richmond, north Yorkshire, was the handknitting of woollen stockings and caps. Most hosiers who organised it lived in the town, with the knitting done in the countryside by women and children as well as by men with another means of livelihood. Only the better-off knitters with a few dozen stockings awaiting collection when they died can be identified by their inventories, but the prices and types of stockings produced appear in many hosiers' inventories.[56]

The leather industry was claimed by Clarkson 40 years ago to be one of the forgotten occupations of early modern England, employing more than all others, apart from woollen clothmaking and possibly building.[57] He used 55 leather workers' inventories to sketch the organisation of the heavy and light leather crafts, which Phillips confirmed later was

---

[51] Zell, *Industry in the countryside*, pp.164–86.

[52] Zell, *Industry in the countryside*, pp.199–219.

[53] Phillips, 'Town and country', pp.110–12.

[54] Trinder and Cox, *Yeomen and colliers*, pp.47–64.

[55] The whole question of the lexicon of local dialect words preserved in the probate inventories is as important as it is fascinating. Weiner and Trinder each explore complementary aspects in Chapters 13 and 14, below.

[56] Fieldhouse and Jennings, *History of Richmond*, pp.177–83.

[57] Clarkson, 'Organisation', p.245; Clarkson, 'Leather crafts', pp.25–39.

applicable to the Kendal cordwainers.[58] The former used tanned leather from cattle hides to make shoes and saddles and was more specialised than the latter which used dressed leather from sheep, goats and calves for gloves, belts and purses. It was organised more on a putting-out basis, with those engaged in it being poorer, more flexible and more eager for additional employment.[59] No process used expensive equipment, but tanning needed a large capital outlay because of the long time it took to soak the hides in solutions of oak bark and tanners often farmed as a subsidiary activity.

Probate inventories supply much piecemeal evidence for the great expansion of retail trade in the seventeenth century, with the best detailing the wares which pedlars, chapmen and packmen sold as well as the retail shops, revealing the goods available for purchase in different places for those who could afford them.[60] Cloth and haberdashery dominated most of their inventories, but Shammas disclosed that shopkeepers were selling more groceries and provisions by the later seventeenth century.[61] Mercers were the least specialised shopkeepers, selling a broad range of goods made in other localities and especially abroad, although Cox showed how all were specialists to some degree in her comparison of three very full mercers' inventories from Wellington with 37 others.[62] There 'most were arranged in a systematic way, in what amounted almost to a standard format, doubtless reflecting arrangements in the shop' and were usually appraised at wholesale prices by fellow tradesmen.[63] This topic has not been fully explored yet, but North's chapter makes a significant new contribution to it.[64]

Debts owed to the deceased provide another field for study as well as those owed by them, but because the latter were not required in the inventories, some can be supplemented by probate accounts, as Spufford demonstrates below.[65] Credits or 'debts owed to' were often listed incompletely by appraisers who had to act quickly after the death

---

[58] Phillips, 'Probate records', p.32.

[59] Clarkson, 'Organisation', pp.245–56.

[60] Thirsk, *Economic policy*, pp.120–2; Spufford, *Small books*, pp.83–110, 120–3; Hey, *Packmen*, pp.191–3, 201.

[61] Shammas, *Pre-industrial consumer*, p.235.

[62] Vaisey, 'Probate inventories and provincial retailers', p.105; Trinder and Cox, *Yeomen and colliers*, pp.20–41, 116 n.20, 278–80, 302–8, 314–21; Dyer, *City of Worcester*, pp.86–7.

[63] Trinder and Cox, *Yeomen and colliers*, p.27; see also Chapter 6, below.

[64] Chapter 15 on merchants and retailers of Cornwall, below.

[65] Debts are also considered by the Coxes in Chapter 2 and by Hodges in Chapter 16 on widows, but the topic is discussed at much greater length in Peter Spufford's Chapter 11 on long-term rural credit.

without time to check them, unless a shop book was available. Identifying the bad from the good debts took time and was rather subjective so that appraisers and executors tended to play safe by overestimating the 'desperate' ones.[66] However, these credits were not just for goods or services supplied, but also for loans to relatives or investments and so help to prove how much the early modern economy relied on credit.[67] Dyer used the debt statements of sixteenth-century Worcester tradesmen to map the elliptical-shaped area dominated by the city's market.[68] The customer base of two specialist traders in Chester, an upholsterer and a staymaker, covered a much wider area than its average traders in the eighteenth century, while further north, the credits of a Kendal pewterer reveal that he traded over the whole of Cumbria.[69]

Urban occupations

Inventories have been used to explore the range and diversity of urban occupations either alone or in conjunction with wills.[70] In 1660–1750, for example, 28 per cent of Wellington's inventories belonged to trades or professional men, but only 9 per cent in the adjacent parishes, which turned to the town for more specialist trades and services, such as baker, butcher, surgeon and surveyor.[71] Kenyon compared Petworth's standing as a market centre in west Sussex with three nearby towns by aggregating the surviving tradesmen's inventories and the total trades in each.[72] Its 140 tradesmen's inventories and 55 trades in 1610–1760 were almost identical with Horsham's, but Midhurst's 127 inventories covering 38 trades and Arundel's 87 inventories indicated their lesser importance.

Inventories never covered the full range of a town's occupations, as the city of Lincoln demonstrates. There from 1661 to 1714 appraisers assigned 63 different occupations or professions to 197 deceased, but Johnston identified 18 more occupations from the contents of a further

[66] Hoskins, 'Elizabethan merchants of Exeter', p.80.
[67] Holderness, 'Credit in a rural community', pp.94–115; Holderness, 'Widows in pre-industrial society', pp.435–42; Spufford, *Contrasting communities*, pp.80, 212–13.
[68] Dyer, *City of Worcester*, pp.68–70.
[69] Mitchell, 'Development of urban retailing', p.262; Phillips, 'Town and country', p.120.
[70] See Chapter 3 by Goose and Evans, pp.57–63.
[71] Trinder and Cox, *Yeomen and colliers*, pp.8, 19.
[72] Kenyon, 'Petworth', pp.103–7.

379 inventories (30 per cent of which were for women) and related probate documents.[73] However, when he turned to other sources in the same period, such as parish registers, the total occupations detected doubled to 166.[74] The Lincoln appraisers 'were not apparently very interested in ascribing occupations'.[75] Many had several jobs from which the appraisers chose just one or none, avoiding most occupations related to barley and drinking in Lincoln, where the inventories identified only three maltsters and one brewer, while Johnston discovered a further 14 and 24 respectively. Some other crafts, such as tailors and carpenters, however, resist detection in inventories which did not name them because their tools were worth relatively little and their customers often provided the materials on which they worked so that the poorer trades were always under-represented.[76]

Although their coverage was far from complete and the quantities often too small to sustain sound statistical analysis, inventory valuations have supplied insights into the economic circumstances of urban tradesmen and craftsmen, as Dyer's descriptive survey of Tudor Worcester's diverse occupations demonstrated from 817 inventories.[77] These showed that the wealthiest trades included clothiers, tanners, innkeepers and brewers, the pewterers were comfortably prosperous, the bakers were getting richer, there was a wide range of wealth among the butchers and smiths and the barbers and tailors were in decline. Hoskins reported that a sample of London merchants from around the same period appeared some four times better off than those from Bristol or Exeter.[78] But other towns are not so well endowed with inventories. Although the single largest body of evidence available for Reed's study of Ipswich from 1583–1714 was 222 inventories, they provided little

[73] Johnston, *Probate inventories of Lincoln*, pp.xxv–xxx. See also Havinden, *Household and farm inventories*, pp.5–7, where as many occupations and statuses were deduced from the contents of the inventories (111) as were specified in either the inventories or wills (111).

[74] The analysis of occupations from wills is pursued in a separate section in Chapter 3, above, pp.57–63.

[75] Johnston, *Probate inventories of Lincoln*, p.xxv.

[76] Johnston, *Probate inventories of Lincoln*, pp.xxxviii, xlv; Munby, *Life and Death*, p.xxvi; Trinder and Cox, *Yeomen and colliers*, p.65; Zell, *Industry in the countryside*, pp.115–16, reported that bakers, butchers and the building trades were all heavily under-represented in his inventory sample for this reason.

[77] Dyer, *City of Worcester*, pp.98–103, 120–32, 136–40, 142–8, 158. Transcripts of unusually detailed inventories for 21 different tradesmen's occupations appear in Dyer, 'Probate inventories', pp.8–60.

[78] Hoskins, 'Elizabethan merchants of Exeter' pp.77–8. The median personal estate for the London merchants was £7,780.

insight into the organisation or development of most trades and no more than 'some flickering light' on the town's economy.[79] Ipswich was the country's second most important shipbuilding port in the early-seventeenth century, but it still has no inventories for shipwrights, ropemakers or sailmakers.

House size and rooms

Good probate inventories can be so detailed that they provide modern readers with a temporary illusion of accompanying the appraisers from room to room round a house with all the possessions apparently left undisturbed since the owner's death. But scholars intent on extracting from selected inventories reliable information about early modern housing and living conditions must cope first with their diverse and inconsistent recording of detail and the unknown proportions excluded. The pioneering study of houses and their contents was published by Emmison in 1938, based on 166 Bedfordshire inventories from 1617–20.[80] His analysis included valuations of their household goods, ranging from 6 per cent valued at over £40 to 28 per cent under £5. Rooms were named in nearly two-thirds of these dwellings, with the five largest housing three gentlemen and two parsons in over ten rooms. The 32 houses with five to ten rooms belonged mainly to yeomen and husbandmen and a few craftsmen; all contained a hall, 27 a kitchen, 22 a buttery, 15 a dairy, 20 a parlour, of which 16 had beds, while most houses had two or three chambers with beds as well. Over 30 more dwellings had four rooms, although in some the fourth was not for living, but for making butter and cheese or sifting flour. Almost all the rest, including those with inventories which did not specify rooms, were probably simple cottages with two or three rooms, although it was often difficult to establish the precise number when it was unclear which lofts or chambers were used for sleeping or storage.

Steer followed in Emmison's footsteps and wrestled with similar problems in his detailed study of 250 inventories from Writtle, Essex, for 1635–1749. His thorough analysis of 217 houses with 1,866 rooms included all service or work rooms, but not barns and other outbuildings, and did not infer the existence of rooms from indirect evidence, such as chambers over a buttery or parlour without mention of the downstairs room.[81] Overall Writtle's houses ranged from one to

---

[79] Reed, 'Economic structure', pp.103–10, 115.
[80] Emmison, *Jacobean household*, pp.3–49.
[81] Steer, *Farm and cottage inventories*, pp.1–51.

22 rooms, with two-thirds having from four to ten. Spufford's work suggests that in the 1660s houses were smaller further north, with over two-thirds having two to seven rooms in Cambridgeshire, but no more than two to five rooms in Lincolnshire.[82]

Hoskins was more interested in the development of houses over time. He argued that there was 'a revolution in the housing of a considerable part of the population' in rural England between 1570 and 1640, which entailed both 'the physical rebuilding and modernisation of the medieval houses' and 'a remarkable increase in household furnishings and equipment'.[83] He illustrated this from Wigston Magna's inventories for 1561–1600 when kitchens were added to many houses, some rooms were boarded over to create upstairs chambers, accessed by ladder, and glazed windows first appeared.[84] By the next century houses under seven rooms (excluding service ones) conformed almost invariably to a fixed plan. Two-roomed houses had a hall and parlour, with a chamber over as the third and either a kitchen, buttery or second chamber for the fourth. Five- and six-roomed houses had three lower rooms with two or three chambers above. Greater diversity appeared only among houses with seven rooms or more.[85] In Suffolk by the 1670s parlours were no longer used for sleeping in the larger houses and kitchens were becoming main living rooms.[86]

Barley consolidated the study of rural housing when he argued that Hoskins' concept of a 'great rebuilding' had outlived its usefulness because inventories helped show that improved housing did not peak until the late-seventeenth century.[87] There were also significant regional variations reflecting different standards of living, with most testators under Charles II living in five to eight rooms in Kent, four to eight in Nottinghamshire and two to six in Yorkshire. Further north and west, in such counties as Durham, Cheshire and Cornwall, similar calculations were not so valid because most houses were smaller and few inventories itemised their contents by room.

---

[82] Spufford, 'Significance', pp.53–4, 63. These figures are based on her Table 2 which has been recalculated by omitting the dubious category.

[83] Hoskins, 'Rebuilding', p.131.

[84] There was a sudden increase in the installation of glass windows in Worcester in the later 1560s and a striking acceleration from the later 1580s; in East Anglia they appeared a generation earlier, but much later in Devon, see Dyer, *City of Worcester*, p.157; Hoskins, 'Rebuilding', p.139 n.1; Platt, *Great rebuildings*, pp.16–21.

[85] Hoskins, *Midland peasant*, pp.285–94.

[86] Garrard, 'English probate inventories', pp.66–8.

[87] Barley, 'Rural building', pp.652–67, 677–8. For a fuller discussion and the idea of a second great rebuilding after the Restoration—see Platt, *Great rebuildings*, pp.1–2, 23–7, 138, 150–7.

Alcock's study of Stoneleigh near Coventry added a new dimension to inventory studies by matching many to ordinary extant buildings from 1530–1750 with the help of very detailed estate records.[88] His correlation of various room-by-room inventories with related architectural plans and drawings provides a unique insight into many individuals' circumstances and the development of a whole community over three centuries. Although the survival of two or more inventories for the same building showed the recorded rooms often varied by one or two, he calculated house sizes and estimated the actual number of smaller homes from other available sources. The inventories alone implied that two-fifths of Stoneleigh's houses had under six rooms in 1600–1750, but when rescaled this proportion rose from a half at the start to four-fifths by the end because so many new cottages were built after 1700.[89]

Studies of urban housing from inventory data usually prove more elusive because town houses were more varied in size and pattern and more often subdivided, especially in the larger cities, so that it is often unclear whether urban inventories cover all or part of a house. Small scale studies of single towns can provide numerous insights into the locality, but so far no clear regional pattern in urban housing development has emerged. Hoskins demonstrated from fewer than 50 inventories how small the houses were in Elizabethan Leicester, where the original basic two- or three-roomed single storey house had often acquired chambers above and the occasional second floor by the later sixteenth century.[90] In Banbury, Oxfordshire, houses with five rooms or fewer conformed to a standard pattern and comprised three-fifths of those which could be identified accurately from 1590 to 1650, but accounted for just half of a smaller sample from Stockport, Cheshire, in the 1660s.[91] In Exeter houses were much more varied, with two-roomed ones being common in the lesser streets, but ten to nearly 20 rooms occurred in houses with three to five floors in the main streets.[92] Earle used 375 inventories from the London Orphans' Court to show that two-thirds of these 'middling sort of people' had from five to eight rooms between 1665 and 1720.[93]

Dyer compared the house sizes of four Midland towns in 1530–1700 from 1,900 inventories, by using the rather crude mean number of

[88] Alcock, *People at home*, pp.12–19.
[89] Alcock, *People at home*, pp.54, 94–6, 121–2, 200–1.
[90] Hoskins, 'Elizabethan provincial town', p.103.
[91] Dannatt, 'Banbury', pp.73–7; McKenna and Nunn, *Stockport*, p.22.
[92] Portman, *Exeter houses*, pp.23–30, 36–7.
[93] Earle, *Making of the English middle class*, pp.209–12.

rooms per house.[94] It revealed substantial increases in the later sixteenth century from six to eight in Coventry and five to seven in Derby, but not in Birmingham or Worcester. Worcester, with many attics and cellars, had a seven-room mean and its rebuilding appears to have occurred already before 1530, but Birmingham's five rooms remained unchanged until the later seventeenth century, when its mean house size rose to just six, the same by then as in Coventry. Dyer's room-name analysis suggests that the hall survived much longer in Birmingham and Derby and the parlour in Coventry and Derby. In Norwich, Priestley and Corfield concentrated on changing room use because 871 room-by-room inventories from 1580 to 1730 could not be related to any surviving contemporary building.[95] Here as elsewhere, multi-purpose living rooms gradually gave way to more specialist cooking, sitting and sleeping rooms, with more wash-houses and garrets as well, but such trends cannot be dated precisely. The recorded size of these houses, which belonged mainly to craftsmen and tradesmen, remained virtually constant. Just over three-fifths had between four and nine rooms, falling to two-fifths if those inventories which did not identify individual rooms were assumed to have had three rooms or fewer, as Shammas has suggested.[96] Unfortunately, problems such as these make many direct comparisons between such separate studies difficult.[97]

An alternative approach to house size in Richmond, Yorkshire, related the number of hearths recorded in the 1673 Hearth Tax to the number of inventoried rooms and showed the median rose consistently from two rooms per house for one hearth houses to four for two, five for three, seven for four and so on.[98] These are comparable to the medians for Cambridge of three to four rooms for two hearths and five to six for three and four hearths, although as always medians ignore all exceptions.[99] In Cambridgeshire the medians were substantially higher, with three rooms per one-hearth house, rising to nine for four hearths, and so indicating that fewer rooms in rural houses were heated.[100]

---

[94] Dyer, 'Urban housing', pp.207–18.
[95] Priestley and Corfield, 'Rooms and room use', pp.97–114.
[96] Shammas, *Pre-industrial consumer*, pp.161–4.
[97] Hoskins, *Midland peasant*, p.292 n.1; Spufford, 'Significance', p.54 n.1; Dannatt, 'Banbury', pp.77–80; Alcock, *People at home*, pp.58, 60, 84; Portman, *Exeter houses*, pp.32–5; Dyer, 'Urban housing', p.209.
[98] Fieldhouse, 'Hearth tax and social structure', pp.14–15.
[99] Goose, 'Economic and social aspects', p.334. I am very grateful to Nigel Goose for providing me with this unpublished information.
[100] Spufford, 'Significance', p.63; Styles, 'Social structure', p.157.

However, Green's exposure of the diversity of one-hearth chargeable houses in west Cornwall revealed one limitation of this approach.[101]

Household contents

Probate inventories provide a plethora of detail about their household contents, but their patchy nature and inconsistent survival make attempts to quantify them elusive, especially for ordinary households.[102] Many historians have therefore used descriptive accounts to illuminate the household goods of particular localities and have made more progress in identifying changes in wealthier people's standards.[103] Some detailed tabulations lack coherent analytical frameworks, such as Dannatt's breakdown of Banbury's furniture or the 12 main categories for Stockport's 1660s inventories, but a more successful approach to quantification concentrated on the appearance of new consumer objects in inventories.[104]

Weatherill's study of some 3,000 inventories belonging mainly to the lesser gentry, professions, merchants, farmers and craftsmen showed that the range and quantity of their household goods increased substantially from 1675 to 1725 in eight widely-scattered areas. She focused on the frequency with which they recorded 17 different objects from three main groups, with most having the basic tables, pewter and cooking pots throughout. Between one and two in five inventories recorded books, silver, table linen, earthenware and looking glasses in the 1670s, with the last two doubling in the next 50 years, while the others remained unchanged. Fewer than one in ten inventories had clocks, pictures, window curtains, knives and forks, china and utensils for hot drinks in 1675, but thereafter ownership of all expanded rapidly.[105] The main difference between provincial towns and rural areas lay in the acquisition of newer more decorative goods, such as window curtains for greater privacy and saucepans with handles used for cooking on enclosed stoves.[106] In addition, 'the indicators of the new modes of eating and drinking were virtually unknown in the countryside', but not in the major towns.[107] The Cumbria sample was the poorest of all, with

---

[101] Green, 'One-hearth homes', pp.11–16.

[102] Johnston, *Probate inventories of Lincoln*, p.lxxv.

[103] Steer, *Farm and cottage inventories*, pp.11–31; Trinder and Cox, *Yeomen and colliers*, pp.90–113.

[104] Dannatt, 'Banbury', pp.90–1; McKenna and Nunn, *Stockport*, pp.52–7.

[105] Weatherill, *Consumer behaviour and material culture*, pp.25–42.

[106] Weatherill, *Consumer behaviour and material culture*, pp.75–7.

[107] Weatherill, *Consumer behaviour and material culture*, pp.77–83.

its rural households having the fewest pictures and other semi-luxury items.[108]

The inventories of Earle's 'middling Londoners' show that their homes were transformed in the same period. By the early-eighteenth century most were more comfortable and lighter, with many more upholstered and cane chairs. They were also better lit, with mirrors in nearly every room, and hung with lighter and more attractive textiles, especially in furnishing the better beds. By the reign of Queen Anne pictures, ornaments and clocks were prevalent throughout many houses and forks, coffee-pots and tea-kettles had become common place. The average value of their linen cupboards' contents (with 36 sheets, 89 napkins and 15 table-cloths) was greater than their kitchens' entire contents, which changed little. Somewhat surprisingly, the poorer homes' domestic goods, excluding plate and jewellery, averaged £60–70 in value in 1665–90 but rose by only £10 after 1690, while the average value of those with over £100 actually fell. At the same time very few of the wealthiest had a coach or a stock of wine, like Samuel Pepys.[109]

Johnston's study of household contents in 510 Lincoln inventories revealed very little change from 1660 to 1714, with quantifiable increases only in looking glasses and grates which burned coal, but very tenuous evidence for improved soft furnishings or other domestic objects. However, he identified four main subgroups among its inventoried citizens when he analysed the total value of their household goods, including plate which was the most impressive item of household display.[110] The fifth with furnishings worth less than £6 when they died, had attained 'a barely adequate standard of comfort' and the next fifth (with £6–15) 'a level of modest comfort'. Domestic goods accounted for one-third of both groups' personal estates, but only one-fifth for the next quarter valued at £16–35. They 'had apparently satisfied normal aspirations' in their furnishings, which were most superior in bedding, bedroom furniture and linen. The remaining third above £35 'exhibited varying degrees of luxury', culminating in 'ostentatious affluence' for the one per cent with more than £200 of household goods.[111] Earle's 'middling' folk in London inhabited a much more affluent world.

The surviving inventories from the Durham coalmining parish of

---

[108] Weatherill, *Consumer behaviour and material culture*, pp.58–9.
[109] Earle, *Making of the English middle class*, pp.290–301, 280.
[110] Johnston, *Probate inventories of Lincoln*, pp.lxxiv–vii, lxiv.
[111] Johnston, *Probate inventories of Lincoln*, pp.lxviii–ix.

Whickham were so patchy over some 150 years that Levine and Wrightson could not analyse them with statistical rigour, but concentrated instead on the types of household goods contained in the most detailed ones 'as a means of ascertaining the general level of living standards' of the main social groups.[112] From just eight Elizabethan copyholders farming 18 to 46 acres, one smallholder and four cottagers, they showed that all had 'a domestic life-style of considerable simplicity,' with the main difference between them being the quantity rather than the types of their goods.[113] From the 1660s onwards, three broad social groups emerged from the greater quantity of surviving inventories, with domestic goods valued at over £15 for the minor gentry and more substantial farmers, between £13 and £6 for the lesser farmers and various craftsmen and under £5 for the rest. Carpets, chamber-pots, china, silverware, pictures and looking glasses were found mainly in the houses of the top group; feather bedding, cupboards, cushions, napkins and various pewter items were common in the middle group, while the living standards of the lowest category differed little from the Elizabethan copyholders. Together with those excluded from the probate process they accounted for most of Whickham's householders and so warned 'against exaggerating the extent of plebeian participation in the new "consumerism"'.[114]

In west Cornwall Arkell's analysis of 153 householders from 1660 to 1685 identified household goods worth £10 and £20 as more appropriate cut-off points.[115] Only the local gentry and richer yeomen, with over £20, had more than a basic range of furniture. Households below the £20 level used chests for keeping their clothes, dressers or sideboards for their eating vessels and sat on benches or the odd chair at tableboards set on frames. Tablecloths, silver spoons and brass candlesticks were confined to those above £10, who often slept on feather mattresses with finer sheets and larger bedsteads than those below £10. Beds and bedding accounted for almost two-fifths of the value of their household goods as did their cooking equipment. In a sample from three other areas, the bedding proportion was comparable, but cooking was valued at no more than a fifth, like other furniture, with eating vessels at just over a tenth.[116]

---

[112] Levine and Wrightson, *Making of an industrial society*, p.89.

[113] Levine and Wrightson, *Making of an industrial society*, pp.90–1.

[114] Levine and Wrightson, *Making of an industrial society*, pp.147, 231–9.

[115] Arkell, 'Household goods', pp.22–6.

[116] These proportions are based on a sample of 61 inventories with household goods valued at £50–100 or £10–19 from Essex, Gloucestershire and Lichfield: see Table 4.2 below, p.100.

Shammas studied the ownership of consumer durables over two centuries and two continents, concentrating in England on five samples totalling 1,150 inventories from Oxfordshire, Worcestershire and East London between 1550 and 1730. About a quarter of their probated wealth was devoted to consumer goods, which included clothes, with more for the poorer people and less for the wealthier ones and farmers. Because the prices of many goods, such as fabrics, were then falling most households continued to acquire more consumer durables. After 1730 there was a widespread rise in their ownership in the American colonies, but the sharp decline in probate coverage in England at the same time prevented Shammas from identifying similar developments there.[117] Styles was not so cautious, maintaining that the trend among the English middling sort of acquiring consumer goods intensified throughout the eighteenth century.[118] Shammas' attempt to discover how far early modern households met their own main consumption needs was less successful because many poorer homes with spinning wheels, for example, used them to earn money.[119]

Other possessions

Inventories are a promising source for studying many other possessions, such as clothes, food and weapons, which are usually tackled on a limited scale. Wearing apparel features frequently with a single valuation at house clearance prices and often was valued together, frustratingly, with the deceased's purse.[120] However, appraisers occasionally exceeded the call of duty by providing valuations for individual items of clothing. Such inventories can be invaluable, especially when studied with those of some retailers, detailed bequests of clothes or those relatively few probate accounts that record children's or apprentices' clothing.[121]

In post-Restoration London Earle used nine detailed inventories to show that the basic middle class male wardrobe (valued between £10 and £20) was three suits with accessories, although many accumulated more, such as a merchant with five complete suits and 17 shirts. Their outer garments were normally made of wool or worsted with linen shirts and drawers and some silk stockings and handkerchiefs. The

---

[117] Shammas, 'Changes', pp.185–94, 199; Shammas, *Pre-industrial consumer*, pp.86–100, 6.
[118] Styles, 'Manufacturing', p.537.
[119] Shammas, *Pre-industrial consumer*, pp.18–40.
[120] Spufford, 'Limitations of the probate inventory', pp.149–50; Johnston, *Probate inventories of Lincoln*, p.lxxiv; Vaisey, *Probate inventories of Lichfield*, p.34.
[121] Dannatt, 'Banbury', pp.99–100.

women's minimum was also three complete outfits with accessories, but their clothes were invariably more expensive because many more were made of silk.[122] In addition, women's clothes were omitted more often than men's because they tended to bequeath them more to their relatives and friends.[123] The evidence from elsewhere and for earlier periods highlights just how exceptional London's living standards were. The average value of a testator's clothing in Shakespeare's Stratford was 30 shillings.[124] At Uffculme, Devon, it was £2 in the late-sixteenth century, rising to £3 in the seventeenth.[125] In general, richer people spent more money, but less of their wealth, on their clothes, but clothing values alone do not indicate social standing because there were enormous variations in individual wardrobes.

Food appears even more intermittently in the inventories because the appraisers were not concerned with perishable goods, but only saleable quantities of preserved foodstuffs.[126] The existence of some foods can be inferred from the listing of such processing equipment as salting troughs for salted meat or the grocery stock of nearby retailers. The most commonly named foods were flitches of bacon and cheese.[127] In south Shropshire, beef and bacon were mentioned in one in four inventories from 1660–1700, but only in one in ten in the first half of the eighteenth century, suggesting that less salt meat was then kept through the winter.[128] Occasional references to butter, honey, sugar loaves, salt and tongue occur elsewhere and even more rarely to onions, apples, bread and gingerbread, which provide fleeting glimpses into food consumption, but never in sufficient quantities for valid statistical analysis.[129]

References to arms and armour occur most in the Elizabethan period and decline during the seventeenth century.[130] They cover a wide range

---

[122] Earle, *Making of the English middle class*, pp.284–5.
[123] Vaisey, *Probate inventories of Lichfield*, p.35. The inventories should have listed all bequests in theory, but in practice they often did not.
[124] Jones, *Family life in Shakespeare's England*, pp.56–9.
[125] Fraser, 'Costume', pp.96–8.
[126] Tucker, 'Houses', pp.84–5; Moore, 'Probate inventories', p.13; Chapter 2 above explains why only traditional stored foods were normally included in most inventories: see pp.30–1.
[127] Johnston, *Probate inventories of Lincoln*, p.lxxiv; Vaisey, *Probate inventories of Lichfield*, p.32.
[128] Trinder and Cox, *Yeomen and colliers*, p.103.
[129] Jones, *Family life in Shakespeare's England*, pp.82–3; Steer, *Farm and cottage inventories*, pp.23–4; Johnston, *Probate inventories of Lincoln*, p.lxxiv; Cash, *Devon*, pp.xix–xx.
[130] Kenyon, 'Petworth', p.71.

of weaponry from swords, rapiers and daggers to pikestaffs and halberds, bows and arrows, pistols and various muskets.[131] After 1660 'the paucity of weapons in the inventories makes it difficult to accept that the Civil War had taken place so recently'.[132] Most later guns were described as birding or fowling pieces and were designed for hunting, but so far no regional study of such weapons over time has been undertaken.[133]

The uneven distribution of musical instruments in probate inventories suggests that domestic music making flourished more in some areas and at different times. The proportion of London households with at least one instrument fell from one in seven in 1660–80 to one in 17 a generation later, perhaps reflecting the growth of professional concerts.[134] Then music making clearly flourished in the cathedral city of Lincoln with 14 different instruments appearing 42 times.[135] Stockport in the 1660s mustered at least five virginals, but an old one was the sole instrument from over a century at Writtle, Essex.[136] Only two people in Stratford were recorded in Shakespeare's time with an instrument: a surgeon's widow with clothes valued at over £12 had a fiddle and a very cultured gentleman a virginal, two viols, a cittern, a recorder, a flute and some music books.[137] His was one of the very few inventories to mention a recorder or flageolet despite their popularity in the late-sixteenth century.[138]

Few Elizabethan inventories listed books, but they appeared more often later; in early-Stuart Banbury about one in ten indicated books, while in later Stuart Lincoln it was over two in five.[139] Normally only the Bible was mentioned by name, although other religious works were identified occasionally such as Foxe's *Book of Martyrs*.[140] The few who possessed books in any quantity were either clergymen or gentry, whose collections were sometimes appraised by specialists. Most appraisers were uncomfortable describing or valuing books, which explains why Spufford found 'it is impossible to get an accurate impression of the number of households with Bibles from the inventories'.[141] Often books were not

[131] Dannatt, 'Banbury', pp.91, 95–6; Flower-Smith, 'Arms and the men', pp.111–14.
[132] Johnston, *Probate inventories of Lincoln*, p.lxxiii.
[133] Trinder and Cox, *Yeomen and colliers*, p.101.
[134] Earle, *Making of the English middle class*, p.296.
[135] Johnston, *Probate inventories of Lincoln*, p.lxxiii.
[136] McKenna and Nunn, *Stockport*, p.44; Steer, *Farm and cottage inventories*, p.48.
[137] Jones, *Family life in Shakespeare's England*, pp.49, 64.
[138] Spufford, *Small books*, p.48.
[139] Dannatt, 'Banbury', pp.97–9; Johnston, *Probate inventories of Lincoln*, p.lxxiii; see also Adams, *Lifestyle and culture*, p.xxii.
[140] Vaisey, *Probate inventories of Lichfield*, pp.36–7.
[141] Spufford, *Contrasting communities*, pp.210–11.

considered worth listing in Cambridgeshire in the 1660s; nor were Bibles necessarily entered separately. The more popular chapbooks worth only a few pence new were listed very rarely in probate inventories, apart from those of a few shopkeepers or chapmen who sold them.[142] In short, like other items discussed above, inventories are far from perfect for studying the prevalence of books, but used with other sources they can provide insights into the extent and type of reading at some levels of society.

Wealth and social structure

At first sight probate inventories appear tailor-made for studying social structure and the distribution of wealth. This assumes that their total valuations approximated to the overall wealth and social standing of most deceased, but warnings against doing so are frequent and uncompromising. 'Probate inventories can seriously underrate a man's total wealth.'[143] They 'are not a reliable guide to the total wealth of any individual, nor can they be used for comparative analysis of relative wealth, unless ... the person concerned owned little or no land'.[144] 'Probate inventories do not provide information concerning the "wealth" of testators but they do indicate something of the standard of comfort in which they lived.'[145] 'There are problems inherent in using the estate values given in probate inventories as indicators of an individual's wealth and social status.'[146] 'There is often a considerable gap between the gross personal estate and the net estate.'[147] The spread of wealth in each status group was so wide 'that it would be impossible to determine rank simply on the basis of wealth alone'.[148]

The cumulative force of these arguments led many historians to qualify the wealth that inventories recorded. Terms such as personal estate, estates according to value, property or assets were all applied to probate values.[149] Others used personal wealth, probate, moveable, inventoried, known or net wealth.[150] The precise meaning of some

---

[142] Spufford, *Small books*, pp.48, 120–5.

[143] Reed, *Buckinghamshire*, p.ix.

[144] Moore, 'Probate inventories', p.12.

[145] Rowlands, *Masters and men*, pp.47–50.

[146] Priestley and Corfield, 'Rooms and room use', pp.94–5.

[147] Hoskins, 'Elizabethan merchants of Exeter', pp.78–9.

[148] Overton, *Agricultural revolution*, p.38.

[149] Hoskins, 'Seventeenth century', p.151; Whetter, *Cornwall*, p.12; Pickles, 'Agrarian society', p.65; Hudson, 'Land', p.29.

[150] Erickson, *Women and property*, pp.41–3; Spufford, 'Limitations of the probate inventory', p.161; Goodacre, *Transformation*, p.151; Garrard, 'English probate inventories', p.57; Alcock, *People at home*, pp.182–4.

phrases is not very clear because they were rarely defined, but they were often used as virtual substitutes for 'wealth' or interchangeably with it.[151]

Wealth alone was also adopted by some authors such as Cressy, who argued that, despite their vagaries, 'inventories give an adequate indication of the distribution of wealth'.[152] Zell concluded unreservedly that probate inventories were superior to taxation returns as a source for studying the changing distribution of wealth or the relative wealth of the different trades in the Elizabethan Weald.[153] His conclusions were based on different inventory valuation bands and means and medians, unlike many other analyses which used a single comparator. In those instances Fieldhouse and others argued that, although both have their limitations, medians are normally more reliable than means unless the samples are very large.[154] However, both Spufford and Rowlands warned against making comparisons with either yardstick alone since status groups overlapped at the edges and the range of valuations found among the same trade could be as significant as its simple mean or median.[155] Similarly, under Hoskins' influence, MacCaffrey asserted that 'the composition of fortunes is more significant than the totals'.[156]

An alternative view holds that because 'total inventorial wealth is not always an accurate indicator of life style,'[157] a person's real status or living standard is often, but not always, reflected better by the total value of their household goods.[158] Two wealthy Cheshire landowners illustrate this. Sir Henry Delves' total of £6,600 included domestic furnishings worth nearly £1,000 and industrial investment of almost £4,000, but, while Sir Thomas Grosvenor's inventory of £3,300 neglected all his industrial property, his household goods amounted to nearly £2,000 and imply a much more lavish life-style.[159] Not surprisingly, Alldridge created his pyramid of wealth for Restoration Chester from its 1660 Poll Tax assessments rather than its surviving inventories.[160]

---

[151] Spufford, 'Significance', pp.53–64: Mitson, 'Significance', p.33; Jones, *Family life in Shakespeare's England*, pp.40–1.
[152] Cressy, *Literacy*, p.137.
[153] Zell, *Industry in the countryside*, p.146; Zell, 'Wealth', pp.208–10.
[154] Fieldhouse, 'Hearth tax and other records', p.80.
[155] Spufford, *Contrasting communities*, p.39: Rowlands, *Masters and men*, p.48.
[156] MacCaffrey, *Exeter*, pp.264–6.
[157] Reed, 'Economic structure', pp.116–17.
[158] Levine and Wrightson, *Making of an industrial society*, p.158; Fieldhouse, 'Hearth tax and other records', p.80; Kenyon, 'Petworth', p.81, who was also aware of a 'significant number' of inventories where the reverse was more applicable.
[159] Hodson, *Cheshire*, p.74.
[160] Alldridge, 'House and household', pp.40–2.

Table 4.1 Social status from a sample of probate inventories, 1675–1725

Social status	No.	Women	Rural	Inventory total		Household goods		(8)
				mean	median	mean	median	
	N	%	%	£	£	£	£	%
Lesser gentry	122	7	61	320	154	55	38	25
Yeomen and larger farmers	952	5	95	165	104	23	17	16
Husbandmen and smaller farmers	332	13	96	32	30	8	7	23
Labourers	28	3	82	16	13	5	5	38
High status trades	152	5	37	193	79	39	27	34
Intermediate trades	344	11	40	157	85	32	33	39
Low status trades	435	2	62	92	45	19	14	31
Widows and spinsters	217	100	59	82	30	18	13	43
Unknown	320							

Note: Column (8) represents the median of household goods as a percentage of inventory total.
Source: Weatherill, *Consumer behaviour and material culture*, Table A2.2, p.212.

Weatherill explored these problems further in her sample of 2,902 inventories from eight parts of England for 1675–1725.[161] Omitting widows, spinsters and those without occupations reduced this total to 2,365, of whom only 156 were women. Yeomen without another stated trade and farmers accounted for a half, with the gentry another 5 per cent and husbandmen 3 per cent. The next fifth comprised eleven trades with between 4 and one per cent each, including shopkeepers, blacksmiths, shoemakers, weavers, mariners and butchers. The final fifth contained 95 different occupations, each well under one per cent and most with just a few representatives. Weatherill aggregated them all into eight or ten groups in three alternative ways. Her preferred approach used social status criteria rather than economic sectors or Gregory King's inconsistent mixture of occupational and status groups. Table 4.1, using her social status groups, shows that the medians for household goods of the yeomen, husbandmen and gentry indicate a lower standard of living than the medians of total probate wealth.[162] The relative standings of those in the higher status and intermediate trade groups differ according

[161] Weatherill, *Consumer behaviour and material culture*, pp.208–14.
[162] In these calculations Weatherill counted farmers with inventories valued at over £60 as yeomen and those under £60 as husbandmen. Her approach limited the labourers to just one per cent, unlike Everitt who identified 8 per cent as labourers in 1560–1640 by counting all country people with no social status and inventories valued, for example, at under £15 in 1610–40 as labourers, see Everitt, 'Farm labourers', pp.413 n.1, 419–20.

to both means and medians because those at the top of the former, including the clergy and professions, were much more wealthy, while those in its middle and tail were not so well off as the intermediate ones.

By contrast, Spufford revealed 'a very considerable economic division . . . between the wealth owned' by labourers (median £15), husbandmen (£30) and yeomen (£180) in Cambridgeshire in the 1660s, although the median for yeomen in two different parishes was £48 in the fens and £299 on the chalk.[163] When Erickson compared these results with nine other studies from the 1580s to 1720s, assuming constant proportions of the inventoried, she detected 'a broad correspondence of wealth' in agrarian social levels, with various medians for labourers ranging from £13 to £28, husbandmen £22–83 and yeomen £104–229.[164] However, these figures do not allow for the exclusion from the probate process of many poorer labourers and husbandmen nor for the increasing trend for husbandmen to be called yeomen, but at different times across the country.[165]

Spatial comparisons of the apparent wealth of different areas or of the same areas over time are often more robust. Beier demonstrated economic stagnation in Elizabethan Warwick by comparing the average value of its inhabitants' goods with a sample from the Arden Forest. At the start, the town inventories were worth on average 50 per cent more, but by the end this gap had disappeared.[166] The 'real' value of the average Worcester testator's property was the same in 1550–69 as in 1600–19 after allowing for inflation.[167] Whetter showed how the distribution of wealth in Cornwall changed from 1600–20, when the mean value of the inventories from the east of the county was a fifth higher than elsewhere, to 1680–1700 when those in the east were worth one-third less than in the centre.[168] Ripley's study of the city of Gloucester and its hinterland in 1660–1700 showed that the mean personal wealth of those in the city (£244) was three-quarters more than those in the countryside (£137) and over half more than that for the nearby market towns.[169] Meanwhile, Pickles compared the fortunes

[163] Spufford, *Contrasting communities*, pp.37–9, 156.
[164] Erickson, *Women and property*, p.41.
[165] Chapter 9 by Evans, below; Moore, *Goods and chattels*, p.22; Stone, 'Literacy', p.107 noted that husbandmen had virtually disappeared from the Gloucestershire marriage licence records by 1680, but not in Oxfordshire until 1720.
[166] Beier, 'Social problems', p.52.
[167] Dyer, *City of Worcester*, pp.158–9.
[168] Whetter, *Cornwall*, p.14.
[169] Ripley, 'Village and town', p.178.

of those living in the Yorkshire town of Otley with its rural neighbourhood in mid-Wharfedale to disclose that, although the median value of their personal wealth in the 1680s was almost the same (about £38), by the 1730s it had fallen by a half in the countryside (to £18) but had risen by a half in the town (to £57).[170] Marshall's study of the rural highland and lowland areas of Cumbria demonstrated no difference between the two in the period 1661–90, when the mean value of farming inventories in both was £71, and again very little difference in 1721–50.[171] But direct comparisons between such totals are inadvisable until the composition of each sample and the assumptions behind their analyses can be ascertained.

Regional comparisons

More light is thrown on the hidden diversity of inventory valuation totals by comparing balanced samples of almost equal size from Cornwall, Essex, Gloucestershire, Staffordshire and Yorkshire, chosen from the 1660s to 1680s to eliminate the problem of changing prices. All are sufficiently detailed for their possessions to be subdivided into six main categories, with the few surviving inventories of over £1,000 omitted to prevent them skewing subsequent calculations. Unlike Weatherill's study, male and female inventories are treated separately, with a composite female group from all areas. The national rural/urban ratio of about three to one is reflected, as the Staffordshire group comes from the city of Lichfield and the Yorkshire one includes some from Otley.[172]

Table 4.2 reveals some significant differences in the inventoried wealth of the five areas. Those from Gloucestershire and Essex appear to be much better off, although a higher cut-off point for probate may account for the former, where only a quarter of its inventories were

---

[170] Pickles, 'Agrarian society', pp.64–5.

[171] Marshall, 'Agrarian wealth', pp.505–8.

[172] The samples have been extracted from appropriately detailed inventories of the 1660s to 1680s in Moore, *Goods and chattels*; Steer, *Farm and cottage inventories*; Vaisey, *Probate inventories of Lichfield*. A similar selection was made from copies of the inventories from mid-Wharfedale for 1686–92, which May Pickles very kindly provided me with and on which she had based part of her article 'Agrarian society' (see p.64 n.15). The west Cornwall data comes from inventories held in the Cornwall Record Office and were analysed by members of the Penwith Local History Group in connection with the research undertaken for their book *West Penwith at the time of Charles II* (ed. Beaufort-Murphy). E. Clee, G. Green, I. Green, C. Harry, J. Nankervis, M. Perry and A. Wright very generously gave of their time unstintingly.

Table 4.2 Regional comparisons of probate inventory samples 1660s–1680s, from five counties in six categories

Males	Household goods %	Apparel and money %	Credit %	Leases %	Farming %	Trade %	Mean value £	Inventory totals Total N	A N	B N	C N
W. Cornwall	17.2	2.9	7.7	32.0	37.7	2.6	82	79	7	25	47
Mid-Essex	21.6	5.6	11.1	0.0	60.8	1.0	128	80	13	27	40
S. Glos.	15.3	12.1	15.4	27.4	29.2	0.5	158	80	20	41	19
Lichfield	37.0	8.8	18.2	4.4	20.5	11.2	84	85	11	27	47
Mid-Yorks	14.7	3.5	17.3	9.8	50.0	4.7	85	80	4	34	42
Total males	20.5	7.3	14.0	15.1	39.7	3.3	107	404	55	154	195
All females	20.6	14.9	35.7	5.4	20.5	2.9	69	81	7	22	52

Note :Inventory values: A = £200–999; B = £50–199; C = £1–49
Source: See footnote 172 of this chapter.

Table 4.3 Male inventories from five counties 1660s–1680s in six categories analysed by three main probate wealth groups

Inventory value group	Household goods %	Apparel and money %	Credit %	Leases %	Farming %	Trade %	Mean value £	No. N
A £200–999	15.2	7.7	14.4	20.1	39.3	3.3	407	55
B £50–199	23.7	6.4	15.3	10.3	41.2	3.1	107	154
C £1–49	35.7	8.6	7.4	7.9	36.2	4.1	23	195
Total	20.5	7.3	14.0	15.1	39.7	3.3	107	404

Source: See footnote 172 of this chapter.

valued at under £50. Conversely, the mean value of the female inventories was only two-thirds of all male ones. The percentages in the table derive from the aggregate value of each category and its subdivisions follow Johnston in including plate among the household goods, but not clothes because so many inventories valued purse and apparel jointly.[173] The figures for credit ignore debts owed by the deceased and fail to distinguish between the good and bad ones so that, when credit contributes substantially towards the total, overall probate wealth is often exaggerated. But at least these data provide a fair guide to the extent of lending at the time.[174]

Household goods contributed one-fifth of the total probate value for both men and women, although it was almost double for Lichfield's males and just 15 per cent for the Yorkshire and Gloucestershire samples. Table 4.3 shows that for the better-off male inventories worth over £200 it was also 15 per cent (with a mean value of £61) and as much as 35 per cent (mean value £8) for those under £50. Apparel, money and credit accounted for half the value of the women's possessions but only a fifth for the men, apart from over a quarter among those from Gloucestershire and Lichfield and a mere tenth in west Cornwall. Credit alone was twice as important for all men with inventories above £50 as below it.

It is well known that farmers in the west of England often leased their property for three lives or many years, while in the east they rented it for much shorter terms at higher rents, but the impact on inventory values has yet to be explored.[175] By law probate inventories covered

[173] Johnston, *Probate inventories of Lincoln*, p.lxiv.
[174] This treatment of debts in calculating inventory valuations is, of course, similar to the approach of many historians such as Cressy: see above, n. 152.
[175] Hoskins, *Age of Plunder*, pp.58–9.

only leases for years and not lives until 1741.[176] However, west-country custom had long treated three–life leases as if they were for 99 years, calling them 'chattel leases'.[177] Because they had to pay large lump sums or fines at the outset, often financed by loans, their tenancies could be of considerable value when they died.[178] This explains the 30 per cent inventory value for leases from Cornwall and Gloucestershire, where farmstock was only slightly more valuable. There leases contributed half the value of inventories worth over £500, a quarter for those between £100 and £500 and a sixth between £25 and £100. By contrast, the Essex sample had no leases at all and its farmstock was even more dominant than in Yorkshire, where leases made up the difference. In addition, nearly one-fifth of the probate value of both the 106 yeomen and 29 husbandmen identified in the whole sample derived from leases. Those who rented land on short leases at much higher rents did not trouble their appraisers, but instead needed more income during their lifetime to pay their rents.

Conclusion

During the last half century inventory studies have transformed our understanding of many aspects of early modern society and economy, such as farming practices, outwork manufacture, retailing, credit, differing life-styles and house contents. Nonetheless, they still have considerable potential for further expansion by researchers aware of why some approaches are more successful than others and their endemic problems are not insuperable, if treated with care and discretion. Selected areas should always be large enough to produce adequate-sized samples for targeted subgroups or issues and be designed for comparison with other areas and sources. Assessments of wealth should recall that probate valuations are based solely on personal estates and ignore the life cycle, all income and any real estate and must accept that single comparators, such as medians or means, are merely approximations. In these circumstances, the current drive for precise quantification should be curbed by drawing firm conclusions only from clear-cut differences and comparable samples.

[176] See above, Chapter 2, p.32.
[177] Cash, *Devon inventories*, pp.xxiii–xxiv; Hey, *English rural community*, p.73.
[178] Clay, 'Lifeleasehold', pp.83–7; Hoskins, 'Rebuilding', p.141.

5

Using Probate Accounts

AMY ERICKSON

Introduction

Probate accounts is the (non-contemporary) term used to describe two very similar early modern documents: the executor's account, filed in cases where the deceased left a will; and the administrator's account, filed in cases of intestacy.[1] The executor or administrator filed an account of the estate for which they were responsible in the church court, usually about one year after the death in question. The account set forth the value of the personal estate, as it had appeared in the inventory. The executor or administrator (hereafter referred to as the 'accountant') was 'charged' with that amount. He or she then listed all disbursements out of the estate. These usually included funeral costs, debts owed by the deceased, and the court's costs for processing the will, inventory and account. A wide variety of other expenses might appear, from rents, taxes and tithes to marital property settlements, children's apprenticeship, and labourers' wages. For all of these payments the accountant 'prayeth', 'craveth' or 'demaundeth' allowance from the responsible court official, the probate ordinary. The account was the final stage in the process of administering an estate. It served two functions: to acquit the accountant of further responsibility for the debts of the dead man; and to ensure that the residue or balance of the estate was distributed either according to the will or according to law.

Wills have been used for 50 years to study the vast majority of the population below the level of the gentry. Some two million wills survive from early modern England. However, wills convey only the

---

[1] I am grateful to the staff of record offices in Lincoln, Chichester, Northampton, Taunton, Dorchester, Winchester, and Cambridge University Library's Manuscripts Department for their assistance. A version of this article also appears in Sogner, *Fact, fiction and forensic evidence*. An earlier version appeared in Martin and Spufford, *Records of the nation*.

Table 5.1 Surviving probate accounts in England and Wales

Record Office	Number	Dates
Aberystwyth	44	1620–1693
Aylesbury	7	1617–1684
Bristol	133	1575–1783
Bury St Edmunds	44	1521–1818
Cambridge: Record Office	12	1700–1823
Cambridge: University Library	202	1561–1730
Chester	275	1569–1807
Chichester	1,217	1578–1714
Dorchester	103	1599–1702
Gloucester	138	1601–1834
Hertford	549	1556–1753
Huntingdon	340	1597–1825
Ipswich	1	1754
Leicester	369	1639–1687
Lichfield	1,361	1576–1850
Lincoln	6,044	1524–1853
London: Greater London Record Office	172	1666–1816
London: Lambeth Palace	116	1555–1756
London: Public Record Office	c.10,568	1665–1754
Maidstone	13,586	1568–1740
Northampton	196	1668–1816
Norwich	206	1626–1824
Oxford: Bodleian	96	1577–1720
Oxford: Record Office	845	1547–1810
Preston	307	1574–1799
Reading	1,661	1564–1783
Taunton	927	1577–1748
Trowbridge	1,696	1567–1827
Truro	393	1600–1650
Winchester	451	1569–1716
Worcester	667	1583–1825
York: Borthwick	536	1606–1855

Source: Peter Spufford, British Record Society Probate Accounts Index Project

testator's intentions, not what actually happened. They are generally only an incomplete record of the testator's property. And it seems they were more likely to be made by wealthier people. At most one-third of the population made a will (the same proportion which makes one today). The million or so inventories which survive provide detailed snapshots of individual possessions, but no indication of how those goods were acquired or what happened to them. Only about 43,000 accounts are extant, less than 5 per cent of the number of inventories. Table 5.1 lists all known accounts and their location. The British Record Society, in a project funded by the Economic and Social

Research Council, has now abstracted some 34,000 accounts located in the 31 provincial record offices, and will shortly publish a name and occupational index on microfiche.[2] In addition, over 10,000 accounts from the Prerogative Court of Canterbury, held in London, remain to be abstracted. There are also relatively small numbers in other record offices which are awaiting repair. At least eight record offices (including those in Aberystwyth, Durham, Exeter, Leeds, Norwich, and Nottingham) have inaccessible accounts, unindexed and scattered amongst large numbers of other probate documents. In addition to being few in number, accounts are also the most chronologically limited probate document. Although the earliest account listed in Table 5.1 dates from 1521 and the last from 1855, in fact usable numbers only exist between 1570 and 1720. Figure 5.1 charts the number of surviving accounts by year. The total absence of accounts during the Commonwealth, when only the central probate court was operating, is clearly shown and was common to all probate documents. Where the survival pattern of accounts differs from those of wills and inventories is in the dramatic decline after 1685, as shown in the dotted line in Figure 5.1.[3]

Geographically, accounts do not appear to exist outside of England, Wales, and the North American colonies (except in the different form of accounts for orphans). In different parts of England, the proportion of the eligible population for which an account was created may have varied considerably. The collection of accounts in Kent, covering the Diocese of Canterbury, is probably the most complete, since the accounts were bound into chronological volumes shortly after filing. These accounts may represent one-fifth of the adult men who died in the diocese in the later seventeenth century, and perhaps a somewhat larger proportion in the first half of the century.[4] Another means of measuring accounts against population is by the Hearth Tax returns. On the basis of these returns, John Houghton in 1693 published estimates of the number of households in each county.[5] Table 5.2 shows the number of surviving probate accounts, the number of estimated households, and the ratio between them. However, most collections of accounts relate not to a whole county, but only to a part of it. For

[2] Jacqueline Bower and Peter Spufford have generously shared with me their draft introduction to this work, on which I have relied in the following discussion and throughout this article.

[3] 1 Ja. II. c.17. For a detailed examination of the survival of accounts in the Diocese of Lichfield and Coventry, see Chapter 12, below.

[4] Spufford, Brett and Erickson, *Probate accounts*, pp.liv–lv.

[5] For a discussion of the calculation of households, see the appendix to Glass, 'Two papers on Gregory King', pp.216–20.

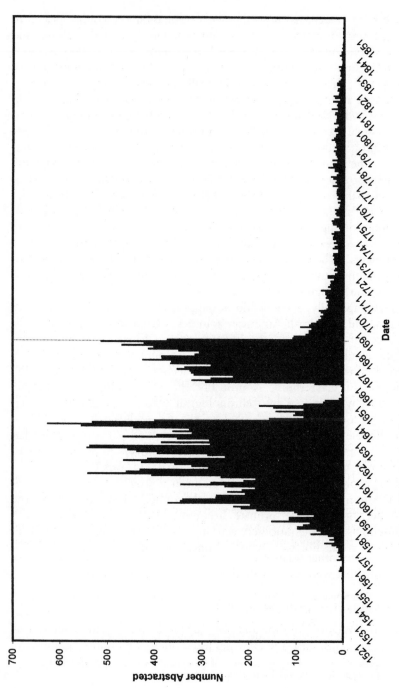

Figure 5.1 Annual number of probate accounts, England and Wales

Table 5.2 Ratio of probate accounts to households by county

County	Dates	Number	'Houses'	Ratio
Kent	1568–1740	13,601	39,242	34.6
Lincolnshire	1524–1853	5,989	40,590	14.8
Berkshire	1564–1783	1,765	16,906	10.4
Sussex	1578–1711	1,221	21,537	5.6
Wiltshire	1567–1827	1,453	27,093	5.4
Oxfordshire	1547–1810	925	19,007	4.9
Huntingdonshire	1597–1825	354	8,217	4.3
Hertfordshire	1556–1753	519	16,569	3.1
Worcestershire	1583–1825	536	20,634	2.6
Leicestershire	1639–1687	379	18,702	2.0
Somerset	1577–1748	929	49,808	1.9
Hampshire	1569–1716	449	26,851	1.7
Cornwall	1600–1650	396	25,372	1.6
Cambridgeshire & Isle of Ely	1561–1823	225	17,347	1.3
Gloucestershire	1601–1834	282	26,764	1.1
Cheshire	1569–1807	275	24,054	1.1

Source: Peter Spufford, British Record Society Probate Accounts Index Project

example, in Kent, between 34 and 35 accounts appear to have been made for every 100 households in the entire county between the later sixteenth and the early-eighteenth centuries. However, the accounts relate only to the Diocese of Canterbury, or east Kent, which accounted for 53 per cent of the county's population.[6] So the true ratio is nearly double: 65 accounts for every 100 households. In counties other than Kent, with more haphazard account survival, we have no choice but to use the household estimate for the entire county, always remembering that these ratios represent a minimum estimate of the number of accounts that were ever made. Therefore in Lincolnshire, 14.8 accounts survive for every 100 households, and 10.4 accounts for every 100 households in Berkshire. These proportions are not inconsiderable. But in more than half of English counties—those which are *not* listed in Table 5.2—less than one account survives for every 100 households over a century and a half. So the survival of accounts is extremely patchy. It is unlikely that any county other than Kent preserved intact even the majority of accounts that were ever made there (see below, pp.115–16).

The content of probate accounts

Despite limitations of time and place, accounts are extremely interesting for two reasons. First, the expenses listed offer extraordinary glimpses of

[6] Spufford, Brett and Erickson, *Probate accounts*, p.lxxi.

daily life at a social level very rarely found in other records of this period. And second, they provide unrivalled economic information, particularly in conjunction with corresponding wills and inventories.

Disbursements out of an estate naturally started with funeral costs.[7] The amount spent was generally between £1 and £2, but varied widely with an individual's wealth. Payments are recorded for beer and cakes for the celebrants, bread given to the poor, and gifts of gloves or rings for mourning friends, as well as for sermons read, bells tolled and gravestones erected. Accounts also detail the cures or 'physic' administered in the last illness (often involving sack and spices), and money laid out for 'fire and candle'. Large amounts were paid to 'chirurgeons' and the occasional apothecary, much smaller fees to the omnipresent pauper women who nursed and watched with the dying, before stripping and cleaning them.

The deceased's holding had to be maintained, crops sown or reaped, animals cared for. Servants had to receive their annual wages, labourers their daily rates; stock had to be fed, rented out, or butchered. The deceased may also have owed back wages, rents and taxes—whether to the king, the parish, or the manor, or for the highways or the dike reeves in the fens.

Orphaned children required clothing, board and schooling, or they had to be 'put out' or apprenticed. Sometimes these costs are listed in a lump or annual sum; sometimes they are itemised—down to a bodice, a pair of drawers, or pens and ink. Clothing, usually for children but sometimes for adults, was listed both ready-made and in terms of yardage, buttons, thread and tailoring.[8] There is also evidence on the retail price of a wide range of foodstuffs and household goods. Unlike inventories, which record the second-hand resale value of goods, accounts list prices new.

Accounts provide evidence of an extensive rural debt and credit market before the eighteenth-century county bank.[9] In addition to 'shop' credit for purchase of goods, many types of bills and bonds in common use appear, along with the rates of interest charged and the terms of the loans. In the two largest account collections which have been abstracted, half of all Lincolnshire men's accounts mentioned such borrowing on specialty, and a quarter of Kent men's accounts.

Accounts often give clues about individual landholding unavailable in

---

[7] The first book-length study to use accounts was Gittings, *Death, burial and the individual*, which examined funerals as social occasions.

[8] On the relative expenses of girls and boys, see Erickson, *Women and property*, pp.49–60. Houlbrooke also uses accounts in *Death, religion and the family*.

[9] See further Spufford, 'Les liens du crédit', pp.1359–73, and Chapter 11, below.

inventories or wills: the listing of rents owed both before a man's death and by his survivors afterwards suggests the number of landlords a tenant held from, and occasionally specifies the type and size of holding. Accounts also detail the division of the residual (after debts) estate belonging to someone who died intestate. This is our only information on inheritance among the two-thirds of the population who did not make a will. (Approximately three-quarters of accounts relate to the property of those who had not made a will.) Accounts can also change the way we interpret wills. For example, sometimes a certain child was not even named in a parent's will or received only a shilling by bequest. Previously it might have been assumed that child was being cut off. But if an account survives it may explain the circumstances, giving details of any settlement made during the parent's lifetime on that particular child, or the child's inheritance of land, or a marriage portion, or a legacy from a grandparent, none of which are mentioned in the will. Accounts and wills together thus give a more complete picture of property division within the family, and accounts on their own provide much-needed evidence of how the law of intestate division was practically applied in cases where the dead man did not leave a will.

Although church courts had legal jurisdiction only over moveable goods, they played a crucial mediating role in the overall distribution of property, and are essential to assessing the impact of the well-known common law practice of primogeniture on the transmission of wealth. Accounts show that at least until 1670 if one child—usually but not always the eldest son—received freehold or copyhold land according to common law or manorial custom, then the church court normally awarded to the non-inheriting children an inordinately large share of the moveable property in compensation. The heir to land was allotted only a token sum in cash. These pecuniary details throw light not only on the economic but also on the emotional structure of the relationships between parents, sons and daughters, and substantially recast the practice of primogeniture.[10]

The relationship between spouses, traditionally dominated by the common law idea of coverture, is also illuminated by the appearance in accounts of marriage settlements. These contracts safeguarded the wife's right to her personal property, which she otherwise lost to her husband upon marriage. In accounts they are found at a social level at which such legal arrangements were not previously thought to have existed.[11]

Wives' role in the management of family finance is also highlighted.

[10] See further Erickson, *Women and property*, Chapter 4, pp.61–78.
[11] See further Erickson, *Women and property*, Chapter 8, pp.129–51.

Although both contemporary treatises and twentieth-century discussions invariably refer to the executor or administrator, most accountants were women, referred to in the documents themselves as the executrix or the administratrix. Nearly 90 per cent of all accounts relate to the estates of men, the majority of whom were married. Most married men who made wills named their wife executrix, at least until the eighteenth century. And the widow of an intestate man had a legal right to the administration of his estate unless she chose to renounce it. (Some women did renounce their right, particularly in those cases where a husband's debts outran his assets and his estate threatened to end up in the negative.) Hence 60 per cent of all those filing accounts in court were female. The majority of accounts filed for women's estates were for widows, and nearly all of the remainder for 'virgins' or 'spinsters'. Married women could not legally own any moveable goods, which obviated the need for probate procedure on their death.

The accounting process

Much has been said to cast doubt on the efficacy of the seventeenth-century church courts. But these comments draw quite uncritically on contemporary propaganda to monopolise more business for the common law courts. It is often forgotten that contemporary criticisms were invariably levelled at the courts' enforcement of morality, and not at its 'civil' functions of marriage and probate. Documentary investigations have demonstrated the widespread acceptance of ecclesiastical marriage jurisdiction in this period. For probate jurisdiction, the evidence of accounts suggests that the church courts maintained a level of control over property division that at least equalled that of the common law courts.

The administration of estates was enforced by the church court's usual apparitors, paid by fines collected from the offending parties. When a date was set, the dead man's creditors and legatees were called to appear in court at the account's passing by a notice posted in the parish church and by a proclamation from the apparitor (or in London by a newspaper announcement). The accountant was allowed to deduct all these administrative costs from the estate, including her sureties' dinner on the day of the court appearance, and travel (guides, horse-hire, or ferrying in the fens), which varied with the distance the accountant lived from the nearest probate court. Journeys might also be required to retrieve and pay debts. Elizabeth Lawrence, widow of a husbandman worth £50 at his death in 1679, lived in Toynton St Peter, some 30 miles from the court at Lincoln. Elizabeth paid the debts her husband owed to 25 men and 5 women who lived in her own and six other parishes up to 20 miles distant. Some of these—to the woollen draper and the butcher, for example—were probably shop debts; one was secured by bond and two were fiduciary ('for the use of' a third party). The average amount of the debts themselves was only slightly over £1, and while Elizabeth probably sent messengers with payment rather than going herself, the relative cost in messengers was high.[12] Elizabeth Steevens *alias* Cox, the accountant of her mother's £33 estate in 1639, was granted more than most by the court at Bath when she claimed £8 for 160 days of her husband's travel in his mother-in-law's business.[13] However, she does not specify that this was done after her mother's death: the two may have done business together previously. In these relatively uncommon cases where a son-in-law assisted with administration, or even filed the account in court, all business still had to be conducted in the daughter's name. Similarly in the more common case of a new husband assisting his wife to file the account of her previous husband's estate: all legal transactions were in her name.

Administrative costs could also be affected by legal changes, like the 1678 Act to bolster the flagging wool trade which required all bodies to be wrapped in woollen rather than linen for burial. Whether certified by affidavit or, as Elizabeth Daulton did, by giving Goodwife Whitehead a shilling to go to the justice and swear that Elizabeth's husband had been buried in woollen,[14] the proof required a small fee. Failure to comply resulted in a hefty fine, distributed to the poor: in 1685 the accountant of Hester Wood in Lincolnshire paid £2 10s. in penalty for burying Hester in linen.[15]

A sale of the dead person's goods added to the administrative costs, involving payments to a drummer, a crier, and a man for keeping accounts on the day.[16] Some accounts still have attached a list of items

---

[12] Thomas Lawrence, £50/-3 (1680) Toynton St Peter, Lincolnshire Record Office (hereafter LRO) Ad Ac 43/128. This and all subsequent references to accounts give the following information: Name of deceased, Status (if known), Charge/Balance (to nearest pound), (Date), Parish, Record Office and Reference.

[13] Alice Cox, £33/-14 (1639) Chelwood, Somerset Record Office (hereafter SRO) D/D/Ct/C16.

[14] Robert Daulton, £29/7 (1680) Carlton le Moorland, LRO Ad Ac 43/101.

[15] Hester Wood, £117/68, Messingham, LRO Ad Ac 44/139.

[16] For example, Mary Thurban, £28/9 (1629) Arundel, West Sussex Record Office (hereafter WSRO) EpI/33/1629. Sales occurred especially for the estates of women, since their households more often had to be liquidated for the maintenance of orphaned children.

disposed of on the day of the sale.[17] If an item sold for less than its ascribed value in the inventory, the difference could be claimed as an allowance in the account, in the same way that if a sheep died after the inventory was taken its value could be deducted from the account. Crop overvaluation between inventory and account has been correlated to periods of low corn prices by the British Record Society study of accounts.[18] On the other hand, sometimes the amount with which the accountant was 'charged' is *greater* than the inventory total because the sale prices exceeded those estimated in the inventory. In some cases these additional sums significantly augmented the value of the inventory. Maurice Greenfield's accountant in Sussex in 1682 made an extra £42 in the sale of Maurice's estate, nearly half as much again as his inventory was valued.[19] Accountants also reported goods and debts which the inventory appraisers had inadvertently overlooked. The Sussex widow Alice Hill, for example, whose husband's inventory came to £46 in 1635, reported an additional £8 bond and £5 worth of goods which had been overlooked, plus £4 worth of books sold before the inventory was even taken.[20] The fact that accountants declared windfall profits as often as losses suggests the church courts took account administration seriously. The number of people involved in valuing inventories, estate sales, and credit transactions must have severely limited the opportunities for fraud.

The court's own fees amounted to approximately £1 15s. The fees for probate of a will and for intestate administration were comparable.[21] In the case of particularly impoverished accountants, the court might abate part of its fees. This happened particularly in Cambridgeshire and Lincolnshire, where more accountants were left in debt than elsewhere. The fees might be reduced by as little as 3s. or cut to as much as half the normal fees, but there was no standard abatement level: the balance of the account was not always negative in cases of abatement, and fees on accounts with comparable or even lower balances were sometimes not abated. These inconsistencies suggest that the court was weighing individual circumstances in each case, perhaps including the accountant's own financial situation and the number and age of the surviving children.

[17] For example, Ann Holwell [no totals] (1622) Westonzoyland, SRO D/D/Ct/H31, and Anne Elliott, £55/–24 (1728) Bridgewater, SRO D/D/Ct/E18.

[18] Spufford, Brett and Erickson, *Probate accounts*.

[19] Maurice Greenfield, £146/17, Shipley, WSRO EpI/33/1682.

[20] Robert Hill, £46/25, Petworth, WSRO EpI/33/1635.

[21] 21 Hen. VIII, c.5; Swinburne, *Briefe treatise* (1635) Pt.6, p.72; C[onsett], *Practice of the spiritual*, pp.422–3.

With reference to the payment of debts and expenses, the court had clear guidelines, laid out by Henry Swinburne in the late-sixteenth century. Any debt out of the estate amounting to more than £2 had to be substantiated by an acquittance or a cancelled bond at the passing of the account. (Acquittances sometimes survive pinned to the account.) Smaller amounts might be attested to by the accountant's oath.[22] She was to pay debts in specific order: first to the crown; then legal judgements and condemnations; statutes merchant and recognisances; obligations; and finally simple bills and merchant (shop) books. Debts without specialty (not in writing) the accountant was not legally bound to pay at all,[23] although she often did, especially those which had been confessed by the dead man in his lifetime or on his deathbed.

As for posthumous expenses, Swinburne directed that 'the most sumptuous and delicate expences are not to be allowed, but honest and moderate, according to the conditions of the persons'.[24] Theoretically, an accountant might have tried to claim non-existent debts and expenses larger than she had actually paid, in order to make a profit from the allowances. But judging from the courts' attention to sums, the success of dishonest accountants must have been limited. Deductions deemed inappropriate were crossed out and the addition, although as erratic as one ever finds in this period, was clearly double-checked. In Margaret Parkinson's 1604 account of her husband's estate before the court at Ely, for example, marginal notes indicate that some of the accountant's claims were allowed by the court but others were not. The final balance was crossed out and recalculated five times.[25] In 1618 it was alleged against Agnes Crow, of the Isle of Ely, that at least some of the debts she claimed in her account of her husband's estate had in fact already been paid by him in his lifetime.[26] Such false expenses would have allowed the accountant to reap a larger residue than appeared in the account balance, but also required extensive co-operation by payees to provide the supporting bonds, shopbooks and acquittances required by the probate court.

The efficacy of ecclesiastical probate jurisdiction is further attested by the tenacity of the court in its pursuit of accountants. Occasionally an account was delayed longer than one year after receipt of an estate, in the event that both parents of a minor child were dead and the

---

[22] Swinburne, *Briefe treatise* (1635), p.89.

[23] Swinburne, *Briefe treatise* (1635), p.78.

[24] Swinburne, *Briefe treatise* (1635), p.90.

[25] Richard Parkinson, £81/52, Whittlesey, Cambridge University Library (hereafter CUL) EDR A12/1/1604/15.

[26] Alexander Crow, £19/2, Elm, CUL EDR A12/1/1618/4.

accountant was personally required to bring up the child, and waited to file the account until the child was of age. These estates were brought to account as many as 15 years after the death in question, and of course the minor child who subsequently came of age was key to enforcing administration in these cases.[27] The court also had to be persistent, since a high death rate produced a high turnover of estates. In one Sussex example, Charity Figge *alias* Vincent *alias* Chandler proved the will of her first husband Chandler, a victualler, in October 1605, and that of her second husband Vincent, who died of plague, within two years following. But in John Vincent's inventory had been accidentally included £11 worth of goods belonging to his dead son by a previous wife, also named John. When son John's own wife died, her administrator, in October 1607, complained to the court that the £11 of John Vincent the younger, of which his wife in turn had been rightful administratrix, was in the hands of Charity Chandler *alias* Vincent. So five months later, now married a third time, Charity was called to account by the ordinary yet again for that £11 belonging to her dead husband's dead son's dead wife's administrator.[28]

Probate accounts as an historical source

Probate accounts appear internally consistent, and the church courts generally in control of the process. But their use as a historical source is complicated by the problem that we do not know under what circumstances an account was originally required by the court.[29] Two reasons in particular which might have caused the ordinary to require an account would suggest a bias in the surviving documents. The first is circumstances of actual or potential conflict over the estate. But aside from a few spectacular instances—like the Cambridgeshire widow Frances Richardson, in possession of her husband's £566, who in 1674 defended four actions at common law and a suit in Chancery in London—evidence of litigation is rare in probate accounts.[30] Only about 10 per cent of accounts mention litigation, and suits over payment of specific debts to or from the deceased were far more common than

---

[27] For example, Alice Hobbs, £21/7 (1619) Othery, SRO D/D/Ct/H64, and Susannah Keen, £142/–67 (1711) Bleadon, SRO D/D/Ct/K9.

[28] Will of William Chaundler, WSRO STC1/15/219b and accounts of John Vincent, elder, £11/–6, WSRO EpI/33/1608 and Elizabeth Vincent, £67/53, WSRO EpI/33/1607, all in Midhurst.

[29] See Chapter 2, above, pp.35–6.

[30] Robert Richardson, £566/–192 (1674) Chesterton, CUL EDR A12/2/1673/1.

litigation over the management of the estate. In 1,500 accounts examined, only two contain evidence of accountants accused of unethical procedures.[31] But these cases only came to light because papers in the dispute were inadvertently filed with the account. We need a thorough investigation of the separately-filed ecclesiastical cause papers in order to understand the nature and frequency of suits over probate and administration. The archives in both York and Maidstone, which hold sets of ecclesiastical cause papers together with the relevant accounts, would be a good place to start.[32]

The second possible reason that the court might have required the filing of an account is the estate's actual or potential liability to debt. If this were the case, then the economic interpretation of accounts would be substantially altered. However, overall only about a quarter of all accounts ended in debt, and there were many different reasons for that debt.[33] So the court would have been extraordinarily inaccurate in its target group if it was calling principally potential debtors to account. While the selectivity of probate accounts' survival is not clear, there is no pattern to suggest its being anything other than random, at least prior to 1685, when the law changed and the number of accounts plummets.[34]

Certainly it seems likely that different courts and different officials over time within the same court enforced accounting to varying degrees. The Diocese of Canterbury accounts may be complete, but in other courts we must assume that accounts were only kept for a short time before discarding them, since their survival appears accidental. At York, for instance, over half of the 58 accounts extant up to the mid-seventeenth century are for individuals whose names begin with 'S', so somehow the 'S' file (and the smaller 'H' and 'N' files) escaped the cull. In other places, such as Bristol and Winchester, accounts survive in chronological rather than alphabetical clusters.

The survival of accounts is certainly patchy relative to that of wills and inventories, but no obvious bias appears in the estates they deal with, such as suspect management or likelihood of debt, which might

---

[31] Agnes Crow was mentioned above. The other one was Martha Onn, relict of Lincolnshire husbandman Bartholomew, who was successfully sued in 1632 by Bartholomew's new administrator 'for her rashe administringe of his goods'. This man then charged the litigation costs to Bartholomew's £9 estate. LRO Ad Ac 23/76.

[32] The only book addressing this issue is Addy, *Death, money and the vultures*, which unfortunately only scratches the surface.

[33] See the discussion in Chapter 2, above, pp.34–6.

[34] See the discussion in Chapter 2, above, p.36.

cast doubt on the wealth of information they contain for local history.[35] There are also seven collections of over 1,000 accounts, which should allow for more quantitative social and economic analysis. Probate accounts cover a wide range of social strata, principally agricultural, since the three-quarters of extant accounts which have been analysed originate predominantly in rural areas and towns. (The as yet unexamined accounts originating in the Prerogative Court of Canterbury will represent a different clientele.) The bulk of known accounts represent more the 'middling' than the wage-earning sort, but this varies with different courts. Accounts may contribute to the assessment of changing social structure over time, and the economic fortunes of these groups. For example, the number of men identified as yeomen in accounts increases dramatically over the seventeenth century. However, regional variations in nomenclature need to be borne in mind: 'labourers' appear regularly in Lincolnshire accounts, but are completely absent in west Sussex, where 'husbandmen' are correspondingly poorer in relation to those identified as yeomen. Of course, many testators and most intestates did not identify their social status, but accounts permit the most precise possible assessment of their economic status (always excepting a complete listing of land ownership, which did not fall within the probate remit).

It has been argued that accounts are a more accurate measure of individual wealth than inventories because they reflect the value of the estate after debts were paid.[36] The difference between the 'charge' and the balance of the account was often dramatic. The median values of east Kent yeomen dropped by approximately 75 per cent, and by 97 per cent in the difficult years of the 1620s; Lincolnshire yeomen's estate values fell by 63–69 per cent.[37] But the actual difference between the initial and final value of an estate was always unpredictable, bearing no consistent relationship to the size of the estate, to the dead man's marital status, or even to the presence of children to be maintained. A large drop in the value of the estate did not necessarily signify a man in difficult circumstances. Some men may have maintained high levels of rent arrears, for example, because they could afford to and found it financially beneficial, rather than because they were struggling. A prosperous businessman maintained mutually acceptable credit with his customers over many years, but when the shop book was called in at his

---

[35] See further Gittings, 'Probate accounts', pp.51–9, and Bower, 'Probate accounts', pp.51–62.

[36] Spufford, 'Limitations of the probate inventory', pp.150–4.

[37] Spufford, Brett and Erickson, *Probate accounts*.

death some customers would necessarily default. The resultant 'desperate' debt may have had little to do with the actual economic position of either businessman or customer.[38]

Whether accounts represent individual 'real' wealth more accurately than inventories depends on what is meant by 'real' wealth. To measure the social standing of a man within his community, one might want to take his inventory value as representative, and calculate from his account the level of his credit (debts for goods and services) and his borrowing (debts on specialty). It has been suggested with reference to the few inventories which list debts the dead man owed, that the value of these debts ought to be *added* directly to the total value of the inventory (instead of subtracted, as they would be in an account), since debts reflected the credibility of the dead man in the community.[39] Certainly accounts confirm that yeomen, and to a lesser extent husbandmen, did indeed owe more debts—that is, were granted more credit—than labourers. But a direct addition of money owed to money possessed would surely overestimate even the man's own view of his reputation, let alone the view of those in the community who may have been persuaded to give him credit or loans for many reasons other than simply his reputation—kinship and friendship, to name only two possibilities.

If by 'real' wealth one means what a man left to sustain his family, then certainly the balance of the account is more representative than the 'charge'. A man's credibility dies, if not with him, then very soon after. To a widow, her husband's debts were of limited use as a notional asset representing his reputation in the community. His debts signified a very concrete reduction in the level of her subsistence, regardless of whether they were for the payment of goods and services, rents, or the result of borrowing. It is certainly possible that she may have been able to negotiate continued credit, but if that happened then the matter would not have appeared in an account.

Expenses in raising children are perhaps the most difficult to interpret, when these are calculated annually. Certainly if an eldest son or a widow took over a tenement, then the upkeep of minor children would continue to be paid out of the farm's profits, as it had been in their father's lifetime. So to set the cost of raising children over a period of years against the static personal estate, valued at a particular time in the agricultural year, would be to misrepresent the dead man's personal wealth.[40] However, annual expenses in childrearing seem to appear only

[38] I am indebted to Nancy and Jeff Cox for these examples.
[39] Moore, 'Probate inventories', p.12.
[40] I owe this example to Nancy Cox.

rarely in accounts filed by widows or eldest sons. They are charged against the personal estate in cases where the child's guardian is not kin or was not responsible for the child prior to its parent's death. In these cases the family holding may have been disposed of. It is my impression that the one-time expense of 'putting forth' or apprenticing a child to a different household may be found in any account, but is more common in estates administered by more distant kin and unrelated men. It will be interesting to check these generalisations in further account studies.

The interpretation of accounts in determining an individual's 'real' wealth must be flexible and transparent, both as to what is meant by 'real' and as to how different types of deduction are being assessed. Consideration of all kinds of debts a man might owe and even the expenses following his death becomes crucial to understanding the transmission of wealth and how it supported his family and the community.

Finally, there are a few practical points to be considered when working with accounts. First of all, not every single probate account is a mine of fascinating information. Accounts were the formulaic copy made by the clerk of the 'scratch' notes that the accountant brought into court. Very occasionally these scratch copies survive with the final document, preserving language quite different from that of the court: in referring to the deceased's young daughter, for example, the accountant's 'wench' becomes the clerk's 'maid'. Local accounting styles vary. Many accounts are cut-and-dried. Some clerks went so far as to draw up the forms in advance, leaving blank spaces for the names of the dead man and accountant, place of residence, and expenses, the latter grouped under general headings of 'funeral', 'debt', and so forth, without room to itemise. This fill-in-the-blank type of account may be detected where the clerk used a different colour ink for the variables, or in references to the deceased as 'he' when the deceased is patently 'she', or conversely if the accountant is referred to as 'she' when in this particular case it happens to be a 'he'. Many of the Dorset accounts were only ever half-finished and are missing dates. The content of accounts varies too: Lincolnshire men's social status is frequently specified; Northamptonshire has many accounts or parts of accounts in Latin, despite the fact that they all date from after 1665, and very few of them specify social status; Somerset accounts have no Latin, frequent law suits, rarely give the disposition of the residual estate, and contain a degree of detail on funeral arrangements unmatched by accounts anywhere else.

The quality and condition of the account collections vary widely. In Lincoln the accounts were long ago bound in volumes, only vaguely in date order and with much overlap, and accompanied by a hand-written index in the same haphazard order as the volumes. In contrast, Chichester has recently restored all of its accounts; they are ordered by year, and alphabetically within year. There is even an index on microfiche, comparable to the ones available for inventories and wills, sorted both by name and by parish. Maidstone is the only office which has microfilmed its probate accounts, but it did so many years ago and the quality is poor. On the other hand, in Taunton the accounts are now in such frail condition that microfilming is impossible. The new British Record Society Index volume will provide a starting point for searching all of the collections outside of London.[41]

The value of probate accounts is inestimable, for their proliferation of details on social and economic aspects of ordinary people's lives, from midwives' fees through marriage contracts to burial ceremonies, and covering most of the essentials—food, clothing, rent, medicine, and inheritance—in between, and for the opportunities they provide for quantitative analysis, both on their own and in conjunction with wills and inventories. Although the probate poor relation, 43,000 is certainly a sufficient number of documents to ask many and varied questions of the source, to learn from accounts all that they can tell us about the people who made them.

[41] Spufford, Brett and Erickson, *Probate accounts*.

6

Prices from Probate Inventories

MARK OVERTON

Almost all probate inventories give valuations for the goods and chattels they list. When a valuation is given for an individual item, rather than for a group of items collectively, and a quantity is also given for the item, then it is possible to divide the valuation by the quantity to produce a unit valuation for the specific item. Historians have often speculated as to whether these unit valuations can be treated as prices. Some think they underestimate prices, while others think that unit valuations calculated in this way do indeed reflect the local market prices for the items concerned. Hitherto there have been few attempts to calculate unit valuations from inventories, and, when the exercise has been undertaken, it has involved relatively small numbers of inventories.

This chapter draws on the findings from a project directed by the author and funded by the ESRC on prices from probate inventories in early modern England.[1] The project produced over 200,000 unit valuations from inventories, which provide the information to investigate the relationship between these unit valuations and prices in some detail. After a brief discussion of the methodology of the project, this chapter explores the relationships between unit valuations and prices by comparing unit valuations with independently produced price series and by looking at the evidence for internal consistency in inventory valuations. Finally, unit valuations are related to testators' wealth and social status.

The objective of the project was to produce price series of domestic goods for early modern England. Unit valuations were collected from inventories for the counties of Hertfordshire, Lincolnshire and Worcestershire for the period 1550–1750. This gave a sample with a

[1] ESRC Award B00232211, 'Prices from probate inventories in England 1550–1750'. I am grateful to the staff working on the project who collected the inventories discussed here: Linda Crust and Brenda Webster for Lincolnshire and Bridget Taylor for Hertfordshire and Worcestershire.

broad temporal and geographical coverage, representing prices in a variety of households; both rural and urban, agricultural and industrial, and from the relatively poor to the very rich. Within each record office three inventories were used (where possible) for each month of the year for the periods covered. Strictly speaking the project needed to sample prices or unit valuations, but in practice it was only possible to sample inventories. Only entries from inventories which could be used to calculate a unit valuation were recorded, so, unfortunately, the project did not result in the collection of complete inventories and the usefulness of the data is restricted to the study of prices.

An important part of the project was its computing methodology. Inventories were virtually copy-typed into a portable computer in the archives, following a few formatting rules, and then analysed by custom software specifically written for the analysis of probate inventories. This software has been described recently in print,[2] but the computing programs used for the analysis of inventories have now been developed into a more 'user friendly' software package for the computer management and analysis of probate inventories, and are now freely available for general use.[3]

The unit valuations collected have been used to compile three kinds of price series. *Major series* have been produced for the most common items. These are continuous for the entire period (sometimes with the exception of the 1640s and 1650s when probate business was taken away from the church courts) and are computed as ten-year averages for most items. There are 44 major price series, grouped into five categories: agricultural products, goods made of metal, textiles, goods made of wood, and capital goods. *Intermittent series* are for those items not listed frequently enough to yield a series of ten-year averages. There are 31 of these, and although they are calculated as 50-year averages it is still possible to get a good indication of price changes over a 200-year period, though short term fluctuations are necessarily lost. The third category are not really series at all, but *unit valuations* for items which appear very infrequently in inventories.

Prices are computed by taking the averages of unit valuations for a particular item from a collection of inventories. It is desirable to

---

[2] Overton, 'Computer management system', pp.10–17.

[3] As part of a project funded by the Leverhulme Trust; 'Household economies in southern England 1600–1750'. The programs were written by Mark Allen and comprise a package for the complete management of probate inventories. They are available free of charge. Further details from the author: Professor M. Overton, Department of Economic and Social History, University of Exeter, EX4 4RJ, UK.

Table 6.1 Unit valuations of cupboards from Lincolnshire, Hertfordshire and Worcestershire

	Lincoln			Worcs.			Herts.		
	N	Mean	S.D.	N	Mean	S.D.	N	Mean	S.D.
1550–1559	82	0.26	0.15	87	0.15	0.09	67	0.24	0.16
1560–1569	122	0.33	0.21	101	0.17	0.12	80	0.30	0.23
1570–1579	159	0.32	0.20	103	0.21	0.19	107	0.35	0.26
1580–1589	150	0.43	0.24	131	0.23	0.16	82	0.40	0.25
1590–1599	122	0.48	0.28	132	0.21	0.15	59	0.41	0.21
1600–1609	123	0.44	0.26	93	0.26	0.17	89	0.39	0.26
1610–1619	95	0.62	0.30	92	0.23	0.15	159	0.42	0.26
1620–1629	96	0.52	0.27	49	0.26	0.20	106	0.47	0.27
1630–1639	86	0.57	0.28	53	0.30	0.19	70	0.49	0.26
1640–1649	53	0.62	0.27	39	0.31	0.19	15	0.44	0.29
1650–1659	20	0.56	0.20	4	0.41	0.36	6	0.28	0.15
1660–1669	41	0.48	0.25	5	0.26	0.19	22	0.51	0.29
1670–1679	47	0.40	0.26	44	0.20	0.14	14	0.45	0.28
1680–1689	27	0.37	0.18	39	0.22	0.18	15	0.22	0.12
1690–1699	16	0.33	0.14	50	0.20	0.14	8	0.20	0.13
1700–1709	2	0.12		29	0.15	0.09	10	0.20	0.14
1710–1719	15	0.25	0.18	24	0.17	0.12	1	0.25	
1720–1729	10	0.19	0.14	23	0.13	0.07	6	0.33	0.32
1730–1739	12	0.20	0.22	2	0.09	0.06	3	0.10	0.05
1740–1749	23	0.24	0.24				1	0.20	

Notes: N = Number of unit valuations   S.D. = Standard deviation

minimise the variance around this average; in other words to keep the range of unit valuations as narrow as possible. This means that the description of items used to calculate a price should be as precise as possible. Appraisers of inventories vary in the level of detail they specify about particular items and are often frustratingly vague. To calculate a price using a large number of unit valuations it is often necessary to use items with vague descriptions, or to lump more detailed descriptions together, which leads to a larger variance. To get a small variance items need to be described as precisely as possible which results in fewer unit valuations being available. A balance has therefore to be struck between prices calculated from items with detailed descriptions but with relatively few unit valuations on the one hand, and prices calculated from described more generally but with a relatively large number of unit valuations. Table 6.1 gives the number of unit valuations, and the means and standard deviations for the distribution of unit valuations for cupboards by 10-year periods for the three counties. There are fewer observations for the later period, partly because cupboards were going

Table 6.2 **Unit valuations of bacon flitches in Worcestershire, 1550–1739 (£)**

	N	Mean	S.D.	Median
1550–1559	11	0.09	0.04	0.07
1560–1569	13	0.09	0.30	0.08
1570–1579	26	0.11	0.05	0.10
1580–1589	31	0.13	0.04	0.13
1590–1599	40	0.18	0.06	0.17
1600–1609	36	0.21	0.08	0.20
1610–1619	50	0.27	0.09	0.25
1620–1629	42	0.30	0.09	0.32
1630–1639	34	0.39	0.13	0.38
1640–1649	40	0.49	0.19	0.47
1650–1659	3	0.56	0.08	
1660–1669	11	0.50	0.14	0.50
1670–1679	60	0.48	0.14	0.50
1680–1689	56	0.48	0.16	0.50
1690–1699	72	0.55	0.17	0.50
1700–1709	23	0.58	0.17	0.50
1710–1719	29	0.61	0.16	0.63
1720–1729	28	0.65	0.23	0.64
1730–1739	3	0.40	0.18	

Note: S.D. = Standard deviation

out of fashion, but also because the number of inventories extant declines over time. 'Cupboard' is a general description, and the standard deviations are generally quite high, reflecting a wide range of values within each period. In contrast, Table 6.2 shows some measures of the distribution of the unit valuations for bacon flitches (one of the few food goods found in inventories) for Worcestershire. There are far fewer instances of bacon flitches being recorded but the standard deviations are proportionately lower than for cupboards. Table 6.2 shows the median as well as the mean and the comparison of the two indicates that the unit valuations are fairly normally distributed around the mean within each period.

Valuations and prices

What do these 'prices' computed from valuations actually represent? Are they an accurate reflection of market prices or merely notional values? Before discussing this it is important to realise that *absolute* price levels are usually less important in historical analysis than *relative* prices. What is of most significance therefore is not whether inventory prices are exactly the same as the actual prices the items concerned would fetch when sold, but whether the *trend* of inventory prices follows the trend of sale prices. As long as the trend of a particular inventory price series bears a constant relationship to the trend of sale prices over time we can calculate proportionate price changes, in order to say, for example, that the price of cupboards doubled between the 1550s and the 1630s. Indeed, many long-term price series are expressed as index numbers rather than as absolute values to allow comparisons between different commodities. Thus, as long as the relationship between inventory prices and sale prices is consistent we can make such comparisons, to show, for example, that whereas cupboards doubled in price between the 1550s and the 1630s, the price of bacon flitches rose over threefold. Furthermore, as long as the difference between inventory prices and sale prices is the same in different places or regions, then we can compare price levels across regions at one point in time.

According to the law the appraisers of an inventory were bound to value items according to the price they would fetch at auction. Thus in interpreting these prices it helps to think of prices fetched by everyday items at auction today, particularly in their relation to new prices. The important point is whether the inventory valuations do reflect auction or other market prices or whether the appraisers simply recorded notional or wildly erratic valuations.

Richard Burn, in his *Ecclesiastical law*, followed Swinburne in considering:

> the inventory shall be made in the presence of some credible persons, who shall *competently understand the value of the deceased's goods*: for it is not sufficient to make an inventory, unless the goods therein contained be particularly valued and appraised by some honest and skilful persons, to be the just value thereof in their judgements and consciences, that is to say, at such price as the same may be sold for at that time.[4]

Historians working with inventories have paid relatively little attention to prices or unit valuations, perhaps because an early authority on inventories, Steer, thought Essex inventory valuations 'ridiculously low', although he offered no evidence as to why he thought this was the case.[5] Unit valuations in inventories are indeed lower than the prices of new goods (because very few inventories include new goods), but that does not mean that they are underestimates of the second-hand, or auction

---

[4] Burn, *Ecclesiastical law* (1763), 2, p.652, following Swinburne, *Briefe treatise* (1590), p.220.

[5] Steer, *Farm and cottage inventories*, p.5.

value. More recent commentators disagree with Steer and generally consider inventory valuations to be a fairly accurate representation of local prices. Johnston for example, argues that, 'wherever it is possible to check the validity of valuations they seem to be generally consistent and closely related to the conventional prices of the time', while Trinder and Cox think that for their Shropshire inventories 'Few items are appraised at values which are totally at variance with the general levels'.[6] Moore considers most goods are given a second-hand value, except for crops, livestock, food for the market, and scrap metal for which second-hand values are effectively current values.[7]

None of these verdicts, however, is based on much empirical evidence.[8] Thus Moore justifies his claim by stating that 'most appraisers would have had serious qualms about falsifying a document made under solemn oath'.[9] Some limited empirical work has been done by Cox and Cox, comparing the prices of horses at Bridgenorth Fair with those calculated from Shropshire inventories and by comparing the inventory price of pewter with an index published by Hatcher and Barker. They conclude that 'our case is that appraisers generally valued goods realistically in terms of their sale potential', and 'with some exceptions valuations were properly made in line with market prices', although their conclusions are based on a small sample size.[10]

It is worth pausing to consider who would gain and who would lose from over- or under-valuations. If goods were under-valued then creditors of the estate (people to whom the deceased owed money), and legatees would gain if they were paid in goods rather than cash. If goods were sold and these people paid in cash, they would receive what they were due, but the residue of the estate would be less than it would have been had goods been sold for their true value. Thus those inheriting the balance of the estate (the heirs) would receive less than they should. If goods were over-valued then the converse would be the case: legatees and creditors would lose if paid in over-valued goods, heirs would gain since the balance of the estate would be larger.[11] Given this balance of

---

[6] Johnston, *Probate inventories of Lincoln*, p.lxxix; Trinder and Cox, *Yeomen and colliers*, p.6.

[7] Moore, 'Probate inventories', p.14.

[8] For example Atkinson *et al.*, *Darlington wills and inventories*, pp.14–18, ask the question about valuations but do not appear to answer it.

[9] Moore, 'Probate inventories', p.16.

[10] Cox and Cox, 'Valuations' (1985), pp.467, 471; 'Valuations' (1986), pp.85–100.

[11] Addy, *Death, money and the vultures*, pp.74–83, discusses this issue although is rather confused.

interests there is no reason to suppose that inventory valuations are likely to be either over- or underestimates. Indeed, as Burn points out:

> But as to the value of the goods upon the appraisement, it is not binding, nor very much regarded at the common law; for if it is too high, it shall not be prejudicial to the executor or administrator; and if it be too low, it shall be no advantage to him.[12]

The ultimate arbiter of valuations was the jury at the ecclesiastical court. Undoubtedly some valuations must have been fraudulent. It is possible to point to a number of cases where inaccurate valuations are discussed at an ecclesiastical court, and occasionally an administrator's account mentions an inaccurate value.[13] In a study involving a large number of inventories random fluctuations around the mean do not matter very much; what matters is if there is systematic bias in a particular direction.

Before presenting the empirical evidence from the current project it is worth mentioning that most of the other problems that beset the historian using inventories are of little consequence in their use for the calculation of prices. For example, it does not matter that goods might be omitted from an inventory; nor that there might have been goods in the deceased's house that he did not own but could use. Possible biases which might come from the distribution of social groups in a collection of inventories, or from the distribution of moveable wealth, will be discussed below.

Comparisons with other prices series

The best test of the accuracy of a series of prices from inventories is to compare it with an independent series for the same commodity in the same place. This is usually impossible because there are so few such independent series: indeed, this is one of the attractions of inventories as a source for the history of prices. However, several comparisons can be made for the prices of agricultural commodities, thanks to work of the contributors to the *Agrarian history of England and Wales*. The price series in Volumes IV and V (covering the period 1550–1750) are based on a wide range of sources and do not appear to include any prices from inventories.[14]

[12] Burn, *Ecclesiastical law* (1763), 2, p.652.
[13] For example, Lincolnshire Archives Office Ad. Ac. 42/64 (for an inventory made in 1674). For probate accounts see Bower, 'Probate accounts', pp.51–62.
[14] Bowden, 'Statistical appendix', in *Agrarian history IV*, pp.814–70; and Bowden, 'Statistical appendix', in *Agrarian history V*, pp.827–902.

Table 6.3 Comparisons between inventory agricultural prices and those from the *Agrarian history of England and Wales*

	Wheat per quarter	Barley per quarter	Oxen per beast	Cows per beast	Ewes per beast	Lambs per beast	Horses per beast	Swine per beast
Correlation coefficients 1550–1749	+0.96	+0.93	+0.91	+0.95	+0.97	+0.96	+0.36	+0.96
Average price difference 1550–1649 (£)	0.30	0.01	0.03	0.44	0.08	0.09	5.89	1.39
Average price difference 1650–1749 (£)	0.35	0.02	2.37	1.58	0.05	0.03	4.16	3.82

Results of comparing these prices with inventory prices[15] from the Hertfordshire, Lincolnshire and Worcestershire inventories are given in Table 6.3. The table shows that the product moment correlation coefficients between inventory prices and *Agrarian history* prices are all above +0.9 (with the exception of horses) which indicates that the series move very closely together; that is relative changes in inventory valuations follow relative changes in market prices. However, Table 6.3 and Figure 6.1 also show that there are absolute differences between the prices from the two sources. Thus for wheat, over the entire 200-year period of the comparison, inventory prices are consistently less than market prices by some 30 (new) pence per quarter. This difference is easily explained because inventory prices are farm-gate prices and therefore exclude the cost of transporting the grain to market. Moreover, market prices refer to grain of merchantable quality, whereas inventory valuations include grain that would not be fit to sell but only suitable for feeding to animals on the farm. For barley, however, there is no such price differential. This is surprising. It might suggest that less barley was marketed than wheat, but it is also possible that the *Agrarian history* series understates market prices for some reason.

Further doubts about the accuracy of the *Agrarian history* prices are raised when comparisons are made with livestock prices. The *Agrarian history* price series used for the comparison are derived by combining the series from two volumes, although these series overlap for 10 years from 1640–1650. As Table 6.3 and Figure 6.2 show, the 'base series' for oxen for the periods before and after 1640 are probably not compatible

---

[15] Hereafter 'inventory price' is used to refer to the mean from a set of unit valuations from inventories.

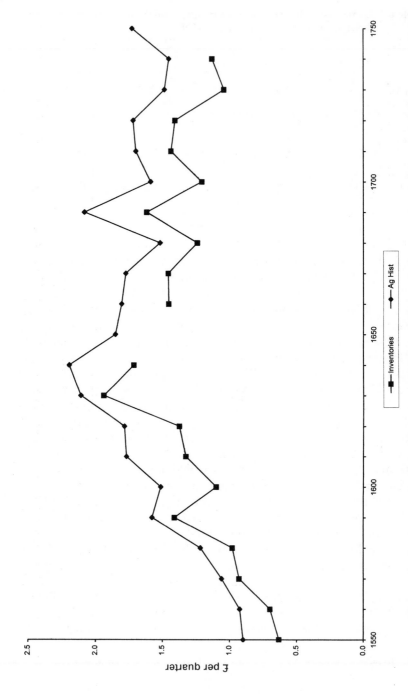

Figure 6.1 Wheat prices from inventories in Hertfordshire, Lincolnshire and Worcestershire (10 year means) compared with wheat prices from the *Agrarian history of England and Wales*

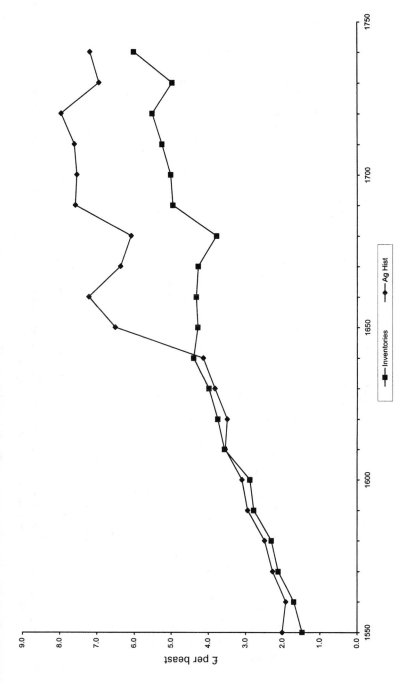

Figure 6.2 The price of oxen from inventories in Hertfordshire, Lincolnshire and Worcestershire (10 year means) compared with oxen prices from the *Agrarian history of England and Wales*

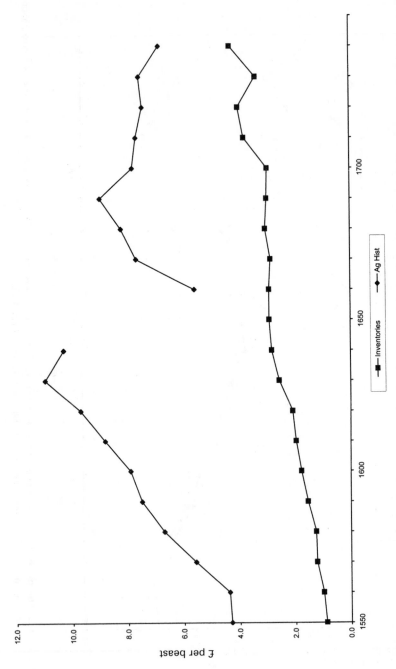

Figure 6.3 The price of horses from inventories in Hertfordshire, Lincolnshire and Worcestershire (10 year means) compared with horse prices from the *Agrarian history of England and Wales*

because of the marked jump in price. For swine the divergence in the absolute level of prices in the two series is even more marked, but here the explanation is that the *Agrarian history* series is based on the price of boars (the most expensive animal) whereas the inventory prices are derived from valuations for swine of all types (some 6,000 unit valuations). But for both oxen and swine the correlations with inventory prices are very high, meaning that the two series share the same pattern of fluctuation.

For horses, Table 6.3 and Figure 6.3 show that not only is there a large absolute difference in the prices of the two series, but the correlation between them is much lower. The inventory prices are compiled from 7,358 separate valuations, including both farm horses (the majority) and riding horses. It is not clear from the *Agrarian history* how many prices are used to compile the index for horses, or where they come from (although for 1500–1640 the series appears to be based on material from Oxford colleges). Given the large number of valuations on which the inventory prices are based it is likely that the inventory prices are the more accurate.

Thus at this point the attempt to compare inventory prices with 'market prices' runs into trouble because of suspicions about the accuracy of the 'market prices' already available. With livestock prices at least the suggestion is that inventory valuations are a more accurate reflection of prices than are the series from the *Agrarian history*. Nevertheless, since most series are so highly correlated, the problem lies in the comparison of absolute levels rather than trends. Because inventory prices do vary in line with the other series we can at least feel confident that appraisers were not recording notional prices and were following the ups and downs of market prices.

The only other commodity for which it has proved possible to make a comparison with an independent series is pewter. Rogers records the price of new pewter and Hatcher and Barker have compiled an index from his data.[16] As Table 6.4 and Figure 6.4 show, the trend followed by the two series is very close and the correlation between them is +0.92. The absolute difference between them (inventory prices are 60 to 70 per cent of Rogers' prices) can be accounted for by the fact that the price of new pewter includes a component for workmanship whereas the second-hand inventory prices are probably just for the value of the metal, given that the unit valuations used are for pewter the appraisers valued by weight. Furthermore, Rogers' series is based heavily on pewter purchased by Oxford and Cambridge colleges which

---

[16] These are recorded in Hatcher and Barker, *History of British pewter*, p.276.

Table 6.4 Comparisons between mean unit valuations from inventories for pewter and new pewter prices from Rogers (£ per 10 pounds)

	Lincoln	Worcs.	Herts.	Index	Rogers
1550–59	0.19			0.19	0.36
1560–69					0.40
1570–79	0.29			0.29	0.32
1580–89	0.25		0.23	0.24	0.30
1590–99	0.22			0.22	0.33
1600–09	0.30			0.30	0.37
1610–19	0.34	0.24	0.38	0.32	0.47
1620–29	0.36	0.32	0.33	0.34	0.52
1630–39	0.39	0.40	0.34	0.38	0.55
1640–49	0.50	0.40	0.46	0.45	0.61
1650–59					0.62
1660–69	0.44	0.38	0.37	0.39	0.60
1670–79	0.40	0.34	0.37	0.37	0.54
1680–89	0.35	0.30	0.29	0.31	0.46
1690–99	0.32	0.30	0.23	0.28	0.44
1700–09	0.29	0.31	0.22	0.27	0.46
1710–19	0.31	0.31	0.31	0.31	0.46
1720–29	0.30	0.30		0.30	
1730–39		0.25		0.25	
1740–49	0.28			0.28	

might be expected to buy pewter of higher quality than that found in households represented by inventories. But as with agricultural commodities the trends of the two series are very close.

Beyond these examples there are few other series of market prices which can be compared with inventory prices. Virtually the only source for such comparisons are in the work of Rogers and Beveridge and their prices are usually wholesale contract prices at institutions, usually for raw materials rather than for fabricated articles. Some comparisons can be made, for example between the prices of cloth in inventories and those recorded by Beveridge (from the Lord Chamberlain's Department, Winchester College, and Westminster School), but the prices of these series seem suspiciously constant over long periods of time. In any case it is very difficult to be certain that prices for similar types of cloth are being compared.

Internal evidence of consistency

Since so many price series based on inventory valuations cannot be checked with independent series, especially for manufactured domestic

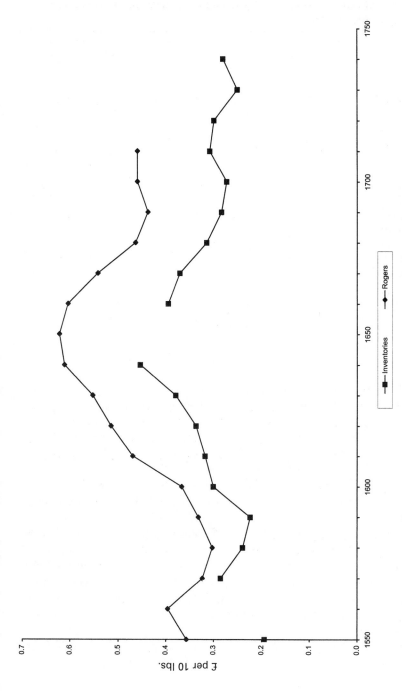

Figure 6.4 The price of pewter from inventories in Hertfordshire, Lincolnshire and Worcestershire (10 year means) compared with the price of pewter from Rogers' *History of agriculture and prices*

Table 6.5 Mean unit valuations and quality of items from Worcestershire and Lincolnshire (£)

	Bedsteads		Coffers		Sheets	
	Old	All	Old	All	Old	All
1575–99						
Worcestershire						
Mean	0.07	0.16	0.07	0.09	0.11	0.18
Median	0.05	0.06	0.04	0.08	0.10	0.15
Lincolnshire						
Mean			0.16	0.60	0.14	0.27
Median			0.14	0.50	0.11	0.23
1625–49						
Worcestershire						
Mean	0.15	0.37	0.06	0.10	0.20	0.28
Median	0.08	0.33	0.05	0.10	0.18	0.25
Lincolnshire						
Mean			0.22	0.66	0.21	0.42
Median			0.17	0.50	0.20	0.40
1675–99						
Worcestershire						
Mean	0.13	0.32	0.07	0.10	0.16	0.28
Median	0.10	0.25	0.06	0.10	0.15	0.25

Note: 'Old' also includes 'worn', 'sorry', 'bad' etc.

items, it is necessary to find some other way of checking inventory prices. The most obvious is to see whether valuations are consistent with respect to the quality of the items being valued. Appraisers frequently used adjectives to indicate goods of inferior quality, such as 'old', 'worn', 'broken', 'poor' and so on, and so it is possible to discover whether prices reflect these descriptions.

The first example of this exercise is shown in Table 6.5 where, for Worcestershire and Lincolnshire, prices are given for bedsteads, coffers and sheets where they are described as 'old', 'worn', 'bad', or in similarly pejorative terms. In order to have sufficient information these prices are averages for 25-year periods; the gaps in the table indicate that sufficient information (20 unit valuations or more) is not available. In all cases the mean and median prices for items described as 'old' are lower than for the same items not so qualified. Quite clearly, therefore, appraisers' valuations reflected their descriptions of quality and were not standard or notional prices.

A second example, shown in Table 6.6, compares the prices of sheets of different quality. Sheets are very common in inventories, and

Table 6.6 **Mean unit valuations of sheets in Hertfordshire, Lincolnshire and Worcestershire (£)**

	Linen	Flax	Hemp	Harden
1550–59	0.24	0.21	0.11	0.09
1560–69	0.29	0.27	0.16	0.10
1570–79	0.32	0.33	0.17	0.12
1580–89	0.36	0.35	0.21	0.14
1590–99	0.40	0.37	0.22	0.14
1600–09	0.42	0.44	0.26	0.16
1610–19	0.48	0.45	0.29	0.17
1620–29	0.51	0.48	0.29	0.20
1630–39	0.51	0.53	0.35	0.21
1640–49	0.59	0.60	0.34	0.22
1650–59	0.56		0.39	0.21
1660–69	0.40	0.49	0.30	0.14
1670–79	0.59	0.51	0.31	0.16
1680–89	0.61	0.42	0.26	0.17
1690–99	0.35	0.47	0.33	0.19
1700–09		0.53	0.39	0.19
1710–19	0.30	0.44	0.32	0.22
1720–29		0.36	0.35	0.15

appraisers frequently recorded the material they were made of. Those of highest quality were linen or flax, sheets made from hemp were of much lower quality, and the lowest quality sheets were described as 'harden', meaning they were made of tow from hemp. Table 6.6 shows the mean prices for four categories of sheets using inventories from all three counties in the study for 10-year periods. Once again, the trend is very clear: the higher the quality, the higher the price.

These examples could be multiplied, and demonstrate that appraisers' valuations were related to their descriptions of the quality of the items they were valuing. Moreover, the trends in valuations for most commodities are remarkably consistent between the three counties in the study, further suggesting that their valuations were following market or auction prices.

Sample bias

A final set of considerations have to do with the more general characteristics of the collections of inventories producing prices which may introduce bias into the price series. Tables 6.7 and 6.8 show how valuations for three common commodities, coffers (or cupboards), sheets and cattle, varied between people of different status. It might be

Table 6.7 Valuation and status: examples from Worcestershire inventories (mean unit valuations in £)

	1550–74	1575–99	1600–24	1625–49	1675–99	1700–24
Coffers						
Labourers			0.07			
Husbandmen	0.07	0.07	0.08	0.09	0.06	
Yeomen		0.10	0.11	0.09	0.10	
Gentlemen		0.14				
Sheets						
Labourers	0.09		0.21	0.28		
Husbandmen	0.12	0.19	0.23	0.28		
Yeomen	0.19	0.28	0.31	0.37	0.32	0.25
Gentlemen	0.21	0.27	0.26	0.32	0.30	0.45
Cattle						
Husbandmen	0.87	1.29	1.61	2.15	2.04	1.95
Yeomen	0.95	1.30	1.95	2.22	2.26	2.15
Gentlemen		1.73	2.18	2.62	2.28	2.31

expected that those of higher status would have more highly valued goods, and indeed this is the case. On the whole, the goods of gentlemen are more highly valued than those of yeomen, who in turn have more highly valued goods than husbandmen or labourers. No doubt in many cases this reflects variations in quality: those of higher status had higher quality goods. But people of high status also had higher valuations for goods for which one might expect relatively little variation in quality. Cattle, shown in Tables 6.7 and 6.8, is one such example, and there are similar rises in value moving up the social hierarchy for commodities such as bacon flitches. This raises the intriguing possibility that people of high status had their goods more highly valued as a matter of principle.

Given that unit valuations do vary with status it is necessary to take the distribution of status groups into account when making comparisons between prices from different groups of inventories, either over time, or between regions. This is difficult because the meaning of status labels changed over time and varied between regions. However, it is comparatively simple to adjust for variations in total moveable wealth between samples of inventories. Table 6.9 shows that mean unit valuations vary with the total moveable wealth in the inventory as recorded by the appraisers. For the same three items prices are calculated from inventories in four categories of total wealth based on the quartiles of the wealth distribution (shown in Table 6.10). The wealthier an individual the more highly valued were his or her possessions. As with

Table 6.8 Valuation and status: examples from Lincolnshire inventories (mean unit valuations in £)

	1550–74	1575–99	1600–24	1625–49	1650–74	1675–99	1700–24	1725–49
Coffers								
Labourers			1.26	1.02				
Husbandmen	0.59	0.84	1.09	1.35	1.49	1.29	1.51	
Yeomen			1.16	1.62	1.40	1.22	1.67	2.49
Gentlemen						1.56	2.17	3.64
Sheets								
Labourers	0.20	0.22	0.30	0.39	0.28			
Husbandmen	0.20	0.23	0.31	0.30	0.36			
Yeomen	0.25	0.31	0.38	0.40	0.39			
Gentlemen		0.53	0.47	0.42	0.49	0.71		
Cattle								
Labourers	0.82	1.23	1.47	1.60	1.88	1.41		1.46
Husbandmen	0.92	1.24	1.64	2.09	1.95	2.10	2.49	2.60
Yeomen	0.79	1.48	1.66	2.23	2.23	2.37	2.65	2.91
Gentlemen	1.10	1.92	2.09	2.82	2.84	2.73	3.07	3.76

Table 6.9 Valuation and wealth: examples from Lincolnshire inventories (mean unit valuations in £ by quartiles of total moveable wealth)

	1550–74	1575–99	1600–24	1625–49	1650–74	1675–99	1700–24	1725–49
Coffers								
Min–LQ	0.19	0.20	0.39	0.58	0.42	0.33	0.18	0.18
LQ–Median	0.26	0.42	0.51	0.63	0.52	0.43		
Median–UQ	0.34	0.47	0.64	0.74	0.61			
UQ–Max	0.36	0.57	0.68	0.61	0.40			
Sheets								
Min–LQ	0.15	0.34	0.27	0.31	0.29	0.27		
LQ–Median	0.18	0.23	0.29	0.35	0.30	0.42		0.23
Median–UQ	0.17	0.28	0.37	0.38	0.45	0.33		0.30
UQ–Max	0.22	0.31	0.36	0.52	0.50	0.50	0.60	0.30
Cattle								
Min–LQ	0.85	1.36	1.59	1.98	2.08	1.85	2.44	2.56
LQ–Median	0.98	1.53	1.88	2.53	2.51	2.33	2.79	2.68
Median–UQ	1.10	1.79	2.19	2.59	2.83	2.80	3.31	3.20
UQ–Max	1.39	1.94	2.54	3.30	3.21	3.48	3.92	3.85

Notes: LQ = Lower Quartile UQ = Upper Quartile

Table 6.10 Total inventory valuations (as recorded by appraisers) in Lincolnshire

	Total	Total with valuation	Min (£)	LQ (£)	Med (£)	UQ (£)	Max (£)
1550–74	933	797	2	17	33	59	612
1575–99	822	695	1	28	55	111	725
1600–24	733	631	2	35	73	144	1,718
1625–49	636	544	5	49	100	189	2,061
1650–74	517	485	2	66	133	246	2,860
1675–99	749	735	1	81	153	296	6,550
1700–24	431	406	6	103	211	403	2,510
1725–49	608	574	1	65	150	316	5,546

Notes: LQ = Lower Quartile Med = Median UQ = Upper Quartile

the status comparisons this undoubtedly reflects the quality of items being valued, but again it might be the case that the wealthy had their goods more highly valued as a matter of course.

Preliminary results

A great advantage of the new prices series from inventories is that they overcome many of the problems in the existing series which stem from the work of Beveridge and his researchers in the 1930s, and from Rogers in the last century:[17] the vast volume of material that this work generated is still the basis for most of the 'new' price series published since, with the notable exception of those in the *Agrarian history* volumes. The most frequently used price series for the early modern period, compiled by Phelps Brown and Hopkins, is based almost entirely on Rogers and Beveridge.[18] Much of their work is still of great value but it does have some shortcomings. Most of the prices from both Rogers and Beveridge are wholesale prices from institutions; Oxford and Cambridge colleges, and government departments. Thus they are not really the same as market prices since these institutions may often have had special contracts with their suppliers. Although there are a large number of *transactions* in Rogers' and Beveridge's work, relatively few institutions or individuals are represented. The difference between wholesale and retail prices can be quite marked, as Rappaport has shown for food prices in London.[19]

[17] Beveridge, *Prices and wages*, vol. 1; Rogers, *History of agriculture and prices*.
[18] Phelps Brown and Hopkins, 'Seven centuries', pp.296–314,
[19] Rappaport, *Worlds within worlds*, pp.123–61.

Table 6.11 Prices from Hertfordshire, Worcestershire and Lincolnshire inventories (index numbers 1550–1749=100)

	Metal A[a]	Metal B[b]	Wood[c]	Textiles[d]	Capital[e]	Agric.[f]
1550–59	62	97	52	65	52	59
1560–69	85	121	72	78	64	54
1570–79	75	107	73	83	69	60
1580–89	89	112	86	85	66	67
1590–99	86	111	88	99	73	87
1600–09	89	101	100	99	70	88
1610–19	112	104	111	110	95	98
1620–29	108	100	115	117	105	98
1630–39	132	129	133	125	97	117
1640–49	135	92	136	129	130	119
1650–59			136	121		114
1660–69	132	124	134	106	114	115
1670–79	117	99	130	110	136	110
1680–89	134	96	106	105	136	102
1690–99	111	70	104	99	124	117
1700–09	104	75	96	100	150	103
1710–19	106	85	97	92	125	113
1720–29	105	68	91	111	140	113
1730–39	86	62	70	106	114	103
1740–49	81	79	65	70	172	105

[a] Brass pots, brass candlesticks, dripping pans, frying pans
[b] Andirons, chaffing dishes, pewter plates, unspecified plates
[c] Bedsteads, chairs, chests, coffers, cupboards, tables
[d] Blankets, coverlets, cushions, napkins, pillowberes, sheets, tablecloths, towels
[e] Furnaces, harrows, ladders, maltmills, ploughs and gear, spinning wheels
[f] Wheat, rye, barley, oats, cattle, horses, sheep, pigs

Many categories of goods are missing from the Rogers and Beveridge series, most notably the prices of consumer goods, or fabricated items for domestic consumption. Rogers' and Beveridge's 'industrial prices' are in fact mostly the prices of industrial raw materials, and industrial price indices constructed from them, by Doughty and O'Brien for example, are really indices of raw material prices.[20] The greatest merit of the new prices from probate inventories is that they cover such a wide range of commodities excluded from existing series. Finally, the Rogers and Beveridge series are for new goods whereas most transactions in

[20] O'Brien, 'Agriculture and the home market', pp.773–800; Doughty, 'Industrial prices', pp.177–92, who constructs an index of industrial prices from Rogers and Beveridge for bricks, tiles, lime, lead, pewter, canvas, cloth, candles, charcoal and paper.

early modern England probably involved the sale of second-hand goods which the inventory prices represent. Table 6.11 shows six price series from the inventories in the study (expressed as index numbers) which provide the basis for a re-examination of many aspects of the economy of early modern England.

Conclusion

It is not the intention to undertake that re-examination here. Rather, the purpose of this paper has been to show how price series may be calculated from probate inventories and to investigate whether they are an accurate reflection of market prices. Where reliable independent series of market prices are available (for agricultural commodities and pewter) the evidence suggests that inventory prices follow the trend of market prices, although their absolute level may be lower than market prices. But this is not necessarily because appraisers were under-valuing; inventory prices are lower because they refer to second-hand goods, or to farm-gate agricultural prices. Where independent price series do not exist, all that can be done is to check prices for their consistency with respect to descriptions of quality, and it is clear from a number of examples that appraisers related their valuation of items to their descriptions of quality. It seems highly probable, therefore, that for most commodities prices calculated from unit valuations in inventories are an accurate reflection of sale prices. However, as with so many statistics generated from inventories, the larger the number of inventories the more reliable are the averages produced. A single inventory may be the subject of many possible sources of error, including erroneous valuations, but most of these errors will cancel out, or at least be less distorting, when averages are calculated from a large sample.

PART II

Wills and Probate Accounts

7

Religious Preambles and the Scribes of Villagers' Wills in Cambridgeshire, 1570–1700

MARGARET SPUFFORD

The background

When the first version of this chapter was published in 1971, historians had made little use of wills, which are a mine of information on many aspects of life.[1] Thirsk had drawn attention to wills as 'unexplored', but the only historian who had really exploited wills at all was Dickens.[2] He had used the religious preambles to illustrate the possible religious opinions of over 700 testators in the Diocese of York between 1538 and 1553 to establish the religious convictions of the ordinary villager, be he yeoman, husbandman, craftsman, or labourer, who once in his life, and once only, at the beginning of his will, made a statement which bore on his religious beliefs. Dickens had not engaged with the problem posed by the possible inserting of the opinions of the scribes, rather than the testators, at all.

The first bequest in a will was of the soul. This may appear strange to modern eyes, but the reasoning behind it is made plain in the will of a maltster of Orwell in Cambridge, Thomas Brooke, in 1597, the body of whose will began 'First as thing most precyous, I commend my soule to God the father my Creator'.[3] So a testator with Catholic beliefs may well leave his soul to 'Almighty God, the Blessed Virgin Mary, and the

---

[1] This article was first published in *Local Population Studies*, 7 (Autumn, 1971), and the immediate interest it aroused can be judged from letters in the next issue of this journal. A revised version was printed in Spufford, *Contrasting communities*, pp.320–34.

[2] Thirsk, *Unexplored sources*; Dickens, *Lollards and Protestants*, pp.172, 215.

[3] This phrase is not common form. I have come across it nowhere else. The original wills of the Consistory Court of Ely, which I have used for this study, are bundled under years, by date of probate, in the Cambridgeshire County Record Office. They have no reference numbers.

whole company of Heaven', or some equivalent phrase, and a testator with puritan or Calvinistic beliefs may well leave his soul to 'Almighty God and his only Son our Lord Jesus Christ, by whose precious death and passion I hope only to be saved' or some other similar phrase. Any will which mentions the Virgin, the saints, or the angels may be suspected of Catholic tendencies. Any which stresses salvation through Christ's death and passion alone, or the company of the elect, may be thought of as Protestant. In between, lie a vast number of indeterminate neutral wills, which simply leave the soul to 'Almighty God, my Creator', or in which the stress on salvation through Christ appears so minimal that they cannot be classified. The spectrum of these clauses is very wide; but because of their existence, historians seeking to penetrate the iron curtain which hides the religious opinion of the really humble laity, below the social level of parish priest or minister, in the upheavals of Reformation or Counter-Reformation, sometimes analyse them in an attempt to establish what was going on at the parochial level.[4]

Scribes

Unfortunately there is one major technical difficulty, which has not been given attention in doing this. For most purposes, the content of the will itself is all that matters; the identity of the scribe who wrote it is irrelevant. For this particular purpose, the identity of the scribe might be all-important. A very high proportion of villagers' wills were made in the testator's last illness, on his death bed.[5] It is almost common form to get, at the beginning of a will, a statement that the testator is 'sick in body but thanks be to God of good sound understanding and memory' and extremely rare to get the opposite statement, which headed the will of William Griggs, a yeoman of Orwell in 1649, that he made his will:

> beinge in good healthe of body (but) considering the frailty of this life, although there is nothinge more certaine than death, yett there is nothing more uncertaine than the tyme of the coming thereof . . . now intending the disposition of landes . . . in this tyme of my good health

---

[4] The clause leaving the soul to Almighty God is never as elaborate and lengthy, in a villager's will, as those of the puritan clergy. See, for instance, the wills printed in Marchant, *Puritans and the church courts*, pp.212–15. They none the less contain significant differences. Dickens used these differences effectively in Nottinghamshire and Yorkshire wills to illustrate the progress of the Reformation amongst the laity: Dickens, *Lollards and Protestants*, pp.171–2, 215–17.

[5] A comparison of the date the will was written and the, usually close, date of probate, shows this. See also Chapter 3, above, pp.45–6, and Chapter 9, below, pp.160–2.

and memory for the better quieting and satisffying my mynd and conscience whensoever it shall please God to visit me with sickness.

A man lying on his death bed must have been much in the hands of the scribe writing his will. He must have been asked specific questions about his temporal bequests, but unless he had strong religious convictions, the clause bequeathing the soul may well have reflected the opinion of the scribe or the formulary book the latter was using, rather than those of the testator.

I have therefore considered the whole question of the identity of the scribes who wrote villagers' wills in relation to the historical points to which the identity of the scribe may have been crucial. When old Leonard Woolward of Balsham died in 1578, he wished to leave an acre or so of his free land away from his son and daughter-in-law to each of his three daughters. His son's death followed soon on his own, and his daughter-in-law's indignation induced her to bring a case to the ecclesiastical court.[6] The details set forth in the depositions made there bring home, with extraordinary clarity, the conditions under which wills could be made in the sixteenth century. Leonard Woolward had retired: he was living in the 'low chamber' off the hall in the house of his son and daughter-in-law. He feared that his desire to provide land for his daughters would bring him discomfort, if not maltreatment in his last illness, and that:

> he shoulde not be well-tended and have that he woulde have, and yf enye of his friends or aquintances . . . should write his sayd will, his sayd sonne yonge Leonard . . . woulde know of yt, and so laye on him that he shoulde not or coulde not make his wyll accordinge to his own mynde.

He therefore asked the young barber surgeon, Henry Spencer, who came from Little Wilbraham several miles away, and who was trying to bring him some relief from pain in his last illness, to write his will for him 'as pryvelye as mighte be'. The barber surgeon was ill-prepared for such a task, and, as he said, 'went to the house of John Allen of Balsham and desyred (him) to bestowe him a penne, yncke and paper'. After writing the will alone in the room 'leaning uppon the sayd testators bedd' and reading it aloud to him after he had attempted and failed to read it to himself, Henry Spencer took the will back to John Allen's house, and read it aloud to him and to his wife, and declared it to be

---

[6] Cambridge University Library, (hereafter CUL) Ely Diocesan Records, (hereafter EDR) D/2/11, ff.259–61. I am very grateful to Mrs Owen, then Ely Diocesan Archivist, who drew this revealing case to my attention.

Leonard Woolward's true will. The will itself was duly witnessed by Henry Spencer and John Allen.

It is immediately evident from this that the circle of people who could be asked to write a will was wide. Quite obviously Leonard Woolward had a number of 'friends and acquaintances' whom he could have asked to write his will and he thought first of them, not instinctively of the minister, curate, or parish clerk. The implication is that, as early as the 1570s, there were in a village several members of the community who could write a document at need, even in a village like Balsham, where there were only isolated references to schoolmasters at work.[7] Since he desired secrecy, his choice fell on the doctor, who came from another village altogether. It is obvious therefore that in the search to identify scribes, not only the incumbent or his curate, who may seem the obvious choice, but the local gentry and acquaintances of the testator must be considered.

There is an obvious, major difficulty in identifying the hand of the scribe who wrote a particular will, for the local historian who is not a highly trained palaeographer. Any hand of the late-sixteenth and seventeenth centuries, once educated beyond a certain point to write a reasonably formalised hand, has so many features in common with any other, that the non-specialist may well pause. There is one redeeming feature. A local historian working on a particular community, and on all the surviving wills for that community, is limiting himself so strictly by date and by place that only a small number of scribes are likely to be at work at any one time.

Orwell

The smaller the community, for a pilot study, in some ways the better. Orwell is a small village on the clay uplands of Cambridgeshire. When it was mapped in the 1670s, there were only 55 houses there, so the Hearth Tax was not far out in taxing 52 of them.[8] Between 1543 and 1700, 99 wills of which the originals survive were proved in the consistory court, although until the 1580s the 'originals' were mostly office copies and therefore useless for these purposes.[9]

---

[7] Spufford, 'Schooling of the peasantry', Map I, p.124.
[8] Public Record Office, E179/244/23.
[9] The initial custom seems to have been to return the true original, signed or marked by the testator, to the executors, and retain an office copy for the court. At some point in the later sixteenth century, this custom changed, and the original document was retained for registration, and presumably the office copy was given to the executors.

It is possible to make at least a reasonable guess at the identity of the scribes who were responsible for a surprisingly large number of these wills. Sometimes the scribe was the only witness of one or more wills who could actually sign his name; sometimes his hand was the only one even approximately of the same type in a run of wills, and he was also a witness to all of them. In order to tell whether or not the clause bequeathing a soul to Almighty God was dictated by the testator's opinions, or by the scribe's, at least two wills in the same hand are necessary, and obviously, a much longer run is desirable.

The Orwell wills include half a dozen each written by an identifiable scribe, who only appears to have written one will. They are therefore useless for comparative purposes. Often the scribe's name is unfamiliar to the historian of the parish, and he may therefore have been an outsider, and possibly a notary or ecclesiastical official. There were four pairs of wills by the same scribe, one series of three, by George Holder, a villager who held at least an acre of freehold in the defective survey of Orwell made in 1607, and two very interesting series of four. One of these was by John Martin, about whom nothing is known, and the other by Neville Butler. He had been educated at the Perse School and Christ's College, and was the grandson of a yeoman. He ended up buying the lands of the dissolved Priory of Barnwell, becoming a gentleman, and disappearing from the Orwell scene.

There were also, most usefully for comparative purposes, two longer series, overlapping in date. William Barnard, M.A., Rector of Orwell from 1609 to 1644, who held a licence to teach there, wrote 12 surviving wills during his incumbency. Six wills were also written by Nicholas Johnson between 1614 and 1626. He was one of Neville Butler's father's first cousins, was frequently a churchwarden, and was tenant of 14 acres of copyhold land. Nicholas Johnson, who was described as the 'well beloved in Christ' of Catherine Rutt of Orwell when she made him the supervisor of her will in 1614, probably had his own religious convictions. Not only Catherine Rutt's testimony, but his career as a churchwarden bears this out. In all six of the wills he wrote, the clause concerning the soul is so nearly identical, that if there were any doubt that the scribe's hand had been identified correctly, it would be disposed of. Every one read 'I commend my soul into the hands of almighty God that gave it me . . . when it shall please God to take me out of this present world'. Whatever the opinions of the testator, they did not influence Nicholas Johnson, who started off each will in his accustomed fashion, which unfortunately did not reveal much of his doctrinal position.

Each of the four men who wrote a pair of wills apiece in the seventeenth century, as well as George Holder, who wrote three, also used his own common form. Laurence Johnson, one of the numerous literate Johnson clan, wrote in his horrible hand an entirely neutral phrase at the end of the 1640s: 'I bequeath my soul to Almighty God'. George Holder wrote with slightly more Protestant emphasis in each of his three wills: 'I commend my soul to God the Father my Creator, and his son, Jesus Christ my Redeemer'. John Wicks took up a slightly stronger position again in 1640, and wrote, 'I bequeath my soul to God my Maker expecting (or believing) to be saved by and through the merits of Christ Jesus my Saviour and Redeemer'. Matthew East, at about the same date, wrote more strongly still. Both his wills contain the phrase, 'I commend my soul into the hands of Almighty God who gave it to me assuredly trusting through the death and passion of his son Jesus Christ to be saved'. Ambrose Benning, who appears as 'Mr Benning' in a rental of the 1670s, and was probably a freeholder and a gentleman, again adopted his own formula. Again, if there was any doubt of the correct identification of a hand which only occurs twice, six years apart, it would be resolved by the identical wording: 'I commend my soule into the hands of god my maker, redeemer and preserver, in an assured hope of a joyful resurrection through the meritts of Jesus Christ my saviour.' It appears quite clearly then that each of these half dozen men adopted his own formula, and that the religious conviction of the scribe, not the testator, is apparent in the will.

This provisional conclusion can be taken further, by looking at the series of 12 wills written by the rector, William Barnard, between 1615 and 1642. William Barnard's phraseology was not much more striking than that of his churchwarden, Nicholas Johnson. Eight of his 12 wills bequeath the soul of the testator to 'the hands of God Almighty my Creator, (Saviour) and Redeemer . . . whenever it shall please the Lord to take me to his mercy'. They were all written before 1636. In 1637, he added a new phrase which appeared in three of the remaining wills and strengthened his formula by the expectation of a 'joyful resurrection to life eternall'. But in the will of Richard Flatt, made in 1636, a strongly individual piece of phraseology was inserted within William Barnard's formula. Richard Flatt commended his soul:

Into the hands of God Almighty, my maker, my Saviour and Redeemer, trusting to be saved by the only sufficient merits of Jesus Christ my Saviour . . . when it shall please the lord in mercy to take me out of this world, being fully assured that this my mortal body shall one day put on immortality, and being raised again by the virtue of Christ's resurrection, I shall live forever with him.

Here is a piece of Pauline theological thinking, which is so far outside the scribe's usual formula that it seems for the first time that a testator feels sufficiently strongly for his opinions to come through clearly into his will. In any long series of wills for any one village, there are a large number of individual formulae which occur, and some deviants which fit into no pattern. It looks, from the example of Richard Flatt, as if these deviants can be taken to reflect the genuine convictions of the testator; the rest reflect the opinions of the scribe, who may, of course, have been a villager also.

This suggestion is strengthened by examination of the four wills John Martin appears to have written. Two of the testators, Mary Barton and Elizabeth Adams, whose wills were made respectively in 1678 and 1680, were members of families who were strongly nonconformist.[10] Their wills were witnessed by Simon Grey who was also a nonconformist, as well as by John Martin.[11] The other two wills were written for men who do not appear on the dissenting church lists, or as absentees from church in the episcopal records. Simon Grey witnessed one of the latter as well as those of the dissenters; but it had a purely neutral clause commending the soul of the testator into the hands of Almighty God, its maker, despite being drawn up and witnessed by dissenters. The last of the four was also neutral. The wills of Mary Barton and Elizabeth Adams were highly individual, however. Mary Barton bequeathed her soul into the hands of Almighty God her maker, 'hoping through the meritorious death and passion of Jesus Christ my only saviour and redeemer to receive free pardon and forgiveness of all my sins'. She also spoke of the temporal estate that 'God in his infinite mercy has lent me in this world'. So did Elizabeth Adams, though she felt that her temporal estate had pleased 'God far above my deserts to bestow upon me'. The clause in which Elizabeth Adams bequeathed her soul had the same sense as Mary Barton's, but it was not phrased in the scribe's identical wording. She ended her will with an injunction to her son and principal heir that related worldly prosperity to prudence, which I have not seen duplicated anywhere else. As Solomon said to his son, 'My son fear thou the Lord and the king, and beware that you live not above your living especially in the beginning for that will bring you to wanton necessity, both in the midst and the ending'.

This scribe then, wrote dissenters' wills, which expressed the testators strong sense of justification by faith, but did not dictate the form when a more neutral phrase was required. Neville Butler, likewise, wrote two

---

[10] Lyon-Turner, *Original records*, 1, p.36.
[11] CUL EDR, B/2/6 ff.51–52v.

wills which were neutral and simply bequeathed the soul to God that gave it,[12] but also two in identical wording when more appeared to be called for. Richard Johnson and Robert Bird both left their souls:

> With a right good will ... to god that gave it whensoever it shall please him to take it out of this transitory life hoping by his infinite mercy and the only merryt of my saviour Jesus Christ that it shall again put on this my corruptible body of flesh and that they [sic] shallbe made partakers of everlasting life.[13]

One further interesting point emerges from the Orwell wills. The rector, when he was present as a witness and not as a scribe, was not necessarily deferred to over the form of the clause bequeathing the soul. Roger Davis, clerk, wrote his own will in 1580 and appears to have been a Protestant, for he bequeathed his soul to 'Jesus Christ in faith in whom I hope undoubtedly to be saved'.[14] He witnessed a will couched in similar terms for John Adam, yeoman, in 1569, but the two others he witnessed for John Johnson, husbandman, in 1568, and Edmund Barnard, another husbandman, in 1595, both had neutral clauses bequeathing the soul. John Money, the vicar in 1595, witnessed Katherine Ingry's will in that year, and she also simply bequeathed her soul to Almighty God. Nicholas Butler, who had the same faith in the resurrection of his temporal body that was later expressed by his grandson Neville, as a scribe, both witnessed Katherine Ingry's will along with the vicar, and had his own will witnessed by the vicar; but his faith in the resurrection of his earthly body seems to have been entirely his own, and was not dictated by John Money.

Willingham

Willingham, on the edge of the fens, was three times the size of Orwell. It differed from Orwell, which had no school permanently established

---

[12] Wills of Richard Kettle and Robert Adam.

[13] This example is a confusing one, because the phraseology Neville Butler uses, and his emphasis on the resurrection of the body, echoes almost exactly that of his grandfather Nicholas in 1601 (PCC 74 Woodhall) and of his great uncle Henry in 1594 (PCC 32 Dixy) although his own father, Thomas, wrote a neutral clause bequeathing his soul in 1622 (PCC 18 Saville) and his own will 'all written with my own hand' only expressed his belief in justification by faith, not in the resurrection of the body (PCC 1675, f.42). We may here be getting an example of the scribe's own religious beliefs, rather than the testator's, but it is interesting that he only applies it when it is called for, and does not automatically write a phrase expressing his own opinions.

[14] It ends 'per me Rogerum Davys'.

before the eighteenth century, in having a school founded by public subscription in 1593. This seems to have been based on the work of the first known schoolmaster, Laurence Milford and had a continuous life thereafter.[15] The same features found amongst the Orwell wills are also found amongst the much more numerous surviving wills from Willingham. There are nearly 250 wills written between the 1570s and 1700 by an identifiable scribe, although 15 of these are the only ones by that particular scribe, and are therefore useless for comparative purposes. Amongst the scribes, there are a considerable number of series by the same men. Laurence Milford himself wrote 50 wills between 1570 and 1602, beginning before he was first licensed as a schoolmaster to 'teach young children' in 1580, and continuing after William Norton, the curate, was licensed to teach grammar in 1596. After experimenting with various formulae hoping to 'obtain everlasting joys and felicitie' for the soul in the 1570s and 1580s, he went through a neutral phase before settling down in 1590 to the constant usage of one of his early experimental formulae, 'I bequeath my soul into the hands of God the father, and to Jesus Christ my saviour, by whose merits I hope to enjoy his everlasting rest'. William Norton only wrote four wills, and bequeathed the soul in an unusual Trinitarian form to 'God Almighty, Father, Son, and Holy Ghost'. This was obviously entirely his own.

Laurence Milford was succeeded as the principal Willingham scribe, not by Norton's successor as schoolmaster, John Nixon, who taught and was curate in Willingham from 1608, but by John Hammond, a local gentleman who was lessee of the sub-manor of Bourne in Willingham. He, with a relation of his, Edward, wrote over 30 wills between 1609 and 1639. He also acted as scribe when a petition against the charges of fen drainage was drawn up.[16] His phraseology was again almost identical throughout the wills that he wrote, and he had been very heavily influenced by Milford. He strengthened the Protestant element and added 'by whose only merits and mercies' to Milford's formula. Otherwise he duplicated it. There were only three wills in the Hammond series which varied from the standard opening in any way, and none of them, with the possible exception of his own, was of importance. John Gill, a labourer, who died in 1623 hoped to enjoy everlasting rest 'after this transitory life ended'. Philip Fromant, a husbandman, trusted to obtain 'remission of all my sins'. When John Hammond himself wrote his own will in 1637, it became evident that

---

[15] Spufford, 'Schooling of the peasantry', pp.139–140, 131–3.
[16] British Library, Add. MS 33466 f.190. I am indebted to Mr Dennis Jeeps, of Willingham, for lending me a photocopy of this.

a genuine faith lay behind his standard Protestant formula, for he left his soul to:

> Almighty God my creator, and to Jesus Christ my redeemer, by whose only mercies and merits (Sealed unto me by their blessed Spirit) I trust to obtain forgiveness of all my sins and to enjoy their everlasting rest.

The laity of Willingham are known from other sources to have been particularly zealous Protestants. They probably had secret conventicle meetings in Mary's time, and were anti-episcopal in the late-1630s. From these beginnings, a strong and lasting Congregational church developed under the Commonwealth. Quakerism was present there too.[17] Laurence Milford, either in his work as teacher or as scribe, unfortunately seems to have made such an impact on the people of Willingham that their individual convictions, which were undoubtedly strong in very many cases, are masked, in their wills, by his phraseology.

The early wills of the seventeenth century do provide ample evidence that old Leonard Woolward of Balsham was right to feel he could depend on 'friends and acquaintances' to write his will, if not to keep it secret, for enough villagers acted as scribes in Willingham to prove the point. In all, 50 wills were written by yeomen from the Greaves family, by Henry Halliwell and Henry Bissell, Edward Allen and Robert Stocker, who each wrote several. A further half-dozen wills were written by other villagers who only wrote one apiece. All these wills began either with a neutral clause, or with Laurence Milford's standard clause, or with Hammond's variant on it. Only John Pitts, a woolwinder, stood out in any way. He wrote three wills between 1617 and 1626, all using the Milford phraseology, but his own will, made in 1631, was couched in stronger terms. His soul was left to the 'hands of Almighty God my Creator hoping for remission of my sins by the death and passion of Jesus Christ my redeemer'. Unfortunately John Pitts' own will was an isolated one, written by Thomas Ambler, so it is impossible to tell whether John Pitts made a fuller and more revealing assertion of his faith on his own death-bed, or whether Thomas Ambler was asserting his own beliefs.

The strength of Protestant feeling in Willingham, combined with Laurence Milford's influence, makes the wills of the villagers so consistently Protestant, that as in any orthodox group it is impossible to tell how far individual feeling is involved, even when minor variants in the phraseology do occur, since the sense is so uniform. Occasionally

---

[17] Spufford, 'Dissenting churches', pp.70, 76–7.

individual testators do stand out, just as Robert Flatt did in Orwell. Robert Shilborn wrote the will of Thomas Lambert, who was a husbandman, in 1625, and that of Thomas Bowles, who was a fisherman, in 1632. There was no doubt at all of the strength of the convictions of Thomas Lambert. Shilborn wrote for him: 'I bequeath my soul to God that gave it trusting in the only merits of Jesus Christ my saviour and redeemer for the forgiveness of my sins, and that death shall be an entrance for me into a better life.' The will ended with the desire that: 'The Lord out of his never decaying or failing mercy be a husband to my wife and a father to all my children.' Thomas Bowles's will began with an orthodox phrase, but contained the tell-tale bequest 'To my eldest son William Bowles . . . my bible wishing him to use it to God's glory'.

Although the influence of Laurence Milford at last declined, the Willingham scribes continued each to write their own standard formula. There was one important change. From the 1650s, the testator's customary bequest of his body to the churchyard for burial, which followed that of the soul, was replaced by a phrase leaving the burial of the body to the discretion of the executor or to 'Christian' burial. This may well reflect the growth of the nonconformist element in Willingham. But Congregationalist or Quaker wills cannot be picked out as such from the phraseology.[18] They can sometimes be identified by virtue of local knowledge. Two Henry Orions wrote 13 wills between 1634 and 1648, and 1659 and 1667. They were probably father and son, and of humble stock. There had been no Orions in Willingham in 1603, but the family held 12 acres of arable there in the 1720s. Both men wrote a roughly standardised form of will, bequeathing the soul to 'God that gave it me, and to Jesus Christ my redeemer by whose mercies and merits I hope to have forgiveness of all my sins and to have a Joyful Resurrection at the Last Day'. The emphasis on the resurrection was typical of them; the formula was their own, but some of the testators obviously had religious convictions which were hidden behind the devout but customary formula of the scribes. John Carter, a chandler, whose will was made in 1648, left both his son and his daughter bibles. Mary Marshall, the widow whose will Henry Orion wrote in 1669 left Francis Duckins a bequest of £2. She did not appear to be related to him, and he was a leading Congregationalist in whose house the conventicle met in 1669. This is not proof that the Orions were writing for Congregationalists, particularly since the very last will in the series, in 1667, expressed the,

[18] Lyon-Turner, *Original records*, 1, p.38.

by now, unusual desire to be buried in the churchyard; but there is a suspicion. It is partially confirmed because the Henry Orion alive in the 1720s had his house licensed as an Independent meeting place.[19]

The same suspicion applies to Edward Negus even more strongly. He wrote 43 wills in an educated hand between 1661 and 1693, mostly with a brief clause bequeathing the soul into the hand of God and the body to the ground in Christian burial. Until 1670 he usually wrote, when he came to the disposal of the testator's goods, 'touching such worldly estate as God in his Mercy far above my estates has been pleased to bestow upon me'; after 1670 he dropped this additional clause. But there was no doubt that he was writing the wills of convinced Protestants. In 1669, the will of Edward Hammond, yeoman, who was one of the sons of John Hammond who had acted as a scribe earlier in the century, contained the clause, 'I give unto Edward Negus my book of martyrs'. Deborah Frohock, a Congregationalist widow, left her son Samuel three bibles in 1672. Four of the 12 men who were known to be Congregationalists in Willingham in 1675 had their wills written by Negus;[20] a suspiciously large number of the witnesses appeared charged with absence from church in an ecclesiastical court in 1673. But despite this, individual conviction did not come through Edward Negus's accustomed phraseology, except in the case of two men, William Bowles, a yeoman in 1673, and John Allen a maltster, in 1686, both of whom trusted in a joyful resurrection at the last day. Neither was known from other sources to belong to a particular sect. Negus himself held the lease of a shop in 1665, and does not appear to have been involved in agriculture at all.

Robert Osborne wrote 11 wills between 1665 and 1693 in a village hand, and wrote a much more vivid clause, but one which was still in a common form peculiar to himself, bequeathing the soul 'Unto the hands of God that gave it to me trusting through the merits of Jesus Christ my redeemer, to have a joyful resurrection at the Last Day'. One of the 11 wills was written for one of the Willingham Quakers, and a second was witnessed by another Quaker.

The clauses in wills bequeathing the soul of the testator to God are therefore mainly couched in whatever phrase the particular scribe was accustomed to use and taken alone tell little, or nothing, of the testator's opinions. But just as the strength of Robert Flatt of Orwell's convictions in 1636 broke through his rector's common formula, so also did a

---

[19] This information comes from Mr Dennis Jeeps, who likewise kindly provided me with additional information on Negus.

[20] Spufford, 'Social status', pp.203–11.

handful of the Willingham wills reflect, in the strength of their language, what must have been the strength of the dying man's faith. John Osborne, who only wrote one will in 1668, must have been closely related to Robert, because their hands were so alike. They were perhaps taught by the same person. Even though the single will cannot be compared with any others written by John, it is impossible to believe that anything but the feelings of Thomas Staploe, the testator, lie behind the last and only statement of faith which he ever made:

> I . . . calling to remembrance the uncertain state of this Transitory life that all flesh must yield unto death when it shall please God to call . . . first being penitent and sorry from the bottom of my heart for sins past most humbly desiring forgiveness for the same, I give and commit my soul unto Almighty God my Saviour and Redeemer in whom and by the merits of Jesus Christ, I trust assuredly to be saved, and to have full remission and forgiveness of all my sins and that my soul with my body at the General Day of resurrection shall rise again with joy and receive that which Christ hath prepared for his elect and chosen.

Conclusion

It seems from this analysis as if, for any village, there will often be two or three scribes writing wills at any one time, and a large number over a period of a hundred years. They will range from the lord or lessee of the manor, to the vicar, curate, church clerk or churchwarden, to the schoolmaster, a shopkeeper, or any one of the literate yeomen or even husbandmen in a village who could be called in to perform this last neighbourly office for a dying man. If the village lay near a county town, it was possible for a public notary to be called in, although this I have less evidence for.[21] Most of these scribes evolved their own slightly different formulae for bequeathing the soul, which can be traced through most or all of the wills they were responsible for. If the scribe was an identifiable villager, as he often was, of course, one is still getting irreplaceable information on the doctrinal convictions of the peasantry, since the scribe came himself of humble stock, like the Greaves, or Thomas Pitts, or Edward Negus of Willingham, or Nicholas Johnson or George Holder of Orwell. Even when the rector, like William Barnard

---

[21] Samuel Newton, a public notary, wrote and signed, as such, the will of Edward Daintry the elder, a husbandman of Milton, in 1665; likewise John Brayshaw, a public notary wrote the will of John Foot a husbandman of Milton in 1628. See also Chapter 3, above, pp.49–50.

of Orwell, or the schoolmaster, like Laurence Milford of Willingham, is the scribe, one is still getting information on whatever doctrine is generally accepted at village level. It is a great mistake to assume the docility of the normal parishioner. If the rector of Cottenham, which was a radically nonconformist village in the seventeenth century, felt unable to let his children out to play after one of them had been attacked and scarred for life with a fork in the school yard by a 'sone to an adversary',[22] it is scarcely likely that such an 'adversary' would call on the rector to make his will, while the choice of potential scribes was, as I have shown, wide. It is therefore safe to assume that however near death the testator was, he still exercised a choice over his scribe, as Leonard Woolward did. He probably did not influence the form of the preamble the scribe normally used, unless he had abnormally strong convictions, but he is highly unlikely to have chosen a man who did not hold the same general opinions as himself.

Wills can, therefore, be used as Dickens used them, to show that a swing away from the cult of the Virgin and the Saints in the 1540s continued into the 1550s, but he was entirely right when he wrote 'The results should not be presented in any spirit of statistical pedantry'. The evidence is not statistical. It is wrong for the historian to assume that if he takes a cross-section of 440 wills proved over a particular period, he is getting 440 different testators' religious opinions reflected, unless of course the wills also come from 440 different places. Even then the scribe might have a determining influence. One is still getting evidence on the attitudes of the peasantry to whatever ecclesiastical settlement was in fashion, but it would take a much more stringent analysis to show how much evidence one is getting, and to eliminate more than one of a series of wills written by the same scribe. On the other hand, when a testator had strong religious convictions of his or her own, this may come through, expressed in a variant of the formula usually used by the scribe concerned. If any local historian wishes to study the religious opinions of the peasantry, he should look for these strongly-worded individualistic clauses which occur in any run of wills for a parish, which alone record the authentic voice of the dying man.

---

[22] Taken from an abstract by W.M. Palmer of a letter from the daughter of the rector of Cottenham, who was ejected under the Commonwealth. Bodleian Library, Walker MS C.S. f.17.

8

Attitudes to Will-Making in Early Modern England

CHRISTOPHER MARSH

Introduction[1]

Wills remain one of the principal sources for historians of popular religion, although in recent years their status as authentic statements of individual faith has been called into doubt by several commentators.[2] Few today would agree with Jordan's description of wills, written in 1959, as 'completely honest documents' and 'mirrors of mens' souls.[3] A majority of historians would probably feel rather closer to the position of O'Day, expressed in 1986: 'Far from revealing the religious beliefs of the average testator, wills and their preambles hide them from the historians' gaze'.[4]

With the advent of Reformation doctrines, greater variety came into the wording of will preambles, though they did not develop uniformly. Late medieval wills, while displaying a considerable range in the nature of religious bequests, normally opened with a fairly standardised commendatory clause in which the testator bequeathed his soul to God, the Virgin Mary and the saints. Occasionally this was abbreviated, or expanded to include the naming of individual saints, but major differences were rare. Under Edward VI and, particularly, Elizabeth I, the range of expressions used became comparatively wide. It is for this reason that historians have scrutinised will preambles in the search for evidence of individual piety.

---

[1] This is a substantially abbreviated version of Marsh, 'In the Name of God?'. The alterations have been made by the editors of this volume.

[2] See, for example, Cross, 'Wills as evidence', pp.44–51. For a comprehensive review of the recent literature on wills, see Plumb, 'John Foxe', pp.40–50.

[3] Jordan, *Philanthropy*, p.16.

[4] O'Day, *Debate*, p.157. This subject is also discussed in Chapter 3, pp.54–7 and Chapter 7, above.

From the start, however, there were difficulties. Dickens, aware that wills were perhaps not all they seemed, cautioned historians against analysing the documents 'in any spirit of statistical pedantry'.[5] Margaret Spufford amplified this warning, and changed the nature of the debate by discussing the actual mechanics of will-making, and by emphasising the importance of considering the broader local context in which any particular will was written.[6]

Because the problems remain, an examination of attitudes to will-making in the early modern period, particularly the later sixteenth century, is still required. This chapter will examine the procedures followed in the drafting of wills, with a view to establishing the context in which a testament was set down in writing, and contributes to the debate surrounding the use of printed formularies. Finally, it discusses the motivations behind making a will, as perceived by godly writers and by the men and women they presumed to instruct on preparing for death.

The process of drafting wills

There was a wide variety of reasons for making a testament, and conclusions are hard to reach for the will-making population at large. It was possible, then as now, to decide to make a will on grounds that had little to do with faith; complicated personal affairs, the need, seen in worldly terms, to provide for one's children, a desire to remember close and not necessarily godly friends, a vain urge to influence earthly events after one's death, or a vindictive wish to punish a thankless child. All such concerns could be discussed without reference to God, even in an age when religion in English society was far more pervasive than it is today.

A small but significant minority of wills became the subjects of litigation, most frequently in the ecclesiastical courts. It is to the records of such causes that we must look in an attempt to examine testamentary motivations. The following discussion is based upon over 40 disputed will cases in the dioceses of Ely, London, Exeter, Durham and Winchester.[7] The sample is a relatively small one, not scientifically constructed, and the observations made here are therefore impressionistic.

---

[5] Dickens, *Lollards and Protestants*, p.171.

[6] See Chapter 7, above.

[7] I have used manuscript court records in the dioceses of Ely, London (Essex), Exeter and Winchester. The Durham cases are taken from Raine, *Depositions*.

Testamentary cause records sometimes yield to the historian a
quantity of vivid detail which cannot be guessed at from the wills
themselves. They are essential sources for students of death, and
frequently reveal striking pictures of deathbed scenes and attitudes. It is
often possible to observe the bonds of kinship and neighbourliness in
the face of sickness and death. This chapter is particularly concerned
with what the records reveal of the circumstances of will-making, and
the spiritual motivations, if any, that lay behind it.

There are obviously certain questions of reliability to be considered
when interpreting these records. It can be argued that court records, by
definition, describe those cases which fell outside the accepted
framework of things. In countering this criticism, it is customary to
observe that, even so, such records cast their own perverse light upon
the norms of behaviour and the expectations of local societies.
Furthermore, in many of the cases, different witnesses presented their
own recollections of what were clearly the same events. It does seem
possible to establish a core of truth; this is, after all, exactly what the
courts were seeking to do.

Evidence relating to the physical circumstances of testators at the time
of will-making reveals, not surprisingly, a number of common
characteristics. Most were sick, though by no means all were in the final
throes of disease. The 'darts of death' were perceived to be on their way,
but impact was not always imminent. The vicar of Sutton (Ely) arrived
at the house of William Bateman, 'wheare in a kytecyen . . . he found
the sayd testator sitting by the fyr side'.[8] A widow from Little Shelford
(Ely) was 'lyinge uppon hir bed in a redd kertle haveing a quilte lyinge
uppon hir'.[9] A clerical testator from Swavesey (Ely) was sick 'in his
chamber where he used always to lye hanged with paynted clothes
wherein was iii beds'.[10] There were many similar examples.

The procedures employed in making wills also display common
features. The basic pattern—calling witnesses, making the will, hearing
it read, and ratifying it—was followed in numerous cases. When the
details are examined further, however, there is found to be a surprisingly
wide variety of practices, not all of which will be comforting to
historians who count wills among their chief sources.

The Sutton (Ely) testator, William Bateman, decided to make his will
'in his good health'. The will had in fact been 'conceyved in writing'

---

[8] Cambridge University Library (hereafter CUL), Ely Diocesan Records,
   (hereafter EDR) D/2/6, f.22.
[9] CUL, EDR, D/2/11, f.109.
[10] CUL, EDR, D/2/7, f.256.

some time before Bateman chose to finalise it in the presence of witnesses. Still healthy, the testator summoned several villagers to his home, including his scribe—a layman called Daniel Morton—and the local vicar, Simon Nappe. Morton then read the will to the testator, who acknowledged it as his own. The document was not dated at its original writing but at the point when Bateman ratified it for the last time. Ironically, the testator's commendable foresight was to backfire on the night of his death. It seems that, because of changed circumstances, Bateman had wished to revise his will shortly before his decease. He had, however, been unable to have it set in writing because, as Robert Claybell informed the court, 'one Danyell who should have bene the writer was in Bedd and felt himself not then well and sayd in the morning he would helpe them as earlye as they would'. When Daniel Morton arrived the next day, he may have experienced feelings of guilt at finding the testator no longer 'sitting by the fyr side' but 'dead in a chamber'. Bateman's widow then produced the first will, written by Morton, but another participant in the unfolding drama exclaimed 'whye it skills no matter for that will, For the said William Bateman made another will [by word of mouth] this night and gave his wife all his house goodes lands and Cattells therein'.[11]

The case cautions strongly against assuming, even in the early part of Elizabeth's reign, that a clerical witness was also the scribe. It is also of note that the dating of the written will did not coincide with its composition. The exceptionally pious will of Thomas Merburie, quoted below, is a case in point.[12] This model student wrote or dictated his will 'being in health at this present time both of bodie and mynde', but the document was dated just a few days before probate was granted and therefore very close to the time of the testator's death.[13] This may have happened frequently enough to threaten the validity of comparing the date written on a will with that of burial or probate and concluding that most wills were composed very shortly before death.[14] Indeed, on the face of things, Elizabethan testators do appear to have had an uncanny knack of knowing which particular bout of sickness was the final one.

[11] CUL, EDR, D/2/6, ff.22–7.
[12] See pp.172–3, below.
[13] Manuscript volume of wills proved in the Vice-Chancellor of Cambridge University's Court, 1558–1602, f.62.
[14] See, for example, Chapter 7 above, pp.145–6. Also Plumb, 'John Foxe', pp.40–5. For another statement of this view see Coppel, 'Will-making on the death-bed', pp.37–45. I am sure, however, that Coppel is right to state that most testators chose to make wills because they felt that the sickness afflicting them was potentially very serious.

The common clause 'revoking all former wills by me made' should also be remembered here. Not all testators left their wills until the final hours.

Standard practice becomes harder to identify as more cases are studied. The right-first-time will-making, though fairly common, was far from universal. The preparation of a will was no easy matter, especially if the testator's affairs were complex, and many scribes must have found it difficult to set the will down in perfect form at the first attempt. Consequently, it appears to have been common for a scribe to carry the first draft away with him, for periods ranging from a few days to several months, in order to make a 'fair copy'. Sometimes, scribes still managed to make crucial mistakes, as in the will of John Salmon of Willingham (Ely).[15] The testator had bequeathed to his wife 'all that she brought' with her at marriage. The scribe took the original will home with him, and absently-minded added the words 'household stuff' to the clause, when he wrote the will neatly. The resultant dispute centred on a heifer ('now grown to a good Cowe') which had been part of the bride's dowry, and which defied classification as 'household stuff'.

In this case, the surviving 'original' is in fact the faulty 'fair copy' which was never read before the testator. It bears the witnesses' names all written in the same hand, that of the incompetent scribe. Such examples have been seen as evidence that the true originals were handed back to the executors and only office copies kept by the court.[16] It is clear, however, that the court never saw the genuine original of John Salmon's will. The scribe added further to the local historian's confusion by omitting his own name from the list of witnesses. He perhaps had good reason for wishing to remain anonymous.

On other occasions, the procedure was not of such dubious reliabilty. More often, the fair copy was prepared following discussion between scribe and testator. It was then this copy that was read and witnessed. At Lent in 1570, the vicar of Swavesey (Ely) assisted 'Father Stacy' in the final preparation of his will.[17] The document was then read aloud to the testator. The vicar, according to his own evidence, then 'toke it whom [home] with him to wryte it fayre, & brought it to him aboute Julye following & red it to him in the presence of John Graves'. There were very similar cases in each of the five dioceses under view here.

There were also occasional cases in which the will was written up in

---

[15] Cambridgeshire Record Office, Ely Consistory Court original will, John Salmon (1560). For records of the court case, see CUL, EDR, D/2/4, ff.118–23.

[16] See Chapter 7 above, p.146.

[17] CUL, EDR, D/2/7, ff. 155–8.

its first form by a scribe working at home, unaccompanied by the testator. John Prowse of Brixham (Exeter) decided to summon the vicar, 'for that he . . . felt him self sick and therefore entended to make his will'.[18] The vicar duly arrived, and:

> having passed somme talk about the making of the will the sayd vicare then knowing his minde and that he should doe at that tyme went from him And within a day or two or iii after as he remembreth the sayd vicare came agayne to the sayd John Prowse lyeng sick in his bedd and brought the sayd . . . testament reddye written with him.

We cannot tell at which point the preamble was composed, but the implication is scarcely reassuring. In this case, as in a number of others, it was not the making of the will that was witnessed, but a subsequent reading.

Some of the most striking cases are those which demonstrate that the preparation of a will could be a process of evolution through changing times, a fact which is frequently hidden in the once-for-all document with which the courts usually dealt. Sometimes, the situation changed sufficiently that a clean break was made and a wholly new will written. In other cases, the necessary revisions were not quite severe enough to warrant a fresh start. The last will of a man from Albury (Winchester) was extremely untidy, almost illegible in places, because of extensive amendments made in the late stages.[19] The document was written in three different hands. The Swavesey fair copy to which reference has already been made was just the final stage in a lengthy process.[20] In September 1569, Father Stacy called on Robert Loder 'to beare wytnes of his will makinge'. Stacy was sick in bed, attended by his daughter and one Lawrence Milford. Stacy then made his will, which was 'wrytten and drawen' by Milford. The scribe then went on his way, leaving the will with Stacy's wife.[21]

The following Lent, six months on, Stacy again summoned Loder. Present this time was the vicar, 'Syr Curtis', to whom the testator or his wife delivered the will. Stacy then ordered several alterations. An additional witness was called, and Curtis read the will to the testator, who acknowledged it gratefully as 'the last will that ever he wold make'. At this point the vicar took the will away to make the fair copy, returning four months later, when he said to the testator 'I have brought

[18] Devon County Record Office (hereafter DCRO), Chanter 860. ff.141–44.
[19] Hampshire Record Office, Winchester wills, B81/1–8, (1591).
[20] CUL, EDR, D/2/7, ff.155–8.
[21] CUL, EDR, D/2/7, ff.155–8.

your will . . . will you have it redd?' Stacy agreed and, finally, a process
which had lasted the best part of a year was concluded, in a document
which bore one date and looked for all the world like a straightforward
composition. Sadly, there is no trace of the will in the records today, so
it is impossible to answer procedural questions about the dating of the
document and the fullness of the witness list. One of the implications of
cases like this is that godly advice to people, that they make their wills
while in health, could be impractical. Circumstances could change
rapidly and radically so that old wills became outdated.

The preparation of a will could, then, be a complicated process, and
the testator needed to be in firm control of his or her mental faculties.
Cases in which advantage was taken of a deranged or witless testator
were in fact rare. Many testators were sick when they made their wills,
but they were certainly not putty in the hands of grasping relatives. In
a number of instances, it seems likely that they had actually become,
through old age and sickness, more short-tempered and confrontational
than ever they had been 'in the time of health'. Manipulation was not
rife and few testators had lost either the will or the power to control
events. Robert Thurgood of Meldreth (Ely) was mentally, if not
physically, agile as his will reached its final form.[22] He altered the
document, after careful thought, to remove his wife as executor. He
then faced the unenviable task of keeping his decision secret from her,
and almost found it beyond him:

> after the said testator had confirmed the said will, he . . . did laye it
> in the corner of the windowe to drie and Joyce Thurgood his wyef
> comenge up & takeinge it in her hand & goeinge away with it, he
> the said testator perceivinge it called her, & desyred her to let hym
> have it, wch she dyd, & soe he delivered [it] to this deponent.

It appears that the description 'weak in body though sound of mind' had
an accuracy which one does not necessarily associate with stereotypical
phraseology.

Other participants

Court officials regularly asked deponents to explain the nature of their
relationship with the testator. It appears that, cynical worldliness aside,
men and women with little to gain were frequently forthcoming with
words of advice and comfort. Deponents across the land dropped in on
ailing neighbours to make friendly enquiries about the state of their

[22] CUL, EDR, D/2/9, ff.40–3.

body and mind. As Gilbert Atwell passed the gate of Ellen Serle, of Kirton (Exeter), he met his own brother Nicholas 'and understanding . . . of the sicknes of the widow Searle, lighted from his horse and went into her house to se howe she did'. He continued, 'after some talke betwene them he this deponent persuaded [advised] her to make her will and to distribute somewhat to the poore . . . and she aunswered she had made her will already and it was in George Trowbridges hands'.[23] Six or more assorted friends and relatives were also present during the exchange. Deathbed gatherings of this sort must have been important social occasions, at which reputations for neighbourliness could be made and lost.

Neighbours at a sick person's bedside could be required to ensure that tempers did not become over-heated. When a Shelford (Ely) widow clashed with her grandson concerning a white curtain, it was only 'uppon the intrety of the cumpanye then present' that real fury was forestalled.[24] Interestingly, it was the aged widow, rather than her grandson, who was urged to moderate her conduct. Friends and neighbours played an important role in the preparation of a will, and in the broader atmosphere that surrounded it. Naturally, therefore, testators generally selected their witnesses quite deliberately, basing their choices upon personal friendship and social respect. The testator who was conscious of the need to make his will 'as sure as may be' would also have been aware of the need to call 'credible' witnesses. In particular communities, therefore, the same individuals tend to appear repeatedly at local will-makings.

In most depositions, the exact reasons for a particular choice are not articulated, but at the time of will-making, the testators' servants, wives and children were frequently sent out to request the presence of particular individuals. An Essex man was summoned, 'being the nere neighbour & well willer of the testator'.[25] A witness in another case was told by the testator, 'after much familiar and comfortable speeches had betweeen them, that 'he had sent for him . . . as his special frind that he would have his will made'.[26] Occasionally, witnesses were present for less touching reasons: Roger Hopper happened to walk past a testator's house at the right moment, 'being in the way to see the yought [youth] of Kirkly play at fott ball'. In the majority of cases, however, witnesses—like executors—were chosen quite deliberately.[27]

---

[23] DCRO, Chanter 860, f.381.
[24] CUL, EDR, D/2/11, ff.109–12.
[25] Essex Record Office (hereafter ERO), D/ACD 1, f.1.
[26] ERO, D/AED 1, f.48.
[27] Raine, *Depositions*, p.79.

A reliable scribe could be of crucial significance. The testator needed above all a man who could be trusted to prepare a legally acceptable document. Beyond this basic criterion, factors such as personal friendship, social respect and religious affiliation may have come into play. The testator's choice was further influenced, of course, by the local availability of scribes, and presumably by the amount of money he was prepared to pay in order to employ a good one.

The later sixteenth and seventeenth centuries were part of a very broad period of transition. In medieval villages, the local priest had been the almost inevitable choice as will scribe, through his superior literacy and his extensive experience in what was perceived as a traditional role. By the eighteenth and nineteenth centuries, professional legal experts had come to enjoy a similar dominance. Elizabethan England presents evidence of both of these types, and of a third transitional breed of will scribe—the 'capable' local layman, who wrote wills either as a neighbourly service, or on a semi-professional basis.

There is very little to indicate that 'public notaries' were widely operative in rural England during the reign of Elizabeth. Will-writing in the towns may have been slightly different. In the corporate town of Wisbech (Ely), just one will from some 150 made between 1570 and 1600 was written by a self-proclaimed notary;[28] no similar examples have been found in the wills written in Cambridgeshire villages like Balsham, Shudy Camps and Horningsea.

England's clergymen had not, however, been completely eclipsed from proceedings. In some communities, the minister continued to write most of the wills. In villages where a range of lay scribes was also available, it can perhaps be argued that a decision to involve the minister carried with it a significance that had not been there when he was the only literate man in the community. In a couple of cases, there is evidence that the old reliance on the priest as will scribe retained some of its hold. In 1586, Lancelot Morgan of Walsingham (Durham) summoned several of his friends and declared 'Neighbours, here is neither minister nor clerk at home, and I would make my will, and I pray you to beare witness how I dispose my goods'.[29] With no cleric available, it was felt that the will could not be set in writing. John Hind, a Cambridgeshire husbandman, arrived at a testator's house to find the will already completed; he surmised that it was 'wrytten . . . by William Bylducke [vicar of Little Shelford] for that there was no other clercke then & there present'.[30]

---

[28] CUL, Ely Cons. original will, John Robinson (1597).
[29] Raine, *Depositions*, pp.320–1.
[30] CUL, EDR, D/2/11, ff.109–112.

The pastoral involvement of local clergymen can occasionally be traced in some detail. The enthusiasm displayed by an individual minister in the performance of his duty could obviously have affected the degree to which testators felt conscious of the spiritual importance of will-making. The vicar of Sandon in Essex proudly told the court that, 'according to his duetye', he had visited a sick member of his flock:

> and after he this deponent had godlye enstructed him and perceived him to be readie to die, he this deponent lykewise perswaded him to sett downe order for the desposinge of his goodes and to make his will and the same testator was verie well content therwithall confessinge that it was his onelye desier.[31]

Religious beliefs

The influence of the clergy brings us back to the point from which we embarked: the role of religion in motivating lay-people to write their wills, and the importance of dedicatory clauses. There clearly were those occasions when the presence of a dutiful vicar, with his 'ghostly counsel' and pastoral advice, must have ensured that a testator was conscious of the spiritual reasons for writing a will, but how prominent a place did these reasons occupy in the popular mind?

There is little suggestion that, for the majority of testators, the composition of a dedicatory clause was viewed as a matter of any great significance. Deponents were almost invariably required to express an opinion on the testator's sanity at the time of will-making. It is striking that recollections concerning the composition of the preamble were not presented as evidence in any of the cases studied.

On the other hand, a great many testators would probably have expressed concern if their scribes had simply omitted the dedicatory clause altogether. Wills which displayed no religious content whatsoever were still extremely rare, and were to remain so for many decades.[32] Such wills were, however, accepted by the probate courts.[33] The religious preamble would surely have had a much shorter life than it did if England's testators had no desire at all for its continuing

---

[31] ERO, D/AED 1, f.59.

[32] The wills written in Banbury retained religious expressions at least until the 1730s. See Vann, 'Wills and the Family', p.360.

[33] See, for example, the will of George Wilson, Ely Cons. original will, (1628). The significance of such wills is hard to gauge. Wilson sounded disillusioned, referring to the disposal of 'that little wch god hath lent me'. He may have dropped the dedicatory clause deliberately. In most cases, there is no indication of the testator's reasons for departing from the traditional format.

existence. In most cases, the fundamental religious format could be safely assumed by testators, and there need have been no detailed discussion. When the vicar of Merrington (Durham) arrived at William Kirkus's house, he asked 'Will ye make a will?' and 'what will ye give to the poore man box?', but he did not, apparently, ask for direction on the wording of the religious preamble.[34] The testator probably felt that the vicar could be relied upon to reflect the essential nature of his belief.

The attitude of the courts is also worth discussing. A great deal of scribal time was spent in transcribing will preambles, word for word, into court registers.[35] The precise religious nature of the documents would then appear to have been of some importance to the authorities. It is normal, at this point in the argument, to refer to the case of William Tracy, the Gloucestershire man who was exhumed, in the 1530s, for writing a radically Protestant will preamble. It was, indeed, an important case, but the fact that it seems to be the only one of its kind ever referred to is also revealing. The authorities were not, in general, quite so quick to pounce on such irregularities. Cases where testators made Protestant wills under Henry or Mary, or Catholic wills under Elizabeth, and suffered no posthumous punishment, are far more numerous. In general, the ecclesiastical authorities probably agreed with godly writers in seeing wills as primarily concerned with the disposition of worldly estate according to Christian obligations.

There is, however, nothing here to invalidate the view that an exceptionally expressive and pious preamble does reflect profound and personal faith. Scribes were perfectly well aware for whom they were writing, and by whom they were directed. There is no reason found in these cases to suggest that scribes deemed it fitting to impose long and idiosyncratic clauses upon those who had not asked for them. It may well have seemed a waste of time to do so. Having said this, will-making appears to have been characterised by a surprising degree of variety, and deviant cases are always a strong possibility. It can no longer be considered appropriate to form any but the most timid judgements from individual wills viewed in isolation; the importance of studying the wills of a community in detail, for evidence of custom, stereotypical formulae and striking individuality, can hardly be emphasised strongly enough.[36] The overriding function of the will was to dispose of worldly estate for

[34] Raine, *Depositions*, pp.212–15.

[35] In the Ely diocese at least, there is little evidence that court scribes abbreviated even lengthy preambles.

[36] Acceptance of this argument has been growing in recent years, since it was stated with force by Spufford: see Chapter 7, above.

worldly peace, and a detailed and explicit confession of faith was rarely a primary concern. A basic religious framework for a will was assumed and probably desired, but it was through the bequests that testators performed their Christian duty.

Printed formularies

One of the debates concerning early modern wills has centred on the use of printed legal formularies in the preparation of English testaments. In 1984, Claire Cross wrote an important article on the wills written in Leeds and Hull between 1540 and 1640.[37] She quoted the long and seemingly personal preamble of a Leeds chapman, written in 1566, but noted the existence of two almost identical examples in wills of the early-seventeenth century, one from each town.

Cross traced the source of these later versions to William West's *Symbolaeographia*, published in 1590.[38] The earlier version, she surmised, must have been taken from a similar legal handbook. West would then have borrowed the formula for his own book. Cross concluded, her faith in wills fading, that 'The wide circulation of these Tudor legal formularies would suggest that lawyers and scriveners were in England exercising considerably more influence upon the composition of wills than has hitherto been recognised'.[39] It was a perfectly reasonable argument; West's book was bulky and expensive, containing draft documents of many types, including four versions of will preambles.

West's formulae are not entirely original to him. Alsop has shown that the last and shortest of West's four preambles appears in identical words in *The boke of presidents*, first published in 1543, thus taking back to the later years of Henry VIII the existence of standardised bequests of the soul.[40] Another of West's sources was Thomas Becon's *The sicke mans salve*, which first appeared in the late 1550s and had been reprinted 28 times by 1632.[41] It is written in the form of a conversation between the dying Epaphroditus and four of his friends, during which his exceptionally pious will is written. The health of the testator's soul, charitable bequests, the duty of a dying man to settle his estate and the need to make a will before the eleventh hour are amongst the subjects

---

[37] Cross, 'Wills as evidence'.
[38] West, *Symbolaeographia*. The work was reprinted regularly into the seventeenth century.
[39] Cross, 'Wills as evidence', p.48.
[40] Alsop, 'Religious preambles', p.22.
[41] Becon, *Sicke mans salve*.

discussed. The preamble to Epaphroditus's will is the source of West's longest and most expressive version, which was thus not lifted from a legal formulary but from an immensely popular godly work by one of the English Reformation's foremost writers. The works of other writers, such as William Perkins (1595), William Perneby (1599) and Christopher Sutton (1600), are also concerned with the duties of a dying man.[42]

Other historians had discovered isolated versions of the formula found in Leeds and Hull and concluded that they were looking at evidence of exceptional piety.[43] Cross's discoveries appeared seriously to undermine their position. The common assumption underlying this growing pessimism may, however, be open to question. Is it appropriate to reason that a preamble (or any apparently 'personal' statement for that matter) loses much of its value as evidence of individual belief if it occurs in the exact same form somewhere else? The logic seems based upon what may be a distinctly modern view of the relationship between expressiveness and originality. The latter is all important to many twenty-first century western minds, but the same attitude may not be entirely applicable to early modern society. It was certainly important to a small number of testators that their will preambles were full and expressive, but did it necessarily detract from the worth of their pious pronouncements if they were not original?

Modern computer technology has made it possible to trace all the testators in the Ely diocese (excluding those whose wills were proved in the court of the Archdeaconry of Ely or the Prerogative Court of Canterbury) who described themselves as 'unprofitable servants of God'.[44] This was the label Becon used in *The sicke mans salve*. The results of this exercise provide the final 'angle' from which attitudes to will-making will be examined in this chapter. How, exactly, was Epaphroditus's preamble put to use?

The 'unprofitable servant' label was used on 68 occasions, with the first example dating from 1569 and the last being in the will of a Whittlesey widow named (appropriately?) Faith King in 1693. In many instances the form used by Becon and West was shortened, often drastically. A number of the wills, particularly those later in the run, suggest that the label 'unprofitable servant of God' had assumed an

---

[42] Perkins, *Salve for a sicke man*; Perneby, *Direction to death*; Sutton, *Disce mori*.

[43] For example Spufford, *Contrasting communities*, 341–2; also, Hartley Thwaite in a letter printed in *Local Population Studies*, 8 (Spring, 1972), 64–7.

[44] Dr Elisabeth Leedham-Green and the staff of the Cambridge University Literary and Linguistic Computing Centre made this project possible.

identity of its own.[45] The most revealing cases were those in which the testator shortened the preamble substantially, but was still clearly using one or other of the two sources. Fifteen testators fell into this category, and the significance of their behaviour seems likely to lie in the perception, already discussed, that a long and expressive preamble was somewhat excessive and unnecessary. By the same token, it can perhaps be argued that an unusually full use of the preamble implied genuine conviction.

The chronology of the 68 wills is also informative; there were only five Elizabethan usages, despite the popularity of Becon's *The salve*. West's *Symboleographia* appeared in 1590, but there was a surprising 25-year gap before the formula was used again in the diocese. In 1615, John Thompson of Ely, a gentleman, used a full form of the preamble. He clearly took it from West, whose version differed very slightly from that of Becon. His will began a series of testaments using the formulary, from a wide range of parishes, and the wordings by this date are all closer to West's than to Becon's. The sudden increase in the numbers of testators using the preamble from 1615 is not easy to explain. It seems possible that it had been published in a more readily available form, possibly as a broadsheet.[46]

It is also possible to trace the involvement of individual scribes and to examine the way in which they used the formulary. A number of men adopted a version of the preamble and used it in wills, by no means all of which were written in their own villages. Through the wills written by two generations of the Amye family of south-west Cambridgeshire, the evolution of a will formula can be traced. In 1618, Roger Amye wrote the will of an Ickleton shepherd and included a very full version of West's formula. Four years later he used a shortened version, but added a clause referring to the goods 'wherwith it hath pleased Almighty God to endue me with all & to make me steward of heare in this world & vale of miserie'. The last three words may well have been taken from the Book of Common Prayer, although they appear in Becon. When Roger's two sons witnessed a will in 1639, the words 'unprofitable servant' survived, but the rest of the Becon/West wording was replaced by a new and completely different preamble evolved from the original version. Thomas Amye, one of Roger's sons, used this new preamble for two more wills.

---

[45] The label 'unprofitable servant' is biblical. See, for example, Matthew 25:30, Luke 17:10. If it had found a place in the godly household vocabulary of the day, the credit may have lain more with Becon than with West. *The sicke mans salve* enjoyed a wide popularity that had nothing to do with its incidental role as an occasional formulary: the same can hardly be said of *Symbolaeographia*.

[46] I discussed this possibility with Helen Weinstein.

This fascinating process suggests a far greater fluidity in the way preambles were used than can be detected in the bare fact that some scribes did make use of formularies. In this subset of the 'unprofitable servant' wills, phrases were dropped and added, new expressions were developed, and gradually evolving formulae were passed around—either in manuscript or by memory—amongst neighbours who also served as local scribes. It seems clear that the expressions used must have been the subject of local discussion, though the fact that the apparently 'stock' preamble was such a lengthy form may suggest that we are focusing here on an unusual group of scribes and testators.

Without detailed local research, the discussion cannot be carried much further. It is noticeable that the total number of 'unprofitable servant' wills written by each individual scribe was not large.[47] If they wrote no other wills, then the testators they served were a select group (and possibly an 'elect' group). It is improbable that a large number of scribes were using printed formularies. Even if all 68 of the 'unprofitable servant' preambles had been simply transcribed from West, which they certainly were not, they would represent a very small proportion of the total number of wills written in the diocese. Admittedly, there may have been other printed formularies—particularly in the second half of the seventeenth century—but the much more common process seems to have involved locally composed preambles being passed around among acquainted scribes.[48]

Expressions of profound faith

It is tempting to speculate on the circumstances and motivation of the rare testators who did expound their beliefs at length. The state of an individual's health was an obvious factor, since detailed expressions were unlikely from a testator who lacked both time and energy. The depth of an individual's faith must also have been influential, though not as clearly so as one might expect. It may not have been so much the strength of belief that set unusually expressive testators apart, as the fact that they felt self-consciously pious as they composed their preambles.

In December 1571, Thomas Merburie, a student at Christ's College, Cambridge, made a will which he headed 'I believe in God the father, god the sone, and god the holie ghost, three persons, but one eternall

---

[47] None of the scribes from the Amye family can have written more than five wills using this label. Most wrote only one or two.

[48] For evidence of other seventeenth-century will formularies, see Capp, 'Will formularies', p.49.

and ever lyvyng god, and I do fullie looke to be saved by thys my beleiff'.[49] Merburie drew attention to the uncertainty of life and recalled 'that we are admonished in the 24 of matthew contynuallie to watche for that we knowe not what howr our master wyll come'. Owing to this uncertainty, Merburie had decided to make a will 'whereby god wyllynge yt shalbe evident to all that during my lieffe I held the profession & belief of a trew Christian man, and goddes grace so assistynge me wyll firmlie & stedfastlye die in the same'.

There followed an extraordinarily full confession of faith. The testator stated his belief in salvation through Christ's death, passion, resurrection and ascension, 'whitowt all vayne opinion of any mans merites, which I do utterly rejecte, detest & abhore as marvelous Injurious to the bludd of my saviour Jesus'. Merburie, amongst a great many other things, also expressed an unshakeable belief in his own election: 'I feele inwardlye in my selfe and in my conscience that before all worldes I am predestinate to eternall liefe'. He asked for a modest burial, shorn of hideous papist trappings, and ended with an affirmation of his belief in the certainty of his own resurrection, 'when I shall heare that joyfull voyce, come ye blessed of my father inherite yee the kyngdome prepared for yow before the begynynge of the world'. There can be no doubt whatsoever that the faith expressed in this will was Merburie's own.

Equally instructive was the will of Thomas Adam, an innholder from Saffron Walden, dated in December 1572.[50] Adam made his will,

> considring the manyfold myseries, Calamities, maladies & perills of death emynate in my mortall body & howe sodenly in these dayes the mortalitye or lyfe of man is extinct to the ensample that other may learn to be redy . . . When god shall call them.

This is the most conscious attempt so far found on the part of a testator to influence his neighbours for the better. The phrases were not, apparently, used in other wills written in the same area at this time; they would, then, seem to reflect the personal feelings of the innholder or, less probably, of his scribe. Despite such expressiveness, the dedicatory clause was brief in the extreme. The testator was clearly a man whose faith meant a great deal to him, but he wrote merely 'I bequeath my soul to Almighty God'. Adam agreed with the godly authors who thought that will-making was an unwelcome distraction in the approach

---

[49] Manuscript volume of wills proved in the Vice-Chancellor of Cambridge University's Court, 1558–1602, f.62.

[50] ERO, 336 CR 6.

to death. He made his will in order that he would be able 'to depart well and Chrystyanlye' when the moment arrived. His commendatory clause was neutral by any standards, because he did not regard his will as the appropriate place for a full-blown confession of faith. He may well have made such a confession at another time.

As in the pre-Reformation period, it was the subsequent 'worldly' bequests that really reflected the strength of a testator's faith. In 1586, a yeoman named William Rushbrigg from Emneth in Norfolk made a will which displayed a short and wholly unexceptional dedicatory clause.[51] Rushbrigg demonstrated his piety instead with bequests to his church, his vicar and the poor of his village. If his son died, the will continued, Rushbrigg's entire estate was to be used for the benefit of the poor and the community, despite the implied existence (in the form of a 'cousin') of more distant kin. The testator left money for the erection of an alms-house, the construction of a gate at the church stile, the repairing of the church way, the diking of the river and the building of a bridge, 'for people safely to passe'. Additionally, he requested a burial sermon, four further sermons, and made extensive gifts to the poor. Rushbrigg was evidently thinking clearly when he made his will—so detailed was it in other respects—but he appears to have seen the full expression of his faith in the preamble as something superfluous and unnecessary. His charitable bequests spoke for themselves.

There appears, then, to have been a common body of motivations uniting godly writers and those testators who expressed themselves, whether by words, deeds, or both. Broadly speaking, a will for the godly man was written because it was the Christian's duty before God to settle his estate, of which he had been but a steward, in such a way as to promote peace, 'stay disputes' and glorify God. In doing so, he hoped also to procure himself a degree of spiritual tranquility, essential if he were to die 'Chrystyanlye'. There was also an element, sometimes at least, in which the testator saw it as his responsibility to set an example to others, to lead his neighbours into similarly godly practice. Within this framework of spiritual motivations and choices, a pious and eloquently elaborated preamble can perhaps be classified as 'a thing indifferent'.

Conclusion

This chapter illustrates the wide spectrum of contemporary attitudes to will-making, and in so doing advances the interpretation of wills by

---

[51] CRO, Ely Cons. original will, William Russbrigg (1586). Professor Eric Carlson brought this will to my attention.

historians. The disputed will cases demonstrate that many testators were fully aware that they were performing a Christian duty. Edward Leach of Milton voiced a widespread feeling in 1644, making his will 'because there should be no controversy after my death for my goods and possessions and for the maintenance of love and peace in the world'.[52] This could be seen today as a purely moral duty, but to the seventeenth-century mind such statements carried resonances that were distinctly religious. It is equally clear, however, that the perceived duty did not extend to the inclusion of anything like a full confession of faith in one's will.

It is not appropriate to argue, however, that there was no correlation between the beliefs expressed in a preamble and those held by the testator. Full and expressive dedicatory clauses were more likely from unusually religious testators, and such clauses are undoubtedly evidence of personal conviction. The reverse is not true; short preambles certainly did not invariably reflect lack of strong faith. All Christians were expected to leave their souls to God, but the religious contemplation that went with this act was not often set down for posterity in a document used primarily for the disposal of wealth.

Wills are not a source into which historians can dip for swift and reliable results. When studied with care, however, they can tell us much of lay faith. Local context is all-important if arguments are to be developed fully. Patterns of local giving must not be neglected; even the deeply religious individual was more likely to express his faith through his worldly bequests than through his preamble. The witness lists can also yield invaluable information, enabling the historian to reconstruct local religious networks, albeit imperfectly. Witnesses were, as we have seen, generally chosen deliberately; the 'godly' were naturally more than likely to summon their like-minded friends, as Epaphroditus did in *The sick mans salve*. Becon enabled his readers to observe the final hours of Epaphroditus; the disputed will cases examined here have opened windows, partially at least, through which proceedings at less exceptional will-makings can be viewed. Taken together, the evidence reveals and clarifies many of the problems historians face in interpreting this source. It suggests also that there remains much vital information to be reclaimed from the wills written in early modern England.

[52] Spufford, *Contrasting communities*, p.343.

9

The Occupations and Status of Male Testators in Cambridgeshire, 1551–1800

NESTA EVANS

Introduction

Probate documents, mainly wills and inventories, have been used by a number of historians to study occupations and status. Patten based his work on non-agricultural occupations in Norfolk and Suffolk on those recorded in all wills from these two counties proved in all the relevant courts between 1500 and 1700.[1] However, the hope Patten expressed in 1977 that 'the day is drawing nearer when we shall be able to make a comparative study of the changing rural occupational structure of pre-industrial England at large' does not yet seem to have arrived.[2]

This study of male occupations in Cambridgeshire is based on the surviving wills from the Consistory Court of the Diocese of Ely, which covered all but some 14 parishes in the east of the county. Although many wills do not include an occupational description of the testator, the number which survive makes them a more fertile source for this information than any other class of document. The sheer number of surviving wills has disadvantages as well as advantages. Before the introduction of computers and databases, the prospect of analysing several thousand wills was a daunting one. Even though large-scale analysis has now been made much easier, it still takes up much time and effort, and is costly.

Cambridgeshire lies between East Anglia and the south Midlands, but does not really belong to either region. Having little industry in the early modern period, it never achieved the wealth of Norfolk and Suffolk and remained a mainly agricultural county. Leaving aside the town of Cambridge, no part of the county in 1524 paid as much tax as

---

[1] Patten, 'Changing occupational structures', pp.103–21.
[2] Patten, 'Urban occupations', pp.296–313.

the wealthiest regions of Norfolk and Suffolk.[3] Apart from the Isle of Ely and the fen-edge villages on its borders, arable farming predominated in the county. Writers from Leland to Defoe agreed that barley and malt were the principal agricultural products of Cambridgeshire, and modern studies have confirmed this. Apart from malting, early modern Cambridgeshire had no large industry.[4] The occupations found in Ely Consistory Court wills confirm this picture.

The Isle of Ely, together with some fen-edge parishes such as Soham and Willingham, presents a very different picture from the rest of the county. Most parishes here had a large enough area of fen for 'their economy to be based on pasture rather than on arable farming'.[5] The vulnerability of this region to flooding before the draining of the Fens, begun in the mid-seventeenth century, made large-scale arable farming impossible. Some fen-edge parishes, such as Chesterton and Chippenham, had only a comparatively small area of fen so their farming was mainly arable. Nevertheless their fens were valuable as pasture.

Cambridge and Ely were the only towns of any size in the county. A feature of the smaller market towns is that they are all close to the county boundaries: for instance Linton is near the Essex and Littleport close to the Norfolk boundary. This suggests that Cambridge and Ely dominated their parts of the county.

The Ely probate records database

In 1994–6 the British Record Society published, in three volumes, an index to the probate records of the Consistory Court of Ely.[6] This index begins with the earliest surviving wills in 1449 and ends in 1858 with the removal of probate business from the church courts to the new civil probate courts. In addition to 33,700 wills, it includes inventories, letters of administration, which only survive from the last decade of the seventeenth century, and guardianship documents.

As far as is known the index of Ely probate records is the first to be created from a database. It was an expensive and lengthy process, which was funded by grants from the Marc Fitch Fund and the Economic and Social Research Council. A typescript index, compiled by Clifford and

[3] Sheail, 'Distribution of taxable population', p.120.
[4] Holderness, 'East Anglia and the fens', p.215.
[5] M. Spufford, unpublished typescript of intended first chapter of *Contrasting communities*, pp.55. I am grateful to Margaret Spufford for allowing me to use her unpublished survey of the agriculture of the old county of Cambridge.
[6] Leedham-Green and Rodd, *Index of the probate records*.

Dorothea Thurley, was converted by Elisabeth Leedham-Green, deputy archivist of Cambridge University, into a form suitable for use as a computerised database. Rosemary Rodd and John Dawson, both of the Literary and Linguistic Computing Centre of the University of Cambridge, used the database to create a completely computerised index with computer-generated supplementary indexes and histograms. This database is available for consultation on line, and it was used to create the tables in this chapter. What the database of Ely probate records has demonstrated is the opportunities for analysis created by the ease with which large numbers can be handled by computer. For at least this one region, the material is available to search a large number of probate records in a range of ways. Carlson's introduction to the index to the Ely Consistory Court wills discusses various ways in which the database can be used, but has by no means exhausted its possibilities.[7] Takahashi has also worked on the Ely Consistory records, as part of his study of the proportion of the population that made wills. Amongst his conclusions is that wills 'provide supporting evidence on the crises of mortality in the sixteenth and seventeenth centuries'. This is particularly noticeable in the case of the epidemic of 1557–9.[8]

There were 164 Cambridgeshire parishes in the Diocese of Ely under the jurisdiction of the Ely Consistory Court, but two other probate courts also had jurisdiction in parts of the diocese, and are not included in the following discussion. The Archdeaconry of Ely contained 51 parishes and two peculiars. Fourteen of these parishes were in the town of Cambridge, where the Vice-Chancellor of the University also had his own court, used by members and privileged servants of the University. The privileged persons included some tradesmen, such as stationers, who were useful to the University. The Vice-Chancellor's Court was also available to widows and children of privileged persons living within his jurisdiction, which extended one mile on every side of the parishes of the town of Cambridge.[9] The occupations of testators who used these two courts are not included in the database, which therefore gives only a partial coverage of the county. Between 1551 and 1800 under 3 per

---

[7] I am extremely grateful to Dr Rosemary Rodd of the Literary and Language Computing Centre of the University of Cambridge for producing the data which made possible the construction of the tables used in this chapter, and for responding so quickly to my many enquiries. Carlson, 'Historical value'.

[8] Takahashi, 'Number of wills', p.212; and see Chapter 10, below, pp.200–11.

[9] Thurley and Thurley, *Index of the probate records*. The probate records of the Ely Consistory and Archdeaconry Courts are held in the Cambridgeshire Record Office, while those of the Vice-Chancellor's Court are in the MS room of Cambridge University Library. PCC wills are not included in this chapter.

cent of the wills proved in the consistory court belonged to persons living in the rural parishes of the archdeaconry and no more than half of one per cent came from the town of Cambridge. The men whose wills were proved in the archdeaconry court are likely to have included a much higher proportion of labourers and husbandmen in the rural parishes and of tradesmen and craftsmen from the town of Cambridge than are found in the consistory court.

The survival of probate inventories in the consistory court is poor. There are virtually none before 1663 and after 1751 their numbers drop sharply. For this reason they have been omitted from this study of occupations, even though over six inventories survive for every ten wills between 1663 and 1750.

Women have also been excluded as not only did far fewer make wills, but they are almost always described by their marital status with very few giving an occupation. Between 1551 and 1800, 17 per cent of the wills proved in this court were for women, over 80 per cent of whom were widows. Male testators' wills far more often give occupation or status.

Occupations and status from Diocese of Ely wills

Wills made before 1551 have not been included as the numbers and proportions giving occupations or status are relatively small: less than 6 per cent of male testators before 1501 and 16 per cent in the first half of the sixteenth century. The following analysis of occupations and status is therefore confined to wills made by men between 1551 and 1800, and the discussion of occupations and status is based on the analyses contained in Tables 9.1 to 9.3. The data is predominantly rural as only 1,969 wills were made by Ely men and a mere 199 wills are those of Cambridge residents, while the small towns have a mixture of rural and urban occupations.

Table 9.1 shows that after 1600 the number of surviving men's wills fell while the proportion giving occupation or status rose. This tendency for the percentage of wills with an occupation or status to rise may be due to a change in attitudes. Although we do not know what proportion of the male population left wills, the numbers recorded with occupation or status in the second column of Table 9.1 remained steady in the seventeenth century. The rise in wills proved after 1700 may not be so great as the figures suggest because during the Civil War and Commonwealth first the Prerogative Court of Canterbury, and from 1653 the Court for Probate, took over most of the work of the lower courts.

Table 9.1 Male will-makers in the Diocese of Ely, 1449–1800

	Total	Occ/status total	% occ/status
1449–1500	1,178	68	5.8
1501–1550	2,762	435	15.7
1551–1600	7,043	2,156	30.6
1601–1650	6,806	3,934	57.8
1651–1700	5,974	4,018	67.3
1701–1750	6,631	5,245	82.8
1751–1800	3,684	3,405	92.4

Table 9.2 Occupations or status of male will-makers in the Diocese of Ely, 1551–1750

	1551–1600	1601–1650	1651–1700	1701–1750	1751–1800
Total occ/status	2,156	3,934	4,018	5,245	3,405
Occupational groups					
Gentry	2.2	2.3	4.0	5.6	6.3
Farming – general	67.5	70.3	62.0	56.0	53.9
Farming – specialist	1.2	2.2	2.2	2.4	5.6
Fishing	2.5	1.5	0.2	0.3	0.4
Building	0.8	1.2	1.8	2.1	2.1
Building in wood	2.0	2.3	2.6	2.7	1.8
Woodwork	1.5	1.7	1.8	2.7	2.5
Metal working	1.9	2.0	2.5	2.9	2.1
Textiles	2.3	2.4	2.1	1.6	0.9
Clothing	2.3	3.4	2.8	2.1	2.1
Clothing in leather	1.2	1.2	2.4	2.5	2.8
Leather making	0.4	0.7	1.3	1.2	0.8
Food and drink	2.9	3.8	8.6	12.0	12.3
Transport and distribution	0.4	0.6	1.5	1.5	2.5
Clergy	8.1	3.0	2.3	1.9	0.9
Others	2.5	1.2	1.6	2.2	3.0
Others					
Manufacture	0.3	0.5	0.8	0.7	1.0
Religion	0.5	0.1	0.1	0.2	0.2
Medicine	–	0.1	0.1	0.4	0.6
Law	0.1	0.1	–	0.1	0.0
Education	0.3	0.1	0.1	0.2	0.5
Admin etc.	0.6	0.0	0.1	0.1	0.5
Service	0.6	0.2	0.3	0.4	0.2
Miscellaneous	–	0.1	0.1	0.1	0.1

Status descriptions raise the problem of interpretation, and this is particularly true of yeoman and gentleman. Both were often used as a status rather than an occupational description, and the same can be true of husbandman. It is not unusual for yeomen's wills, and inventories, to give no sign of any involvement in agriculture. In some cases these men

Table 9.3 Percentages of main occupations of male Ely will-makers, 1551–1800

	1551–1600	1601–1650	1651–1700	1701–1750	1751–1800
farming					
farmer	0.1	–	0.3	2.8	22.4
husbandman	36.2	26.9	22.4	11.2	2.0
yeoman	15.1	21.8	31.5	37.1	27.0
labourer	16.2	21.6	7.9	4.8	2.4
shepherd	1.2	2.0	1.5	0.9	0.6
building, wood & metal					
bricklayer	0.1	0.5	0.8	1.0	0.6
carpenter	2.0	2.3	2.6	2.7	1.8
wheelwright etc.	0.2	0.3	0.4	1.1	1.0
blacksmith/smith	1.7	1.9	2.3	2.6	1.8
textiles & clothing					
weaver	1.9	1.9	1.3	0.5	0.1
tailor	1.9	3.0	2.3	1.5	1.3
cordwainer	0.4	0.5	1.8	1.9	2.1
shoemaker etc.	0.3	0.4	0.2	0.4	0.5
food & drink					
baker	0.3	0.5	1.1	1.1	1.3
butcher	1.0	0.8	2.1	2.9	2.0
grocer	–	0.1	0.7	1.2	1.0
innholder/keeper	0.2	0.2	0.7	1.5	2.1
miller	0.5	0.9	1.3	1.5	1.5
victualler	0.1	0.3	1.3	2.2	3.2
transport					
waterman	0.3	0.5	1.0	0.7	0.9
mariner etc.	–	–	0.2	0.4	0.3
Occ/status total	2,156	3,934	4,018	5,245	3,405

may have retired, and it is not uncommon in the seventeenth century to find yeomen living in towns. As Marcombe has noted, the term yeoman does not explain 'what a person actually did . . . a yeoman might as easily be a tradesman as someone connected wholly or partly with agriculture'.[10] On the other hand many men dwelling in small towns owned land and were involved in farming, and some rural yeomen had a trade. Without reading all the yeomen wills it is impossible to tell whether or not they were farmers, but because few lived in towns in this sample, all yeomen have been included under farming in Tables

[10] Marcombe, *English small town life*, p.95.

9.2 and 9.3. Similarly, some men termed gentlemen were actively engaged in trades such as brewing and malting. They formed part of Everitt's 'pseudo-gentry' found in seventeenth-century towns.[11] Another reason why occupational descriptions are not totally reliable, is that dual, or even multiple, occupations were common in rural areas in the early modern period. A single occupational description can disguise as much as it reveals of how an individual testator made his living. Where inventories exist and can be compared with wills, they sometimes give an indication of a broader range of activities than the testator's occupational label, but it is not feasible to undertake such a study with this size of sample, so despite the above caveats a general analysis of occupations found in Ely Consistory Court wills has been undertaken.

Tables 9.2 and 9.3 demonstrate clearly the overwhelming importance of agriculture to the economy of Cambridgeshire, and make it clear that it was not an industrial county. Table 9.2 shows a significant decline in the proportion of testators involved in farming after 1650, but Table 9.3 makes it clear that this was mainly at the expense of husbandmen and labourers. The decline in will-making husbandmen may partly result from a change in terminology, but probably also indicates the squeezing out of the small farmer. In some places, such as Chippenham, this was due to enclosure, but the county as a whole was 'one of the last counties in England to be enclosed'.[12] Elsewhere in the county engrossing led to a drop in the number of small farms; this can be illustrated at Orwell.[13] The period after 1650 also shows a very substantial increase in the numbers of yeomen leaving wills. After 1750 farmers start to replace yeomen and these two groups together total nearly 50 per cent of all wills proved between 1751 and 1800.

At the same time as the percentage of farming testators was falling, Table 9.2 shows a rise in the proportion of wills made by men engaged in most trades and services, the exceptions being textile and clothing occupations. The largest increase occurred in the food and drink trades, which must reflect an increase in retailing after the Restoration. Growing wealth amongst men engaged in these occupations would lead them to be more likely to make wills, and thus increase their proportion as will-makers. Defoe's comment that Cambridgeshire had 'no industries at all' is borne out by the evidence from wills.[14] The failure of weaving and tailoring to expand, shown in Table 9.3, underlines the

[11] Everitt, *Change in the provinces*, p.43.
[12] Spufford, unpublished typescript, p.55.
[13] Spufford, *Contrasting communities*, pp.100–4.
[14] Defoe, *Tour through the eastern counties*, p.122.

absence of a textile industry in rural Cambridgeshire and, apart from malting, there is no evidence of any other important industry in the county. Even so, over the whole period 1551–1750 only 99 testators described themselves as maltsters or malt makers.

With the exception of the food and drink trades, the growth in the proportion of tradesmen's and craftsmen's wills is fairly small. By 1750 the two largest trades in the food and drink group were butchers and innkeepers or victuallers. Table 9.3 reveals the relative expansion of a number of different trades, sometimes followed by a decline; a discussion of some of these follows. A particularly interesting group of occupations is that connected with water. These include boat builders, watermen and fishermen. The total number of testators with water-related occupations is small, with these three occupations totalling only 386. This may indicate that many who followed these trades were too poor to leave a will, but it is also likely that for fenmen fishing and transporting goods by water were part-time occupations. There were many inland ports in the Isle of Ely and the northern part of the old county of Cambridgeshire, and the town of Cambridge was a major inland port until the nineteenth century. The numbers of watermen and boat builders declined after 1750, probably due to the mid-eighteenth-century improvements to fen drainage, and to roads following the building of turnpikes. Fishers and fishermen were most numerous in the century 1551 to 1650 (totalling 115); the sharp fall in their numbers thereafter (only ten in 1651–1700) must be a result of the draining of the fens. The first phase of this began in 1631 and was completed by 1652.

Labourers

The differences between the arable and fen regions, described above, are important for an understanding of the numbers of Cambridgeshire labourers who left wills; after agriculturalists and artisans they are the third largest group for the period 1551–1750. Labourers have been included in the farming group in Table 9.3, but this may be misleading as the term labourer can cover a wide range of skilled and unskilled jobs. It is perhaps better seen as a status label rather than a job description. Between 1551 and 1750, only one labourer's will out of 1,767 was made by a Cambridge resident, so this discussion is unavoidably biased towards rural areas and agricultural labourers. The large number (849) of labourers' wills dating from 1601 to 1650 is very striking, forming 20 per cent of all wills proved in this half century and 48 per cent of all labourers wills for 1551–1750.

If the term labourer was used in the seventeenth century as a status

Table 9.4 Percentages of labourers' wills in three Cambridgeshire regions

	Isle of Ely %	Fen edge %	Other parishes %
1551–1600	39.1	27.7	33
1601–1650	33.6	25.4	41

label, then the rise and fall of the Cambridgeshire labourer may be connected with smallholding and ancillary occupations rather than the demand for labouring. This was particularly true of the Isle of Ely and the fen-edge parishes, where alternative employments were available. Landless men or those with two acres or less could make a living by other means far more easily here than in arable regions. The fens offered opportunities for grazing and fattening livestock, cutting reeds, making hay, cutting turf for fuel, fishing and wild fowling, and crafts such as basket making. The rise in the number of landless householders in Willingham, a fen-edge parish, between 1575 and 1603 tends to support this hypothesis.[15]

The increase in housing in fen and fen-edge villages was probably a contributory factor in the rise in will-making labourers, just as it is likely that the later draining of the fens had a dire effect on the economy of the same group. However, the economic and social conditions peculiar to the Isle of Ely and the fen-edge parishes do not explain why considerable numbers of labourers' wills are also found in the rest of the county. It can only be suggested that manorial control was generally weak there too and so allowed the fragmentation of tenements.

Table 9.4 shows that in the second half of the sixteenth century the highest percentage of labourers' wills came from the Isle of Ely, while in the following half century this position was held by the southern half of the county. Table 9.5 provides a more detailed breakdown for the first 50 years of the seventeenth century, a crucial period for the decline of will-making labourers in the fens. What Table 9.5 makes clear is that a fall in labourers' wills began after 1620 in the Isle of Ely, the region most affected by the draining of the fens. The fen-edge parishes were similarly affected, but labourers' wills from the parishes in the third group continued to rise until 1640.

A count of the number of labourers who left wills in the neighbouring county of Suffolk underlines how unusual are the Diocese of Ely figures. The Archdeaconry of Suffolk Court, in the eastern half of the county, proved 151 labourers' wills between 1444 and 1700,

[15] Spufford, *Contrasting communities*, p.149.

Table 9.5 Will-making labourers in three Cambridgeshire regions, 1601–50

	Isle of Ely		Fen edge		Other parishes	
	No.	%	No.	%	No.	%
1601–10	50	40.0	28	22.5	46	37.0
1611–20	100	41.0	64	26.5	78	32.0
1621–30	65	31.5	55	26.5	87	42.0
1631–40	57	30.0	41	21.5	93	48.5
1641–50	14	21.5	28	43.0	23	35.5

Note: labourers' wills are not found for all parishes in the county.

while from 1354 to 1700 the western Archdeaconry of Sudbury proved those of 446 labourers.[16] Few Suffolk labourers are likely to have made use of the Norwich Consistory Court. These figures are insignificant compared with the 1,529 labourers' wills proved by the Ely Consistory Court between 1505 and 1700.

Market towns

Table 9.6 presents an analysis of the occupations and status of the inhabitants of two small market towns between 1551 and 1750. Linton is in south Cambridgeshire very close to the Essex border, while Littleport lies just to the north-east of Ely and near the border with Norfolk. The latter is only a short distance from the Great Ouse to which it was linked by a canal. Both places were small market towns and both lie on the edge of Cambridgeshire, but in other ways they are very different with Linton standing on chalk and Littleport in the peat fens. Throughout the 200 years covered by Table 9.6 Linton was far better provided with shops and tradesmen than Littleport, and the latter was clearly a more agricultural community. The numbers of labourers fell in both towns, but were always greater in Littleport than in Linton. These differences must reflect the geographical positions of the two towns. Littleport was more isolated than Linton before the draining of the fens, while the latter had the advantage of being a natural centre for a number of small villages, as well as being on a road which led to Saffron Walden and from thence to an important road to London.

Very few Cambridge residents' wills were proved in the Consistory Court, as most of them had to use the Court of the Archdeacon of Ely. Goose discovered that as many as nine in ten of the Cambridge wills

---

[16] Serjeant and Serjeant, *1444–1700* and Serjeant and Serjeant, *1354–1700*.

Table 9.6 Percentages of occupations/status in two market towns, 1551–1750

	Linton	Littleport
1551–1600		
gentry	0.0	3.7
yeoman	12.0	18.5
husbandman	28.0	51.8
labourer	12.0	18.5
trades/shops	32.0	0.0
1601–1650		
gentry	0.0	1.0
yeoman	26.5	15.5
husbandman	13.0	43.5
labourer	5.6	22.0
trades/shops	53.0	15.5
1651–1700		
gentry	3.8	0.9
yeoman	32.5	30.0
husbandman	3.8	40.0
labourer	2.0	6.5
trades/shops	52.0	23.5
1701–1750		
gentry	7.0	5.0
yeoman	15.5	44.5
husbandman	7.0	9.5
labourer	2.2	4.2
farmer	1.0	0.0
trades/shops	56.0	35.5
Totals of all occupations/status		
1551–1600	25	27
1601–1650	53	96
1651–1700	52	106
1701–1750	84	115

were proved in the archdeaconry court between 1500 and 1700. During these two centuries the leading occupations in the town were strongly orientated towards the service, food and clothing trades; shoemakers and tailors were particularly important in the third group.[17] Goose writes of Cambridge that 'Rarely was textile production of such minor significance in a pre-industrial town', and adds that its second key function, besides serving the University, was as a centre of trade.[18]

[17] Goose, 'Economic and social aspects', p.125.
[18] Goose, 'Economic and social aspects', pp.139–40.

Conclusion

In the absence of any comparable database of wills it is difficult to make any precise comparisons with other work on occupations in the early modern period. Wills, marriage licences and depositions in church courts are amongst the sources used by Cressy in his study of literacy and its relationship to status and occupation in Tudor and Stuart England. His table, based on deponents in the courts of five dioceses and covering six counties and London between 1560 and 1700, shows that, apart from London and Middlesex, women were never more than 20 per cent of deponents.[19] The social distribution of London deponents is not comparable with that of any other part of England. Just as in the Diocese of Ely, farming occupations formed the largest group in the dioceses of Norwich, Exeter and Durham, followed by tradesmen and craftsmen. However, the percentages of tradesmen and craftsmen in all three were much higher than in Cambridgeshire, while farming occupations were lower. These differences could be a result of different economies, but it is perhaps more likely that the social structure of deponents in church courts differs from that of testators, with a bias towards the better off.

Patten used wills for studies of occupations in rural East Anglia and its towns. His article on rural occupations covers 1500 to 1700, but excludes agricultural ones. His sources are wills and inventories from the Consistory Court of Norwich and the four archdeaconry courts in this diocese, together with the wills of East Anglians proved in the Prerogative Court of Canterbury between 1500 and 1700. The survival rate of inventories in the consistory court records is much better than for the archdeaconry courts. Patten divides occupations into three groups: distributive trades, artisan-retailers and manufacturing trades. His study demonstrates that non-agricultural occupations were widely distributed throughout East Anglia, and that the number and range of occupations increased over the two centuries.[20] Norfolk and Suffolk differ from Cambridgeshire for they were more densely populated and were the home of a major industry, the manufacture of cloth of various types. Patten's work on English towns from 1500 to 1700 also concentrates on East Anglia and tabulates the rise in the number of trades and occupations over two centuries.[21]

Tawney's study of occupations in Gloucestershire in 1608 is based on a printed muster roll, but in spite of differences can be used for

[19] Cressy, *Literacy*, p.114.
[20] Patten, 'Urban occupations', pp.296–313.
[21] Patten, *English towns*, pp.254, 273, 283.

comparison with Cambridgeshire in the early-seventeenth century.[22] The Gloucestershire document is a snapshot of the male population of the county in one year, but covers an age range almost as wide as that of male testators. Bristol is excluded, and due to evasion the return is almost certainly not exhaustive. Of the 19,402 men in the returns a status or occupation is given for 17,046 (88 per cent), only some 4,000 less than the number of wills which form the subject of this chapter. The towns of Gloucester, Tewkesbury and Cirencester are dealt with separately by Tawney, and have been omitted from the following discussion.

Seventeenth-century rural Gloucestershire was a very different county from Cambridgeshire; textiles, mining and iron-working were all important in the former. As a result the percentage engaged in agriculture in Gloucestershire is markedly smaller, 49.5 per cent in 1608 against 70.3 per cent in Cambridgeshire in the period 1601–50. Husbandmen greatly outnumber yeomen in Gloucestershire with 3,774 of the former and only 927 of the latter. Tawney has classified 1,831 of the 1,962 labourers as agricultural workers.[23] He found that some of the smaller towns, such as Chipping Camden and Winchcombe, had a high percentage of men whose occupations were agricultural; 30 per cent for the former and 39 per cent for the latter. The joint percentages for yeomen and husbandmen who lived in the two small Cambridgeshire market towns of Linton and Littleport in the first half of the sixteenth century are consistently higher than these, even though labourers were included in the two Gloucestershire towns. The figures are 39.5 per cent in Linton and 59 per cent for Littleport; if labourers are added, the figures are 45 per cent and 81 per cent (see Table 9.6 above). This suggests that the small towns of Gloucestershire were more urbanised than those in Cambridgeshire.

The existence of a computer database for the Ely Consistory Court wills has made possible this study of occupations and status in this diocese. The quantity of data available, nearly 19,000 wills with an occupation or status recorded in a period of 250 years, makes this database at present unique. This preliminary study based on the wills of the Ely Consistory Court has shown some of the many possibilities opened up by a computer-generated database. The field is open for surveys of other aspects of early modern society in the county of Cambridge as well as detailed parochial studies.

[22] Tawney and Tawney, 'Occupational census', pp.25–64.
[23] Tawney and Tawney, 'Occupational census', p.59.

10

Fertility and Mortality in Pre-Industrial English Towns from Probate and Parish Register Evidence

NIGEL GOOSE

Introduction

Demographic analysis of English pre-industrial towns is fraught with difficulty. Simple attempts to establish population totals at individual points in time from tax or ecclesiastical returns involves making a number of more or less educated assumptions about omissions from the listings concerned, some of which have recently been shown to be of only limited value for demographic purposes.[1] Parish registers present familiar problems in both town and countryside: incomplete survival, lapses in the standard of registration and possible long-term under-registration of births due to delay between birth and baptism.[2] But the fluidity of urban populations renders their use even more problematic, and poses particular difficulties for the more sophisticated techniques of demographic analysis: family reconstitution may not be viable in an urban context, particularly when towns were composed of numerous small parishes.[3] There are additional question marks over the value of

---

[1] Phythian-Adams, 'Urban decay', pp.170–3; Goose, 'In search of the urban variable', pp.183–4 and n.102; Goose, 'Ecclesiastical returns', pp.46–7; Dyer, 'Bishops' census', pp.19–37; Goose, 'Bishops' census', pp.43–53.

[2] Flinn, *European demographic system*, pp.5–9; Wrigley and Schofield, *Population history*, pp.15–32, 89–102; Schofield, *Parish register aggregate analysis*, pp.8–9.

[3] Palliser, *Tudor York*, p.114; F. Lewis and M. Power, unpublished paper on the possibilities of reconstitution in Liverpool delivered to Early Modern Economic and Social History Seminar, Institute of Historical Research, 12 November 1993; Schofield, 'Representativeness and family reconstitution', pp.121–5; Finlay, *Population and metropolis*, and reviews by T. H. Hollingsworth in *Economic History Review*, 35 (1982), p.306 and P. Laxton in *Urban History Yearbook 1983*, pp.186–7; Wrigley, 'How reliable', pp.571–95.

urban marriage register data, for some urban churches were used quite regularly by inhabitants of surrounding rural parishes. All of these problems have left English pre-industrial urban demography in its infancy, with no clear understanding of the process and mechanisms of population change.[4]

Given the difficulties posed in an urban context by conventional source materials, it is perhaps surprising that greater use has not been made of probate evidence. One concerted attempt to use wills is Gottfried's regional study of East Anglia between 1430 and 1480, which provides some valuable data to set alongside the selective manorial or monastic evidence, and the indirect indices provided by price and wage trends, that have for so long been the main weapons in the medievalists' demographic armoury.[5] For the early modern period, however, there is no comparable survey, and probate evidence has seldom been used for demographic purposes. There are two notable exceptions: Slack's work on mortality crises, which uses wills to supplement parish register evidence, and Fisher's seminal article on the mortality crisis of the later 1550s, recently the subject of renewed scrutiny.[6] Other than this, the industry of Takahashi in counting the number of wills that survive has helped further to underline the temporal distribution of mortality crises identified by Slack on the one hand and Wrigley and Schofield on the other, besides revealing the spread of will-making down the social scale by the end of the sixteenth century.[7] There has, however, been no systematic attempt to use early modern wills to measure changing levels of fertility or nuptiality, apart from a couple of very brief considerations of the numbers of children they reveal for the towns of Worcester and Lutterworth.[8]

This chapter will explore the possibility of using wills to enhance our understanding of early modern urban demography. It will offer an analysis of fertility trends and mortality crises in the three large towns of Cambridge, Colchester and Reading between 1500 and 1700, using all extant wills and parish registers, comparing and contrasting the relative

---

[4] For a fuller discussion of such issues see Goose, 'Urban demography', pp.273–84. For a more recent contribution focusing upon York, Galley, *Demography of early modern towns*, and forthcoming review in *Bulletin of the Social History of Medicine*.

[5] Gottfried, *Epidemic disease*.

[6] Slack, *Impact of plague*; Fisher, 'Influenza and inflation', pp.120–9; Moore, ' "Jack Fisher's 'flu": a virus revisited', pp.280–307; Zell, ' "Fisher's 'flu" ', pp.354–8; Moore, ' "Jack Fisher's 'flu": a virus still virulent', pp.359–61.

[7] Takahashi, 'Number of wills', pp.187–213.

[8] Dyer, *City of Worcester*, pp.34–5; Goodacre, *Transformation*, pp.62, 64.

value of the two sources. The long term population trends in these towns, their respective ability to grow by natural increase, and the trends in fertility that can be tentatively estimated from parish registers, will be compared with the changing numbers of children recorded in wills. A similar exercise will be conducted regarding levels of mortality as revealed in parish registers and in the number of wills proved annually. Whilst the methodological problems involved in the use of wills for these purposes will be highlighted, it will be argued that they can profitably be used alongside parish register evidence to provide a fuller picture of early modern demographic conditions and trends, sometimes confirming the results that the registers reveal, sometimes compensating for incomplete registration of vital events.

The towns

Cambridge, Colchester and Reading were all towns of the 'second-rank' in the urban hierarchy, clearly distinguishable from simple market towns in terms of size, economic complexity and influence, and in the sophistication of their social, political and administrative structures, but lacking the regional role that has been assigned to 'provincial capitals' such as Norwich, Exeter or York. Towns of this stature, besides possessing features common to all towns worthy of the name, generally exhibited economic specialisms, and in this respect they present interesting contrasts. Cambridge, besides being a university town, was a centre of internal trade of the first importance, exemplified by the great Stourbridge Fair which ran for three consecutive weeks, described in 1589 as 'by far the largest and most famous fair in all England, whence very much use is derived as well by the merchants dispersed throughout the whole realm . . .'.[9] It was also an inland port, trading in corn, coal and other goods via the river network which extended to King's Lynn.[10] Reading was a textile town, concentrating upon production of traditional broadcloths and kerseys, though towards the later seventeenth century it was finding a new orientation as a collecting, processing and distributing centre for agricultural produce.[11] Colchester was also a cloth town, but one that successfully made the transition from woollen to worsted production in the later sixteenth century, and was also a port active in both coastal and overseas trade.[12] Despite these

[9] Maitland and Bateson, *Cambridge borough charters*, p.97.
[10] Goose, 'Economic and social aspects', pp.139–42.
[11] Goose, 'Decay and regeneration', pp.53–74.
[12] Goose and Cooper, *Tudor and Stuart Colchester*, pp.76–87.

Table 10.1 The population of Cambridge, Colchester and Reading, 1520s–1670s

Date	Source	Cambridge	Colchester	Reading
1524/5	Exchequer lay subsidy	2,600	3,500	2,600
1534	Oath of fealty		3,700	
1563	Bishops' census	3,000		
1570s	Parish registers		4,600	
1584	Householders in High Ward			2,650
1587	Vice-Chancellor's estimate	5,000		
1620s	Inmate census	7,750		
1620s	Parish registers		11,000	6,200
1674	Hearth Tax	7,900	10,400	
1670s	Parish registers			5,400

Notes: For the methodology employed to arrive at these estimates see Goose, 'Economic and social aspects', Appendix 2, pp. 429–36. A correction factor of 25 per cent has been added to the original Cambridge figure for 1563 in the light of more recent research.

contrasts, they shared one experience in common with most of the larger provincial towns of early modern England, and this was the rapid growth achieved in the later sixteenth and early-seventeenth centuries, shown in Table 10.1. Modest expansion in the second and third quarters of the sixteenth century was followed by distinct growth in the following 50 years, a trend that is fully endorsed by the growing number of vital events (baptisms, burials and marriages) recorded in the parish registers for each town, after which population stabilised or declined slightly.

The sources

These towns were not selected for the comprehensiveness of their demographic evidence, and their parish registers vary markedly in quality.[13] Reading comprised just three large parishes, but while the register for St Mary survives from the 1540s, and that for St Giles from the 1560s, data is only available for St Lawrence from the early-seventeenth century. Only two of the 14 Cambridge parish registers are extant from the start of registration in 1538, four are available between the 1560s and 1580s, ten from the 1590s, and—perhaps unusually—all 14 through from 1605–40. Typically, registration deteriorates in the 1640s and 1650s when only five registers were well kept, and improves again after 1660. Colchester is a different matter. Only three of the

---

[13] For full details see Goose, 'Economic and social aspects', Appendix 3.

town's 16 registers are reliable through from the 1560s to 1640, although others provide useable data for shorter periods, and no reliable information survives after 1640.

Even the generally well kept registers have gaps: for example, those for St Mary, Reading, are deficient in 1557 and 1562–4, both well known as years of widespread epidemic disease. Nothing can be done to correct the burial figures for such years, although when a gap in registration appears arbitrary, not corresponding with any known mortality crisis, these can be made good by interpolation from the average figures for surrounding years. It must also be recognised that demographic conditions could vary markedly between parishes within individual towns, and thus a careful eye must be kept on the sample of parishes in view at any time, particularly to avoid undue bias to the poorer, suburban parishes.[14] Further than this, no additional correction factors have been applied to the raw data the registers contain. This may mean that recorded baptisms do not accurately reflect births, for any delay between birth and baptism, given the high rates of infant mortality in the period, will mean that a proportion of infants died before they could be baptised. The estimated shortfall, however, calculated from rural evidence, is just 2 per cent for 1550–99, 3.4 per cent for 1600–49 and 4.1 per cent for 1650–99, so the impact of this factor is likely to be fairly marginal.[15]

The first advantage of probate evidence is in terms of coverage. Wills survive, in varying numbers, for each of these towns throughout the period 1500–1700, a total of 6,195: 2,185 for Cambridge, 2,634 for Colchester and 1,376 for Reading. There are no gaps in the series. All wills proved in archdeaconry, consistory and prerogative courts have been examined and their numbers for each 20-year period, alongside the percentage proved in the Prerogative Court of Canterbury, are presented in Table 10.2.[16] But while wills survive for each of these

---

[14] Goose, 'Household size and structure', pp.355–6; Slack, *Impact of plague*, pp.112–13.

[15] Wrigley, 'Births and baptisms', p.281; Wrigley and Schofield, *Population history*, p.97.

[16] Wills consulted here include all of those relating to inhabitants of these towns proved in the Archdeaconry Court of Ely (Cambridge University Library, hereafter CUL, EPR Archd.), Consistory Court of Ely (CUL, EPR Cons.), University Vice-Chancellor's Court (CUL, UA, VC probate, bundles 1–17), Archdeaconry of Berkshire (Berkshire County Record Office, MS wills Berks), Salisbury Consistory Court (Wilts County Record Office, uncatalogued), Archdeaconry of Colchester (Colchester Record Office, hereafter CRO, D/A CR & CW), Archdeaconry of Essex (CRO D/A, ER & EW), Bishop of London Commissary Court (CRO, D/A BR & BW), and the Prerogative Court of Canterbury (Public Record Office, registers Moone to Pett).

Table 10.2 Wills proved in Cambridge, Colchester and Reading, 1500–1699

	Cambridge		Colchester		Reading	
	No.	% PCC	No.	% PCC	No.	% PCC
1500–19	39	100	136	11	33	82
1520–39	127	18	88	10	38	47
1540–59	208	3	150	4	130	19
1560–79	105	15	166	15	89	18
1580–99	231	13	257	15	121	25
1600–19	330	20	356	13	122	26
1620–39	357	18	382	16	198	26
1640–59	238	46	302	40	184	73
1660–79	300	20	427	13	205	53
1680–99	250	20	370	21	256	50
Total	2,185	20	2,634	18	1,376	39

towns throughout 1500–1699, their number varies. Relatively few are extant for Cambridge 1500–19 and for Reading 1500–39, in each case averaging under two per year, compared to approaching six per year in Colchester. In 1520–59, however, 335 Cambridge wills survive, compared to just 238 in Colchester, despite the fact that Colchester was the larger of the two towns. For all three substantially more wills survive by the early-seventeenth century, but in Cambridge the numbers failed to keep pace with population growth, while in Colchester the proportion was virtually identical in both 1520–59 and 1600–39. For early-seventeenth-century Reading, fewer wills survive per head of the population than for either of the other towns.

The small number of surviving wills for Cambridge and Reading in the early-sixteenth century is further reflected in the heavy preponderance of PCC wills shown in Table 10.2, the measurement of which provides a valuable test of undue bias in the sample towards the very wealthy.[17] The high percentages for each town in the period 1640–59 reflect the impact of the Civil Wars and Interregnum upon the ecclesiastical courts rather than any bias in the sample. The habit of using the PCC appears to have lingered in late-seventeenth-century Reading, but many of these wills reveal only a modest level of wealth, indicating that this was merely an administrative anomaly, not an indication of a biased sample.

While examination of wills proved in each level of ecclesiastical court will achieve the most comprehensive coverage, it is clearly not possible

---

[17] The proportion of PCC wills is very low for Cambridge and Colchester in the period 1540–59, but the numerical difference in numbers between this and the successive period is small, and the results are not distorted as a consequence.

to overcome the fact that the evidence is inherently socially selective. Calculations for Cambridge and Reading, which provide relatively comprehensive burial evidence for the early-seventeenth century, suggest that, assuming half of all recorded deaths were of children, approximately 12 per cent and 10 per cent of adults respectively left wills, and the proportion in the early-sixteenth century was considerably lower still. Will-makers were, however, predominantly men, and hence the proportion of adult males leaving wills was substantially higher, approximately 19 per cent and 17 per cent respectively. The relatively poor are not wholly unrepresented, for some testators followed quite humble occupations, though it is equally clear that there was a pronounced skew towards the wealthier inhabitants.[18]

Social selectivity is but one of the problems involved in using wills for demographic purposes. Sex selectivity is another, for married women were not allowed to leave a will without permission from their husband, and such instances are rare. Child deaths, obviously, very rarely feature in will evidence, and these factors pose particular problems for the employment of wills as an index of mortality. As a guide to fertility they present additional difficulties. As infant and child mortality was so high in pre-industrial England, a count of children mentioned in extant wills can stand as only a weak surrogate for a true measure of fertility. But children that were living at the time of their parents' death may also have been excluded from the will where their portion had already been granted (married females in particular), or when a will was hastily drawn up as death approached, and hence they cannot always be relied upon to provide a true picture of replacement rates or completed family size.[19] Testators also feature in this evidence at very different stages in their life-cycles, and hence changes to age-specific mortality levels could also affect the results.

One particular worry is that female children may have been substantially under-represented, and hence it is important to test for this. Table 10.3 shows that females are slightly under-represented in each town for much of the sixteenth century, although to a lesser extent from 1540 onwards, apart from Reading in the period 1560–79.[20] By the

---

[18] See also the recent remarks of Zell on this topic: ' "Fisher's 'flu" ', p.355.

[19] Females were clearly under-enumerated in fifteenth-century East Anglia: Gottfried, *Epidemic disease*, p.26.

[20] A sex ratio at birth of 105 is an acceptable estimated norm: Wrigley, *Population and history*, p.16. Greater exposure to risk produced by the employment of male children and young adults might be expected to balance any greater care afforded them in a male-orientated society, and hence a sex ratio in the region of 100 or a little over can be taken to suggest reliability of the will data.

Table 10.3 Sex ratio of children mentioned in wills (males per 100 females)

	Cambridge	Colchester	Reading
1500–19	200	138	110
1520–39	98	136	143
1540–59	108	109	101
1560–79	110	113	146
1580–99	115	101	101
1600–19	108	97	95
1620–39	90	93	94
1640–59	114	84	84
1660–79	106	104	78
1680–99	95	94	91

seventeenth century the balance had swung, and given that there is no reason to suppose that males might be under-represented in wills, figures as low as those found in late-seventeenth-century Reading might indicate the emergence of an imbalance between the sexes, possibly due to sex-specific mortality patterns, or simply changing inheritance practices, a topic worthy of more consideration in its own right.

Although Table 10.3 reveals that female children were not regularly and seriously ignored in wills, the discussion of fertility in the following section will offer two calculations: one of the total numbers of children mentioned, and another of the number of sons per male testator. The problem of apparently childless testators remains, however, for it is impossible to tell if they were truly childless, had already granted their children's portions, or had simply dictated the briefest of wills as death approached. For this reason, it was felt necessary to offer two calculations of the number of sons per male, one including and another excluding those wills that mention no children. These tests and refinements go only part of the way towards revealing weaknesses in the data, however, and no attempt has been made to detect instances of remarriage, or to compare generations at even approximately the same stage in their life-cycle, simply because it is impossible to do either with confidence.[21]

Fertility

We can now turn to consider the trends in 'fertility' that the will evidence reveals, in the knowledge that tests for under-recording of

---

[21] Cf. Gottfried, *Epidemic disease*, who is more sanguine and hence attempts a more sophisticated analysis than that offered here.

Table 10.4 Mean number of children mentioned in wills, 1500–1699

	Cambridge			Colchester			Reading		
	Total*	S1**	S2**	Total	S1	S2	Total	S1	S2
1500–19	2.4	1.5	0.8	2.4	1.4	0.8	2.6	1.4	0.9
1520–39	2.1	1.0	0.4	2.1	1.3	0.8	2.7	1.6	1.0
1540–59	2.3	1.2	0.7	3.0	1.6	1.1	3.3	1.7	1.3
1560–79	3.2	1.7	1.2	3.2	1.7	1.2	2.9	1.6	1.1
1580–99	3.1	1.6	1.0	3.4	1.7	1.1	3.3	1.8	1.2
1600–19	3.1	1.7	1.0	3.3	1.7	1.1	4.0	2.0	1.4
1620–39	2.7	1.3	0.8	3.3	1.6	1.0	3.5	1.7	1.2
1640–59	3.0	1.7	1.0	3.6	1.6	1.1	3.4	1.6	1.0
1660–79	2.9	1.5	1.0	3.1	1.6	1.1	3.2	1.4	1.1
1680–99	2.6	1.4	0.8	2.7	1.4	0.8	3.4	1.6	1.1

Notes:
* Figures for mean number of children exclude testators mentioning none. Widows are excluded where their spouse's will is extant to avoid double counting.
** Sons per male (S1) excludes testators mentioning no children.
** Sons per male (S2) includes testators mentioning no children.

females and for bias towards the wealthiest inhabitants suggest that the period 1500–19 should be ignored for Cambridge and Reading, whilst for Colchester in 1500–39 and Reading in 1520–39 and 1560–79 only the data for males can be relied upon. Only those wills that provided a clear indication of numbers of children were employed in this analysis, reducing the total number to 4,296, of which 3,217 mentioned children.

The data for Cambridge in Table 10.4 indicate a slight upward movement in the figures for average numbers of children and sons per male in wills proved 1540–59, and a much more marked increase in the subsequent period. The figures stabilise in the late-sixteenth and early-seventeenth centuries, with a quite pronounced decline in 1620–39, followed by recovery and renewed decline in the second half of the century. Both the absolute figures and the trend are similar for Colchester, although here the upward shift occurred slightly earlier in the sixteenth century and the plateau was maintained for longer, with clear decline only setting in towards the end of the seventeenth century. The Reading figures for average numbers of children fluctuate more noticeably in the sixteenth century, but if allowance is made for the likelihood of an undercount in 1520–39 and 1560–79, indicated by the skewed sex ratios for these periods, the data indicates an upward movement early in the sixteenth century, followed by stability prior to a significant rise in the late-sixteenth and early-seventeenth centuries, and then steady decline through to 1660–79. The peaks achieved in the Reading figures for the early-seventeenth century, however, stand significantly above those for either Cambridge or Colchester.

How do these trends compare to the demographic experience of these towns as revealed by parish registers and other sources? Table 10.1 provided an outline of their growth across these two centuries, the key feature of which was the speed with which each town grew in the later sixteenth and early-seventeenth centuries, all three more than doubling in size within the space of approximately 50 years. In general terms this corresponds well with the evidence from wills presented in Table 10.4 for both average numbers of children and sons recorded per male testator. For the earlier sixteenth century both Cambridge and Colchester grew moderately, while the population of Reading remained stable, and this too appears to be reflected in the earlier upward shift in the numbers of children recorded in the wills data for both of these towns. The early-seventeenth century fluctuations shown in the will evidence cannot be closely compared to population trends, but the long-term tendency for their populations to stabilise or decline slightly from roughly the second quarter of the seventeenth century again finds reflection in the trends shown in Table 10.4.

While the changing numbers of children mentioned in wills appear to confirm the long-term general trends of population movement, how do they compare with baptism/marriage ratios calculated from parish registers? The baptism/marriage ratio has long been a conventional tool of aggregate demography, but it is in fact a rather poor measure of fertility, encompassing many factors that affect both marriages and births.[22] In particular, the remarriage level, which will be strongly influenced by trends in mortality, can seriously distort the figures, while no allowance can be made for the fact that the population was far from closed, but subject to the influence of migration. Given these difficulties, small fluctuations in these figures should be ignored.

The baptism/marriage ratios presented in Table 10.5 indicate an upward shift for each town towards the latter part of the sixteenth century, as did the data from wills, followed by gentle decline from the early-seventeenth century, the trend fluctuating more erratically in Colchester, and to a lesser degree in Reading, than it did in Cambridge. The plateau achieved in early-seventeenth-century Reading, however, stood well

---

[22] Chambers, *Vale of Trent*, pp.52–4; Eversley, 'Survey of population', pp.403–4; Sogner, 'Aspects of the demographic situation', pp.137–8. For a critique of the method: Wrigley and Schofield, *Population history*, pp.189–90; Schofield, *Parish register aggregate analysis*, pp.20–1.

Table 10.5 Baptism/marriage ratios in three towns, 1550–1675

Date	Cambridge	Colchester	Reading
1550	–	–	3.1
1555	–	–	2.6
1560	–	–	2.3
1565	–	–	2.3
1570	–	2.8	2.5
1575	3.2	2.6	3.1
1580	3.8	2.9	3.4
1585	4.2	3.6	3.5
1590	3.4	4.6	3.5
1595	3.4	4.0	4.0
1600	3.8	3.6	4.7
1605	3.6	3.3	4.9
1610	3.4	2.5	4.2
1615	3.5	3.5	4.4
1620	3.2	4.4	4.3
1625	3.0	3.3	4.6
1630	3.2	3.3	4.6
1635	3.3	3.6	4.3
1670	3.0	–	3.5
1675	–	–	3.6

Notes: Baptism/marriage ratios calculated using 10 year half-overlapping periods.
Lines between rows indicate a change in the sample of parishes employed. On no occasion do these changes affect the trend shown.

above that found in the other towns, and was sustained for longer, a feature that also stood out clearly from the will evidence, while the fragmentary data for the later seventeenth century also appears to mirror the decline from the early-seventeenth century peaks shown in Table 10.4.

Although it is not possible to present the full data here, the trends revealed in Table 10.5 also correspond well with the respective ability of each town to achieve natural growth through a surplus of baptisms over burials.[23] Cambridge achieved natural increase in every quinquennium from 1576 to 1600, with baptism/burial ratios as high as 1.87 in 1576–80 and 1.70 in 1581–85, after which natural decrease set in. In Colchester the sparse register information available reveals a degree of natural growth through from 1560 to 1590 apart from one quinquennium, with a more erratic pattern emerging after 1590, producing just a small natural surplus across the early-seventeenth century as a whole. Reading was very different, in that the strong

[23] For further details, Goose, 'Economic and social aspects', pp.258–71.

natural increase which emerged in 1566–70, producing peak baptism/burial ratios of 1.72 and 1.63 in 1581–85 and 1586–90 respectively, was sustained through the early-seventeenth century, only one quinquennium, 1596–1600, exhibiting a natural deficit, and this of only three in the two extant parish registers.

It is tempting to try to relate the details of these trends to the will data and baptism/marriage ratios revealed in Tables 10.4 and 10.5, but although quite close correspondences can be discovered—for instance in the patterns exhibited in the early-seventeenth-century Colchester figures—this level of analysis is probably inappropriate given the various shortcomings of both the data and methodology. Broader correspondences, however, might have more significance, and we have seen that the onset of sustained population growth in each town, their respective baptism/marriage ratios and their varying abilities to achieve natural growth, are all compatible with the changing numbers of children revealed in the analysis of wills, the discrepancy between Cambridge and Colchester on the one hand and Reading on the other standing out particularly clearly. It is very tempting, therefore, to conclude that fluctuations in fertility did, at the very least, play a part in determining the rate of expansion or contraction in these towns. Nevertheless, it must be recognised too that changing *mortality* conditions, through their effect upon completed family size and remarriage levels, could also help to explain the trends revealed here.[24]

Mortality

We can now turn to the use of wills to indicate changing levels of mortality, 'crisis mortality' in particular, entering upon far more familiar, well-trodden ground. The social selectivity of wills has already been emphasised, and thus they are unlikely to provide an accurate indication of the severity of mortality crises that were themselves socially selective, such as those caused by plague or famine.[25] The number of wills proved in any one year, even a 'crisis' year, is relatively small, and thus modest increases can easily produce a doubling of the average number proved. For more precise statistical calculation of the severity of mortality crises parish registers must be employed, and the conventional multipliers

---

[24] In particular, it is almost certain that levels of mortality were lower in early-seventeenth century Reading than in Cambridge, which itself must have contributed to at least some degree to the higher numbers of children revealed in wills in the former town as compared to the latter: Goose, 'Urban demography', pp.281–2.

[25] Slack, 'Mortality crises', p.14.

pioneered so long ago by Schofield (2.0 for a 'major crisis', 1.5 for a 'minor crisis') provide the most appropriate measure for individual parishes or towns, although once again the size of the population in view must be taken into account.[26] Wills do, however, allow the identification of at least some crisis years prior to the commencement of burial registers in 1538, and supplement the often inadequate parish register data for the mid-sixteenth and mid-late-seventeenth centuries. The annual level of wills proved in each town in all relevant ecclesiastical courts in the sixteenth and seventeenth centuries is shown in Figures 10.1–10.3, while crisis mortality calculated from extant parish registers is displayed in Table 10.6.[27]

The low annual number of wills proved in the very early-sixteenth century, and the high proportion of those for Cambridge and Reading proved in the PCC, make it difficult to comment upon the data, although numbers were very high indeed in Colchester in 1502 and well above average in Cambridge in 1521 and across the years 1529–32. The mortality crises of the 1540s and 1550s stand out very clearly. Both Colchester and Reading were affected in 1540, a year of high mortality in London, Lichfield, and Essex and Berkshire more generally, and while Slack has assumed that this was an outbreak of plague, the absence of any reference to plague in corporation records, and its impact upon the generally wealthier will-making population, might warn us to leave the question of its cause open.[28] The early 1540s appear to have been generally unhealthy in each of these towns, with a particularly sharp rise in the number of wills proved in Cambridge in 1544–5, 1545 producing the highest annual total for the town in the entire sixteenth century.[29] This was another year of generally high mortality across the country, as well as a year of dearth, while the Cambridge Group's national parish

---

[26] Schofield, 'Crisis mortality', pp.10–22. It is for this reason that far lower thresholds for the identification of a 'crisis' are appropriate for large populations such as the Cambridge Group national sample of 404 parishes than for individual parishes or towns: Wrigley and Schofield, *Population history*, pp.332–6.

[27] Detailed calculations of crisis mortality on a parish by parish basis were too extensive for inclusion here, but will be referred to as appropriate in the text, and can be found in Goose, 'Economic and social aspects', Tables 4.14–4.16, pp.303–7.

[28] Slack, *Impact of plague*, pp.57, 60–1; Goose, 'Economic and social aspects', pp.316–7.

[29] Burial registration commences for the parish of St Mary in Reading towards the end of 1538, and although poor or suspect registration in the early 1540s has led to its exclusion form the tabulations presented below, the number of burials was high in 1540, as well as in 1543–4.

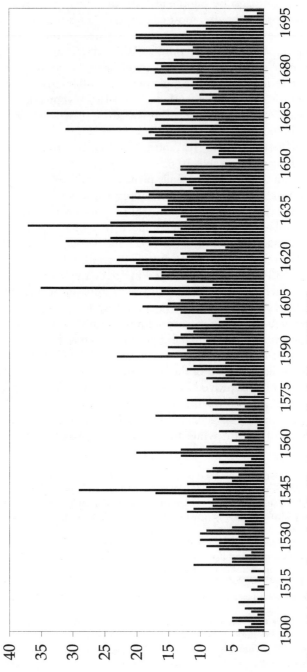

Figure 10.1 Annual number of wills proved in Cambridge, 1500–1699

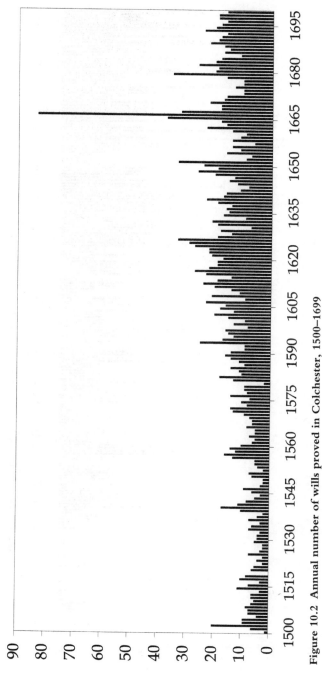

Figure 10.2 Annual number of wills proved in Colchester, 1500–1699

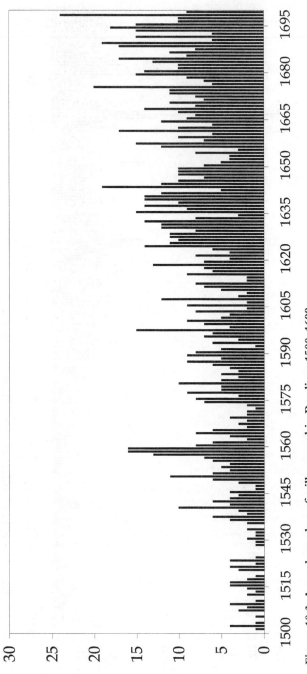

Figure 10.3 Annual number of wills proved in Reading, 1500–1699

register sample also indicates successive years of high mortality in the early-mid 1540s, a period of sustained difficulty that deserves closer attention.[30] A relatively small blip in the probate series is evident for Colchester in 1550–1, Cambridge in 1551–2, and a more noticeable peak in Reading in 1550–1, reflecting the effects of the last outbreak of sweating sickness in England, and confirming its relatively modest impact, both in general and upon towns in particular, already revealed by parish register analysis.[31] The two Cambridge parishes of St Benedict and Little St Mary also show its impact, and its presence and rapid effect is confirmed by Henry Dylcock, Fellow of Christ's College, whose will was 'wryten in the time of the sweat . . . daylye seinge and howrlye hearing tell of soden death every where . . .'.[32] It had no pronounced effect, however, on burial registration in St Mary, Reading, nor St Leonard's, Colchester.

The 'influenza' epidemic of the late-1550s, probably a combination of typhus and plague following hard upon the poor harvests of 1555 and 1556, has been the subject of considerable scrutiny, and stands out clearly in Figures 10.1–10.3, indicating that each town suffered at least two consecutive years of high mortality. Its impact is confirmed by the, still limited, parish register data for Cambridge and Reading shown in Table 10.6, and more modestly in a minor crisis apparent in St Leonard's, Colchester, in 1560. The burial evidence reveals that in the two small Cambridge parishes for which data survives mortality rose by a factor of 2.3 in 1558. Cambridge will evidence, however, suggests a more drawn-out epidemic, probably lasting from 1556–9 inclusive, and producing increases over the eight-year average in the number of wills proved of factors of 2.6, 4.0, 2.6 and 1.8 for these four years respectively. For St Mary in Reading the parish register reveals high mortality across 1558–9, producing mortality ratios of 2.0 and 1.7, while wills again suggest a more extended epidemic lasting from 1557–9 inclusive, and producing increases in numbers of wills proved by factors of 2.6, 3.2 and 3.2 respectively. The parish register evidence for Colchester is extremely poor for this period, though the parish of St Leonard's gives a hint of high mortality, while wills provide clear evidence of high mortality lasting through the period 1556–60. Comparison of the number of wills proved with the eight surrounding years produces multipliers of 2.6, 3.2, 2.4, 2.8 and 2.0 for these five years respectively.

---

[30] Slack, *Impact of plague*, p.57; Wrigley and Schofield, *Population history*, Table 8.12, p.334; Clay, *Economic expansion*, I, p.40.

[31] Wrigley and Schofield, *Population history*, Table 8.12, p.334; Dyer, 'English sweating sickness', pp.362–84.

[32] CUL, UA, VC, probate, will of Henry Dylcock, fellow of Christ's College, 1551.

Table 10.6 Crisis mortality in three towns from parish registers

Date	Cambridge Multiplier	N=	Colchester Multiplier	N=	Reading Multiplier	N=
1547	2.3	15				
1552	1.9	13				
1558	2.3	16			2.0	20
1559					1.7	19
1570			1.5	36		
1574	2.2	41				
1582					1.7	30
1586			1.6	39		
1588	1.8	100				
1593					1.6	46
1596					2.2	51
1597			2.5	45	2.3	59
1602			1.7	49		
1603			2.6	51		
1604			2.8	51		
1605	1.6	153				
1608					1.7	143
1610	2.2	222				
1624					1.7	136
1625	2.1	253	2.3	75		
1626			2.8	75		
1630	2.3	274				
1638	1.5	295				
1643					2.9	85
1644	1.5	268	–		–	
1658	1.5	185	–			
1665	1.5	247	–			
1666	3.2	254	–			
1675	–		–		2.2	148

Notes: The multiplier represents the conventional Crisis Mortality Ratio, calculated on the basis of average mortality in the eight surrounding years, excluding any other year that also exhibits mortality at crisis level. All years where the ratio reached 1.5 or over are included in the table.

N = represents the eight-year average upon which the multiplier is based, and hence gives an indication of the register coverage represented in any crisis year.

The Cambridge and Reading data include a fluctuating sample of parishes, though two of Reading's three large parishes are included from 1565, and at least five of the 14 Cambridge parishes from the same date. The Colchester figures are based upon just three of the town's 16 parishes—St Botolph, St Mary at the Walls and Lexden—for which registers survive through from 1561 to 1640.

This data strongly supports the argument for an extended epidemic rather than a dramatic impact in any single year, and this may in turn help explain why it did not attract the attention of contemporaries that might have been expected.[33] One must not, however, get carried away by the size of the multipliers that can be calculated from wills, for the number for each town shown in Figures 10.1–10.3 is relatively small. Nor can the number of wills proved give any more than an impression of the number who actually died in any one year. In Reading, for example, 45 wills were proved in 1557–9, some 30 more than normal, but this is impossible to convert to a measure of mortality. For this we must turn to our parish registers. In the parish of St Mary in Reading, there were 72 burials in the two years 1558–9 which stand out as crisis years in Table 10.6. If we estimate that St Mary accounted for roughly one-quarter of the town's population at this date, which stood at approximately 2,600, the overall level of mortality in the town would have been roughly 11 per cent, and the parish exhibits a crude death rate in 1558 of 60/1000, very close to the Cambridge Group's back projection estimate for 1558/9 of 65.[34] It is possible, therefore, to harmonise a steep rise in probates with a death rate of relatively modest overall proportions.[35]

This is not in any way to diminish the epidemic of 1556–60: epidemics by the sixteenth century never carried off substantial proportions of the population, either nationally or regionally, even if their local impact was occasionally severe, and thus the fact that this outbreak was the only one able temporarily to halt the upward movement of English population stands as clear testimony to its significance. There are three reasons why it exerted such a powerful influence. First, it was less socially selective than many other diseases, as contemporaries themselves noted, which is one reason why it shows up so clearly in the probate evidence.[36] In Cambridge, for example, the

---

[33] A view supported by both Zell and Moore: Zell, ' "Fisher's 'flu" '; Moore, ' "Jack Fisher's 'flu": a virus still virulent', pp.359–61.

[34] Wrigley and Schofield, *Population history*, Table 8.11, p.333.

[35] Determination of the extent to which population fell over the course of the period 1556–60, which has caused such controversy, is extremely difficult even at the local level. My own best guess for Reading would tend towards the lower end of the suggested spectrum, closer to Wrigley and Schofield's 5–6 per cent than to Moore's 16 per cent: Zell, ' "Fisher's 'flu" ', pp.357–8; Moore, ' "Jack Fisher's 'flu": a virus still virulent', p.359.

[36] It is also possible, indeed likely, that its impact upon the more elevated social groups served to maximise disruption of the recording of vital events in parish registers, and those that do survive may well be an inherently biased sample in consequence.

epidemic carried off William Gill, alderman, and William Robinson, bailiff, both in 1556, John Lyne, alderman, in 1558, besides several burgesses. Amongst the university population to succumb were Rowland Swinbourne, clerk and master of Clare Hall, Dr Nicholas Shaxton of Gonville Hall, suffragan to the Bishop of Chichester and John Fuller, clerk, whose inventory was valued at over £622. Second, it was less geographically selective than many other diseases, and although some regions escaped more than others it was clearly very widespread and affected urban and rural areas alike. And finally, it endured, chipping away at the population, to a greater or lesser degree in different communities, over a period of six years, a feat that no other extended outbreak was able to equal to quite the same degree. This is the basis for Fisher's stimulating hypotheses concerning its economic impact, but its social impact deserves attention too, for the first recorded assessment for the relief of the poor in Cambridge was made in 1556 in conjunction with a survey of the 'three states of the poor sort' and inquiry into recent immigrants. Similarly, in 1557 a compulsory poor rate was levied in Colchester upon pain of imprisonment, some 15 years ahead of equivalent national legislation, and poor immigrants were more closely regulated.[37]

The value of wills as evidence of mortality crises declines after 1560 as parish register evidence becomes increasingly available, although the registers themselves are, as noted above, occasionally far from perfect: for example, the temporary breakdown in registration of vital events in St Mary, Reading, in 1563–4, a notable plague year, has certainly obscured a significant mortality crisis here.[38] Figures 10.1–10.3 do, however, appear to indicate that *persistently* high mortality at crisis level did not recur in these towns during the sixteenth century, perhaps with the exception of Cambridge in 1587–9. They also suggest that Cambridge experienced greater deviations from the trend than did either Colchester or Reading, while in the early-seventeenth century mortality fluctuations in Reading are less pronounced than in either of the other towns. This accurately reflects the results of parish register analysis across the period 1561–1640. If we treat consecutive years of high mortality as single crises, and add in the 'missing' Reading crisis of 1563–4, in these 80 years Cambridge experienced seven crises, Colchester five and Reading six, mortality doubling on four, three and probably two occasions respectively, with the Reading outbreaks more

[37] Cooper, *Annals of Cambridge*, 2, p.110; CRO, Morant MSS, D/Y 2/2, p.37; Slack, *English poor law*, p.60.
[38] Slack, *Impact of plague*, Table 3.3, p.61.

commonly of shorter duration than those in Colchester. Calculation of the 'excess' mortality produced in crisis years for these three towns in the years 1606–40 underlines the contrast, producing figures of 10.3 per cent, 8.7 per cent and 3.4 per cent for Cambridge, Colchester and Reading respectively, and helping to explain why Reading alone remained able to achieve a substantial natural surplus across this period.[39]

Despite the fact that will evidence is socially selective, it does identify the majority of outbreaks of epidemic disease that are apparent from parish registers, both locally and nationally, despite the fact that plague was by far the most common culprit, and was a disease that impacted most violently upon the poorer, suburban areas of towns.[40] But there are exceptions. The Cambridge evidence suggests that in 1605 and 1638 wills fail to reflect the high mortality indicated in the parish registers, although the outbreak of plague that hit hardest in 1605 actually began in 1604, a year which saw a notable if not remarkable rise in the number of wills proved, and the failure of these numbers to continue to rise would be compatible with the tendency for the wealthier urban residents to flee to safer havens once it was clear that plague was established. Plague was without doubt again the culprit in 1638, producing crisis mortality ratios of 2.0 in Great St Andrew, 2.6 in Barnwell and 3.6 in All Saints, and this crisis would have escaped notice if will evidence had been relied upon alone. The devastating outbreak of 1665–6 is only reflected in the probate data for the latter year, possibly a product of the time lag between death and probate in such a busy period for the ecclesiastical courts.

For Colchester, the 1586 crisis does not show up in the will evidence, while that of 1602–4, which continued in the parish of St Mary at the Walls into 1605, is only weakly represented. This was a period of extended crisis mortality across the town, the product of endemic plague, with mortality ratios as high as four and five in some parishes in particular years, the severity of which could not possibly be established from will evidence alone. Analysis of individual parishes reveals that the crisis of 1586 actually extended from 1586–8, and as it coincided with poor harvests and evidence of famine in some parts of the country, its failure to find reflection in the will evidence might suggest a similar cause here, particularly as the corporation were moved to raise a forced loan for the purchase of Baltic rye in September

---

[39] Goose, 'Economic and social aspects', Table 4.17, p.310.
[40] Slack 'Introduction', p.8; Goose, 'Household size and structure', pp.354–6. This confirms the conclusion reached by Takahashi from his analysis of wills proved in the PCC, Consistories of Ely and Worcester and Archdeaconry of Leicester: 'Number of wills proved', pp.200–4.

1586.[41] High mortality in both 1586 and 1588 was, however, particularly a feature of the parish of St Mary at the Walls, not one of the town's poorer parishes, while neither the seasonality of deaths nor the trends in baptisms conform to Appleby's criteria for the possible existence of famine, and high mortality may have been due to plague, or to a combination of plague and 'the burning ague', or one of the other fevers reported to be prevalent in these years.[42]

In Reading the crisis of 1582 is not reflected in the number of wills proved, although it is quite clear in the parish register for St Mary, with a particularly sharp rise in mortality in September.[43] The harvest was good in 1582, however, and the existence of plague in London again points the finger at this most common culprit. Closer inspection of the parish registers reveals why the number of wills proved is low in 1608, despite clear evidence in the registers of a high death rate. The high mortality evident for the town as a whole by 1608 actually began in St Lawrence and St Mary in 1607, a year which did see a small increase of probate activity, and this is again compatible with the tendency for the wealthy to flee plague-affected towns, although it might also be the product of the migration of the disease to the poorer parish of St Giles by the latter year. On the other hand, mortality in both St Lawrence and St Mary in 1607 was very heavily concentrated in March and April, a seasonality far from typical of plague, while the more severe mortality which afflicted the poorer parish of St Giles in 1608, a year when plague was noted to be active in the town, shows the characteristic late summer/early autumn peak. This was most probably a 'mixed' crisis, therefore, the early stages of which were less socially selective than the second phase, producing the contrasting trend in probates and parish registers between the two years.[44]

In some years will evidence appears to indicate high mortality which is not reflected in the parish registers. These include 1569, 1617 and 1661 in Cambridge, but closer inspection of the registers for individual parishes reveals high mortality in many parts of the town in both 1617 and 1661, just falling short of a crisis level for the town as a whole. For Colchester the years 1582, 1593, 1616, 1648 and 1651 all produced significantly above average numbers of wills proved, but no crisis

---

[41] CRO, T/A 465/122, Assembly Book 12 September 1586.

[42] Goose, 'Economic and social aspects', pp.318–19; Appleby, *Famine in Tudor and Stuart England*, pp.8–9; Slack, *Impact of plague*, pp.73–5.

[43] It is somewhat odd that Slack omits to list this as a crisis in Reading, although the town is included amongst his tabulations: *Impact of plague*, Table 3.4, p.62.

[44] Cf. Slack, *Impact of plague*, p.67, where it is argued that this was an extended outbreak of plague.

mortality ratio as high as 1.5 across the town as a whole. 1582–3 was, however, a year of high mortality in two parishes, while in 1593 St Mary at the Walls experienced mortality 1.5 times above the nine-year average. There is no indication in the registers of high mortality in 1616, while by 1648, the year of the siege of Colchester, the registers cease to be of any use. Because of this the will evidence again comes into its own in the later seventeenth century, providing graphic evidence of the *relative* scale of mortality in 1665–6, but with just 152 wills proved in 1665–7 (83 of these in 1666) little indication of its true magnitude. Contemporary reports fill the gap, the death roll being variously given as 5,259 for the 17 months between August 1665 and December 1666, of which 4,731 were from plague, and 5,034 for the 67 weeks from September 1665 to 21 December 1666, of which 4,526 were from plague.[45] Roughly half of the town's population died in this outbreak, rendering it in proportional terms the most destructive epidemic experienced by any large provincial town in the early modern period, and under 3 per cent of these left a will. In Reading it is more difficult to identify peaks and troughs because of the lower number of wills proved and generally flatter trend, though the figures for 1607, 1618 and 1661 appear significantly above average. The crisis of 1607–8 has already been discussed, while in 1617 and in 1661–2 registers for one and two individual parishes respectively indicate mortality significantly above average. Wills, therefore, often provide indications of higher than usual levels of mortality that are not apparent from parish registers across a town as a whole, but may be confined to a particular parish or group of parishes within it.

Conclusion

As a source for the determination of levels of fertility wills have profound shortcomings, but this is equally true of simple aggregate analysis of parish registers. Although suffering from serious social and sex selectivity probate data does, however, have distinct advantages in terms of chronological coverage. The results of its analysis presented here correspond well with the trends in growth and in natural increase or decrease revealed for these three towns, in broad terms at least, while Reading stands out in both sets of data, exhibiting very different demographic characteristics from Cambridge or Colchester in the early-seventeenth century. In this period the figures for average numbers of

[45] British Library, Stowe MSS, 840, ff 44–5; Essex Record Office, D/P 200/1/6 (unfoliated). See also Goose and Cooper, *Tudor and Stuart Colchester*, p.68.

children and sons per male in Reading stand substantially above those for Cambridge in particular, reinforcing the idea of a variety of urban demographic experiences rather than a simple conformity to a conventionally accepted pattern, and perhaps indicating that differences in fertility may have contributed as well as variations in mortality. To measure mortality, it is clear that parish register data is far superior to will evidence, allowing levels and trends in mortality to be established with a high degree of confidence for most years, besides providing information on burial seasonality that can help to elucidate probable causes of death. Although major leaps in mortality do commonly show up in the probate evidence, there are occasions when mortality crises could not have been identified from wills alone. Nevertheless, the fluctuations in numbers of wills proved in individual years between these three towns do appear to correspond to the extent to which they experienced mortality crises as indicated by parish register data. Furthermore, by dint of its social selectivity, the very *failure* of will evidence to reflect high mortality in a particular year as shown in parish registers may help to shed light on the causes of that mortality by inviting closer analysis. Most importantly of all, wills provide evidence for the period before parish registration began, for the mid-sixteenth century when register survival is poor, can invariably be relied upon to plug gaps in parish registration, and are particularly useful in the period of the Civil Wars and Interregnum when parish register evidence declines drastically in quality, as well as for the later seventeenth century when registration was again often poor, in some towns at least.

Urban demography is a difficult undertaking, for the available evidence is patchy in coverage, highly variable in quality and often difficult to interpret. The more sophisticated techniques of demographic analysis are extremely difficult to apply in an urban context, but even aggregate methods have severe drawbacks in the context of populations that are highly mobile, open and commonly subject to unusually high levels of volatility, particularly with respect to death rates. The best strategy, therefore, in any attempt to elucidate the structures and processes of early modern urban populations is to use as wide a range of evidence as possible, and this will involve sources that allow the calculation of population sizes at fixed points in time such as tax returns and ecclesiastical censuses, parish register analysis and—for all its evident shortcomings—probate evidence as well, not in place of these other sources but as a valuable supplement to them.

11

Long-Term Rural Credit in Sixteenth and Seventeenth-Century England: the Evidence of Probate Accounts

PETER SPUFFORD

Economic and social historians in England have been using probate inventories extensively since 1945 for a wide variety of purposes.[1] Amongst other things they have been intrigued by the large number of debts in these inventories owed to the deceased at his death. This has aroused suspicion of the size of the network of rural debt and credit in seventeenth-century England.[2] Unfortunately, these inventories give a one-sided picture of debt, for they normally only give the debts due to the deceased, not those due *by* him or her.[3] In 1590 Henry Swinburne, in the first edition of his standard *Briefe treatise of testaments and last willes*, laid down that it was correct practice to omit the debts owed by the deceased from his inventory, and that there could be risks to the accountant if they were included. Inventories frequently distinguish 'sperate' debts, which the

[1] This is a condensed and revised translation of my 'Les liens du crédit au village dans l'Angleterre au XVIIe siècle'. I would like to thank Dr Amy Louise Erickson, Dr Jacqueline Bower, Mr Matthew Brett and Mrs Nesta Evans for their help in the research on which it is based, which was funded by grants from the ESRC and the Leverhulme Trust. For more details of that research see the essay in this volume by Dr Erickson. I would also like to thank my wife, Prof. Margaret Spufford, for her very useful advice. She is particularly pleased that I have at last written the paper on 'Money lending in rural society' that she and the late Dr Jack Ravensdale said that they were intending to write, when *Contrasting communities* was published in 1974, p.80 n.48. It is a footnote that has given her a lot of trouble over the last quarter century.
[2] Holderness 'Credit in a rural community'; Holderness, 'Credit in English rural society; Holderness, 'Clergy as money-lenders', pp.195–210; and Spufford, 'Limitations of the probate inventory'.
[3] Holderness was consciously impeded by this in his innovatory work on credit in rural society, 'Credit in a rural community', pp.94–5, 108.

appraisers *believed* could be recovered, and 'desperate' or hopeless debts, which they did not believe could be recovered.

The courts, when they made grants of probate or letters of administration, required that the executor (or administrator) should report how he, or more commonly, she, had carried out the responsibility of handling the goods of the deceased.[4] Accounts, therefore, once existed as commonly as inventories, with duplicate copies in the hands of the courts and of the accountants who had rendered them. These accounts, where they have survived, provide the other half of the picture, for they give the debts due by the deceased. It is not surprising that the accountants' copies have disappeared, like private copies of wills, inventories and letters of administration. What is much more surprising is that so few of the court copies have survived, unlike wills and inventories.

Where these accounts do survive they give fascinating details of what happened after a death. They always begin by giving the total of the probate inventory value, the sum for which the executor, or administrator, was charged with rendering an account. These accounts often reveal how complete or defective the inventory had been. Occasionally extra items, more debts to be collected for example, were added in, or the goods sold for over the estimated value. More often the inventory value was reduced for a variety of reasons. Sometimes the goods had simply been over-valued, but this happened sufficiently infrequently to give us greater confidence in inventory valuations than many historians have previously shown. The most common reason why the inventory value was too high was simply that debts due to the deceased could not be collected.[5] 'Desperate' debts were normally included in the inventory total, and thus in the 'charge' at the beginning of the account, even if the appraisers did not think that they were collectable. Although a competent and aggressive executor could often get more debts than the appraisers believed possible when dividing them between 'sperate' and 'desperate', it was more often the other way round. However, most importantly for our present purposes, these accounts reveal the extent of the debts owed *by* the deceased, which were actually paid out by the accountants.

[4] Sheehan, *Will in medieval England*, p.218, suggested that the nature of this obligation evolved in the third quarter of the thirteenth century.

[5] We found evidence of over-valuation of the moveables in the inventory in only 1,268 accounts, or 4 per cent of some 34,000 that we examined in over 30 record offices. 243 over-valuations were caused by desperate debts, which had been included in the inventory, but proved not to be collectable by the administrator or executor.

East Kent

The most significant group of accounts to survive in England are those of the consistory and archdeaconry courts of the Diocese of Canterbury, which dealt with probate business for the eastern half of Kent.[6] Around 60 per cent of the population of Kent lived in this part of the county, perhaps some 24,000 households in all.[7] This essay discusses some results of our investigation into rural debt, particularly derived from the extraordinary richness of the Kent accounts, together with some examples of the material to illustrate what can be discovered. The 13,565 east Kent probate accounts surviving from the period from 1569 to 1740 reveal that practically all the individuals concerned left payments outstanding at their deaths for such purposes as rents or tithes, rates or taxes, or wages to servants. However, I was not looking for *this* sort of indebtedness, but for deliberate borrowing. Even sums paid out by the accountants specifically described as 'debts' do not always indicate deliberate borrowing, for so much ordinary business was carried out on credit. 11,009 of these east Kent accounts reveal that the deceased left debts, described as such, to be paid. Only 2,577, barely a sixth of them, record no such debts. If the example of those caught at the moment of death was at all typical of those still alive, then it was patently normal in east Kent in the seventeenth century to be living at least in part on other people's money. The median number of debts recorded was three. It was as uncommon to leave more than nine debts to be paid as it was to leave none at all. Some, however, were indebted to quite a considerable number of people at the time of their deaths. Amongst the Kent accounts, 568 people (just over one in 20) left over 20 debts for their executors or administrators to pay off. In this Kent was not atypical. In the country as a whole we found 1,674 people, out of around 34,000, who left 20 or more debts to be paid (again approximately one account in every 20 examined), including 184 people with 50 or more debts, and even 15 who left 100 or more debts.

The names of the creditors whom the accountant paid are virtually always given, except sometimes when they were owed very small sums, which have been grouped together. Unfortunately the reasons for the debts are not always given in the same way. In fact, in the accounts we have looked at with close attention, unspecified debts were much more

---

[6] These are now in the Centre for Kentish Studies (hereafter CKS), formerly the Kent Archives Office, at Maidstone.

[7] I am indebted to Dr Bower for this estimate, derived from the records of the Compton Census of 1676.

common than debts whose origin was specified. We believe that most, but not all, of these unspecified debts were for goods supplied to the dead man or woman, although in surprisingly few cases were any of the debts specifically explained as debts for goods supplied to the deceased.[8] This is 'surprisingly few' in view of what we know of the normality of supplying goods on credit, often extended credit, in late-seventeenth-century England. All published volumes of probate inventories provide numerous examples of tradesmen who have died with outstanding payments due to them for goods they have supplied on credit. The probate inventory and account of Sylvester Widmere (1668), a mercer of Marlow in Buckinghamshire, shows that he had supplied goods on credit to over 230 named customers, and had himself similarly purchased on credit from his own suppliers the goods that he supplied on credit.[9]

Most dramatically, Muldrew when working on the records of the Guildhall Court of King's Lynn found that, over a four-year period, 1683–6, all, or almost all, of the 2,000 or so households in the small town of Lynn were involved in at least the initial stages of litigation over debt. The great majority of pleadings concerned unpaid sales credit that had been extended, often orally, on goods bought and sold.[10] It seems that the origins of the large number of unspecified debts were simply not specified because it was taken for granted that creditors were normally those who had supplied goods on credit, and since these were normally oral arrangements, there were no written papers to quote.

Although most debts paid by accountants were informal, and probably oral in origin, in 3,667 east Kent accounts (just over a quarter of the whole number surviving, and a third of those with debts), there were debts involved for which the deceased had been bound by written obligations, 'bonds', 'bills', or 'specialty'. The largest group of these were described as 'bonds' and were the normal written method of securing a loan in the seventeenth century. Among the east Kent accounts there were 3,474 (26 per cent of the whole number surviving), in which the accountant expressly said that she or he was paying a 'bond'. Yet more formal than ordinary bonds were recognisances of

---

[8] Only 62 of an initial trial run of 344 Archdeaconry Court of Canterbury probate accounts for 1671–5, worked on by hand in preparation for using the computer, contained debts specifically explained as debts for goods supplied to the deceased. CKS, PRC2/35/1–270 and PRC2/36/1–72.

[9] Reed, *Buckinghamshire*, pp.21–46.

[10] Muldrew, 'Credit and the courts', pp.23–38. A major book on credit, particularly short-term sales credit, in early modern England is currently in the press.

debt registered or enrolled in staple courts under the Statute Merchant of 1285. Although this had been the most common form of formal obligation in the later middle ages, many fewer were entered into in the seventeenth century, and only a few accounts referred to such enrolled debts.[11] Less formal than bonds were other written records of debt, for example simple 'bills' or entries in merchant books. These were known generically as 'specialties'. In 355 of the east Kent accounts the accountants said they were paying debts 'on specialty'. In 193 cases out of the 355 these were accounts in which there were no references to bonds, but in 162 accounts there were also references to bonds. Least formal of all were loans made for which there was no 'specialty or writing'. These should have been the last to be paid, according to Henry Swinburne, who explained in 1590 that executors should pay the debts of the deceased according to a strict order—firstly debts to the prince, secondly recognisances upon statute merchant, thirdly debts arising from court judgements, fourthly obligations (on bond), fifthly debts due upon simple bills, or merchant books, or other like specialties, and finally, if at all, those for which the creditors have no specialty or writing. In the fourth edition, in 1677, his editor amplified all these categories, and pointed out that it was dangerous to pay debts without specialty or writing, except for servants' wages, until all other creditors had been satisfied.[12]

Other groups of surviving accounts, smaller than that from east Kent, show much the same proportions. According to Erickson, of all the 165 Northamptonshire accounts (1665–85), 47, again just over a quarter, have debts described as on bond, specialty or mortgage. Where she was able to follow up the unspecified debts in probate accounts, a few turned out, rather surprisingly, to be for loans on bond, as well as those for goods supplied.[13] In other words the visible quarter of the accounts in which the accountant declared that the debt was a consequence of deliberate borrowing is only a minimum. Loans made upon bonds were thus a normal part of everyday life and the way that it was financed in the countryside and small towns of eastern Kent in the seventeenth century, as in Restoration Northamptonshire.

Detailed examination of a group of 75 accounts of the 1670s from

---

[11] For example, when Ellenor Latham accounted in 1622 for the moveables of her late husband George, a gentleman of Belton All Saints in Lincolnshire, his debts included £100 that he had borrowed from Richard Pishey, gent. of London 'on Statute' and £2,000 from the widowed Lady Francis Pyerpoynt, also 'on Statute'. Lincolnshire Record Office (hereafter LRO) Ad/Ac/8/29.

[12] Swinburne, *Briefe treatise* (1590), Part 6, Chapter 16.

[13] Personal communication.

the Diocese of Canterbury revealed 37 in which the accountants were paying off a total of 158 formal bonds. Thirty-eight of them were bonds for £10, while 14 were for sums under £5; the smallest was for 11s. Only seven in this group were for over £50, including two for £100 and the largest for £150. Formal bonds were frequently for round sums of money. Other batches of bonds examined produced similar results. The range of formal loans in any one of the 47 Northamptonshire accounts was from £5 to £264, with a median of £50. Men, or their families, could be ruined by very small bonds. When John Aves, of Chippenham in Cambridgeshire, died in 1676 his goods were appraised at £9 6s. 2d., but, since he owed a baker of a neighbouring parish £4 10s. on bond, his household possessions were put up for auction by the parish. His widow purchased the cradle in the sale.[14]

For England as a whole, in 870 accounts the accountants said that they were paying debts on 'specialty'. So large a bulk of these were from before the Civil Wars that it would seem that there was a change of terminology in the middle of the century.[15] The term 'specialty' has only been noticed in three accounts after 1689. Since many 'specialties' were 'bills', I was tempted to include them, with 'bonds', as 'obligations', in my calculations.[16] I have, however, treated both them and mortgages separately.[17]

Probate accounts can also give some indication of the way that this sort of borrowing had grown and at what period. Probate accounts survive for east Kent in sufficiently large numbers, nearly 12,000 in all, between 1582 and 1641 and between 1665 and 1684, to be worth breaking down by decades. More than 1,700 accounts survive from many of these decades. The global proportion of 26 per cent of east Kent accounts which show accountants paying off borrowing on bonds and bills, when broken down over time, shows a very striking growth in borrowing between the 1580s and 1620s. After this period of growth, there followed 60 years in which there was a more or less static proportion of accounts in which accountants paid off bonds and bills, as Table 11.1 shows. Bower, in her work on Kentish yeoman, has found that yeomen borrowed more commonly than other rural inhabitants in

---

[14] Spufford, *Contrasting communities,* pp.210, 339.

[15] Of those that can be dated, 656 examples of debts 'on specialty' came from 1642 or earlier, and 151 from 1661 or after. In a sample of accounts from the 1620s there seems to have been no perceptible difference in the scale of the debts 'on specialty' and of the loans on bond.

[16] In 1677 the editor of the fourth edition of Swinburne's *Briefe treatise,* Part 6, Chapter 16, explained that 'bills' are also 'of the nature of obligations'.

[17] Mortgages rarely came into the probate accounting process. See below p.221.

Table 11.1 Probate accounts from the Diocese of Canterbury showing evidence of deliberate formal borrowing on bonds and bills

Decade	Number of accounts	% with formal debts	Yeomen		
			Decade	Number of accounts	% with formal debts
1582–1591	717	6	1581–1590	36	0
1592–1601	1,700	10	1591–1600	65	3
1602–1611	1,281	16	1601–1610	18	11
1612–1621	1,865	26	1611–1620	61	25
1622–1631	1,700	34	1621–1630	56	45
1632–1641	1,720	30	1631–1640	49	49

Civil War and Interregnum. Local probate courts temporarily suspended

Decade	Number of accounts	% with formal debts	Decade	Number of accounts	% with formal debts
			1661–1670	150	47
1665–1674	1,358	31	1671–1680	190	42
1675–1684	1,494	33	1681–1690	117	48

Note: Nearly 12,000 in all, 1582–1641 and 1665–84. The same figures are displayed as a histogram in Spufford, 'Les liens du crédit', p.1364.

east Kent. When over 30 per cent of the general population of those for whom probate accounts survive had borrowed on bond, over 40 per cent of yeomen had done so. The rise in borrowing by yeomen took place at the same time as their neighbours.[18]

Interest rates

In the 1680s Samuel Pepys, the diarist and secretary of Charles II's navy, put together a large collection of cheap print.[19] He included *The Country-Man's Counsellor or Every Man made his own Lawyer* amongst his selection of small practical works.[20] This was a 24-page octavo work aimed at a very wide, and even poor, rural market. It was marketed at 2d., the price of a loaf of bread. It gives the forms of a Latin bond, and of an English bill obligatory, both for loans of ten pounds. Ten pounds was a relatively slight sum in the 1680s, when, according to inventory

---

[18] Bower, 'Kent yeoman', pp.149–63.
[19] Now housed in Magdalene College, Cambridge. See Spufford, *Small books*, pp.130–55.
[20] Bound in his second volume of 'Penny Merriments', pp.783–806. The edition that he collected is internally dateable to around 1686.

values in Kent, it was less than the value of two cows with their calves, or three acres of wheat ready to harvest.

The *Country-Man's Counsellor* explained how interest payments were to be expressed in such formal bonds. The *Country-Man's Counsellor* said that, when drawing up a bond, the sum to be repaid should include the interest. Some of the handful of cancelled bonds which survive with the accounts appear to follow this advice. The account exhibited in 1589 by his widow, of her administration of the moveable goods of William Davis, a chapman of Winslow in Buckinghamshire, had two cancelled bonds attached to it for irregular sums. They were for £28 4s. and for £21 16s. 10d. respectively.[21]

On the other hand, the pattern of making bonds for the round sums actually borrowed, is the one that very frequently appears in accounts. Consequently, in many accounts the interest, forbearance or 'use money', is mentioned separately, if any was outstanding at death. We can therefore sometimes deduce the rate of interest involved in bonds, when they were paid off by the probate accountants.

The rate of interest in England dropped continuously from the sixteenth to the eighteenth century. The rate paid on bonds was generally, but not always, at the legal maximum. By the Usury Act of 1571, which re-legalised the payment of interest, the permitted maximum was 10 per cent.[22] In most of the accounts of the next four decades, from which a rate of interest can be deduced, it was indeed 10 per cent. However in one account, of 1599, an illegal 14 per cent was charged on a bond, but in another, of 1611, only a generous 4 per cent was charged. The next Usury Act, of 1623–4, in force from 24 June 1625, reduced the maximum rate of interest for new bonds to 8 per cent, and an accountant duly paid 8 per cent in 1641. The Commonwealth Usury Act of 1651, confirmed by the Restoration Usury Act of 1660, reduced the maximum once more, this time to 6 per cent.[23] Again the accounts of the second half of the seventeenth

---

[21] Hertfordshire Record Office, ASA 25/4807. At the time of his death William Davis was keeping a shop at Winslow from which he sold not only linens and other textiles, but also grocery, small haberdashery, and mercery, including hats.

[22] An Act of 1545, 37 Hen. VIII, c.9, enacted because of 'ambiguities', had already specified a maximum legal rate of interest of 10 per cent, 'tenne pounds in the hundred for one hole yere' for both loan or 'forebearance' of money, and for mortgages. It had, however, been repealed by 5 & 6 Ed. VI, c.20, an act that forbade the taking of any interest at all after 1 May 1552, since it was 'by the worde of God utterly prohibited'. The act of 1571, 13 Eliz. I, c.8, returned to the 10 per cent of 1545.

[23] Usury Act of 5 August 1651, in force from 29 September. See Firth and Rait, *Acts and ordinances*; 12 Ch. II, c.13.

century show that bonds generally bore interest at the maximum legal rate. The 158 bonds referred to in the group of accounts of the 1670s, carried interest at 6 per cent per annum. This is apparent since the accountants were frequently paying off arrears of interest as well as the principal. This was normally the interest for six months which makes it look as if interest was usually then paid half-yearly. I have only noticed two accounts, in 1671 and 1683, that reveal bonds which bore interest above the legal maximum, at 8.75 per cent and 10 per cent respectively. In the seventeenth century rates were even lower in the Netherlands, as English observers repeatedly complained, giving Dutch merchants an enviable advantage.[24]

Probate accounts, like inventories, give no indication of real property. It was wealth in the form of houses and land which provided the ultimate security which enabled some rather than others to borrow on bonds. There was normally no specific security offered, although the credit-worthiness of borrowers could be bolstered by guarantors. This was a cause of uncertainty to Alice Bromfield when administering the goods of Daniel Bromfield of Daresbury in Cheshire in 1665, as she could not render a complete account since she believed that he was 'suerty' for several bonds and bills to the value of at least £200, although she had not been asked to make any payments.[25] If obligations could not be met by the borrowers themselves, the sureties were called on, sometimes with ruinous results.[26] The important thing was that such bonds were enforceable by law, and that the courts were prepared to enforce payment, under penalties, including imprisonment for debt.

These bonds were not mortgages, which were normally larger and were predominantly secured on real property. As such, they did not normally come into the probate accounting process. However, leases, cattle and other goods were occasionally mortgaged, and other accountants used money from moveables to pay off mortgages on houses and land rather than sell them. Mortgages are mentioned in only 70 out of the 13,586 Kent accounts, while under one per cent of the

[24] Spufford, 'Access to credit', pp.305, and 317–19.
[25] Cheshire Record Office, Daniel Bromfield W.C. 1664.
[26] John Egerton, first Earl of Bridgewater, for most of his adult life a very rich man, died overwhelmed with debt in 1649, because he had guaranteed the borrowings of his son-in-law William Courteen, whose two ships sent to the East Indies were captured by the Dutch in 1643. His son, the second earl, had to mortgage his estates extensively to satisfy the bond-holders, and it was not until 1673, 24 years later, that he was free of the burden of debt, over £71,000, inherited from his father, most of which was a consequence of Courteen's disastrous voyage. Hamilton, 'Bridgewater debts', pp.217–29.

accounts from the whole of England mention them, of which the majority date from after 1685.

Reasons for borrowing

There seem to have been a number of occasions in the life-cycle when those engaged in farming would be likely to borrow. First of all in early manhood when setting up, as the example of William Wraight shows. He was still a young unmarried yeoman when he died. He was primarily a sheep farmer with around 130 sheep in his inventory plus their lambs. His moveable goods, mainly the sheep, came to £112 10s., and two-thirds of the value of his livestock had been financed by borrowing on bond.[27] Following on from this, further borrowings would allow for increases in the scale of farming, so that additional land could be taken on, either purchased or leased.

Borrowing, however, was not always for positive investment and advancement. It could take place to stave off ruin, either because of individual fecklessness or incompetence, or because of unforeseeable calamities, ranging from individual illness to general disasters like the harvest failures of the 1590s.

Much later in the life-cycle family expenditure could necessitate renewed borrowing. There was not only borrowing for dowries, but also for sons, either to apprentice them, or to set them up as farmers in their own right. For example one Lincolnshire yeoman, Thomas Appleby of Thornton Curtis, set up his four sons and a daughter with cash gifts of £150 each in his lifetime, but after his death in 1664 a fifth son had to be paid his promised portion by his widowed mother.[28] Finally the terms of a will, by which a father required the elder son who inherited the land to pay out sums to set up his brothers, often imposed on him the obligation of borrowing, although not necessarily at once. Money for stock and equipment on the one hand and for dowries on the other were also the two greatest occasions of borrowing in rural England in the seventeenth century.

Whether or not the indebtedness was permanent there were often times in the process of executing a will or administering the moveables of an intestate when money was short. Henry Harnett, a married yeoman, with an adult son to act as his executor, was involved in mixed farming. His very substantial house had a milkhouse, two butteries and

---

[27] William Wraight of Warhorne in Kent Wills, CKS, PRC17/76/338; Inventory. PRC11/49/215; Account PRC2/41/111.

[28] Spufford, 'Limitations of the probate inventory', p.170.

a cheesehouse. His house had, besides these, and the hall, parlour, kitchen, brewhouse and granary, no fewer than six chambers, including one each for the men-servants and the maids. This scale of farming, and this standard of living, was maintained by heavy borrowing. He had borrowed no less than £400 on bonds at 6 per cent, half of it from relatives, and his son had to borrow a further £100 on bond, for a short time, to cope with winding up his father's affairs, which were not in a good state.[29] In 1610 Elizabeth Warren, the widow of a Cambridge vintner, had also to borrow when administering her dead husband's complicated estate. In conjunction with Raphe Warren, a London grocer, she signed and sealed bonds with very short terms, two for £70 and two for £40. Two of these were conditional penal bonds, by which the debtors agreed to pay a large penalty, in these cases the sum owed was doubled, if they were late in making their repayment.[30] Such bonds were already under attack in 1610, as courts more and more refused to enforce such large penalties since they could be interpreted as breaching the limits of usury legislation.[31] Penal bonds continued to be written, however, for much of the seventeenth century.

Lenders

The evidence from inventories suggests that lenders were much less numerous than borrowers. Trinder and Cox in a study of 846 probate inventories made between 1660 and 1750, in the Ironbridge area of Shropshire, noted that 92 inventories contained references to money out upon bond, out at interest, or which for some other reason they were led to think had been invested.[32] In other words only 11 per cent of this group of Shropshire people were lending on bond or other formal instruments at the same period that 30 per cent of the Kent people for whom accounts survive in Kent were borrowing in this way. Unless there was a marked difference between Shropshire and Kent, this would suggest that borrowers on formal instruments were three times more common than the lenders.

The only single clear group of lenders suggested by our accounts was the members of the borrowers' own families. Examples from seventeenth-century Kent include John Swaineland, whose goods were administered by Edward Prescott. Edward and John's wives were sisters.

[29] Henry Harnett of St Lawrence in Thanet: Inventory, PRC1 1/49/15; Account, PRC2/4 1/55.
[30] Cambridge University Library (hereafter CUL), VC Acc 1/57.
[31] Melton, *Sir Robert Clayton*, pp.52–3, 132–3.
[32] Trinder and Cox, *Yeomen and colliers*, pp.18–19.

Edward's account of John's goods included repayment of £300 which John had borrowed on bond from George Young of Canterbury, the brother of the two wives. The account of the goods of Richard Tritton, who had married Edward Prescott's sister, reveals that Edward was his principal creditor, and that he had also borrowed £7 from his father-in-law John Prescott.[33] Holderness, in an analysis of 42 Lincolnshire accounts, found that 40 per cent of lenders could be identified as relatives by blood or marriage.[34] The importance of family members in providing investment has also been stressed by those working from inventory and other evidence. For example, the diary of Isaac Archer, the post-Restoration minister of Chippenham in Cambridgeshire, reveals the importance of family members for him. As a young man he was constantly in financial trouble and was bailed out by loans from aunts without heirs, while later in life he was himself a lender, on bond, to others including his son-in-law.[35] Loans within the family had all sorts of advantages besides security and there could be a strong charitable element both in lending or in borrowing—although this rarely went as far as Mr Smith of Clare College, Cambridge University, who began dictating his will in 1633 with the instruction: 'There be 2 bonds in my Studdy betwixt my father in Law & mee, I will that they be both burnt'.[36] The importance of the family in providing investment in seventeenth-century England merits detailed study. One of the problems for historians is to be able to recognise who are kin. Cressy has made us aware how wide the network of kinship was that was recognised at the time, which in most cases will be invisible to us.[37] It has recently been re-emphasised by Spufford and Takahashi.[38]

Apart from that, most of the lenders in my sample were designated with the appellation 'Mr', which, in the 1680s, still implied an element of social deference in England. Many, but not all of these were gentlemen investing surplus rents, not merely in the acquisition of additional land, but also in lending on bonds at 6 per cent. The inventory of Robert Weedon Esq., of Fawley, Bucks., drawn up in 1703 illustrates the activity of one such gentleman in lending money. At his death he had 35 loans outstanding. Two of the largest sums that he had lent, for £500 and £300 respectively, were formally secured by

---

[33] CKS, PRC2/24/85, and PRC2/24/148. I must thank Dr Bower for drawing my attention to these two interlocked examples.

[34] Holderness, 'Widows in pre-industrial society', p.441.

[35] Storey, *Two East Anglian diaries*.

[36] CUL, VCC A/C 2/71.

[37] Cressy, 'Kinship and kin interaction', pp.38–69.

[38] Spufford and Takahashi, 'Families', pp.379–411.

mortgages, while five of the smallest sums, four of £5 and one of ten
guineas, were merely on 'notes under hand', informal IOU's. In
between were 27 bonds and bills. The three largest of these, running up
to £200, did not reach the level of the two mortgages. It was
presumably not thought necessary, at this level, to bind the borrowers'
lands into the credit arrangements. The two smallest, for £10 and £5,
overlapped the informal notes. The bond was the preferred form of
formal obligation for sums in between £20 and £100. These bonds
were generally for round numbers of pounds, £20, £30, £50, £80,
£100, with interest not included in the sum to be repaid, but additional
to it. What is particularly interesting about this inventory is that it gives
the dates at which the bonds were drawn up. Like mortgages,
borrowing on bond was a long-term way of raising capital, and the
lender was looking for a long-term income from interest. Although 15
of Robert Weedon's loans had been made in the five years before he
died, 18 were over ten years old, including four over 20 years old, and
two over 30 years old. He had been investing since the 1680s to gain an
income for the rest of his life.[39]

In a very few cases in our sample we are aware that the lenders were
among the borrowers' landlords. In most of them, however, the lists of
names of landlords and those of lenders do *not* coincide. The clergy must
be considered along with the gentry,[40] and it is not yet clear how many
of these lenders designated as 'Mr' will turn out to be clergy. The diary
of Ralph Josselin, like that of Isaac Archer, reveals him as a lender.
Other studies have emphasised the role of widows as investors,[41] and of
'aged' yeomen and even husbandmen who, having divested themselves
of their farming goods and stock, laid out their money on loans and
mortgages and, it is fair to assume, lived off the interest.[42]

This does not exhaust the range of rural investors and it is very clear
that whenever anyone in rural England had money to hand they did not
leave it lying idle. Guardians of minors put portions and dowries out at
interest for their charges. In 1619 Edward Brewster, the guardian of the
two daughters of Symon Holte, a husbandman of Burgh le Marsh in
Lincolnshire, invested part of the £180 balance of the account for them
at 10 per cent, the then maximum legal rate of interest.[43] When they

---

[39] Public Record Office, PROB5, 1018, printed in Reed, *Buckinghamshire probate
inventories*, pp.280–4.
[40] Holderness 'Clergy as moneylenders'.
[41] Holderness. 'Widows in pre-industrial society', pp.435–42; see also Chapter
16, below, pp.318–21.
[42] Spufford, *Contrasting communities*, p.80.
[43] LRO, Ad/Ac/15/1.

had charge of their own money, slightly older orphaned girls put their own dowry money out at interest in the same way.[44]

In addition there was a certain amount of investing by townsmen in the surrounding countryside, particularly by those who, by the nature of their occupation, had a widespread clientele. For example Israel Jacob of Canterbury, who died in 1692, lent on a large scale in rural Kent. He was an apothecary, one of a family of apothecaries and physicians, probably of Flemish origin. His marked success in business presumably generated the surplus cash, which he was frequently able to invest in the country. His activities have been picked up by Bower in probate accounts from 1660 onwards. They occur frequently from the 1670s to his death. He appears in the accounts as a provider of medical attentions to the dying, and a supplier of 'Naples biskett' and other refreshments for funerals, as well as a lender on bond.[45]

Contacts

The next puzzle is to determine how borrower and lender were put in touch with one another. The necessary contacts for investing within the family need no explanation, nor do those within the hinterland of a market town. Much, but not all, of the borrowing of John Formeston of Redbourn in Hertfordshire can be explained in these ways. When his widow Jane accounted in 1637 for the moveables of her late husband, she had paid off sums that he had borrowed on bond from a variety of people. Not only had he borrowed £80 from his grand relative Thomas Formeston, citizen of London, but also smaller sums from humbler neighbours in the same part of Hertfordshire: £20 from Adam Hobbs a weaver of Flamstead, £10 from Nicholas Slowe a husbandman of Ayot St Laurence, and £25 from Richard Beomond of Studham, just into Bedfordshire. The contacts for all these loans are easily explicable, but Jane had also repaid £70 borrowed from another London citizen and £10 from Roger Challenor of distant Shrewsbury.[46]

Other connections were also useful for borrowing and lending, such as membership of small religious or ethnic groups. Marsh has found evidence for lending between members of the Family of Love in Cambridgeshire at the end of the sixteenth century and the beginning of the seventeenth.[47] Bower has used a number of accounts that reveal

---

[44] For example Margaret Graves of Willingham in Cambridgeshire did so, Spufford, *Contrasting communities,* p.142 n.66.
[45] Bower, 'Probate accounts'.
[46] Hertfordshire Record Office A25/4925.
[47] Marsh, *Family of Love.*

the extent of investment between members of the small General Baptist congregation in Dover, and within the alien community of Dutch and Flemish immigrants based on Sandwich.[48]

A sizeable amount of investment nevertheless took place between parties who had no personal contact immediately evident to the historian. Brokers certainly existed. They were most often scriveners, who, like notaries elsewhere in Europe, combined loan-broking with conveyancing.[49] Holderness has only discovered isolated examples of country attorneys in Lincolnshire, who acted, like their London counterparts, as brokers, arranging loans both on mortgage and on bonds.[50] In 1956 Pressnell had already identified the arrangers of credit, the money-scrivening attorneys, as one of the main sources of country bankers in the eighteenth century, along with wholesalers and yarn masters, whose distinctive contribution to country banking was the ability to remit funds to and from London.[51]

Conclusion

It is clear that Kentish, and indeed English, rural society at large was penetrated through and through with habits of formal borrowing and lending in the period immediately before the emergence of a country banking system there, and had been since at least the 1620s. I believe it was a necessary precondition that such use of credit should reach a critical mass before there was room for a banker, but cannot yet spell out how this network of formal loans on bonds was transformed into one in which one party deposited money with a banker, and the other party borrowed it from the banker, rather than borrowing directly, on bond, from the first party. It was certainly a long drawn-out process.

Those who lived in provincial England had had no difficulty in investing or in borrowing for at least two centuries before country banking came into existence. It is a fanciful myth to believe that rural English men and women normally hoarded spare money in the thatch or under the floorboards. They only did that when caught unawares by

---

[48] Bower, 'Congregation'.

[49] The Usury Acts of 1571, 1623–4, 1651 and 1660 term the arrangers of loans alternatively as Scriveners, Brokers, Solicitors or 'Drivers of Bargaynes for Contractes'.

[50] Holderness, 'Widows in pre-industrial society', p.438, cites such broking activities in Lincolnshire by David Atkinson of Louth and Benjamin Smith of Horbling, some of whose working papers survive.

[51] Pressnell, *Country banking*, pp.36–44.

civil war or threat of foreign invasion. They knew better. Spare money was to be invested not hidden. And if borrowed it was to be put to work. The probate accounts give us some insight into how ubiquitous debt and credit networks were in rural England from at least the late-sixteenth century onwards.

12

Understanding Probate Accounts and their Generation in the Post-Restoration Diocese of Lichfield and Coventry to 1700

ANNE TARVER

Introduction

It has been proposed that there is potential for remedying some of the limitations of data from probate inventories by the use of probate accounts.[1] These accounts were produced when the administrator or executor had completed their task and showed the final financial summary of the value of the estate after all debts had been paid. It could be thought that sufficient numbers of probate accounts survive in enough detail to provide suitable complementary information to balance that given in inventories, which, by ignoring real estate and debts, presented a slightly rosy statement of the deceased's financial affairs. Probate accounts provide a wealth of information that can include details of medical costs of the deceased in their final illness, and the funeral costs are often itemised. Debts were also itemised, and included monies borrowed on security, purchases made for everyday items, expenses of raising children, rents due to landlords, parish dues of various kinds, and finally bequests made to friends and relatives. These would be totalled by the accountant and subtracted from the initial inventory value. This moment of truth often showed a financial chasm between the cosy optimism of the inventory and the cold reality of the cash left in hand. Probate accounts too have their limitations. At Lichfield these include a small proportion giving the occupation of the deceased and a strong tendency to group all the debts together as a lump sum.

The purpose of this chapter is twofold. First, to examine the provenance, survival, form and potential use of probate accounts that

---

[1] Spufford, 'Limitations of the probate inventory', pp.153–4; Spufford, Chapter 11 above, p.214.

were generated by accountants of both testate and intestate estates during the post-Restoration period in the extensive Diocese of Lichfield and Coventry. Second, to consider the number of accounts generated in relation to the major probate legislation passed between 1670/1 and 1685,[2] and to examine its effect upon the number of probate accounts exhibited in the diocese between 1661 and 1699.

This paper will begin by putting the probate accounts into the broad context of the area of the diocese, and the overall number of accounts produced will be reviewed. The structure of the ecclesiastical courts through which these documents were produced will be considered and the provenance and survival of the accounts will be discussed in relation to the courts.

The form and number of these accounts will be examined within three time periods, pre-1671, 1672–85 and post–1685 in relation to the legislation previously described. Some of the areas of major interest that can be explored through these records will be considered, and the summary will review the potential and limitations of the Lichfield accounts.

The Diocese of Lichfield and Coventry

The post-Restoration Diocese of Lichfield and Coventry, shown in Figure 12.1, covered a very large area of the west Midlands. The diocese included the old counties of Staffordshire and Derbyshire, as well as the northern parts of Warwickshire and the northern and eastern parts of Shropshire. The diocese was divided into four archdeaconries, two of which were almost coterminous with the old counties of Derbyshire and Staffordshire. The areas of Warwickshire and Shropshire in the diocese each formed an archdeaconry, that of Shropshire being known as the Archdeaconry of Salop. Despite the apparently extensive physical nature of the diocese, a quarter of the total number of parishes in Staffordshire were outside the jurisdiction of the bishop in either peculiar jurisdictions or extra-parochial areas. Smaller areas in each of the other archdeaconries were also outside the jurisdiction of the bishop.

Number of accounts produced 1661–99

Comparatively few post-Restoration probate accounts survive in the Lichfield records. The total number of extant accounts is only 831 for

---

[2] The research on the material post-1680 formed part of a Leverhulme-funded project on the Consistory Court records of the Diocese of Lichfield and Coventry, 1680–1860.

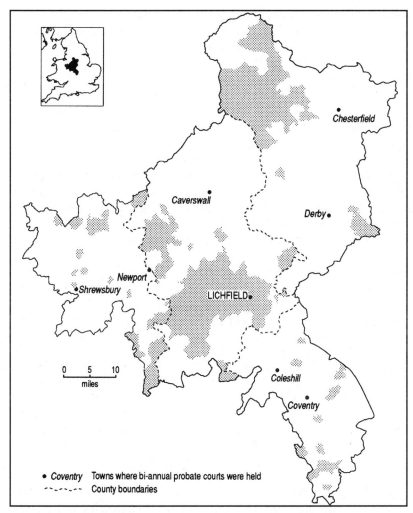

Figure 12.1 Peculiars and extra-parochial areas within the rural parts of the Diocese of Lichfield and Coventry

the years between 1661, when the courts resumed business after the civil war, and 1699. For a diocese of the size of Lichfield, this is a very small number. To put this into a simple context, the total number of recorded probates in the calendar of wills and administrations in the diocese in 1680 was 704. There were 876 in 1681 and 707 in 1682. The maximum number of accounts remaining from a single year was 111 for 1682. The values of these estates ranged from £2 15s.[3] to nearly £6,200.[4] To what extent this reflects document loss or lack of production will be considered in terms of the provenance of these accounts.

The probate courts

The church courts of every diocese fulfilled three functions—administration, jurisdiction and visitation. All of these functions involved probate matters, and at Lichfield the system seems to have been very efficient in the period under discussion. The extant, detailed, records of the probate courts for two small areas cover two short time periods, but would suggest great attention to detail. Their business included the granting of probate to executors and granting letters of administration to those who wished to administer an intestate's estate, entering into bonds where necessary. The production of an account seems to have been compulsory for those entering into an administration, and a date was given on the Lichfield bonds by which this had to be completed. The accounts that were exhibited in the normal probate courts can simply be described as 'standard' accounts. If an executor or an administrator died before completing their task, the probate had to be taken back to the consistory court, which would grant permission to another individual to complete the winding up of the estate. This simply led to the production of what can be described as a 'secondary' account, whereby a single account included the separate estates, or parts of estates, of two individuals. This can be illustrated by the account of George Short and William Addams in winding up the estate of Isaac Burgess, an oatmeal-maker from Snitterton, Derbyshire, in 1680.[5] They had to include Isaac's accounts of his duties as bailiff to Mr Smith who owned the local mill. Reference was made in the account to the supply of a load of cinders for the repair of Mr Smith's mill dam.

In this very large diocese probate courts were held not only at Lichfield, but undertook a bi-annual circuit. Spring and autumn probate courts were held at two towns in each of the counties of Derbyshire, Shropshire and Warwickshire. These towns were Derby, Chesterfield, Shrewsbury, Newport, Coventry and Coleshill. The Staffordshire probate courts on this circuit were only held at Caverswall, with the

---

[3] Lichfield Joint Record Office (hereafter LJRO) B/C/5/1698/104, Anne Statham, widow of Shirland (Db).

[4] LJRO B/C/5/1692/37, William Marriott, of Scarcliffe (Db).

[5] LJRO B/C/5/1680/7, Isaac Burgess of Darley (Db).

main probate court at Lichfield in session throughout the year. Prior to the Civil Wars, probate court books were kept for the Lichfield diocese as a whole, recording every grant of probate and administration. After the reinstatement of the courts in 1661, these volumes ceased to be produced. They were replaced by a system of recording grants of probate listed in separate county books.

Thirty peculiar jurisdictions were also entitled to hold probate courts. Twelve were in the hands of prebends of the Cathedral, and 11 were manor courts. The peculiar courts proved wills and conducted instance business where required, behaving exactly like other ecclesiastical courts, although they lacked the sophisticated registry facilities of Lichfield. The chances of documentary survival from such jurisdictions is slim. These courts too would have demanded probate accounts, although the survival rate would be very small indeed.

The main jurisdiction courts of the diocese were held by the bishop in the form of consistory courts, usually sitting twice a month in the cathedral at Lichfield in the east side of the north transept of the cathedral.[6] It was to these courts that testamentary causes, concerning the validity of wills and the non-payment of legacies, were brought. The probate accounts that were exhibited before these courts fall into two categories—'disputed' accounts and 'accounts exhibited with inventories'. These were very different from the standard forms, reflecting their different origin and purpose.

The vast number of documents generated by all of these courts required accessible storage for their preservation. The post-Restoration registry in the cathedral close housed the documents of both probate and jurisdiction courts, which were consulted regularly by the court proctors, under the supervision of the diocesan register and his deputy. The rich and extensive documentation of all of the probate courts of the Lichfield diocese is now housed in the Lichfield Joint Record Office and consists of wills, inventories, administration bonds and associated probate papers.[7] These documents were carefully folded prior to their filing in the registry. A search of this vast documentation for a sample period between 1670 and 1685 shows that the bulk of probate accounts were not filed amongst the papers of each decedent as a matter of course. The registers of the Lichfield courts undertook their duties assiduously in all other areas of business, and records relating to a single cause heard in the consistory court were all stored together. It appears

[6] Shaw, *History and antiquities*, I, plan of Lichfield Cathedral by Harris, opposite p.244.
[7] LJRO B/C/10.

that probate accounts were simply stored with the consistory court records in this diocesesan registry, rather than with those of the probate courts. On a practical level, the bulk of the accounts would have been generated between one and two years after the time of probate and it is thus unlikely that they would have been filed together. It would have been a very time consuming task to link them with the earlier documents. It still is.

Provenance and survival of the accounts

Quorum nomina [names of whom] citations were issued through the office of the vicar general of the diocese, calling individuals to attend the bi-annual probate court, listing their names by parish within each deanery. The citations were delivered by the apparitors of the bishop, and returned, annotated, to the registry in Lichfield. The bi-annual courts were held primarily for the granting of probate for those who could not get to the Lichfield court. Standard accounts were either endorsed with the name of the probate court through which they had passed, or the name was added to the bottom of the account, with the date on which it was signed. The maximum number of courts in the diocese from which documents were produced per year was 15, including Lichfield. The highest number of courts represented in the standard accounts in any one year was only 11, and in many years documents are only recorded for eight of these courts, suggesting possible document loss.

Reasons for the reluctance to produce accounts become visible on the *quorum nomina* citations. In addition to requests for individuals to take up probates, the citations also requested that accounts be brought into the court. Annotations by proctors and apparitors give us some idea of why accounts did not appear in any great numbers. Mention is made of goods distrained by landlords, in lieu of unpaid rent, which left no goods or estate to be disposed of. Other accountants simply left the parish, or were moved on by settlement being made elsewhere under the poor law. Others were unable to get to the court. Ellen Hawkesley alleged 'That her husband died so much in debt that all his Goods would not pay his debts by many pounds'.[8] Some names were crossed through, and some of these have the word 'Exp' [expedited] beside them, indicating that the appropriate action had been taken.

A final factor in the explanation of the low number of accounts could

---

[8] LJRO B/V/4, Probate Court *Quorum nomina* citation, Nov. 1679, Chesterfield (Db).

be the cost of exhibition of the account in court. The Warwickshire county book shows the cost of exhibiting an account to have been 6s. 8d., with some abatements of fees. A small proportion cost 3s. 4d., and one or two as little as 1s. 8d., suggestive of a carefully constructed sliding scale of fees. How it was decided that Thomas Yorke should administer the estate of Clement Gulliver we shall never know but he may well have been a creditor of Clement, a tailor. The grant of administration for Clement Gulliver's £14 estate appeared in the Warwickshire county probate book in 1684. The grant cost 4s. in the probate court held on 9th April in Coventry.[9] The costs of using the probate courts for merely exhibiting the account may well have tipped the scales against the final, formal, exhibition. It would have been prohibitive for estates of small value, but costs were waived in some instances so that the account could be exhibited in *forma pauperis* [pauper's form] if it was legally necessary to exhibit an account. It is impossible to escape the feeling that these matters were carefully weighed by accountants. The possibility of exhibiting accounts 'extrajudicially', must also be considered. There is no reason why civil lawyers should not have been involved in the swearing of affidavits to the truth of an account, leaving no trace in the diocesan records.

The volume of work passing through the probate courts would be very difficult to assess without two surviving contemporary probate books.[10] Both of these books date from the late-seventeenth century, one for Derbyshire[11] and one for Warwickshire.[12] The Derbyshire book lists the fortnightly business that took place between November 1678 and August 1681. During this time only four accounts were exhibited, one in 1679 and three in 1680. The paucity of accounts becomes apparent when seen against the 151 grants of probate and 125 letters of administration recorded overall in the book. Accounts were only exhibited for 1.4 per cent of all estates for which probate had been granted. This small number of accounts also needs to be seen against the lack of records of the bi-annual courts held at Chesterfield and Derby at this time, which should have been listed in the county book. It may be that this book simply records Derbyshire probates heard at Lichfield.

The Warwick probate book lists business for the slightly longer period from May 1679 to November 1684, including the bi-annual probate courts held at Coventry and Coleshill, and some of the pages

[9] LJRO B/A/18/4, Warwickshire Book, 1679–85. LJRO B/C/5/1680/7, Clement Gulliver.
[10] LJRO B/A/18, County Probate Books.
[11] LJRO B/A/18/10, Derbyshire Probate Book, 1678–81.
[12] LJRO B/A/18/4, Warwickshire Book, 1679–85.

are actually headed '*apud* [at] Lichfield'. Over the four years that the book was in use, 581 grants of probate and 420 letters of administration were granted in the county and only 127 accounts were exhibited, an overall average of 12.7 per cent. This scrap of evidence would support the suggestion that a very small number of accounts were being produced. Even if a further 11 courts were producing accounts, the overall numbers would still remain very small. The dates of the original probate for both of these counties range from a few months to a few years previous to the exhibition of the account.

Form and potential uses of probate accounts

The content of probate accounts was subject to legal constraint. Canon law respected the wishes of the deceased, but where no instructions had been given it was very difficult to know what to do. The problems of the disposal of the surplus of intestate estates had been a thorny one throughout the medieval period, and each diocese simply developed its own custom of proportional division between widow and children. The matter was finally resolved by a temporary act of parliament passed in 1670, effective for seven years from 1671, described as an 'Act for the Better Settling of Intestates Estates', but popularly known as the Statute of Distribution.[13] In this act the division of the surplus monies was nationally defined. This legislation required the administrators of these estates to undertake two legal acts. The first was to enter into a bond with the official of the court, from June 1671, providing two sureties for the administration. The second task was to exhibit an account before the judge or his surrogate in the probate court at a given date, usually two years later, to show what monies had been paid out and to whom. The balance was then divided between the widow and any surviving children. This would officially and publicly signify the end of the probate process.

This temporary act was renewed on two occasions, and made permanent in 1685, when the earlier necessity to enter into a bond was retained, but accounts were only to be exhibited at the request of relatives or creditors.[14] In response, the production of standard accounts ceased abruptly at Lichfield.

The exhibition, or legal submission for inspection, of an account in court, for either testate or intestate estates, served three purposes. First, to make the affairs of the decedent public, second, to demonstrate

[13] 22 & 23 Ch. II, c.10.
[14] 1 Ja. II, c.17.

openly that all debts had been paid. Finally, it would define the amount of the estate that was available for distribution. This would ensure that it was possible to carry out the division of the surplus of intestate estates according to the custom of the diocese. The fact that the *'quietus est'* [it is quit] appears on the bottom of some surviving accounts demonstrates that these were inspected after completion. This would confirm by *'restat in manibus'* [remains in hand] that the sum in the inventory exceeded the account by a given figure. In other words, the balance was a positive one, and there was money to be distributed according to the custom of the diocese. The document was signed by the surrogate of the court to indicate that the estate had been wound up to the satisfaction of all present, after which time there was to be no further discussion or argument. A high proportion of the Lichfield accounts were produced for intestate estates, although this included a small number produced by those acting in place of executors who had renounced their duties.

Contemporary law books tell us little about the practicalities of producing an account and the form it should take. The contents of accounts have only been specified on one occasion, by Swinburne, and then only to executors. He felt that 'moderate expenses were to be allowed according to the condition of the persons' and that 'sumptuous and delicate expenses are not to be allowed'.[15] The debts of the deceased were to be paid in strict order, as discussed by Erickson.[16]

The Lichfield accounts begin with a paragraph giving the background to the account. The name of the accountant is given, stating their relationship to the deceased, whether they were acting as executor or administrator to the named decedent and where he or she lived. The 'onus' or charge was stated, being the value of the inventory of the deceased's goods. The debts at Lichfield were listed in a standard order. Funeral charges were listed, usually as a total, followed by the debts of the deceased. These debts were often merely totalled, and in a high proportion of cases no indication was given of the names of creditors. Debts of less than £2 could simply be sworn before the judge and may not have been recorded on the account. Those accounts which only identified one or two creditors may represent those where a public acknowledgement of payment was necessary. Finally, the legal fees incurred in the probate courts were given. The expenditure was totalled and deducted from the charge to give the balance of the account, either as a total to be distributed or as a negative balance to be redressed by the accountant.

[15] Swinburne, *Brief treatise* (1677), pp.228–9.
[16] Erickson, 'Introduction to probate accounts', p.278. See also Chapter 5 above, p.113 and Chapter 11 above, p.217.

As we have seen from Swinburne, the requirement was obvious, and some of the reasons behind the reluctance to exhibit the account have been discussed. The importance of agreement was emphasised by Swinburne, who noted that any ecclesiastical official who allowed accounts to be passed before all parties were satisfied was liable to be suspended *'ab ingressu ecclesiae'* [from entering church] and thus from administering or taking the sacrament for a period of six months.[17] William Nelson confirmed this necessity for agreement when he noted that common lawyers were not interested in probate business 'because none was left out of the Agreement, who could pretend a Right to any share'.[18] It was this necessity for agreement which may have limited the contents of the accounts to those contentious matters that required public resolution.

The potential uses of Lichfield probate accounts are curtailed by the problems of linking the accounts with the inventories. The lack of occupations stated on the account removes the information from its socio-economic context. The overall extent of the values of estates and their debts can be examined. Another field for exploration is that of relationships between administrators and the deceased. Who acted as an administrator of intestate estates? Were they relatives or creditors, and were estates with negative balances left to creditors rather than the family? Did these relationships change over time? Disputed accounts tend to focus on the items in dispute, concentrating on the matter in hand. Accounts with inventory give much more information, and often relate to individuals living alone, and these comparatively unusual items give a rare opportunity to reconcile the inventory and account.

The Lichfield probate accounts

A total of 831 probate accounts dating from 1661 to 1699 has been identified amongst the cause papers of the Lichfield consistory court. Although these accounts originated in two separate courts, the probate and the consistory, they were all filed with the consistory court documents. The distribution of these accounts over time is discussed in three separate periods relative to contemporary legislation. The annual totals are shown in three figures. Note that the number of accounts with positive and negative balances does not always match the total number of accounts in any year. This is because some accounts have totals for either the charge or discharge missing and the balance cannot be ascertained.

---

[17] Swinburne, *Brief treatise* (1677), p.379.
[18] Nelson, *Lex Testamentaria*, p.20.

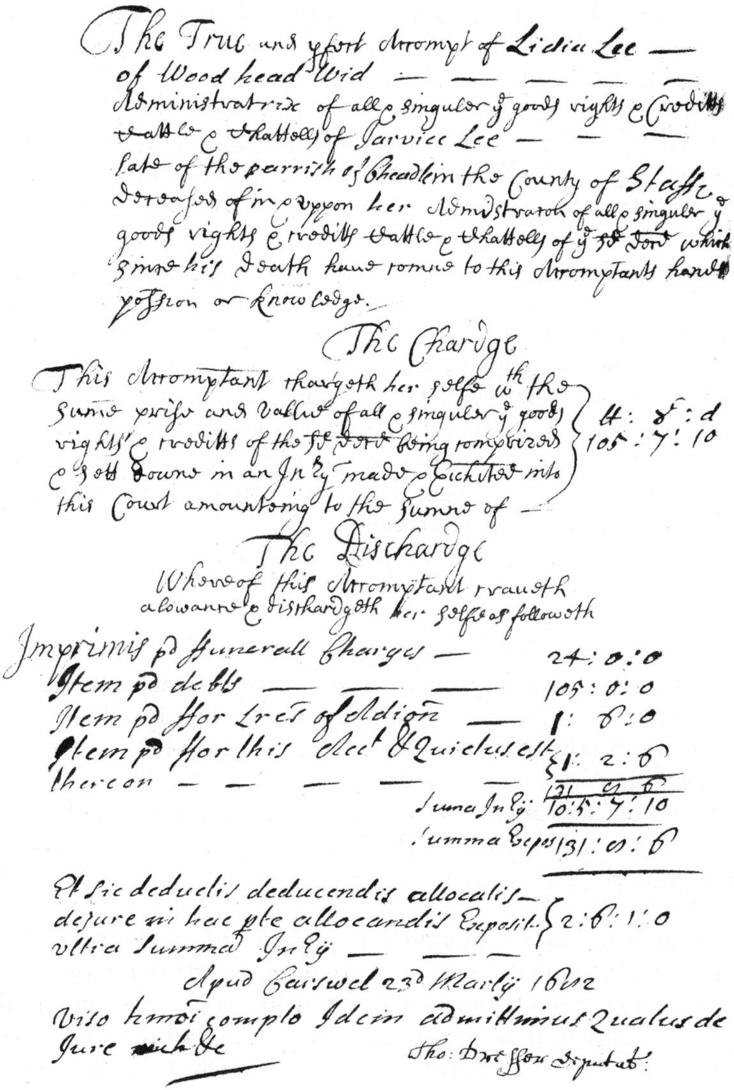

The True and perfect Accompt of Lidia Lee —
of Woodhead Wid —
Administratrix of all & singuler ye goods rights & Credits
cattle & chattells of Jarvice Lee —
late of the parrish of Cheadle in the County of Staff &
deceased of in & uppon her Administracon of all & singuler ye
goods rights & credits cattle & chattells of ye sd Decd which
since his death have come to this Accomptants hands
possession or knowledge.

The Charge

This Accomptant chargeth her selfe wth the summe prise and vallue of all & singuler ye goods rights & credits of the sd Decd being comprized & sett downe in an Invry made & exhibited into this Court amounting to the summe of — li : s : d 105 : 7 : 10

The Discharge

Whereof this Accomptant craveth allowance & dischargeth her selfe as followeth

Imprimis pd ffunerall Charges —	24 : 0 : 0
Item pd debts —	105 : 0 : 0
Item pd ffor Lres of Adcon —	1 : 0 : 0
Item pd ffor this Acct & Quietus est thereon —	1 : 2 : 6
	131 : 2 : 6
Summa Invij	105 : 7 : 10
Summa Expens	131 : 02 : 6

Et sic deductis deducendis allocatis de jure in hac pte allocandis Expendit ultra Summam Invij — 2:6:1:0

Apud Carswel 23d Martij 1682

Viso hmoi compto Idem admittimus Qualus de Jure debe

Tho: Dreffton Deputat:

Figure 12.2 An example of a Lichfield standard account

The standard accounts were usually written by a court clerk on a small sheet of paper 10″ by 7″ with a single fold, and using a 'fill in the blanks' format, a notable example of a tidy mind at work. The name of the decedent, and their administrators or executors, as well as the amounts of money involved were duly entered later. In a high proportion of the accounts, the occupation of the deceased was not given. The two hands that were involved in the production of these documents would appear to have been those of the court officials. Certainly, these accounts were not written by the accountants themselves, and the surviving copies must have been those that had been ingrossed by the court. The name of the appropriate probate court where the standard account was exhibited and the date were added at the foot of the sheet, together with '*restat in manibus*' or, ominously, '*comptans exposit ultra vires inventoria summa*' [account exceeds the total of the inventory by some considerable amount]. This type of account was produced until 1685.

The accounts surviving at Lichfield may or may not represent the true state of the decedent's affairs, or the accountants perceptions of them. They may simply represent a written compromise between the parties, signed by the accountant. It could be suggested that a number of accounts were simply agreed privately between the parties, for reasons that have been discussed earlier.

1661–1671

The system for the production of accounts in the Lichfield diocese was obviously in place well before any legislation was proposed. Accounts were being produced where there was a positive balance with monies available for distribution, rather than accounts where bills could not be met, suggesting voluntary exhibition.

The 148 viable accounts[19] produced during this period (out of a total of 155) were the work overwhelmingly of administrators of intestate estates (136) prior to the legal requirement to enter into a bond. The bulk of these accounts, 76 per cent, showed a positive balance, with monies available for distribution. The number of executors' accounts was minuscule, only 12 such accounts were produced between 1661 and 1671, and these were, in nine cases, in deficit. This would also suggest that executors were very much fewer in number, and seldom exhibited accounts due to agreement being reached within a family group. It may be possible to link sudden rises in numbers with local mortality crises, particularly the 67 accounts in 1667, but as yet there is no immediate explanation for the increase in 1664. During this period there were very few disputed accounts produced in the consistory court.

---

[19] A viable account for the purpose of this chapter is one that has the onus and discharge stated, and which shows a positive or negative balance. Those that balanced exactly have not been included.

Figure 12.3 Numbers of probate accounts exhibited annually in the Lichfield diocese, 1661–71

Nine causes have been identified over this period, and would, of course, relate to problems with the work of the executor or administrator of the estate.

The potential use of documents from this period is limited by the lack of evidence of occupations to establish the social framework in which these accounts were produced. One indicator is the value of estates for which accounts were drawn up and these will be discussed shortly. Accurate figures for the numbers of these accounts for each diocese over time can demonstrate the extent to which the legislation influenced their production. Knowledge of the courts of origin of the accounts can also help our understanding of the administrative structures within different dioceses. Did other dioceses maintain bi-annual probate courts, such as those at Lichfield, or did they rely on administrators and executors coming to the central probate court? Both the range of values of estates, and the overall picture of debt in the community over different time periods, can be picked up from these accounts. For the small number of accounts that can be linked back to the original probate documents, particularly to inventories, more information can be gleaned. Where the debts are listed rather than totalled, the use of the document is greatly increased, particularly where debts on specialty can be traced. It is unfortunate that the bulk of these accounts also relate to intestate accounts, where there are no wills to compare with the intention of the deceased regarding the dispersal of their estate.

1672–1685

There was a notable increase in the number of accounts exhibited following the 1670/1 Statute, reviving their rather erratic production in the Lichfield diocese. In proportion to the size of the diocese, there were very few accounts passing through the courts in any single year. The most significant increase began in 1672, which is where it would be expected to occur, when the number of accounts rose to 77. This then droppped back to around 20 per year. The numbers gradually increased from 1680, the largest surviving group dating from 1682, when 111 accounts survive. The number of accounts rose sharply in 1684 and 1685 as a result of local ecclesiastical politics. At this time the courts were under the jurisdiction of the Metropolitan, during the suspension of Bishop Wood.[20] The very sharp decline in numbers in 1686 was evidence of the reaction to the Statute of Distributions when it was no longer necessary to exhibit an account.

[20] Between July 1684 and May 1686.

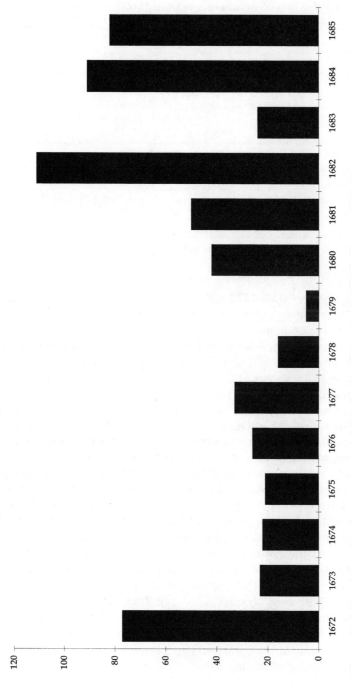

Figure 12.4 Numbers of probate accounts exhibited annually in the Lichfield diocese, 1672–85

Table 12.1 Value of probate accounts exhibited, 1680–99, by county

Charge, £*	Derbyshire		Warkwickshire		Staffordshire		Shropshire	
	Pos	Negs	Pos	Negs	Pos	Negs	Pos	Negs
1–50	58	24	31	8	60	21	29	13
51–100	38	6	26	4	41	14	20	7
101–200	42	13	16	5	17	9	8	3
201–300	11	0	6	1	7	2	3	1
310–400	4	0	2	0	3	0	3	0
401–500	2	1	2	0	0	0	0	0
501–600	0	0	2	1	1	0	0	0
601–700	1	0	1	0	1	0	0	0
701–800	0	0	0	0	1	0	0	0
801–900	0	0	0	0	0	0	0	0
901–1000	1	0	0	0	1	1	0	0
1000+	3	1	0	0	0	0	0	0
Total	160	45	86	19	132	47	63	24

Note: *These represent viable accounts only.

Altogether between 1672 and 1685, 623 accounts were exhibited in the Lichfield diocese, of which 599 were viable for analysis. A sample of 400 standard accounts was used to trace the social groupings of the deceased for the period between 1680 and 1685. Searching through the probate documents revealed the occupation or status of only 188 individuals, 52 per cent of the deceased. The largest category was that of yeomen, 54, with a further four in that group giving dual occupations. Thirty-eight husbandmen were identified, but no labourers. Of the 31 womens' estates, 26 were those of widows. The next most numerous group was that of gentlemen, whose estates yielded 15 accounts. These may have been lawyers rather than gentry. The remaining accounts were drawn up for a wide range of craftsmen and the clergy. The maximum number of accounts in any of these very small groups was four.

The values of accounts exhibited between 1680 and 1699 have been analysed by county to give a broad picture of this aspect of the court business over the last two decades of the century, and are shown in Table 12.1. Accounts worth up to £50 seem to have been the most commonly exhibited, forming 42 per cent of the total number of accounts. Those worth between £51 and £100 form 27 per cent of the total, and those worth between £101 and £200 form another 20 per cent of the total. Negative balances were found in an average of 25 per cent of accounts at these values. This proportion of negative balances declines with the increasing value of estate, but the numbers are too small to make statistical sense. Estates worth in excess of £500 are very rare; these were usually taken to the Prerogative Court of Canterbury, probably relating to the property of those with land in more than one diocese. The accounts from Derbyshire and Staffordshire represent the estates of men making money from mining and trade. The three Derbyshire accounts worth £1,000+ were all created for the same individual's highly complex estate, by an executor who died during the process of sorting matters out, whose work was then taken over by an administrator.

At a county level smaller accounts, those worth less than £100, formed 60 per cent of the Derbyshire total, 66 per cent of those for Warwickshire, 76 per cent of those for Staffordshire and 78 per cent for those from Shropshire.

1686–1699

Following the dramatic drop in the number of accounts produced after 1685, their character changed. Standard accounts disappeared completely. Only 53 accounts were produced between 1686 and 1699, and these were of the more detailed types derived from the disputed causes in the consistory court, in the manner specified by the Statute of 1685. Forty 'disputed' accounts were produced in testamentary causes, and the remaining 13 accounts were of the 'exhibited with inventory' type. The form of both of these accounts is very different from that of the standard account. Many of these accounts run to several pages, using widely differing formats. Some accounts and inventories were written on the same sheets of paper, but they were still written out by the court proctors and signed by the accountants. Five were not viable for analysis because of totals missing from either the inventory or the account.

Accounts for intestate estates still predominated, with 32 in this category. Of the remaining 16 executors' accounts, 13 showed negative balances, explaining their appearance, and the remainder were in credit. In no year in this period did the accounts number more than eight, and in 1697 no accounts appear.

In spite of their small numbers, these documents give, in most cases, a great deal of detail relating to the subject under dispute. Accounts 'exhibited with inventory' generally provide the balance of information sought after in terms of individual wealth that can be linked to occupation. Most inventories and accounts relate to those who died in old age, and who had probably settled their children. One small but fascinating group is that of suicides—the affairs of those who died suddenly can provide a snapshot of the individual in the prime of their

Figure 12.5 Number of probate accounts exhibited annually in the Lichfield diocese, 1686–99

life. This type of account occurs in such small numbers as to be unusable for statistical purposes, but can still provide narrative details of named individuals.

'Disputed' accounts can either represent a legal endpoint in a cause or be produced during the progress of the cause. In some disputes, two or three accounts were generated. In causes relating to subtraction of a legacy two types of account could be produced. If a minor was suing the accountant through a guardian, the account would focus on the cost of bringing up the individual concerned and their siblings, if any. If the plaintiff was an adult, then the account would focus on the costs of the funeral, the number of debts, legal fees, and travel to and from the court. In both cases they are much more detailed than the earlier standard form of account and can provide a great deal of reasonably comparable information on debt, funeral practices, and the provision of legacies for differing individuals of widespread social groupings.

The church courts could only demonstrate particular items in which the estate had not been well managed. Canon law was constrained in many ways by having to adhere closely to the matter in dispute. The courts had no power to enforce payment of monies owed, such business belonged to the realm of the civil lawyer. Accusations of fraudulent administration seldom appeared before the later eighteenth century, but this would generate a very different set of items in the account, with questioned items featuring prominently, often with the names of creditors and their occupations.

Disputed accounts and 'accounts exhibited with inventory'

In a short chapter it is not possible to deal in great detail with all the information that can be derived from disputed accounts and those exhibited with inventory. The most important types of information that can be obtained from this small Lichfield series include funeral customs, building repairs and details of the upbringing of children. It is this last group that will now be considered.

Information relating to the upbringing of children can be found in two types of accounts, generated as a result of 'subtraction of legacy' causes in the consistory court. In disputed cases, children who felt that they had not received their dues from the family estate, however small it may have been, were entitled to sue the accountant for their legacies. Causes were sometimes brought by a guardian on behalf of a minor, worried by the possibility of fraudulent administration of the goods. The cause would be brought through the consistory court of the diocese, and the defendant—the executor/trix—would have to produce an account to show why there was no money forthcoming. The usual answer was that all of the money left by the deceased had been spent on the upbringing of the family. Accounts were presented in different forms and ranged from lump sums spent on individually named offspring to minute details of items of shoes and clothing purchased, and pocket money given to the child.

One of the smaller accounts, that of Sarah Smith alias Clews, one of the executors of Elizabeth Clews, widow, of Stramshall in the parish of Uttoxeter, Staffordshire, began with a charge of £13 6s. 4d., and was submitted in 1699. The maintenance of four daughters ranged from £2 10s. to £6 over a period of 9 to 18 months after the death of their father. The two youngest daughters, who had received maintenance for 15 and 18 months, were suing Sarah Smith for their share of the estate. The sum spent on the eldest child included diet and maintenance whereas that for the other three children included diet, maintenance and clothes. The total spent on maintenance came to £17 10s. and the whole account was overspent by £10 5s. 6d.

Schooling was included in a number of accounts, for girls as well as boys. The three children, two daughters and a son, of Samuel Wood of Allestree, Derbyshire, were all given maintenance, clothing and schooling for six, nine and eight years respectively at a cost of £8, £22 and £20. Sarah, the eldest daughter, took her mother to court for her share of the estate, which resulted in the production of an account in 1691. The total of £50 10s. left an overspend of £6 10s. over the inventory to be found by their mother and her new husband.

Their problems were minimal compared with those of Sarah Cox and her husband John who had to find £46 19s. to maintain Sarah's seven children by her previous marriage. The childrens' father had lived at Caldwell, Derbyshire, and Sarah must have remarried within two years of her previous husband's death in 1691. A contract to pay £8 for the apprenticeship of Thomas Corbet had to be honoured and he had to have two suits of clothes when he 'went out an Apprentice' at a cost of £2. Dorcas, Ann and William were provided with meat, drink and clothes for two years at a cost of £24. Sarah presented problems of her own. Having been maintained for 15 months with meat, drink and clothes she had to be provided with clothing 'at her going twice out to service'. This was expensive at £6. Mary and John Corbet had also been provided with clothes since their father's death, almost two years previously, at a cost of £5. Understandably, there was no mention of schooling in this account, which had an initial charge of £19 16s. and was submitted in 1693.

In a complex cause relating to a tertiary account, Deborah Norgreave alias Slaney, of Baxterley, Warwickshire, took Edward Slaney to court at Lichfield in 1691. Edward had acted as executor of the estate of Stephen Slaney, deceased, who had in turn been brother and administrator of the estate of Deborah's father, John Slaney of Baxterley in Warwickshire. John had left goods and chattels worth £40 12s., but his daughter's maintenance, nursing, and clothing for ten and a half years had cost £63. Nursing and other charges when she was 'ill of the smallpox' had cost a further £1 4s. and £1 1s. 8d. was paid to the chirurgeon. When she left her uncle's care she had been given clothing worth £2 10s. and 15s. in cash. Edward's problems had not ended. He had to pay a further 16s. 8d. for 'charges when the said Deborah was released from an arrest in Tamworth'. She was obviously strapped for cash, and attempting to obtain any legacy to which she was entitled.

Elizabeth Bickley of Middle, Shropshire, presented her account in 1699. She is one of the rare individuals for whom we can find a character reference. Richard Gough described her rather waspishly as 'more commendable for her beauty than her chastity, and [was] the ruin of the family'.[21] Her husband William had left goods and chattels worth £126 9s. 10d. and despite Gough's comment she had managed to leave a positive balance of £105 12s. 7d. The four children, one son and three daughters were all maintained with meat and drink, although only William attended school. The cost of his upbringing was £2 2s. 6d. with a further 4s. 10d. for two pairs of shoes. Elizabeth's maintenance cost was £1 10s. and her sister Susanna's only 10s. Clothes were made for Elizabeth and Anne Bickley at a cost of 6s. Unfortunately no indication is given of the length of time over which they were maintained. The largest item of expenditure was £5 given to Thomas 'upon contracting of marriage betwixt him and Judith the daughter of Robert Wilkinson as part of his portion'. This last item was a legally important confirmation of the payment of his portion.

The estate of Thomas Wedgwood, of Burslem in Staffordshire, was administered by three executors, Margaret his widow and John and Thomas Wedgwood also of Burslem, a potter. The account was presented, with the inventory, in 1698. The maintenance of seven children is accounted for, and represents the financial capacity of a wealthier family. The estate was worth £294 6s. but was still overdrawn when all the maintenance and creditors had been paid. Seven children were maintained for a period of up to nine and a half years. Margaret and Margery had received 'maintenance, lodging, washing and clothing', for a whole year each at a cost of £5. Thomas had been kept

---

[21] Gough, *History of Myddle*, p.206.

for two and a half years at a cost of £12 10s. Catherine, Sarah and Mary
were maintained on the same terms, but including schooling, for three
years, nine years and three months and nine years and six months
respectively, the costs escalating from £30 to £92 10s. and dropping to
£75 for Mary. Her funeral added another £5 to the disbursements of
the executors. Timothy Wedgwood was maintained with schooling for
five years at a cost of £50 and apprenticed to Mr Bell of Congleton for
the sum of £13. The terms of the agreement stipulated that his family
should pay for his clothing over the seven-year apprenticeship and this
added another £17 10s. to the overall maintenance costs of £305. The
estate was £120 18s. 2d. overdrawn, money that had to be found by the
executors. The account was generated as the result of a demand by
Margery for her share of the estate.

One of the most detailed accounts of individual children came from
accounts made by Thomas Bache, curator *ad lites* [at law] of Michael
Green, a minor, son of Walter Green of Bonningale in Shropshire.
Thomas Bache was probably asked to undertake the production of an
account by virtue of his literacy and the complexity of the situation.
Michael and his guardian were both illiterate. There was no inventory
produced of the goods of the deceased, in fact these had to be assembled
from the widow, to raise the cash for Michael Green's upbringing. The
value of the goods eventually totalled £14 15s. 11d. His father had been
involved in agriculture and in business, and £5 1s. 2d. was spent upon
correspondence and loss of time in dealing with this. No costs were
given for food, medicine or lodgings. His father's house was not in good
repair and £1 2s. 6d. was spent on a variety of tradesmen's bills,
including the thatcher. Expenditure on clothing, including the weaving
and dying of cloth, knitting up and footing of stockings and mending a
shirt came to 10s. 6d. New shoes and repairs of the old ones came to 8s.
3d. Small luxury items including ale for 2d., tobacco for 3d., shoe
buckles and a penknife for 6d. would suggest that Michael was in his late
teens, although 2d. worth of gingerbread would suggest a younger and
sweeter tooth. Michael was already given to borrowing money,
although on a small scale, at sixpence a time. In spite of such a small
charge, the account was £3 7s. 8d. in credit which was handed over to
Richard Mason, Michael's guardian.

The most fascinating of all the accounts prior to 1700 is that of Mary
Finch, alias Draper, of her first husband's estate, exhibited in 1696.
Robert Draper was the last of the line of the Draper family who had
lived at Culland in the parish of Brailsford, Derbyshire, since 1498. The
family was entitled to bear arms and was obviously of the lesser gentry
of the county. Mary was christened in December 1680 and her sister

Dorothy was buried in August 1683, leaving Mary as the sole heiress. Her father was buried in December 1689, just over a week after Mary's tenth birthday. Her mother remarried and seems to have been determined that her daughter would make a suitable marriage. Her late husband's funeral was an elaborate one, with torches, mourning rings and gloves, and £10 10s. 3d. was given to the poor. Mary's upbringing for the next six years followed a similar degree of opulence when compared with the maintenance of other children. She moved to Lichfield and then to London. Her education included dancing and spinet lessons and numerous new clothes, including silk stays trimmed with silver lace. This fortunate young lady was also provided with pocket money.

Accounts exhibited with inventories provide a more complete view of the affairs of the deceased but, once again, will only contain items upon which agreement had been reached after negotiation. They usually survive without any accompanying documents, and show a negative balance. These accounts actually provide a more accurate statement of the economic affairs of the deceased in that the expenses of child-rearing have not been included. Both accounts and inventories were always ingrossed by the clerks of the court, and the signatures of the accountants are usually given, demonstrating their literacy, or lack of it.

Thirteen accounts were produced for exhibition with inventories and these are strongly linked to individuals living alone, boarding or tabling with others. Their inventories do not mention room names but there is only sufficient furniture for one person, together with limited cooking equipment. The accounts mention occasional bonds and monies owed to semi-official bodies. The accounts do, in fact, demonstrate clearly why most of them were exhibited—to illustrate the satisfactory completion of the probate process for an individual with few, or no, relatives.

Conclusion

The wisdom of executors making a probate account was pleaded by Swinburne in his *Brief Treatise*: 'if the Executor have well and faithfully executed his office, and fully discharged the trust reposed in him, what should move him that he should not willingly make a due account thereof, and thereby obtain an acquittance?' Such a statement would suggest that executors did not always provide a final statement voluntarily, although they may have been compelled to produce an account 'at the instance or promotion of such Legataries and Creditors invocating the office of the Judge'.[22] Swinburne's plea obviously went unheard at Lichfield. Sensible though it may have been to produce an account, it seems to have been unpopular in the diocese. Nelson's statement that 'none was left out of the Agreement, who could pretend a Right to any share' would suggest that these accounts probably were not the work of a single individual, but of a number of people settling the account amongst themselves to their satisfaction.[23]

Regrettably the Lichfield probate accounts do not survive in sufficient detail or quantity to redress the failings of the probate inventory. The logistics of linking the two items are complex and time-consuming in the numbers that would be needed for a viable analysis. However, the survival of the probate court records and a small number of the administrative records of the courts can throw light on the reasons why so few were produced and why so few remain. The numerous contemporary reasons for the failure to produce an account may provide the necessary explanations for the comparatively small numbers of these documents at Lichfield. One of the most important findings to arise from the Lichfield material has been the identification of different types of account, their dating and contents.

The realisation that these accounts were produced by a group of people, rather than simply the accountant, suggests that they do not always include every item that historians would wish. Certainly real estate is not listed, nor are debts itemised in a way that would give a clear picture of the overall credit situation. So few accounts were exhibited in proportion to the total number of probates passing through the courts that conclusions drawn from these figures may not be valid. However, the extent of debt can be established in a small proportion of the population, and the role of creditors in the probate process examined. The question of who acted as administrators for intestates is one field where further work is needed.

However, the most rewarding area is that of the disputed accounts and those exhibited with inventory. The specific detail that can be obtained from these can provide the only source of a great deal of information on subjects that have hitherto been difficult to locate, and also for individuals well down the social scale.

---

[22] Swinburne, *Brief treatise* (1677), pp.376–7.
[23] Nelson, *Lex Testamentaria*, p.20.

PART III

Probate Inventories Plus

13

The Language of Probate Inventories

EDMUND WEINER

Introduction

This study is a sketch of the main features of the language of probate inventories. Rather than draw on disparate material from a wide range of published probate inventories, I have selected my examples from two collections, one from Yorkshire in the north of England and one from Warwickshire in the west Midlands.[1] From these I shall draw some general conclusions both about the language of the communities in which probate inventories were written and about the English language as a whole in the period 1500–1700. I shall consider the language of probate inventories under the three headings of the written forms, the word stock, and grammar.

The written forms

Needless to say, the language of most probate inventories looks pretty alien to most modern readers, even if they are accustomed to Tudor literature. This effect is chiefly due to their spelling. The modern reader constantly, but on the whole unconsciously, contrasts the spelling of probate inventories with modern standard English spelling (SES). But SES, of course, has evolved from earlier spelling conventions, and to understand fully the spelling of probate inventories we need to know a little about the spelling of Middle English, the relationship between the latter and emerging SES, and the relationship of both to the phonology of the London-based 'standard' language.[2] We also have to take into

---

[1] Brears, *Yorkshire Probate Inventories* (hereafter Brears) and Alcock, *People at Home* (hereafter Alcock). Both collections represent just a subset of the actual or potential material from their localities, Brears containing probate inventories that had come into the keeping of the Yorkshire Archaeological Society, and Alcock 55 (out of a total of 428 documents for the parish of Stoneleigh) selected for qualities quite other than linguistic.

[2] Phonology, the science of vocal sounds; system of sounds of a language.

account the phonology of the non-standard regional dialects which continued to flourish at least until the Industrial Revolution and the close of our period.

The language of English texts from the early-Tudor period is scarcely distinct in spelling from that of the preceding era. The arrival of printing in the 1470s did not at first alter scribal conventions, and indeed the possibilities of variation in the spelling of individual words were exploited to enable the printed line to be more easily justified. But between the middle of Henry VIII's reign and the middle of Elizabeth I's many of the conventions that are now fundamental to SES began to be adopted in printed books; the essential principles of SES were discernible in some printed works by 1590; and by 1650 the system was virtually universal in print (though the imitation of printed practice in private manuscript did not prevail for another century). In order to compare inventory spelling with SES it will be necessary to list the main features of the latter in some detail.[3]

A. Vowel spellings:

1. The use of the digraphs *oo*, *ee* to represent only the long high vowels, as in *doom* and *deem*, and not (as in Middle English) the long mid vowels as well (see 2).[4]

2. The use of the digraphs *ea*, *oa* in closed syllables to represent the Early Modern English long mid vowels, as in *great* and *groat*.

3. The partly systematic use of 'silent *e*' to show that the vowel in the preceding syllable is conventionally 'long', e.g. in *mate, mete, mite, mote, mute*, and the corresponding disuse of non-functional silent *e*.

4. The use of *y* at the end of a syllable but *i* medially for the long or short *i*-sounds (whereas in Middle English the reverse was often the case), e.g. in *crying*, Middle English *criynge*, and the concomitant replacement of syllable-final *ie* by *y*, e.g. *happy day* for *happie daie*.

5. The preservation of a written distinction (lost in pronunciation by 1600) between (i) the long mid vowel *o* and the diphthong *ow*, e.g. in *sloe* and *slow*; (ii) the long vowel *a* and the diphthong *ai* or *ay*, e.g. in *mane* and *main*; (iii) the long vowel *u* and *eu* or *ew*, e.g. in *due* and *dew*; and (iv) the originally long vowel of certain words like *double* and *trouble* and the short vowel of *tub*.

6. The absence of a written distinction (developed in speech before

---

[3] This list is not complete; a number of minor and less clear-cut features are omitted.

[4] Digraph, a group of two letters expressing a single sound.

1500) between (i) the *a* of *hat* and the *a* of *hall, talk,* and (ii) the *o* of *hop* and the *o* of *hold*.

B. Consonant spellings:

7. The use of double consonants to show the shortness of a preceding vowel, e.g. in *matter, summer,* and the corresponding disuse of non-functional double consonants (except as in 8).

8. The non-functional doubling of final *f, l, s,* and *k* (as *ck*), e.g. in *chaff, small, glass, crack*.

9. The preservation of a written distinction between pairs of sound sequences which have merged in speech, such as (i) *wr-* as in *write* and initial *r-* as in *rite*; (ii) *stl-* as in *bristle* and medial *ss-* + syllabic *l* as in *mussel*; (iii) initial *wh-* as in *whey* and *w-* as in *way*; (iv) *s* before a *y*-sound as in *passion* and *sh* as in *cushion*.

10. The use of a non-functional letter to expand to three letters a word that would otherwise contain fewer (so *tie, owe, ewe* beside *sty, mow, new; add, egg, inn* beside *bad, leg, bin*); 'grammatical' words such as pronouns, prepositions, and basic verbs, are exempt from this principle (e.g. *by, my, we, us, in, go*).

Probate inventory spellings deviate from SES in three main ways: the arbitrary misapplication of a small number of standard spelling rules (both those listed above and others that predate SES); the continuation of archaic spellings; and the use of 'phonetic' spellings (which will be more carefully defined below).

In many, but not all, inventories there is a sprinkling of spellings which are perhaps best explained as the misapplication of common rules of spelling which are usually observed by the writer. The commonest kinds are:

1. Unnecessary *e* in vowel combinations, e.g. *Liveing* (1695), *sawecers* (1660), *cherene* churn (1630), *yeareinge* (1612), *payeinge* (1612).[5]

2. Unnecessary double consonants, e.g. *coltte* colt (1556), *stolles* stools (1537), *housse* hose (1557), *blancket* (1557), *stircke* (1578), *horsse* (1625).[6]

3. *k* for *c* before non-front vowels, *Kowhouse, Kowe* (1612)· *kanapy* (1638); *ch* for *c* before non-front vowels, *chushinges* (1612); *c* for *k* before front vowels, *cettles* (1697), *Cimlinge* kimnel (1632); *g(e)* for *j*

---

[5] Alcock, p.85; Alcock, p.112; Alcock, p.126; Brears, p.72; Brears, p.73.
[6] Alcock, p.24; Alcock, p.31; Alcock, p.27; Alcock, p.32; Brears, p.46; Brears, p.76.

before non-front vowels, *gyrken* (1559), *vergeues* (1578); *g* for *j* before front vowels, *gackettes* (1558).[7]

A number of characteristically late Middle English spellings, discarded in SES in the sixteenth century, continued to be used by inventory writers. Each of the typical archaisms in the list below is preceded by the number of the relevant principle in the SES list above.

SES 1, 2. Single vowels often occur where SES has digraphs, e.g. *broche* broach, *sheres* shears (1597), *chesepress* cheesepress, *gese* geese (1697); *stoles* stools (1559), *shetes* sheets (1561), *cote* coat (1596); double *e* and *o* occur (especially in early inventories) where *ea* and *oa* or *o* . . . silent *e* occur in SES, e.g. *hoose* hose (1580), *boorden* of board (1572).[8]

SES 3, 6. Non-functional double consonants and silent *e* at the end of syllables remain common throughout the period, e.g. *cuppeborde* cupboard, *spytte* spit (1556), *calfe*, *piggs* (1695), *knobbs*, *gunn*, *potts* (1720); conversely, we find single consonants and/or absence of expected silent *e*, e.g. *on* one (1542), *wyf* wife (1567), *scomer* scummer, (1585), *uper*, *harowes*, *laders* (1661).[9]

SES 4. Non-final *y* for *i* is common throughout the period, e.g. *hangyng*, *whyt*, *hys* (1537), *Lynnen*, *Swyne*, *kyne* (1662); conversely, syllable-final *ie* continues in use where SES substitutes *y*, e.g. *canopie*, *Daie Howse* (1604), *haie* (1567).[10]

SES 7. Conventional double final consonants are often not used, e.g. *bucskins* (1694), *pres*, *bras* (1596).[11]

SES 10. Disregard of the three-letter principle is common, e.g. *ry* (1607), *ax* (1631), *od* (1717).[12]

A number of other Middle English conventions discarded by SES linger in many probate inventories, e.g. *ei* or *ey* for long *e*, *oi* or *oy* for long *o*, *f* for medial *v*, and *sch* and *ssh* for *sh*.

A large number of non-SES spellings fall into none of the above categories, but can be described as 'phonetic'. This term can be misused; for example as if it meant 'looking more like the modern pronunciation than the SES'. The sense in which I intend it is 'reflecting the actual pronunciation of the writer, where this differed from the pronunciation

---

[7] Brears, p.72; Brears, p.84; Brears, p.71; Alcock, p.122; Brears, p.79; Alcock, p.45; Brears, p.53; Alcock, p.35.

[8] Alcock, p.32; Alcock, p.122; Brears, p.6; Brears, p.11; Brears, p.59; Alcock, p.56; Brears, p.43.

[9] Alcock, p.23; Alcock, p.85; Alcock, p.46; Brears, p.2; Brears, p.17; Brears, p.56; Brears, p.119.

[10] Alcock, p.31; Brears, p.123; Alcock, p.78; Brears, p.17.

[11] Alcock, p.39; Brears, p.59.

[12] Alcock, p.4; Alcock, p.70; Alcock, p.128.

notated by SES'. This category can be subdivided into (i) spellings which reflect general contemporary pronunciation better than SES; (ii) spellings which reflect the regional pronunciation of the community from which the inventory comes; (iii) spellings which reflect general contemporary non-standard English pronunciation.

(i) SES fails to reflect a number of changes in pronunciation that had been completed at least by the seventeenth century and in most cases much earlier. The writings of contemporary scholars give direct evidence for these; moreover, they can be deduced from written texts of many kinds, among which probate inventories are especially good witnesses. Historical linguists generally infer that the merger of two formerly distinct sounds or sequences A and B has occurred when they find that spelling A can be used for sound B and vice versa. Typical evidence occurs in our texts as follows (reference once more is to the SES list above).

SES 5(i). Merger of the long mid vowel *o* and the diphthong *ow* is shown in e.g. *croe* crow (1631), *housse* hose, *loudes* loads (1559).[13]

SES 5(ii). Merger of the long vowel *a* and the diphthong *ai* or *ay* is shown in e.g. *scayles* scales (1580), *wane* wain (1569), *main* mane (1673), *pare* pair (1689), *spaydes* spades (1561), *mades* maids (1561), *baycon* (1567), *wanes* wains (1572).[14]

SES 5(iii). Merger of the long vowel *u* and *eu* or *ew* is shown in e.g. *bruyng* brewing (1537), *puter* (1697), *ure* ewer (1578), *puther* pewter (1596).[15]

SES 5(iv). The merger in certain words of the vowels of *double* and *tub* is shown in e.g. *dublet* (1557).[16]

SES 6(i). The split between the *a* of *hat* and the *a* of *hall*, *talk*, and the merger of the latter with *au*, *aw*, is indicated by e.g. *haull* (1557), *mault* (1616), *hawlle* (1568), *bawke* balk (1570).[17]

SES 6(ii). The split between the *o* of *hop* and the *o* of *hold*, and the merger of the latter with *ou*, *ow* (in *soul*, *low*), is indicated by e.g. *ould* old (1675), *boulting* (1616), *bowting* (1559), *mowde* mould (1561), *boulsters* (1632).[18]

---

[13] Alcock, p.70; Alcock, p.45.

[14] Alcock, p.55; Alcock, p.77; Alcock, p.74.; Alcock, p.98; Brears, p.10; Brears, p.12; Brears, p.16; Brears, p.42.

[15] Alcock, p.31; Alcock 122; Brears, p.50; Brears, p.59.

[16] Alcock, p.27: there are eight other similar spellings, none with *ou*.

[17] Alcock, p.27: there are six similar spellings of 'hall' in this collection; Alcock, p.59: there are 13 similar spellings in this collection; Brears, p.24; Brears, p.39.

[18] Alcock, p.48: there are three similar spellings in this collection; Alcock, p.59: there are eight similar spellings in this collection; Brears, p.6; Brears, p.10; Brears, p.78.

SES 9(i). The merger of initial *wr-* and *r-* is indicated by *wracks* racks (1720).[19]

SES 9(ii). The merger of *stl-* and medial *ss-* + *l* is indicated by *tressel* (1694), *brisel* bristle (1542), *tressells* (1568), *huslement* (1585).[20]

SES 9(iii). The merger of initial *wh-* and *w-* is indicated by *werof* (1569), *wich* which (1628).[21]

SES 9(iv). The merger of *sh* and the combination of *s* and a *y*-sound is shown in e.g. *quyscions* (1552), *quissions* (1632).[22] (The *sh* sound is original.)

(ii) Isolated spellings that are suggestive of the modern regional pronunciation of a word or form are not necessarily 'phonetic' representations of that pronunciation at an earlier date. But if we find spellings of a word, or a group of words containing a particular phonetic sequence, which match the regional pronunciation established from evidence collected in recent times (and in some cases, deduced from local Middle English texts), it is reasonable to believe that the inventory writers were recording the pronunciation of their district rather than that on which the SES of the word is based, especially when the same kinds of spelling occur repeatedly in the inventories of a particular locality.

In the Stoneleigh inventories three types of spelling correspond well with features of west Midland pronunciation known from elsewhere: (1) the development of initial *w* before long *o* in *wottes* oats (1552);[23] (2) *o* for standard *a* before nasal consonants in *condelstyckes* (1556) and *homer* (1559);[24] and (3) *a* for standard *o* in certain other environments, e.g. in *cocklaft* (1682), *parenger* (1675).[25]

Three typical spellings in the Yorkshire inventories accord perfectly with (among other authorities) Harold Orton's twentieth-century survey

---

[19] Alcock, p.149.

[20] Alcock, p.39: there are eight similar spellings in this collection; Brears, p.2; Brears, p.31; Brears, p.56.

[21] Alcock, p.19; Alcock, p.95: there are three similar spellings in this collection.

[22] Alcock, p.46; Brears, p.78.

[23] Alcock, p.47 (also in three other inventories); cf. *wuts* in Wilbraham, 'Attempt at a Glossary', p.31 and Jackson, *Shropshire word-book*, p.491.

[24] Alcock, p.24, also p.45 (1559); Alcock, p.45; cf. such forms as *mon-ondle* man-handle, *onker* hanker, *'ontle* handful, in Salisbury, *Glossary of words and phrases*, and *homber* hammer, in Jackson, *Shropshire word-book*. In Middle English records from Worcestershire, Old English *a* appears as *o* frequently before *m* and *n*: see Sundby, *Studies in the Middle English dialect*, p.258.

[25] Alcock, p.61; Alcock, p.48 (and in five other places); cf. such forms as *crass* cross, *drap* drop, *ladge* lodge, *racket* rocket, in Salisbury, *Glossary of words and phrases*.

of the dialect of adjoining south Durham: (1) spellings with *aw* of words that have *ow* in standard English, e.g. *sawen* sown (1559), *thrawne* thrown (1567, 1578); (2) spellings with *wh* of words that etymologically contain *qu*, e.g. *whie*, *whe*, *whies* (1559), *wheyes* (1578) quey, heifer, *whearnes* (1561), (1570), *wheres* (1596) quern; (3) spellings with *n-* of words that etymologically contain *nd-*, e.g. *tronell* (1567), *trinle* (1596, 1602) trundle or trindle, *cannellstick* (163?), *grinelstones* (1639).[26]

(iii) When we find that documents from a particular area frequently exhibit similar non-SES spellings for a word, and that documents in several other areas exhibit the same feature, it is reasonable to assume that this is no coincidence, but the record of a form that was widespread in non-standard use, but had not penetrated the standard language. Perhaps the most noteworthy is the merger of the unstressed ending *ing* with the endings *in*, *en*, and *on*. Not only are there passim such spellings as *dryppen*, *choppen*, *chaffyn* (1578), but also reverse spellings, e.g. *basinges* (1602), *Kitching* (1639).[27] A form of *cushion* with *qui-* as the first syllable is almost universal in the Yorkshire sample, appears ten times in Stoneleigh (as against eight instances of *cushion*), and is found in documents from other parts of England; this suggests that it was once a supra-regional variant. The occurrence of spellings such as *shutes* suits (1640)[28] indicate that the merger of *s+y* and *sh* was widespread in syllable-initial position, though *sugar* and *sure* are the only words in which it survives in 'standard' pronunciation. An apparently disyllabic spelling of the word *form* in the Yorkshire inventories, e.g. *fowreme* (1567), *furram* (1612), is corroborated in distant Warwickshire in *fourromes* (1552),[29] attesting a perhaps once widespread pronunciation. Spellings such as these underline the known fact that several supra-regional features of early Modern English pronunciation never became 'standard'.

The word stock

The vocabulary of probate inventories is limited in two ways: semantically, to the terms of the household, farm, and shop (a positive limitation, as we shall see); and grammatically, in that nouns and

[26] Orton, *Phonology*; Brears, pp.4, 14, 49: cf. Orton, *Phonology*, Section 144.4; Brears, pp.7, 46, 12, 39, 60: cf. Orton, *Phonology*, Sections 262–267; Brears, pp.15, 59, 67, 68, 86, 92: cf. Orton, *Phonology*, Section 288.
[27] Brears, p.46; Brears, pp.64, 91: the inventories in Alcock are from an area in which the final *g* in *ng* has been preserved to the present day, and hence do not attest this development.
[28] Alcock, p.166.
[29] Brears, pp.14, 67, 68; Alcock, p.46.

adjectives predominate, verbs occur chiefly as participles, and adverbs and conjunctions are rare (a disadvantage for the lexical historian). Everybody is aware of the considerable number of words in probate inventories which are not part of everyday modern standard English, and almost every printed collection contains a glossary. Probably the majority of these words are now obsolete or archaic, owing to the economic and social changes of the last two centuries. There is a natural tendency to think of them also as 'dialect'. I shall presently consider the suitability of this label.

These non-standard words and word meanings fall into two groups. There are, firstly, words and meanings that noticeably occur in inventories from one particular district or region. Generally speaking, these lexical items can be related to the known regional vocabulary of the area in modern times (that is, since local dialect collecting began seriously in the late-nineteenth century), and often as well to the vocabulary of local Middle English texts that antedate the rise of standard English. Here are five words from Tudor and Stuart Yorkshire which were all recorded from south Durham in the 1930s.

gimers (1639);[30] *gimmer* 'ewe between her first and second shearing' is found in Scottish texts of the fifteenth century.

lang settle (1559);[31] *langsettle* 'long bench with arms and a high back' is found in northern texts of the fourteenth century (e.g. *Durham Account Rolls*).

spaynynge (1561), *spaned* (1578);[32] *spane* 'wean' is found in northern Middle English texts such as *Cursor Mundi*.

stee (1561);[33] *sty* 'ladder' is also found in *Cursor Mundi* etc.

tups, *tupps* (1639);[34] *tup* 'ram' is found in northern Middle English texts before 1400.

These words are all examples of 'regional dialect' uses which were never adopted into standard English.

Secondly, there are words and meanings that are not now part of standard English but occur in probate inventories from widely separated parts of the country. Here are six words recorded in the *Oxford English Dictionary (OED)* from fifteenth- and sixteenth-century sources (the middle four down to the nineteenth century) which in the Tudor and Stuart period occur in both our Warwickshire and our Yorkshire collections.

---

[30] Brears, p.89: Orton, *Phonology*, Section 68.3.
[31] Brears, p.5: Orton, *Phonology*, Section 45.1.
[32] Brears, pp.10, 45: Orton, *Phonology*, Section 89.5.
[33] Brears, p.10: Orton, *Phonology*, Section 100.1.
[34] Brears, p.89: Orton, *Phonology*, Section 116.

board-cloth 'tablecloth'.[35]

cob-iron 'one of the irons on which a spit turns'.[36]

harden, herden, hurden 'a coarse fabric made from the hards of flax or hemp'.[37]

hilling vbl. n.[1] 2 'bed-quilt'.[38]

piggin 'a small pail or cylindrical vessel'.[39]

steep-fat s.v. *steep* v.[1] 5 'in the names of vessels used in steeping'.[40]

The probate inventory evidence from two widely separated areas, taken with the *OED* evidence, suggests that these words were supra-regional. Since they are all words relating to everyday items, it is reasonable to assume that they were familiar to a large proportion of the population. However, they hardly feature in literary texts at all (*cob-iron* occurs in a work by Bacon, *ante* 1626, and *piggin* in a work by Herrick, 1647),[41] but the reason cannot be geographical: it must be social. Literature did not record them because they denoted subjects which did not primarily concern the reading and writing classes. Probate inventories therefore preserve a section of the everyday English vocabulary which would otherwise scarcely survive.

There is another notable aspect of vocabulary in probate inventories. Every collection of probate inventories that is carefully studied (by comparison with the *OED*) yields a list of words that have not before been recorded. When different lists are collated, some shared items are usually found, and these then join the above-mentioned category of supra-regional, but non-literary, vocabulary; others remain, for the time being, unparalleled. In the Stoneleigh inventories there are 54

[35] *boardclothes* (1597) Alcock, p.32 (also three earlier examples); *bordclothes* (1567) Brears, p.15. (*OED* has Scottish and Cumbrian evidence.)

[36] *cobyrons* (1597) Alcock, p.32 (and several other examples), Brears, p.6 (1559), Brears, p.12 (1561). (*OED* has Yorkshire, Lancashire, and 'South and East Country' evidence.)

[37] *hurden* Alcock, p.27 (1557); *herden* Alcock, p.45 (1559); *harden* Brears, p.11 (1561). (*OED* has evidence from Durham, Norfolk, East Anglia, Nottingham, Lancashire, and Yorkshire.)

[38] *hilling* Alcock, p.32 (1597); *hillinge* Brears, p.16 (157?). (*OED* has evidence from Lancashire, Sheffield, and Essex.)

[39] *piggin* Alcock, p.97 (1612), *piggin* p.108 (1610); *piggins* Brears, p.15 (1567), *pigin* Brears, p.160 (1689). ('recorded . . . from Northumberland to Hampshire', *OED*, s.v.)

[40] *steepfatt* Alcock, p.59 (1616) (and three other occurrences); *stepefatt* Brears, p.37 (1570), p.52 (1578) (*OED* has only two examples, both northern).

[41] Of the six, the only ones recorded in Johnson's *Dictionary* are *cobiron* (perhaps because of its use by Bacon) and *piggin* ('in the northern provinces, a small vessel'). From our first list, Johnson included only *tup*, with the interesting comment 'this word is yet used in Staffordshire, and in other provinces'.

previously unregistered lexical items, 16 of which are attested in other non-literary documents, four of them quite plentifully.[42] In the Yorkshire inventories at least 15 unrecorded items occur:

borderers (for cupboards), *dishecall, hosser, landsele, mambled* (designating aglets and buttons), *maunded* (designating a skep), *otter staffe, rap* ('to put in a staff'), *raythes*, (coup- or cart-) *rath, shilved* (designating wains), *skelb(o)uses, skreres, strivinge iron, trashment, wodcans*.[43]

It follows that the more the vocabulary of each inventory collection is exhaustively studied, the more will be discovered about the history of 'non-standard' English, not just as a sprinkling of isolated 'dialect' outposts, but as the diffused vernacular of the common people.

Grammar

Probate inventories are of course highly formulaic; the commonest syntactic feature is the noun phrase, with a typical structure of determiner (article, demonstrative, or numeral), an optional modifier (adjective, participle, or adjectival phrase), a noun headword, and an optional postmodifier (which may be a phrase or occasionally a clause); we also find the repeated locating formula 'In the [place]'. We can learn less from them about their writers' grammar than about pronunciation or vocabulary, but they still offer some interesting insights, as the examples below indicate.

The verb phrase: the third person singular present

(1) all sych geres that longyth to the sam (1537).
(2) all that belonges to the bedde (1556).
(3) all that belongest to it (1660).
(4) Debtes which the said Thomas Coxe dothe owe (1580).
(5) an other bed where the Children lyeth (1612).
(6) calves that is spaned (1578).[44]

---

[42] See further Weiner, 'Use of non-literary manuscript texts', pp.235–54.

[43] Brears, p.59; Brears, p.63 (explained as 'a rack for dishes' by the editor); Brears, pp.17, 89, 119, 161; Brears, p.71; Brears, p.36; Brears, p.60 (explained as 'made of basket-work' by the editor); Brears, p.51; Brears, p.34; Brears, pp.16, 91 (explained as 'cart-shelving' by the editor); Brears, p.99; Brears, pp.10, 38 (explained as 'the front boards of a cow stall' by the editor); Brears, p.34; Brears, p.37; Brears, p.40: the *English Dialect Dictionary* gives this word on the strength of mentions in four nineteenth-century north country glossaries; Brears, p.19.

[44] Alcock, p.31; Alcock, p.51; Alcock, p.112; Alcock, p.57; Brears, p.71; Brears, p.45.

From (1), it would seem that the ending *(e)th* was still normal in the west Midlands in the early-sixteenth century, but (2) and (3) suggest that the northern *(e)s*, which had only recently appeared in London English, was being adopted in the second half of the century, except in *doth*, where *(e)th* was retained longer in standard English. Since the *-s* form was usual in northern Middle English for both singular and plural (as (6) shows), *lieth* in (5) looks like hypercorrection, due to a mistaken belief that *(e)th* was the 'standard' (southern) equivalent in the plural as well.

The verb phrase: the past participle

(7) The corne sowed in the feild (1580, also 1631)
(8) Other things forgotten (1694); things forgot (1697)
(9) debts owen to (1570)
(10) lowe backte (1568)[45]

The tendency to substitute regular for irregular past inflections is shown in (7); but (8) shows the variation between past participles with and without *en* in the late-seventeenth and early-eighteenth century. (9) shows the preservation of an old participial form (retained as the adjective *own*). (10) shows the disappearance of the unstressed vowel from the regular past inflection in the mid-sixteenth century.

The noun phrase: relative pronouns

(11) Scheppe, of the qwyche 20 be hoyes (hogs) (1557).
(12) Richard Knowles whoe came from London (1656).
(13) one bed as is in pyces (1578).[46]

(11) is a late example of *the which* (last in literature in the early-seventeenth century); (12) an example of *who* as a relative, which was only northern until the seventeenth century; and (13) of the relative pronoun *as*, which has been non-standard since the same century.

The noun phrase: nominalisation

(14) 3 2-yere oldes and 4 of 3-yere oldes (1569).
(15) one od one (1656).[47]

(14) shows the nominalisation of a compound adjective by the addition of the plural suffix; this is especially interesting since evidence

---

[45] Alcock, pp.57, 70; Alcock, pp.39, 122; Brears, p.40; Brears, p.31.
[46] Alcock, p.28; Brears, p.117; Brears, p.47.
[47] Alcock, p.77 (1569): cf. Brears, p.89, five fower yeare old steares; Brears, p.115.

of the use of [numeral] + *year-old*, as a noun, does not occur in standard English until the nineteenth century.[48] The use of the pro-form *one*, shown in (15), is likewise northern until the seventeenth century.

The adverbial phrase: prepositions

(16) 2 Acres a rye (1597).
(17) In the Chamber below the entry (1607).
(18) apperteyning of Sir Thomas W. (1542).
(19) one Chare . . . with a bull head on yt (1568).
(20) spones with postelles on (1578).[49]

The historic form of *of*, so worn down as to resemble the indefinite article, and seen in (16), was banished from standard English after the seventeenth century; *below* (17) was rather a new preposition in literary English at this time; *of* with *appertain(ing)* (18) is unparalleled in literary English; (19) and (20) show early use of the colloquial construction [noun] *with* [noun] *on/in* (*it*) in place of a relative clause.

If these two collections are typical, then probate inventories, even with their formulaic structure, can offer us information both about grammatical features that were becoming old-fashioned (e.g. 1) and, perhaps more significantly, about features that were new or had not yet emerged in contemporary literary English (e.g. 14).

How different is the language of probate inventories?

Probate inventories of any date between the 1530s and 1730s differ from modern standard English more markedly than contemporary literary texts. This is quite obvious in the spelling system, which, as we have seen, may deviate either through conservatism or through a 'progressive' use of 'phonetic' spellings rather than conventionalised SES. Exact statistics are not available, but it seems as if in a sample of literary texts the proportion of words (tokens) deviating from modern standard spelling runs from 30 per cent around 1540 to 14 per cent a century later, after which deviation is minimal; whereas in our two collections the rate starts above 40 per cent, drops to 30 per cent a century later, and is still around 20 per cent in the 1680s.[50]

The difference is also very marked in vocabulary. In literary texts

---

[48] Nominalisation, turning an adjective into a noun.
[49] Alcock, p.32; Alcock, p.47; Brears, p.2; Brears, p.31; Brears, p.50.
[50] These percentages, and those for vocabulary below, are based on a word-count of literary texts in Görlach, *Introduction to Early Modern English*, pp.341–3, 359–61, 237, 373, 385–7, 397–8, and 273–4.

throughout the period the proportion of words and meanings (again, tokens) that are not part of modern standard English fluctuates around 7 per cent. In our collections it is around 13 per cent until the mid-seventeenth century, and still above 10 per cent at the end of the period. As we have seen, only part of this difference can be ascribed to regional dialect; as much, or more, is due to the presence of supra-regional everyday vocabulary that was absent from literary English. It is fortunate that probate inventories survive to testify to the language of ordinary people.

14

The Wooden Horse in the Cellar: Words and Contexts in Shropshire Probate Inventories

BARRIE TRINDER

Forms and categories

Words in probate inventories are used in very particular ways.[1] A scholar discovering a wooden horse in an inventory made in Bridgnorth in 1693 might rashly conclude that he was examining a list of the chattels of a pioneering manufacturer of children's toys or of a classical scholar planning a re-enactment of the Trojan wars. A careless reading of such an entry as '2 barrels and two horses' which failed to note the context of the item—in a cellar—might result in an over-estimate of the town's equine population. Historians should be grateful to appraisers like those who listed 'horses for the barrels to stand on' in 1728 for defining terms which can otherwise lead to confusion. The forms of an inventory, the order in which goods are listed, the categories which the appraiser consciously or unconsciously selects, the sequences of words which become familiar as many inventories are examined, were shaped

---

[1] The inventories on which this chapter is based have been transcribed since 1972, chiefly by members of adult education groups sponsored by Shropshire County Council and the University of Birmingham School of Continuing Studies. In due course typed copies of all of them will be lodged with Shropshire Records and Research. The original documents are in the Lichfield Joint Record Office (Lichfield diocese and peculiars) and the Herefordshire Record Office (Hereford diocese). I am grateful for the assistance of several hundred people who have worked as members of these classes, and to David Lloyd, Malcolm Wanklyn and Sam Mullins, at various times tutors of classes, for their generous co-operation. I owe a particular debt to Jeff and Nancy Cox of the University of Wolverhampton without whom the project would never have progressed so far, and who, together with colleagues at University College Northampton, have provided helpful comments on the chapter.

not just by legal requirements but also by the customs of the region. A first impression of a group of inventories may be that it shows no signs of order or consistency. A closer investigation shows that there were often customs which were observed over long periods, as well as idiosyncrasies practised in particular places for short spells which may simply reflect the whims of appraisers.

It is the contention of this chapter that probate inventories represent the best source for investigating the material culture of early modern England but its purpose is not to examine particular aspects of that culture—when the dresser appeared or how meat was preserved—but to show how words which may be familiar can take on new and precise meanings in the context of an inventory and to suggest how inventories can be decoded to increase our understanding of the details of the lives of our ancestors.[2]

The chapter is based on the analysis of about 7,000 inventories taken mainly between 1660 and 1750 in a variety of communities in Shropshire, including Shrewsbury, then one of England's principal regional capitals, the coal-mining parishes of the Ironbridge Gorge, the market towns of Ludlow, Shifnal, Bishop's Castle, Wellington and Newport, fertile lowland parishes like Stottesdon, Richard's Castle and Adderley, and remote upland communities around the Clee Hills and the Stiperstones. Such a large and varied sample provides an opportunity to look closely at the ways in which words are used, and to demonstrate patterns which may aid the interpretation of inventories more generally.

Many inventories contain few details, and were apparently made hurriedly to expedite a legal process—but some were composed with meticulous attention to detail, whether relating to the trade of the deceased or to his or her household. The inventory of Joseph Weyman of Ludlow, a perukemaker who died in 1746, lists 136 items of which no more than a dozen relate to his trade, and yet its total value is only just over £36. Most inventories give only passing attention to the wearing apparel or books of the deceased, yet that for Jane Ryder of Shrewsbury, taken in 1770, includes 53 items listing clothing and 18 listing books. One asks why a mousetrap worth just a penny was included on the £6 inventory of Thomas Houlart, labourer of Tugford, who died in 1664. Such detail was provided consciously and for a purpose, even if we cannot now determine what that purpose may have been. By contrast the appraisers of George Smith of Shifnal in 1737 when listing the contents of his buttery noted eight barrels and some drink, and added a concluding item, 'a table and other small

[2] Mather, 1693; Adams 1729; Allen, 1728; all Bridgnorth.

things too tedious to mention', and the inventory of Thomas Adams, mercer, of Newport, who died in 1706, has the rooms of his house simply totalled, while the goods in his shop appear as just one item—worth over £700.[3]

As Weiner's chapter demonstrates, the language of inventories can be of great interest to the etymologist.[4] Shropshire inventories reveal the use of such wonderfully archaic terms as 'pullen', the plural of poultry, and of such curiosities as a monteith, a bowl with notched inner edges in which drinking glasses could hang to cool, which was named after a seventeenth-century Scotsman, the bottom of whose coat was similarly uneven. Nevertheless, the challenge of understanding the inventories of a particular region is not primarily etymological. The meanings of rare and obscure words can usually be traced, with patience. It is more important to understand the ways in which words which are relatively familiar are employed, and to accept, with humility, that many words are used in ways which preclude direct translations into modern English. There are no precise modern equivalents of 'seedness' or 'mit'.

The meanings of some dangerously familiar terms soon become evident. The term press, when unqualified, almost always means a cupboard in Shropshire inventories, in the sense still in current usage in Scotland and northern England. A *pair* of tables will always indicate tables used for gaming of the kind illustrated by Randle Holme. Trams, like some horses, are stands on which barrels are placed in cellars. Expressions like 'a carpet belonging to the table', 'a table and carpet' or 'a side cupboard and carpet' indicate that carpets in seventeenth and eighteenth-century Shropshire were not floor coverings.[5]

The meanings of some difficult words can be determined by study of their contexts. If the word 'cratch' is used at all in the late-twentieth century it is applied to a rack for feeding animals, mounted on the wall of a stable or cowshed. The *Oxford English Dictionary* (*OED*) adds a variety of other meanings: a moveable rack for feeding beasts out of doors, a wooden hurdle used in killing sheep, a frame suspended from the beams of a kitchen and used for hanging bacon, or a device employed in a dairy for draining whey in cheesemaking. Shropshire inventories listing 'beef and bacon on the cratch', 'cheese cratches', a

---

[3] Weyman, 1746, Ludlow; Ryder, 1770, Shrewsbury; Houlart, 1664, Tugford; Smith, 1737, Shifnal; Adams, 1706, Newport.

[4] See Chapter 13, above.

[5] Holme, *Academy of armory*, III, pp.62–5; Aston, 1686, Stottesdon; Welling, 1797, Bridgnorth; Whitaker, 1798, Bridgnorth; Jones, 1750, Cleobury Mortimer; Menlove, 1708, Wem; Fisher, 1680, Shrewsbury; Easthope, 1700, Bridgnorth.

cratch in a butcher's slaughter house, 'cratches for sheep' include all these meanings and more besides. A 'bottle cratch' in a Bridgnorth cellar was probably some kind of rack, and the cratch listed with leather, shoes, seat and lasts in the shop of a Newport shoemaker was presumably a frame useful in the manufacture of footware, perhaps in order to hang a hide in such a way that it remained both flat and aired.[6]

Similarly contexts provide meanings of the word maid. The *OED* acknowledges that, apart from its obvious meanings, it was applied to several inanimate objects, but only identifies its application to a clothes horse, the one meaning which still has some current use. Such items as 'a maid for drying cloaths' indicate that the word was used in this sense in eighteenth-century Shropshire, but the term seems more commonly to have been applied to an iron stand in a fireplace, used for hanging or placing hot objects, 'a maid to hold the pan', a 'smoothing iron and maid', a 'toaster and maid', a 'maid to hang a frying pan' or simply an 'iron maid'. There were also wooden maids, at least one of which was located in a room used for malting. The meaning of a word like maid can only be ascertained from its context, and from comparing it with other occurrences within a large sample of inventories.[7]

The meanings of other words can similarly be deduced from their contexts. The word jack can mean either a leather bucket or a machine to turn a spit. Which is indicated in a particular instance can only be deduced by whether it is in a fireplace or amongst other receptacles for liquids. One Bridgnorth inventory taken in 1664 helpfully distinguishes a 'leather jack' from the 'jack to turn the spit'. The 'parcel of Wedgwood' in the inventory of John Billingsley, bellowsmaker of Birmingham in 1702, obviously does not refer to ceramics in the Etruscan style made in North Staffordshire, but should be interpreted in its context in Billingsley's workshop, together with bolster wood, rough bellowsboards, and various tools.[8]

Inventories which contain few details can be as helpful in gaining understanding from a large collection as those which list multitudes of items, because their very terseness defines the patterns of thinking which appraisers applied to households. A certain Joseph Felton appraised many inventories in Shrewsbury between 1703 and 1716. In more than

---

[6] Grove, 1709, Alveley; Adams, 1729, Bridgnorth; Eccleshall, 1688, Newport; Gilbert, 1760, Bridgnorth.

[7] Wilson, 1742, Shrewsbury; Poyner, 1765, Bridnorth; Scott, 1708, Shifnal; Stretton, 1747, Bridgnorth; Stephens, 1742, Much Wenlock; Atkiss, 1708, Salop.

[8] Broadfield, 1664, Bridgnorth; Billingsley, University of Wolverhampton, *Dictionary of traded commodities database* (hereafter *DTC*).

a dozen households he judged the contents by a simple categorisation: Brass & pewter, Upholstery, Joinery Ware, Iron Ware, Napery, Coopery, Lumber.[9]

A recognition of this kind of thinking provides a key to the understanding of other, more detailed, inventories. Many appraisers thought in terms of particular materials, metals, textiles and various sorts of wooden ware, and their patterns of thinking can be discerned in inventories which are awash with detail. Some appraisers helpfully define their categories. A Shrewsbury inventory of 1678 defines upholstery ware as beds, bolsters, coverlet, curtains, vallances and carpets, and joiners' ware as cupboards, bedsteads, chests, tables, stools and wainscoat. Other appraisers saw the value of houses primarily as the sum of the value of the items in different rooms and some contemporaries of Joseph Felton made inventories which were no more than lists of rooms and values. In agricultural parishes some appraisers gave precedence to the farm outdoors, listing animals, crops and equipment in some detail, while summarising briefly the contents of the house.[10]

The language of inventories reflects the thinking and priorities of appraisers. In deciding how to describe a deceased person in the preamble of an inventory, for example, there was a choice between a word indicating status, like esquire, gentleman, yeoman, husbandman or labourer, and one indicating occupation. In rural Shropshire agriculturalists were universally described by their status—the term farmer is almost unknown on the county's probate documents before 1750. Some men so described are shown by the contents of their inventories or by other probate documents to have followed particular trades. In towns the use of occupational labels was commonplace, but some traders who were obviously butchers, bakers or candlemakers were nevertheless described as gentlemen in preambles of their inventories. Women were defined almost universally by their marital status so that such female traders as Sarah Shakle of Birmingham who made files and died in 1719, and Joan Bourne of Bridgnorth who died in 1674 and manufactured felt hats were described as widows, although the contents of their inventories reveal that they were running substantial businesses.[11]

Appraisers also gave names to rooms. Probate inventories have been

[9] Barker, 1705, Shrewsbury; see also: Bayley 1704; Beale; 1707, Beddow, 1703; McCormick, 1705; Jaundrell, 1706; Morris, 1703; Morris, 1707; Nicholas, 1714, Pugh, 1716; Wheatley, 1705; all Shrewsbury.
[10] Birch 1678; Cole, 1717; Cope, 1720; all Shrewsbury.
[11] Shakle, *DTC*; Bourne, 1674, Bridgnorth.

used by students of vernacular architecture to determine changes in the form of rural buildings. It is certainly possible to plot the appearance of new terms used to describe rooms and of the changing uses of rooms referred to by old names. In Shropshire it is clear that the parlour was used less and less as a sleeping room in the late-seventeenth century, and that in the homes of the moderately wealthy it became more and more common to find a room described as a dining room. Such developments may indicate significant social changes, but if they are to be understood it is necessary to distinguish between the name applied to a room and the functions which it served. This is best exemplified in the word brewhouse. Sometimes the word was used in a literal sense. Thomas Andrews, a wealthy barge owner and innkeeper of Bridgnorth, who died in 1723, had a brewhouse which contained equipment for brewing beer and nothing more. Most brewhouses, however, were used for several purposes, and it is commonplace throughout Shropshire to find them stocked with 'brewing and dairy vessels' or with 'brewing tubs, wash tubs, furnace and boiler'. They were places where many household tasks involving liquids were carried out.[12]

Hierarchies

Appraisers in all parts of England were accustomed to use hierarchical sequences when describing various kinds of animals or artefacts. Recognition of the ways in which such sequences were employed enhances our understanding of the inventories of a region or a particular parish—a hierarchy is a template, within which certain categories may be expected, and an item falling into a certain place in a hierarchy is likely to have a meaning determined by its position. Within such hierarchies some words take on highly specific meanings.

In Shropshire this phenomenon is best exemplified by the ways in which appraisers described herds of cattle. The agriculture of much of the county was primarily pastoral, and in rural parishes the cattle of the deceased most commonly appear as the first items in an inventory. A typical hierarchy, but not a typical herd, is illustrated in the inventory of one of Shropshire's principal seventeenth-century dairy farmers, Richard Furber of Adderley, who died in 1660. His herd, worth just

---

[12] For the parlour see Priestley and Corfield, 'Rooms and room use', pp.93–123; Weatherill, 'Meaning of consumer behaviour', p.214; Tayleur, 1675, Market Drayton, includes one of the earliest dining rooms in Shropshire; Trinder and Cox, *Yeomen and colliers*, pp.16–17; Oakes, 1714, Bridgnorth; Chalenor 1735, Edgmond.

over £300, consisted of 139 cattle, including, 62 cows, 15 twinter beasts, 25 yearling calves and 30 sucking calves.[13]

This sequence, the cows in milk, the two-year olds (and sometimes three-year olds), the yearlings, and the calves, often divided into weaning and suckling calves, is followed in many other inventories, but some use different terms to describe the same categories. A Richard's Castle inventory of 1684 lists: '9 kine, Two three yeare old haifers, four two yeare old bease, four year old bease'.[14]

A Holgate inventory of 1672 includes: '18 kine, 5 two year olds, 7 yearlings, 7 weanling calves, 2 calves'.[15] Here the word kine is used in a specialised sense, unknown to the OED, to mean cows in milk, while the context defines the sex of the animals described by the archaic term 'bease'. This word is used in another form and in another sense in an inventory taken in Moor in 1668 which itemises: '4 Cow Besse, 4 young Besse, 1 yearling Beast'.[16]

This is precisely the same hierarchy, where the term 'besse' takes on the meaning of cows in milk, while the expression 'young besse' means cows more than a year old which are not yet in milk. Another inventory from Moor taken in 1710 is one of several in which the word bullock appears to describe female cattle. It lists: '3 kine, 2 two year old bullocks, 4 year olds, 3 calves'.[17] In particular contexts in other inventories the word bullock is used to mean a young plough ox. A Much Wenlock inventory of 1706 includes two large oxen sold for just over £9 and two lesser bullocks worth £5.[18]

Words can therefore take on specific meanings shaped by their context in an inventory and our understanding of an inventory will be enhanced if we understand the hierarchical sequences which shape the appraisers' thinking. Similar sequences can be observed in descriptions of crops in predominantly arable areas, in the grades of linen, where the most common sequence, in descending order of value, is Holland, flaxen, hempen and hurden, or in lists of brass, pewter or wooden goods.

Coopery ware

One of the categories most readily identified by appraisers was the collection of staved receptacles which formed part of every household.

---

[13] Furber, 1660, Adderley.
[14] Higgins, 1684, Richard's Castle.
[15] Cresset, 1672, Holgate.
[16] Davis, 1668, Moor.
[17] Cowdell, 1710, Moor.
[18] Mason 1706, Much Wenlock. A looser usage of bullock meaning a young beast rather than the modern sense of a castrated bull is acknowledged by the OED.

These vessels might be individually named, or they might be categorised as cooper's (or coopery, cowpery, coupery) ware, indicating their method of manufacture, as treen (or trynning, trinen, trine, trinding, trening) ware, showing that, like joyner's or turned ware, they were made of wood, or as brewing or dairy vessels, identifying their purpose. Curiously, no collective adjective appears to have been employed to identify vessels used for laundry purposes. Such receptacles were superseded in the course of the Industrial Revolution by replacements made from galvanised iron (later from galvanised steel), and in the twentieth century by utensils made from stainless steel, aluminium and above all, since World War II, from polythene. They were used for tasks which, on a domestic scale, were traditionally the responsibility of women, making butter and cheese, malting, brewing, washing clothes, storing provisions, and scalding and bucking (that is, steeping and bleaching) yarn. In a small house such objects might all be in a kitchen, and in a large house in a succession of specialist rooms, a dairy, a malthouse, a washhouse, but most commonly, in houses of all sizes, they were located in a brewhouse. Analysis of staved vessels shows that many different words were used to describe utensils which were used for the same purposes, and that the terms commonly used to describe them could vary considerably over short distances.[19]

Appraisers sometimes grouped artefacts in ways which indicate their common features, 'buckets, tubbs & pailes', 'mitts, stunds, barrells and the like', 'trinen ware as mites, stoonds and the like', 'al sorts of Trinden ware for brewing and milking' or 'barrels, loomes, stonds & other treen & wooden ware'. The varied nature and purposes of such utensils is indicated by an appraiser in Newport who in 1689 grouped together, '5 brewing stunds of different sizes, 2 wort turnells, 2 watering comps, 2 wash tubs'.[20]

The most common term for such a utensil was a tub. In Shropshire tubs were used for washing clothes, containing water for household use, storing grain, bran, meal, salt or feathers, making cheese, preparing and storing butter, brewing beer, salting meat, kneading dough or steeping yarn. One inventory includes a meal tub, a powdering tub,[21] a kneading tub, an ealding (that is, ale) tub, a soaping tub and a feather tub. Others

---

[19] Trinder and Cox, *Yeomen and colliers*, pp.109–11; Holme, *Academy of armoury*, III, pp.107, 335; McDonald, 'Brewhouse in the Ironbridge Gorge'.

[20] Cooke, 1719, Bridgnorth; Price, 1689, Lydbury North; Sayes, 1677, Lydbury North; Harper, 1686, Lydbury North; Amyes, 1663, Much Wenlock; Holmes, 1689, Newport. Wort, infusion of malt which through fermentation becomes beer.

[21] Powdering tub, a tub for salting or curing meat in.

name such items as two old tubs to put corn in, a butter tub with some butter in, and kneading tubs and other tubs necessary for a baker. Many terms synonymous with tub were used in the county, some of them only in particular localities. Such terms may in some times and in some places have indicated vessels with particular characteristics which may have served particular purposes, but close analysis of the inventories shows that they were all used in a general sense, sometimes with adjectives which defined their size, shape or function. Some items, 'brewing tubs *or* mitts', 'tubs *or* stunds' show that these were often regarded as interchangeable.[22]

A 'mit', more commonly a 'mitt' and sometimes a 'mette' was widely used as a synonym for tub. It had a strong association with dairy activities, indicated in such items as 'Tubs, mitts and all other wooden vessels belonging to ye Dayry'. The presence in inventories of numerous kneading mits shows that they were used in making bread. A Bishop's Castle inventory of 1684 refers to two mits for washing and two large ones for brewing with four others. They were extensively used for both brewing and washing. Appraisers distinguished between large and small mits. Some were round and some were oval. The term was used in most parts of Shropshire, but was more common in the south-west than on the Staffordshire border.[23]

The word stund also meant a kind of tub. It is not defined in the *OED*, but was widely used in Shropshire, rather more in the north and east than in the south and west, as a term synonymous with tub. Stunds were principally used for brewing—a Newport inventory of 1689 refers to five brewing stunds of different sizes but other inventories show that the term was applied to utensils used in dairying and laundry work.[24]

The *OED* defines a turnel as 'a shallow oval tub for scalding, kneading or salting'. In Shropshire the use of the term was largely confined to the north and east of the county. No less than 46 are named in the 246 inventories made in Newport between 1660 and 1750. The word appears hardly at all in the inventories of Bishop's Castle, Ludlow and the parishes around the Clee Hills. Every qualification of the word suggests that it was synonymous with tub, mit or stund. There were kneading turnels, scalding turnels, soaping turnels, milk turnels and meal turnels. Turnels varied in size and shape. A Shifnal inventory of 1713 includes a large turnell, a round turnel and a large long turnell. The

[22] Roberts, 1700, Shifnal; Joyner, 1664, Bridgnorth; Griffiths, 1709, Shrewsbury; Hinde, 1651, Newport.
[23] Low, 1721, Stoke St Milburgh; Walters, 1684, Bishop's Castle.
[24] Holmes, 1689, Newport.

word kimnel is similarly defined by the *OED* as a tub used in brewing, kneading and salting. It was used in the same parts of Shropshire as the word turnel, although it is less common. All the qualified uses of the word relate to brewing.[25]

Skeel is another word, duly acknowledged in the *OED*, which indicates a tub for domestic use. It was commonly used in the parishes around the Clee Hills, but rarely appears in northern or eastern Shropshire. Skeels are mentioned in 14 of the 218 inventories of the parish of Stottesdon, and are very common in the inventories of the nearby town of Bewdley across the Worcestershire border. Skeels were used in brewing and for kneading dough, and could be round, long or oval.

The use of the word loom to mean a tub is recognised in the *OED*, but its disappearance from modern currency means that its appearance in inventories can cause confusion, and the unwary scholar who fails to recognise it could inflate a region's domestic textile industry. The word, like turnel, is used principally in Shifnal, Newport and other parishes on Shropshire's eastern border, although it does occur in Richard's Castle at the county's southern extremity. The word loom is frequently unqualified, so that whether it indicates a tub or a machine used for weaving can often be determined only by its context. It was much used in the parish of Kynnersley, where some appraisers were careful to distinguish *weavers'* looms. Otherwise it is only the context of such looms as those in the item '5 barrells, 5 looms, 2 bouks, 1 churn' on a Shifnal inventory of 1699, which shows that they were tubs. All the looms whose function is indicated were used for brewing.[26]

A similarly confusing word is hoop, which is recognised in the *OED* as a measure of corn of varying capacity. Some hoops in Shropshire inventories were clearly used for that purpose. A Tugford inventory of 1693 lists a 'hope to measure by', and a 'measuring hoop' was itemised on a Madeley inventory but some hoops were simply used as containers for wheat or beans. Shifnal inventories of 1686 and 1701 each include both a hoop and a half hoop.[27]

The word coomb, as it appears in the *OED*, or compt, as it most commonly appears on Shropshire inventories—compe and coume are other variations—also indicates a tub, but one used for a more specific purpose. The *OED*, quoting Randall Holme, suggests that it was

---

[25] Scott, 1713, Shifnal; Ball 1667, Newport.
[26] Hooper, 1625, Kynnersley; Baker, 1640, Kynnersley; Smart, 1699, Shifnal.
[27] Strefford, Tugford, 1693; Goodman, 1733, Madeley; Turner, 1686, Shifnal; Perrins, 1701, Shifnal.

principally used in brewing, but Shropshire references indicate that it was more commonly associated with malting. The word is often prefixed with water, weeting or watering, and usually seems to indicate a vessel used for steeping barley before it was laid out on a malting floor. The word was principally used in east Shropshire, and was commonly employed in neighbouring parts of Staffordshire, but it also appears in the grain-growing parish of Stottesdon in south Shropshire.[28]

The most remarkable word meaning this kind of half-barrel that has emerged from the study of inventories in Shropshire is betchin (the most common spelling, but also rendered as betchen, bechen etc). It is a word unknown to the *OED*, but has obviously links with German and Dutch words meaning a basin or similar container. The use of betchin is almost entirely confined to the town of Bridgnorth, where it appears on 97 (20 per cent) of the 484 inventories which survive for the period 1630–1800. The word is used in the 1630s and continued to appear on inventories until the 1760s, but the sample of inventories surviving from the last three decades of the eighteenth century is too small for its absence to be regarded as evidence that it had disappeared from currency. The word is used in none of the inventories of the parishes in the Ironbridge Gorge, only ten miles upstream from Bridgnorth, and in constant communication with the town through trade on the Severn. Almost all the inventories for the rural parishes around Bridgnorth have been transcribed, but no more than four instances of betchins have been found. The meaning of betchin can be determined by its context. Betchins are always grouped with items made of wood, as in the phrase 'betchins, tubs and barrels', and one is specifically defined as part of the treenware. One inventory in 1640 refers specifically to a 'wooden bechchen'. A betchin is sometimes qualified by an adjective indicating its relative size or its function, a great betchin, a washing betchin, a kneading betching or a soaping betchin, indicating that like a mitt or a turnel, it could be used for a variety of household purposes. Betchins came in various sizes and probably in different shapes, since inventories refer to a long betchen and a small betchin.[29]

Coopery is not the only ware described in inventories which can be subjected to this kind of linguistic and functional analysis. The same could be done for other kinds of containers, for the boxes, coffers and trunks, which are included in many inventories although their uses are

[28] Inventories of Abbot's Bromley and adjacent parishes in Staffordshire, transcribed by Sandra Bowdler, formerly of the University of Wolverhampton. I am grateful to Ms Bowdler for allowing me to see these transcriptions.
[29] Parsons, 1694; Lee, 1640; Cocke, 1640; Shenall, 1638; Southern, 1688; all Bridgnorth; Rowley, 1687, Stottesdon.

detailed in only a few, or for the baskets, strawn whiches, whisketts, chipes, cipes and kypes, which held many kinds of goods. The collections of linen, obviously prized in many households, the assortments of iron and brass artefacts to be found in most domestic hearths, the hand tools used in agriculture and horticulture, or the filters and funnels used in malthouses and dairies would show similar results. The Shropshire sample shows that open tubs were to be found in every household in late-seventeenth and early-eighteenth-century England, that they were used for many different purposes, and that the names by which they were known differed markedly over quite short distances. Holme notes that in Cheshire, the terms eston and cruck, both unknown in this sense in Shropshire, were used as synonyms for tub in cheesemaking.[30]

The display of wealth

If analysis of tubs shows how the use of words in inventories varies over short distances, examination of those items of furniture which were used to display accumulated wealth shows how the use of language changed over time to accommodate new domestic customs. Pewter is found on every detailed household inventory in Shropshire. During the first half of the eighteenth century it was increasingly displayed. One of the most significant indications of increasing material prosperity in the period was the evolution of the dresser, a cupboard topped by a flight of shelves on which pewter in excess of normal daily utilitarian requirements might be displayed. The *OED*, while recognising the sixteenth-century use of the word to indicate a sideboard from which food was conveyed to the dining table, does not illustrate its further evolution before the nineteenth century. The first references in Shropshire to furniture of this kind are pewter 'frames' or 'ladders' listed in inventories around 1700, usually in association with cupboards. A Bridgnorth inventory of 1700 refers to 'a pewter frame and dresser with drawers'. By the 1740s it is commonplace to find such entries as the 'Dresser with Drawers, a pewter frame, twelve pewter dishes, nine pewter dishes' which occurs on an inventory from the same town of 1741. Dressers were as likely to be found in the kitchens of the coal miners of the Ironbridge Gorge as in those of the wealthy families of the county town. In the 1750s seven of the 14 colliers in the region for whom inventories survive had such dressers. By examining a large sample of inventories it is possible to discern something of the evolution of new terms to describe new types

---

[30] Holme, *Academy of armory*, III, p.355.

of furnishing. Similar patterns can be observed in the growing use of such luxuries as clocks, pottery, tinware and looking glasses in the first half of the eighteenth century.[31]

Weights and measures

It is natural when studying probate inventories in a scientific age to seek precise metric equivalents for thraves of straw or waxweights of hurden yarn, but such quests may prove futile. Units were often used in ways which may now appear inconsistent. For example, in eighteenth-century Shropshire ironworks it was commonplace for the raw materials fed into a blast furnace to be measured in three different ways: iron ore in dozens, coal in stacks and limestone in tons. There were certainly variations between inventories from different regions in the extent of measurement of commodities, and in the units employed. It is necessary to discover through the examination of contexts how and where units were used, and with what degree of precision.

The extent of apparent confusion is illustrated by a Claverley inventory of 1702 in which there are four bays of barley, three parcels of peas, four loads of oats, seventy strikes of malt and two strikes of threshed corn. In the context of a large sample these entries are less confusing. Throughout Shropshire grain crops stored in the straw were often measured in an understandably approximate fashion by the number of bays of a barn which they occupied, or the number of waggon- or cart-loads which they represented. Stored grain was most commonly recorded by volume in strikes.[32]

In counties where arable farming was more important than pastoral it is commonplace for agricultural inventories to begin with lists of growing crops measured in acres. This was a relatively rare practice in Shropshire and in the Diocese of Lichfield generally. A few inventories from all parts of the county follow this practice, and it may have been customary in some parishes. It is particularly prevalent in the widely separated parishes of Much Wenlock and Richard's Castle. Growing crops were most commonly measured in strikes, indicating the amount of seed which had been sown. In just one instance, in the unenclosed parish of Market Drayton in 1674, growing crops of wheat, rye, barley, French wheat and peas are measured in 'lands', presumably the strips of open fields. The word 'seedness' was sometimes used to refer to a

---

[31] Easthope, 1715, Bridgnorth; Boucher, 1741, Bridgnorth; Trinder, *Industrial Revolution*, pp.186–8; Weatherill, 'Consumer behaviour', pp.216–25.
[32] Barker, 1702, Claverley.

growing crop, not quite the meaning given to the word by the *OED* which defines it as 'the action of sowing'. The meaning is evident from such inventory items as 'two strike seedness of wheat on the ground' or 'one strike's seedness of hardcorn growing'.[33]

The word thrave is widely used in Shropshire inventories in the sense, defined in the *OED*, of a varying measure of straw or fodder, but extended to include crops of unthreshed grain or pulses. A Bridgnorth inventory of 1644 refers to '4 thrave of sheaves of wheat in the barn' while a Bewdley inventory in 1707 lists 'eight & thirty thrave of corn in the straw in the barn'. A Leighton inventory of 1705 includes thraves of corn, oats, barley, peas and vetches, but, perversely in the light of the dictionary definition, loads of hay. A recognition that the word thrave was usually applied in a particular sense makes it possible to distinguish between unthrashed crops and stored grain in many inventories. Appraisers in Moor in 1666 helpfully distinguished '14 thraves of corn in the barn' from '4 bushels of oats in the house'.[34]

The customs authorities measured grain in particular units, malt in quarters, oatmeal in bushels or barrels and wheat in quarters. Superficially it appears that no such order was observed by Shropshire appraisers when considering stored grain. Wheat, rye, barley, oats, muncorn,[35] malt and pulses might be measured in bushels, or alternatively in strikes. The relationship between strikes and bushels is acknowledged by the historian of English weights and measures to be complex, and Holme seems uncertain whether a strike was the equivalent of one bushel or two. The most significant aspect of the Cheshire writer's observations on the topic is his discussion of the term 'measure', which he says was often used instead of strike 'in our county'. This is born out by the Shropshire inventories, many of which from parishes near to the Cheshire border refer to 'measures' of wheat, barley, rye, muncorn, malt and peas, precisely those commodities which were assessed elsewhere in bushels or strikes. Stored crops were appraised with more consistency than appears at first sight. Once threshed they were almost always assessed as strikes, bushels or measures. There were recognised relationships between these three units, which were consistent within particular regions. Analysis of Shropshire inventories shows that the more esoteric units which do not fall within these relationships, the acre of corn in a barn at Shifnal, the day's work of

---

[33] Nagginton, 1674, Market Drayton; Amyes, 1663, Much Wenlock; Cadwallader, 1675, Shifnal.

[34] Onions, 1644, Bridgnorth; Hill, 1707, Bewdley; Worrall, 1705, Leighton; Pinches, 1666, Moor.

[35] Muncorn, a mixture of wheat and rye grown together.

unthrashed barley and the pickle of malt in barns at Newport, the 'cantle of peas in Mrs Pickering's barn' at Stanton Long, were used only rarely. The interest which they arouse detracts from an overall pattern of measurement which was regionally consistent, even if it cannot readily be translated into modern terms.[36]

Throughout Shropshire small quantities of hemp and flax were grown on odd bits of land, and once harvested were processed in the home before being taken to be woven by custom weavers. The units in which these materials were measured at the various stages of manufacture are superficially confusing, but once put in context, and compared with dictionary definitions and descriptions of processes by Holme, they assume a degree of consistency. Raw flax or hemp which had been retted and scutched but not heckled might be described as a parcel 'in the rough' or weighed in pounds or stones. Heckled flax or hemp was measured in knitches (the term used in the *OED*), knitchens, knick, or nitchens.[37] Once dressed, linen yarn was measured in dozens, pounds or skeanes, or more commonly in slippens or slippings. Holme defines a slipping as the amount of yarn which might be wound upon the reel at time, generally about a pound. On some inventories yarn is measured in wax weights, and a Bridgnorth inventory of 1653 lists four 'Huswives pound weight of flax and two Huswives pound weight of hemp'. These were accepted terms which relate to avoirdupois units. Holme explains that a housewife's pound was approximately two wax pounds and that a wax pound was 16 ounces.[38]

Some other commodities were obviously measured consistently. Wool is always measured in pounds or stones, and occasionally in tods, one tod being the equivalent of 28 pounds. Curiously the term was also used in measuring hops, which were more commonly assessed in pounds or hundredweight. A tod of hops in Bridgnorth in 1754 was the equivalent of 35 pounds. Feathers, commonly stored in the home, were measured in pounds or stones, while nuts and salt, both easily assessed in terms of volume, were measured in strikes. Bark and coal were

[36] Zupko, *British weights and measures*, p.132; O'Connor, *Weights and measures*, pp.156–8; Holme, *Academy of armoury*, III, pp. 260, 331, 337; Parkes, 1723, Much Wenlock; Friend, 1676, Newport; Felton, 1723, Newport; Greenhalfe, 1682, Stanton Long.

[37] Trinder, *Industrial archaeology*, pp.134–6; Fowler, 1680, Kynnnersley; Pigott, 1679, Shifnal; Slade, 1684, Stanton Lacy; Pixley, 1694, Shifnal; Preece, 1743, Abdon.

[38] Green, 1713, Shifnal; Harvey, 1701, Newport; Gough, 1665, Bridgnorth; Bourne, 1649, Much Wenock; Harriman, 1721, Much Wenlock; Ferrington, 1671, Shifnal; Holme, *Academy of armoury*, III, p. 107; Wolryche, 1685, Dudmaston; Lewis, 1653, Bridgnorth.

measured in loads. Tallow was normally assessed in stones, but one inventory lists a 'keech' of tallow, a Shropshire dialect word meaning a cake of fat, wax or tallow. Other units of measurement are less clearly understood. 'Three hundred' of broom, doubtless cut and intended for use as fuel, might or might not be the equivalent of three hundredweight. The inventory of John Billingsley, bellowsmaker of Birmingham, taken in 1702, lists 'four loads and two and twenty Dozen of Rough Bellowsboards' at £7 10s per load worth in all £32 15s, from which it may be deduced that a dozen was worth 2s 6d, and that there were 60 dozen in a load. This is a long way from a metric equivalent, but it shows, as do so many Shropshire inventories, that appraisers were more consistent in their use of terms of measurement than a superficial examination of inventories may suggest. Such consistency was regional, and when commodities were placed upon Severn barges to be carried to other parts of the country they were significantly assessed in the Gloucester port books in Winchester bushels or in various London units.[39]

Conclusions

Probate inventories can provide insights into aspects of material culture which are of interest to many species of historian. They were usually made with care, and they deserve respect. The rapid scanning of numerous inventories to find evidence of debts or dairy equipment, a methodology which in the context of vernacular architecture has been described as 'mindless ticking', is not a satisfactory method of approaching these documents and can lead to elementary and sometimes hilarious misunderstandings. It fails to realise the benefits which can accrue from the study of the language of a large sample. The study of contexts within large collections of inventories, based on full-text transcriptions, offers many possibilities. For example, we might enquire with some hope of success whether truckle-, trundle-, low-, field- and servants' beds were synonymous, whether they occur less frequently than previously in the mid-eighteenth century, and, if so, whether their disappearance marks significant changes in relationships between parents and children, or between masters and mistresses and their servants.

The rhythms of a past language become evident as acquaintance with inventories increases. We recognise the frequently repeated sequences of items: 'trines of felleys' (i.e. trains of felloes) in wheelwrights' shops,

---

[39] Dickinson, 1714; Williams, 1754; Baker, 1719; Corbett, 1706; all Bridgnorth; Hawkins, 1660, Newport; Wood, 1708, Stoke St Milburgh; Billingsley, *DTC*.

'grates, fire shovels and tongs' in numerous fireplaces, and 'a joyned tester and sted', followed by 'matt and cord, curtains, vallens [that is, vallances], one feather bed and two feather bolsters, two blankets and one rug' in a typical chamber of a prosperous household.[40] Just as residence in a foreign country provides an introduction to a richness of language which is inaccessible through textbooks or tapes, the study of a large sample of inventories reveals words and phrases which are memorably expressive or even lyrical. Many are simple words used in particular ways, the meanings of which are obvious, even if they are unknown to polite literature. Expressions like 'Yokes and all other tack of team' and 'Lent tilling' appear in many agricultural inventories. A Norbury inventory of 1702 lists 'Grayne Inned and Growing'. Many Shropshire farmers grew crops of mixed grain for bread flour and sometimes for malting. Such crops were commonly called muncorn, maslin or dredge,[41] but individual appraisers identified them as 'blendcorn' in Much Wenlock in 1668 and 'mingled corn' in Shifnal in 1698. Appraisers often categorised ironware in a kitchen, but only one inventory, composed in Edgmond in 1673, lists with the familiar broaches, racks and grate, 'all other Ironage'. An item like 'Wool with other housewifery' in a Bishop's Castle inventory of 1692 expresses volumes about the role of women in rural society. One is puzzled by the team of ducks listed in Shifnal in 1722, and it is to be presumed that the 'Lombardy' itemised with chairs and stools on a Stanton Lacy inventory of 1671 consisted of unwanted items of furniture which had no connection with northern Italy.[42]

The world of the appraiser is not easy to penetrate, and we can never expect fully to understand it. If we are to increase our meagre understanding we have to be prepared to accept disorder, to dive into an ocean of unfamiliar words and expressions, in which after a time we may see enlightening patterns, although much disorder may remain. We need to learn not just an old language but a series of highly localised dialects and practices if we are to realise the potential of probate records as sources for the study of material culture.

[40] Jackson, 1696, Bridgnorth.
[41] Maslin, a mixture of wheat and rye grown together; dredge, a mixture of oats and barley grown together.
[42] Shepherd, 1669, Bitterley; Jacks, 1702, Norbury; Davis, 1668, Much Wenlock; Turner, 1698, Shifnal; Newell 1673, Edgmond; Collins, 1692, Bishop's Castle; Roden, 1722, Shifnal; Taylor, 1671, Stanton Lacy.

15

Merchants and Retailers in Seventeenth-Century Cornwall

CHRISTINE NORTH

Introduction

Probate inventories have for many years been a popular and well-used source. They offer invaluable evidence about patterns and changes in a variety of features of social and economic life, and have been employed extensively as a basis for studying individual parish or town communities and for major regional and national research projects.[1] Two major published works on Cornwall based on probate inventories concentrate respectively on the development of regional building styles and an overview of the county's economy in the seventeenth century.[2] A long-term project at the Cornwall Record Office to list and index the Archdeaconry of Cornwall probate records has identified a potential area for research, other than parochial or town-based analysis or sampling for a broader-based topic, by focusing upon the records of individual trades or occupations drawn from a complete regional collection.[3] Some of the most detailed inventories to survive are those for merchants, haberdashers, mercers and others engaged in the wholesaling or retailing of merchandise. This chapter explores the circulation and retailing of consumer goods in Cornwall in the first half of the seventeenth century and offers an additional regional insight to supplement work previously undertaken on mercers in Oxfordshire, Shropshire and elsewhere.[4] It is based upon analysis of the probate

---

[1] See the general discussion in Chapter 4, above. An important project is currently under way at Exeter University under the direction of Mark Overton, using probate inventories from Cornwall and Kent.

[2] Chesher and Chesher, *Cornishman's house*; Whetter, *Cornwall*.

[3] Cornwall Record Office, *Index to Cornish probate records*.

[4] Vaisey, 'Probate inventories and provincial retailers', pp.103–110; Trinder and Cox, *Yeomen and colliers*, pp.20–41; Tiller, 'Shopkeeping', pp.269–86.

documents of 111 merchants and retailers, 92 of whose probate inventories have survived.

The local context

At the beginning of the seventeenth century the majority of Cornwall's population of around 100,000 lived in farms and hamlets in the countryside and around the coast. Farming provided the main source of employment and income, supplemented by fishing, tin mining and some cloth manufacturing.[5] The structure of society in the seventeenth century was one of 'degree, priority and place'. The nationally observed recent improvement in the fortunes of some social groups was reflected in Richard Carew's perceptive remarks on Cornish society. Cornish gentlemen were seen to be generally modest in their expenditure, though perhaps indulgent of their wives' whims:

> They keep liberal, but not costly builded or furnished houses . . . and delight not in bravery of apparel; yet the women would be very loath to come behind the fashion in newfangledness of manner, if not in costliness of the matter, which perhaps might over empty their husbands' purses.

The 'yeomanry' he saw as no different from 'other shires' but noticed a marked improvement in the way of life of the husbandman, 'who conformeth himself with a better supplied civility, to the eastern pattern', with the ability to maintain himself and his family in 'a competent decency' with money to spend at the weekly market for 'provisions of necessity and pleasure'.[6] The early years of the seventeenth century saw even 'remote' Cornwall ready to keep up with new fashions and able to indulge in a few luxuries as well as the necessities of life.

Analysis of the Protestation Returns of 1641–2 suggests that Bodmin, Liskeard and Launceston were then the largest towns in Cornwall, but none of the Cornish boroughs had more than 1,000 inhabitants or about 200 households. In short, all were very small, an unusual situation compared to most other English counties.[7] Most of Cornwall's towns had been granted royal charters of incorporation as boroughs by 1600, and over 40 places had acquired the privilege of holding markets and

---

[5] Whetter, *Cornwall*; Stoate, *Cornwall Protestation returns*; Pounds, *Population of Cornwall*.

[6] Carew, *Survey of Cornwall*, reprint, pp.136–7.

[7] Clark and Hosking, *Population estimates*, pp.15–24; see also Whiteman and Russell, 'Protestation returns', pp.17–29.

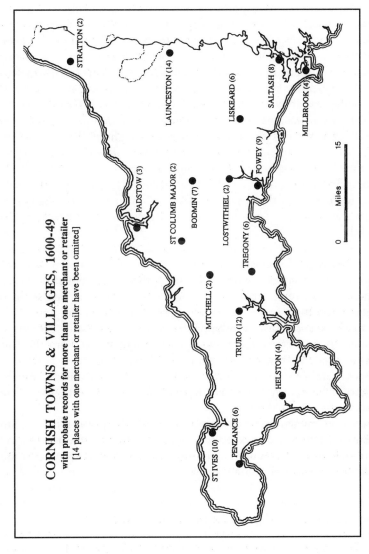

CORNISH TOWNS & VILLAGES, 1600-49

with probate records for more than one merchant or retailer

[14 places with one merchant or retailer have been omitted]

STRATTON (2)

LAUNCESTON (14)

LISKEARD (6)

SALTASH (8)

MILLBROOK (4)

PADSTOW (3)

ST COLUMB MAJOR (2)

BODMIN (7)

LOSTWITHIEL (2)

FOWEY (9)

TREGONY (6)

MITCHELL (2)

TRURO (12)

HELSTON (4)

ST IVES (10)

PENZANCE (6)

0   Miles   15

Figure 15.1 Cornish towns and villages, 1600–49

fairs. In addition, fairs were traditionally held at the time of parish feasts and offered further opportunities for buying and selling. The growth and increasing mobility of the population, combined with developing economic activity, meant that by the early-seventeenth century many towns were experiencing problems with unlicensed trading, a feature that they shared with towns in general.[8] Certainly in Cornwall the corporate towns and boroughs appear to have imposed quite severe restrictions on selling and retailing in an attempt to ensure a monopoly for their own freemen. Liskeard in 1587 required that 'no Burgess or Inhabitant hereafter shall putt up Shop or trade in any mistory or art unless he be first allowed by the said councell, a man sufficiently skilled in his art, of good behaviour and ability'.[9] St Columb Major's town account book records the regular letting throughout the seventeenth century of 'the parish shops', effectively controlling trade and at the same time collecting a substantial annual income from rents.[10] The Corporation of Tregony in 1622 drew up and applied very strict rules for the regulation of the town's markets: even in the early-eighteenth century the borough took swift action against anyone 'keeping shop unlawfully'.[11]

No distinction seems to have been made in the early-seventeenth century between wholesale and retail traders. Most of the domestic manufacturers of goods also held for sale other wares which they had not made themselves, while merchants would expect to sell some of their stock to others for resale. What is not clear is how the towns, and their markets and fairs, developed to accommodate the growth of permanent retail outlets. Certainly, Thirsk suggests that from the late-sixteenth century 'a wide selection of consumer goods', both from domestic manufacture and from imports, was becoming available throughout the country, not only from pedlars and chapmen but from retailers in provincial towns.[12]

Cornwall's geographical situation, used in later centuries to exploit the county's perceived 'difference', made it difficult to reach by land, but provided a convenience of seaborne access denied to many other parts of the country. As Carew put it:

---

[8] Everitt, 'Marketing of agricultural produce', esp. pp.543–63.
[9] Constitutions of Liskeard borough: Cornwall Record Office (hereafter CRO) B/LIS/182. Cornish boroughs merit further study, particularly Liskeard, Launceston and Bodmin where the survival of records is good.
[10] CRO P/36/8/1.
[11] Constitutions of Tregony borough: CRO J/2080.
[12] Thirsk, *Economic policy*, pp.118 ff.

Though nature hath shouldered out Cornwall into the farthest part of the realm, and so beseiged it with the ocean, that . . . the inhabitants find but one way of issue by land, yet hath she in some good measure countervailed such disadvantage through placing it both near unto, and in the trade way between Wales, Ireland, Spain, France and Netherland.[13]

Certainly the estuary of the Fal was one of the main trade routes to the Americas by the seventeenth century, but since no customs office was established there until the 1650s no import records were compiled which identify goods brought into the port.[14] In the early part of the seventeenth century customs revenues collected at ports in Cornwall were in any case included in the returns made for the headport of Plymouth. Much of the Cornish trade seems to have been in tin and fish with only a small involvement in other aspects of commerce.[15] This pattern of trade is discussed by Whetter but the nature of the sources prevents detailed analysis.[16] What is evident from the work of both Whetter and Stephens is that imports into the region for the first half of the seventeenth century included wine, dried fruits, sugar, salt and soap, from Europe, Scandinavia and the New World, and that by the 1630s Fowey, Penzance, St Ives and Penryn were becoming increasingly important, with the corresponding decline of Truro as a port. By the 1650s tar, hemp, canvas, soap, hops, wine, fruit, spirits and tobacco were being shipped into Penryn and Falmouth. Some manufactured and luxury items were brought by sea from London and other English ports, especially Plymouth and Bristol.[17] Inventories of Exeter merchants indicate a regular pattern of trade between that city and Cornish towns.[18]

The documents

This study of merchants and retailers in Cornwall in the period 1601–49 is based on the examination of 111 sets of documents from the records

---

[13] Carew, *Survey of Cornwall*, reprint, p.83.

[14] Fisher, *Ports and shipping*, p.2.

[15] Stephens, 'Foreign trade of Plymouth', pp.125–37.

[16] Whetter, *Cornwall*, pp.147–54.

[17] Fisher, *Ports and shipping*, p.15.

[18] The records of Exeter City at the Devon Record Office include some 200 inventories for the period 1560–1630 of the goods and chattels of citizens who died leaving orphans whose custody was granted to the city by the charter of Elizabeth. They include eight merchants, a mercer, and two apothecaries: those cited are numbers 104, 101 and 143 respectively.

of the probate court of the Archdeaconry of Cornwall. Ninety-two include inventories, most of which are accompanied by other documents, including 50 wills, 29 administration bonds and seven probate accounts. The remaining 19 consist of wills without inventories, four of which have administration bonds attached. They are generally well-written, a few in a particularly elegant hand. Valuations prior to 1610 are almost entirely in Roman numerals, whilst after 1630 there is a noticeable increase in the use of Arabic notation.[19] For the period 1610–30 both systems are used, sometimes in the same document. Valuations are in pounds, shillings and pence: many entries are valued at 13s. 4d., the old English mark, or at 6s. 8d. or 3s. 4d., half and quarter of a mark respectively.

The basis for selection of the probate documents was that the deceased dealt, or apparently dealt, in commodities for resale, rather than being primarily engaged in selling wares which they themselves had made.[20] Merchants are therefore included, as are chapmen, pedlars, mercers, haberdashers and chandlers. Weavers, clothiers and woollen-drapers were only included when their inventories suggested the sale of goods other than those manufactured in their own domestic workshops. Craftsmen selling their own goods, service occupations and purely specialist trades, such as vintners, are all excluded. Occupation or status is specified for 80 of the 111 individuals. Besides the 52 merchants the remainder are variously described as clothier (5), mercer (9), haberdasher (4), chapman (4) or draper (3), with one chandler, one pedlar and one weaver. Three are also described as gentleman and there are five women: three widows, a spinster and one of the mercers. Altogether they come from 28 different locations in Cornwall, although some may have traded quite widely. For example, the inventory of Robert Bennett of Tregony from 1606 mentions trestles, boards, poles and tilts in Helston and Madron as well as a stall in Tregony, so he evidently travelled to other market towns as well as trading from his 'shop'. Unsurprisingly, all but six lived in towns, most in Launceston, Truro, St Ives, Fowey and Saltash, followed by Bodmin, Liskeard, Penzance and Tregony.[21] Of the 52 individuals self-styled or described as merchant, 47 were in chartered boroughs, two in market towns, two in the seaport of Millbrook and only one in a rural parish.

---

[19] Cullum and Wardley, 'Diffusion of the Hindu-Arabic numeral system', pp.3–31.

[20] This selection is narrower than the 'dealing trades' named by Weatherill, *Consumer behaviour*, pp.191–216.

[21] The records for the ports of Falmouth and Penryn, proved in the Exeter diocesan courts, were destroyed during World War Two.

Table 15.1 Merchants' and retailers' inventory values

Value range	Merchants	Others	Total
< £50	7	24	31
£50–199	18	17	35
£200–499	10	8	18
£500–999	1	2	3
£1,000+	2	3	5
Total	38	54	92

These probate records offer a tantalising glimpse of involvement in national and overseas trade. One borough in particular appears to warrant further investigation. The port of Fowey was the base for the trading activities of John Rashleigh, who developed an important Newfoundland fishing industry in the early-seventeenth century, and traded regularly in a three-way voyage via the Mediterranean. The brothers Henry and John Colquite (of Fowey and Golant), both appearing in the probate records in 1607, also had seafaring interests, their inventories listing a crane, ropes and pulleys, stores on the quay and unspecified 'sea stuff'. In 1640 Ambrose White of Fowey left to his son 'all his Spanish books' and is recorded as having 'merchant goods'. Cyprian Goodall, also of Fowey, had shares in two boats—*Bridget* and *William* in 1640: his son Michael was 'presently out of England'. Richard Hurley of St Ives 'went on a viage and then died' in 1633. Estate records of the Rashleigh and Treffry families include the names of many additional merchants and dealers in Fowey.

Table 15.1 reveals the very wide range in the probate inventory values of the moveable goods and credits of these merchants and other retailers. For one-third they were under £50, while for one in twenty they totalled over £1,000, indicating that they included among them men of fundamentally different social standing. Those described as merchants tended to be wealthier than those with other occupational descriptions: only 18 per cent of merchants fell into the bottom category of wealth, compared to 44 per cent of other occupations. Towards the upper end of the scale, however, there is little difference between the two categories: 8 per cent of merchants exhibited an inventory total of £500 or more, compared to 9 per cent of those with alternative occupational designations.

Table 15.2 demonstrates considerable variation in the detail about retailing activities recorded in the inventories, which can render analysis very difficult, particularly for those with only modest recorded wealth. Only 15 inventories provide both an occupational description of the

Table 15.2 Recorded quality of retailing information, by inventory valuation (%)

	<£50	£50–199	£200–499	£500–999	£1,000+
(Number)	(31)	(35)	(18)	(3)	(5)
Detailed 'shop' information	19	26	28	67	20
Brief 'shop' information	52	46	44	33	80
No information	29	28	28	–	–
Total	100	100	100	100	100

deceased as well as detailed information about his wares—quantities, prices, descriptions and values for individually named commodities. Of these 15, the single chandler had fabrics, haberdashery, starch, pitch and match. The two chapmen had grocery goods, small wares and haberdashery, all items that could be carried in hampers, boxes or panniers. Two clothiers possessed all the equipment necessary for making cloth, but one also had soap, tobacco and 'small wares', as did one weaver, in addition to his looms. Three mercers, as well as fabrics and haberdashery, held grocery goods, small wares and tobacco. Indeed, this mixture of goods is found in all the inventories of the remaining six merchants in this group, as well as in most of those without a recorded occupation or status. Although four inventories give an indication of concentration on the sale of hats, the overall impression is one of lack of specialisation. It is difficult, even on close examination of the documents, to make any real distinction between the activities of most of the subjects. The goods carried by chandlers, mercers or merchants do not suggest any standard seventeenth-century criteria for their categorisation. Some descriptions suggest an occupation, but the term merchant, given the higher median level of recorded wealth they displayed, may perhaps be regarded as an indication of socio-economic status rather than a particular activity.[22]

Where no details are given, definitions are even more difficult. Twenty inventories refer to 'shops' or 'wares' with no further information, but give an occupational description of the deceased. The sole draper had only 'wares in the shop', as did the three haberdashers, but one of these also had a warehouse, another had wool bags and a shop with shelves and chests. Four of the five mercers had 'shop wares', the fifth, as well as 'stuff in his shop', had boots and 'clowting leather'

---

[22] Vaisey, 'Probate inventories and provincial retailers', pp.104–7.

for patching. Eleven inventories give neither details of goods nor occupational description. One, however, records 'a chapman's box and small wares', five had 'small wares' specified, three including tobacco; two had 'wares made to sell'. Three were widows, two evidently with goods for retail, but the third, while holding a few pieces of cloth for sale, seems to have been primarily engaged in domestic manufacture.

What this survey does reveal is that, contrary to Whetter's conclusion that during the period 1600–20 'there were no shopkeepers wholly engaged in the retail trade', at least 16 inventories for this period list a wide range of commodities for resale, include no means of manufacturing goods, and specifically mention 'shops' equipped variously with shelves, boxes, scales and weights, and stock and account books.[23] Many more were actively involved in the buying and selling of merchandise than have been identified from their probate records. To begin with, other merchants, haberdashers and retailers are mentioned in these documents as creditors, appraisers or bondsmen. Some wealthier individuals would have had their wills proved, or their administrations granted, in the Exeter diocesan courts, whose records were destroyed in 1942, or in the Prerogative Court of Canterbury.[24] There must also have been poorer tradesmen who are not represented at all in the probate records. The number found in the present survey must, therefore, be regarded as a minimum.

The appraisers named in the inventories are almost without exception from the same town or parish as the deceased. In some cases a close relative helped with the appraisal but business connections are more evident, and may help to explain the specialist knowledge of fabrics, spices and other goods, and their prices and values, demonstrated in the documents. The valuations given were normally at wholesale, rather than retail, prices.[25] The appraisers seem to have had a facility for weighing and measuring a wide range of commodities. Items are recorded by number: dozen, gross, thousand; by weight: ounces, pounds and hundredweights; by capacity: gallons, hogsheads, casks and rundlets. Paper is counted by the quire and ream, while fabrics are carefully measured and calculated by the bolt, bale, yard, piece or ell, depending on the type of material and its place of origin. Nearly every inventory which mentions 'goods in the shop' records the existence of

[23] Whetter, *Cornwall*, p. 134. Whetter's conclusion is drawn from an analysis of a sample of 1,250 Cornish inventories for this period. See also North, 'Fustians, figs and frankincense', pp.32–77.

[24] Twenty-one parishes were peculiars of the Bishop of Exeter: they included Budock and St Gluvias in which lay, respectively, Falmouth and Penryn.

[25] Trinder and Cox, *Yeomen and colliers*, p.28.

some sort of weighing equipment. In one or two instances the appraisers have evidently had access to stock books, as witnessed by phrases such as 'as by the shop book appeareth', or 'as by particulars'. However, since no 'shop books' listing items in stock have been found for the period, information about the commodities in which the merchants and retailers traded seems only to be available in probate inventories, and hence they provide a unique window upon contemporary patterns of consumption in seventeenth-century Cornwall.

The range and variety of goods in these inventories is remarkable, and remarkably consistent throughout the period, though some new items, mainly fabrics and 'made' goods, appear for the first time in the 1630s. Fabrics, trimmings, haberdashery, imported foodstuffs and spices feature in inventories across the whole range of valuations, with an assortment of 'made' goods and small wares. The range of fabrics listed was often impressive. Robert Bennett's inventory, compiled in Tregony in 1606 and valued at about £450, is one of the longest, listing 439 items, 400 being goods for sale, and including more than 60 types of fabric: canvas, dowlas, fustian, say, calico, holland, lawn, jeans, and the more exotically named Philip and China, moccado, changeable buffin, mingled perpetuana, Bologna silk, black billament, tabinet, velvet and tabby grosgrain. He had ribbon, laces, threads, buttons and pins in great quantity and variety. John More of Saltash, whose goods were listed in the same year, stocked 20 kinds of cloth, besides trimmings, haberdashery and an assortment of 'made up' items: stomachers, cauls, taffeta and satin masks, and gloves. His total valuation was £49 19s. 9d. George Selden of Liskeard, who died in 1635 with an estate valued at £360 and is described both as a merchant (in his will) and a mercer (by his appraisers), possessed a range of fabrics which included not only many found in early inventories but also camlean, figuratoes, pyramides, carthagineans, paragons and 'nonesopretties'. He had Hampshire and Bristol cloth, pairs of bodices, and belly pieces. William Sydenham, of Truro, had in 1639 several hundred yards of fabrics; by contrast with George Selden, these consisted almost entirely of woollen and worsted cloths, kerseys, serges and bays, valued at around £150.

Many of the inventories record dried fruits, spices, soap and sugar, while some include hats, stockings and gloves. Pepper was the main spice, and was imported in large quantities: Richard Daniell despatched over 2,000 pounds weight of pepper in one cargo, and it was found in all but two of the inventories which recorded spices. Cloves, ginger, cinnamon, mace and nutmeg were also imported, and feature in seven inventories. Sugar, either refined or bruised, in loaves or powder form, was also found. Food colourings feature quite regularly, including 'sanders', an Indian colouring derived from sandalwood; 'turnsole', which was used to colour jellies and sweetmeats a blue or violet colour; and saffron, which although valued in the inventory of Robert Bennett of Tregony in 1606 at 11s. 8d. per ounce appears in five inventories. 'Hops and other grosserie' feature in the inventory of George Selden. In the longest and most detailed inventories (almost entirely in the first quarter of the century) there are also ABC and grammar books, cittern wires, bowstrings, hawks' bells, playing cards, spectacles, and paper, parchment, galls and sealing wax. Some items had been widely available for many years—traditional woollen cloths, some spices, flavourings and colourings—but there is evidence of newer, more fashionable commodities being stocked, including many of the 'new draperies' and a range of luxury goods.

The composition of inventoried wealth

The possessions included in these inventories and their comparative value is summarised in Tables 15.3 and 15.4. 'Merchandise', 'wares' and 'shop goods', whether listed in detail or merely mentioned, are included in 73 per cent of the inventories, not surprisingly since this was one of the criteria for selection. They represent an overall average of 33 per cent of assessed wealth by value, ranging from just 13s. 4d. in the inventory of John Drew of Launceston in 1629, in the lowest valuation group, to the £570 worth of stock of Henry Stephens of Fowey, whose inventory, valued at over £1,000, was appraised in 1644. For those inventories valued at under £200, 'shop goods' represented 30 per cent of assessed wealth, whilst for those of middling wealth (£200–499) and those at the very top of the scale (£1,000+), the proportion stood slightly lower, at 26 per cent and 24 per cent respectively. No significance can be attached to the figure of 52 per cent for the £500–999 category, for this calculation is derived from just three inventories.

The varying degree to which these merchants and retailers invested in 'shop goods', of course, is partly a reflection of the relative importance of other forms of wealth they held. Turning to consideration of household goods, the most striking feature of Table 15.4 is the high proportion of total wealth held in this category by those in the bottom valuation group (40 per cent), and, to a lesser extent, by those assessed at £50–199 (29 per cent). This is as might be expected: household goods feature in 95 per cent of inventories, reflecting the need for all to equip themselves with the basic necessities of clothing and furniture. Beds and bedding are common throughout, distributed

Table 15.3 Possessions mentioned in inventories, by inventory valuation

Value range	Total	Household		Cash/clothes		Shop goods		Debts due		Leases		Farm		Sea/fish		Tin	
	N	N	%	N	%	N	%	N	%	N	%	N	%	N	%	N	%
<£50	31	27	87	26	84	22	71	6	19	4	13	6	19	3	9	–	–
£50–199	35	32	91	33	94	24	69	27	77	16	46	14	40	9	26	2	6
£200–499	18	17	95	17	95	13	72	17	95	4	22	12	66	5	28	2	11
£500–999	3	3	100	3	100	3	100	3	100	3	100	2	66	–	–	–	–
£1,000+	5	5	100	4	80	5	100	5	100	4	80	5	100	1	20	–	–
Total	92	84	91	83	90	67	73	58	63	31	34	39	42	18	20	4	4

Table 15.4 Comparative value of possessions mentioned in inventories, by inventory valuation (%)

Value range	N	Household	Cash/clothes	Shop goods	Debts due	Leases	Farm	Sea/fish	Tin	Total
<£50	(31)	40	11	30	9	3.5	3.5	3	–	100
£50–199	(35)	29	9	30	15	7	4	5	1	100
£200–499	(18)	19	9	26	22	11	10	3	0.3	100
£500–999	(3)	12	2	52	27	1	6	–	–	100
£1,000+	(5)	13	12	24	35	13	2	1	–	100

through most rooms except the kitchen; towards the end of the period there are fewer beds in parlours. Furniture, textiles and implements for cooking and eating also appear in most inventories, and three-quarters include 'luxury' items, mainly silver spoons, though books, musical instruments and pieces of jewellery are recorded in a few.

Many inventories list in some detail items of furniture and household equipment, without recording their disposition in specific rooms. Thirty-three of the inventories name rooms: most are of the 'hall, parlour, kitchen and chambers over' pattern identified by the Cheshers as typical of the homes of the 'better-off yeomen' of the period, and demonstrate the increasing importance of the parlour.[26] Some houses were clearly more spacious. Several had a buttery and a cellar, there are 'linney rooms', a couple of references to a study, and John Hicks of St Ives had 'timber for erecting a new kitching' in 1639.

Standards of domestic comfort appear from inventory information not to be *invariably* associated with specific occupations: mercers, clothiers and haberdashers appear in all but the two richest value groups, and merchants are included in all five, though none of the four chapmen have inventories valued above £100. In 1608 Andrew Coyler of Saltash, a chapman in the lowest value group, had only a dust bed, a cupboard, a table and a few pans. In 1607 Roger Service, a clothier of St Columb Major in the same group, had a few bedclothes and a threepenny candlestick. Humphry Daniell (1604), a Liskeard merchant with a total valuation of around £80, had in his house only basic bedding, furniture, a cupboard and some pewter and crocks. By contrast John Tremenheere of Helston (1605), Daniell's contemporary, lived in some style, with silver, books and draperies in his house valued at nearly £500, while the home of his richer kinsman, John Uren (1614), also in Helston, contained cushions, rugs, carpets, curtains, silver, brass and pewter. In 1620 Jenkin Daniell's family in Truro enjoyed pictures on their walls, ate off china dishes, and were protected from draughts by curtains at their windows and around their beds. Where a will exists additional information may be present on the deceased's domestic arrangements, and when the wills are taken into consideration, it is clear that there was often a difference between the financial and social status of the merchants and that of the chapmen, clothiers and mercers who dealt in merchandise.

Under the heading of cash and clothes, 'purse, girdle and wearing apparel' are included in 90 per cent of the inventories, consistently representing around 10 per cent of the total value of every group except

[26] Chesher and Chesher, *Cornishman's house*, p.61.

for the £500–999 band, where the cash and clothes values average only 2 per cent of the total. Disappointingly, there is hardly any detail of clothing, and in the majority of inventories money makes up the greater part of the valuation under this heading.

Debts due to the deceased are recorded in 63 per cent of the inventories, either as specific 'shop' debts, or as repayment of loans on bond. 'Debts due' occur in only 19 per cent of the lowest value group, rising to 77 per cent in the next group and an average of 98 per cent of the remainder. Assuming that debts were consistently and accurately recorded, this provides an interesting insight into the means by which business was conducted by merchants and retailers at different levels in the social scale. In the analysis of comparative values in Table 15.4, money due represents 35 per cent in the richest group, falling steadily to 27 per cent in the £500–999 group, 22 per cent in the £200–499 group, and 15 per cent and 9 per cent in the two lowest value groups; but the recovery of £2 owing to an estate valued overall at only £16 must have been as crucial as the repayment of the £240 owed to Edward Chepman of Liskeard (1629) out of his total estate of £853. The inventory of Peter Holman of Fowey in 1644, irritatingly brief, records goods valued at £2,094, including debts good and desperate at a massive £1,030. 'Shop books' are recorded in 17 inventories—bills, bonds and accounts in less than a dozen—but the keeping of credit accounts must have been essential for many traders who would only have been able to sell their goods if they allowed their customers credit. Purchases may not have been dealt with as separate transactions, and some debts must have been outstanding for years. The inventory of Nicholas Grove of Fowey includes an itemised list of moneys owed to him at the time of his death in 1647. The majority were outstanding in the shop book only since the previous year, and include some identified as loans rather than outstanding payments for goods, but 11 had been unpaid since 1642 and 15 dated from the 1630s. An additional business sideline seems to have been the holding of goods in pawn.

The settling by executors of debts due to the deceased, and of money owed, is recorded in detail in three of the seven sets of probate accounts, and considerably amends the impression of wealth created by their respective inventories. Jenkin Daniell of Truro (1620) and Robert Ton of Helston (1614) were apparently well-to-do merchants, Ton's inventory value being nearly £200 including 'debts due' at a modest £17, Daniell's goods being calculated at over £300 only £10 of which was money owing to him. Their widows both presented accounts to the archdeacon's court which showed that more was owed by their late husbands to business creditors than their estates were worth. Bersabee

Ton, having accounted for the funeral with sermon and bells, provided a dinner and horsemeat for her late husband's friends and paid the court expenses, was required to pay out over £125 in settling Robert's outstanding debts; and while Johan Daniell's expenses as executor were modest (less than £10 for the funeral and the costs of administering Jenkin's probate and account) she submitted an itemised account of her husband's debts amounting to over £300, with a note 'this Accoumptant hath disbursed more than she hath received £68 10s. 6d.'. Rose Vigurs of Launceston 'craved allowance' for £650 worth of desperate debts, having already paid out over £500 to named creditors. Her husband's inventory of 1632 records 'debts good and desperate' of £798 which were included in his inventory valuation of £1,050.[27]

Far from all the merchants and retailers in this sample were engaged solely in the movement of goods and commodities: indeed, the majority were also engaged in agricultural activities. In all, 39 inventories record some agricultural involvement, and while most of the farming interests appear in the smaller towns and the rural parishes, merchants and shopkeepers in most of the chartered boroughs also demonstrate some involvement in working the land. This is a feature that figured more prominently in the middle to upper reaches of inventory valuations: of those with inventories valued in excess of £200, almost three-quarters exhibited some farming interest, whilst for the wealthy testators valued at over £500, seven out of eight held leases of land or property. For those of middling wealth (£200–499), the value of leases and farm goods combined (21 per cent of wealth) challenged that held in the form of 'shop goods' (26 per cent); for the wealthiest category, the proportion stood at 15 per cent, again not very far short of the 24 per cent held in 'shop goods'. The proportion owning leases or farm goods declined further down the social hierarchy, where such investments constituted a significantly smaller percentage of total wealth.

The disposition of property deserves further consideration, for here additional information from other probate documents can be brought to bear. Property appears in 34 of the 92 inventories, from the modest 'remainder of a lease, £2' of John Peters of Lostwithiel (1645) to the properties in Helston valued at £231 in John Uren's inventory (1614). Although the criteria for inclusion in an inventory were specific ('chattels' included leaseholds) the peculiar nature both of local borough property holdings (some copyhold, some leasehold) and of the west country preference for leases 'for 99 years or three lives whichever

---

[27] Spufford, 'Limitations of the probate inventory', pp.150–5.

is the longer', must have led to anomalies and inconsistencies in recording.

Some clarification, and additional information, is found in wills; 19 record details of property, ten for possessions already briefly noted in inventories, nine offering new information. William Roche, a self-styled merchant of Kenwyn near Truro, made his will in 1599 leaving a leasehold house and corn mills in Kenwyn, and leasehold property to his wife 'for the better mayntenance of her smaler children' while he was abroad. The will was proved in 1602: his inventory records merely 'leaseholds' valued at £12 13s. 4d. In 1626 Henry Cary's inventory, correctly, does not record his freehold property, but the details in his will of substantial freehold possessions in Cornwall and Devon suggest that his 'wealth' and status as a mercer was greater than indicated by his inventory alone.[28] Other merchants were careful to leave property described as 'shop' to their sons or wives. Overall, the wills examined record the disposition of freehold and leasehold properties in Cornwall, Devon, Warwickshire, Kent and Norfolk.

It would, however, be unwise to place too much reliance on information recorded in probate documents as an indication of the ownership of freehold, or the occupancy of leasehold, property. Family or marriage settlements made during the life of the deceased were a not uncommon way of ensuring the disposal of property as its owner wished. Records of the boroughs and market towns, and of the local gentry estates, may be a more reliable source than the evidence of probate documents alone.[29]

Tin mining interests occur in only four inventories, all in the £50–499 value range. Sea-going activity occurs more frequently than mining, featuring in 18 inventories, and as one would expect is largely represented in coastal towns with a safe anchorage, primarily Fowey, Penzance and St Ives. Those in the lowest value group seem to have been actively engaged in fishing, but the remainder, where described, are identified as merchants. Seven of these, all of whom have unspecified 'merchandise' or 'wares' in shops or warehouses, also have cellars on the quay and interests or shares in boats. This common seafaring theme is also apparent in eight merchant inventories in the far west of the county, where no merchandise is recorded but where all seem to be engaged not only in fishing (they have nets, pressing stones and cellars) but also in the provision or organisation of regular sea

---

[28] Since he owned property in two archdeaconries, Henry's will should have been proved at the diocesan court in Exeter.

[29] See Chapter 3, pp.66–9 and Chapter 17, below, pp.333–5.

voyages. The consistent use of the term merchant to describe this group suggests the need for further investigation.[30] St Ives has a dozen men in the 1630s and 1640s who are described in probate documents as merchants though there is nothing in their wills or inventories to indicate any retailing or warehousing activity. Without exception they have significant investments in fish cellars, boats, salt and equipment, and occupy substantial leasehold premises in the town.

The evidence of wills

It is not only with regard to property holding that wills can be employed to provide additional information. Fifty of the inventories are accompanied by wills, the majority recording financial bequests to wife and children which are frequently complex. Over 30 wills refer to children under 21, several to children still in the womb: death did not always come in old age. Wives are often left instructions on the care and education of children, usually with the support and advice of 'overseers'. Some of these are the children's uncles, a few are referred to as 'trusty and well-beloved friend', while John Hicks of St Ives in 1639 left the care of his family to 'my loving neighbour and gossip'. In 1629 in Liskeard Edward Chepman's seven youngsters were entrusted to the care of their eldest brother 'until they can earn their living', with lump sums when each came of age: his estate was valued at £1,050. Alice Hoskins, who had against her father's wishes married Nicholas Randle, 'an ungodly fellow and an outcast', was in 1641 left 'only £100', an indication perhaps of her father James Hoskins' wealth beyond the £250 worth of possessions recorded in his inventory in Launceston in 1643. Many well-to-do merchants left substantial bequests to parish churches, to the poor, or to 'the lazar people' of Launceston. Some were particularly generous: Robert Cole of Liskeard in 1619 left 40 shillings to the mayor for the use of 'poor artificers' of the town, as did Edward Chepman ten years later. Similar bequests were made by Thomas Gennis in Bodmin (1624) and Daniel Bedford in Helston (1644). Funeral sermons, forgotten tithes and the forgiving of unpaid debts ('several great sums of money' in the case of James Lewarne of Truro in 1626) also feature in the wills of the better-off, though the settlement of their own debts must in some cases have reduced substantially the amount of money available for distribution. Although it has only been possible to touch upon such matters here, many aspects of wealth and

[30] For a discussion on the activities of merchants in the later seventeenth century see Whetter, *Cornwall*, p.153ff.

property holding and its disposition, can, therefore, be further explored through an analysis of the contents of wills, and the combined exploitation of wills and inventories provides a far richer harvest than consideration of either source in isolation.

Conclusion

The conclusions which can be drawn from probate records must be considered in the context of the records themselves. They were not compiled to provide evidence of contemporary life and business, and their limitations must always be borne in mind.[31] Nevertheless, there can be no doubt that, when used with care, they provide a richness of information about the composition of wealth and of various social and occupational groups, and the nature of their business interests, that can rarely be gained from other extant sources.

Detailed comparison between different occupational or economic groups has, however, not been possible because of the varying levels of detail in the inventories. Some record and price every individual ounce or yard of goods, others infuriatingly list only 'goods in the shop'. Some contain no reference at all to the contents of the deceased's house, giving no opportunity to assess and compare his domestic situation with that of his contemporaries. Debts due and owing cannot be adequately calculated from inventory information alone. General trends and an overall picture are the most that can reasonably be achieved. The impact of these limitations has been partly lessened by the use of information from other documents, mainly wills, plus a few probate accounts. Bequests of personal and domestic items sharpen the general picture of early-seventeenth-century households in Cornwall and add some detail to the Cheshers' mainly architectural analysis, even though it has not been possible to take this analysis very far in the present chapter.[32] Certainly in the areas of financial arrangements and the ownership and disposition of property it is essential to examine these records, which can supplement, and occasionally confound, information obtained from inventories alone.

Analysis of these probate documents shows that the Cornish in the first half of the seventeenth century had access to as wide a range of home-produced and imported goods as their contemporaries elsewhere in England. A few at least of the Cornish towns seem to have enjoyed

---

[31] See Chapter 4, above, pp.95–102; also Spufford, 'Limitations of the probate inventory'.
[32] Chesher and Chesher, *Cornishman's house*, pp.42–54.

permanent 'retail' shops, though their owners, like Robert Bennett of Tregony mentioned above, may also have travelled with a market stall to other towns. Those traders with easy access to the sea were from the early years of the century engaged in well-organised seafaring enterprises. There was clearly a vibrant and mobile community engaged in the acquisition and distribution of items for sale, with a complex network of contacts inside and beyond the county and overseas. The inventories of the merchant class demonstrate a liking for, and the ability to acquire, luxury goods for their houses, and to make generous provision for their families. It is also clear that the wealthier merchants and retailers invested more heavily in property and farming, while also relying far more heavily upon credit than did their more humble counterparts.

Further work on the activities of those engaged in seafaring as well as in the handling of merchandise may well revise, and enhance, our perceptions of Cornish merchants in this period. What is clear from the present study is that Cornwall in the early-seventeenth century continued to enjoy and exploit her closeness to Europe so delightfully described by Richard Carew in 1602:

> The nearness helpeth them, with a shorter cut, less peril and meaner charge, to vent forth and make return of those commodities which their own or either of those countries do afford; the lying in the way bringeth foreign ships to claim succour at their harbour, when either outward or homeward bound.[33]

Glossary

Bays, cloth with worsted warp and woollen weft.

Belly piece, a triangular stiffening of pasteboard or whalebone set into the front of a doublet, forming a corset-like ridge.

Billament, usually spelt biliment, woman's head ornament.

Buffin, changeable, buffin is a coarse cloth used for women's gowns; changeable is used to denote a shot material.

Calico, cotton cloth originally imported from the east, named after Calicut in India.

Camelan, possibly camelina, a woollen cloth woven in a basket weave.

Canvas, coarse, unbleached cloth made from hemp.

Carthagineans, possibly carthagena, cotton with a long staple.

Cask, a measure of capacity varying with place, date and contents.

---

[33] Carew, *Survey of Cornwall*, reprint, pp.83–4.

Caul or call, close-fitting cap worn by women.

China, Philip and China, a worsted or woollen stuff of common quality; a woollen textile like camlet, sometimes watered; used for clothing and upholstery.

Cittern, a type of guitar with wire strings.

Dowlas, coarse linen named after Dowlas in Britanny.

Dust bed, dowst, chaff, the husks of winnowed corn. Poor people used these to stuff pillows and mattresses.

Ell, the English ell was 45 inches in length. By the seventeenth century it was mainly used to measure linens.

Figuratoes, a wool fabric used in Norwich in the seventeenth century, similar to bombasine but with large figured effects.

Fustian, coarse cloth made of cotton and flax or hemp, or cotton only. Named after Fostat, a suburb of Cairo where this cloth was made.

Galls, used for making ink.

Hogshead, a capacity varying according to the type of liquid it measured.

Holland, good quality linen cloth.

Jeans, cloth originally made in Genoa.

Kersey, coarse, narrow woollen cloth which does not originate from Kersey in Suffolk, but from an Arabic word for a long, narrow cloth.

Lawn, fine linen.

Moccado, a kind of woollen cloth

Nonsopretties, a linen tape on which were woven figures in colours.

Paragon, kind of double camlet (camlet is a silk and wool mixture).

Perpetuana, mingled. Perpetuana is a durable wool fabric resembling serge and made in many colours.

Philip, see China.

Pyramides, also peramides, paramides, piramides. A seventeenth-century fine narrow English worsted dress fabric, made with two coloured yarns.

Quire, usually 24 sheets of paper, but it could have a smaller number of sheets, even as few as eight.

Ream, 20 quires (see above) which equals 480 sheets.

Rundlet, usually runlet, a cask of varying capacity from one pint to 18 gallons.

Serge, double twilled cloth, sometimes a mixture of worsted and wool.

Tabby grosgrain is mixed silk and cotton, which is ribbed; also a stout silk of rich quality.

Tabinet, a watered wool and silk fabric.

16

Widows of the 'Middling Sort' and their Assets in Two Seventeenth-Century Towns

MARY HODGES

Introduction

Thame and Woodstock were two thriving market towns in Oxfordshire in the seventeenth century. Both had been founded 500 years earlier as 'new towns'—Thame by the Bishop of Lincoln and Woodstock by Henry II. The royal borough of Woodstock was confined within a mere 61 acres, although the hamlet of Hensington was so close that it virtually formed part of the town. By the mid-seventeenth century about 600 people lived in Woodstock and about 1,500 in Thame, which covered over 5,200 acres.[1]

The importance of small towns within the early modern urban hierarchy has long been appreciated, even if the proportion of the urban population living in small as compared with larger towns was diminishing towards the later seventeenth century as the growth rate of the larger centres increasingly outstripped that of the smaller.[2] Nevertheless, there were over 800 market towns in England and Wales in the sixteenth century, and still over 700 in the seventeenth, and towards the end of that century roughly half of English town-dwellers may have lived in towns smaller than 5,000 inhabitants, constituting

---

[1] Articles on the towns appear in the *Victoria County History of Oxfordshire*, Thame in vol. VII, pp. 160–219, Woodstock in vol. XII, pp. 325–430. Population estimates were made by the Woodstock and Thame Research groups using the parish registers, assuming baptism and burial rates of 30 and 20 per 1,000 respectively. These totals have been checked against back projection estimates, and compared with figures that could be derived from Hearth Taxes and the Compton Census, all of which produce similar totals.

[2] Jack, *Towns in Tudor and Stuart Britain*, pp.173–4; Clark, *Small towns*, Table 5.1, pp.97, 99–100.

Table 16.1 Occupations of husbands in Thame and Woodstock, 54 of 64 linked couples

Occupational group	N	%
1. Gentry, professional	7	13
2. Agricultural	19	35
3. Craftsmen	8	15
4. Shopkeepers	20	37
Total	54	100

Note: Group 1 is made up of 5 gentlemen, 1 clerk and 1 scrivener.
Group 2 is made up of 16 yeomen, 2 husbandmen and 1 labourer.
Group 3 is made up of 1 blacksmith, 1 carpenter, 1 collarmaker, 1 currier, 1 fellmonger, 1 glover, 1 salter and 1 weaver.
Group 4 is made up of 6 butchers, 3 mercers, 2 bakers, 2 drapers, 2 innholders, 1 barber, 1 distiller, 1 shoemaker, 1 tailor and 1 tallowchandler.

possibly 14 per cent of the national population.[3] Simple market towns stood at the bottom of the urban hierarchy, typically with populations ranging from 600 to 1,500, occasionally a little larger, with their claim to urban status resting essentially upon their marketing role. The inhabitants of both Thame and Woodstock were thus typical in depending upon the prosperity of their towns as market centres, although their craft occupations and commercial activities were supported by farming, a more important part of Thame life than of Woodstock.[4] As Table 16.1 reveals, over one-third of married male inhabitants were employed in service and retail trades, while three in ten described themselves as yeomen and one in ten gentlemen.[5] Like most small towns, therefore, they were economically and also administratively

---

[3] Everitt, 'Marketing of agricultural produce', p.467; Clark, *Small towns*, pp.1, 90.

[4] The Thame Group designed a method for categorising the occupations. It was decided that this should not be an attempt to reflect class since status at this time was the important factor. The categories are: 1—gentleman, teacher, surgeon, cleric, scrivener; 2—all agricultural occupations including yeoman, husbandman, labourer; 3—craftsman; 4—shopkeeper, innkeeper, victualler; 5—women. In the database we have a table for occupations and another for status where information on 'occupations' such as knight, esquire, almsman. the elder etc. can be stored.

[5] Compare this with Evans, 'Testators'. Evans' figures on occupations in nine Suffolk villages give 28 per cent of occupations not known and 51 per cent in farming. Market towns like Thame and Woodstock are significantly different.

unsophisticated, and possessed a distinctly rural aspect, although there was considerable scope for variation within this broad group, as Patten's East Anglian survey has shown, while it is all to easy to understate their significance.[6] Unfortunately the East Anglian study is one of the few significant surveys of early modern small towns, and despite the recent and very welcome efforts of the Leicester Centre for Urban History, detailed studies of such towns remain very rare indeed.

One of the key reasons for this, of course, is that their relatively simple political and economic structures meant that they failed to generate the range and weight of documentary evidence that larger centres invariably produced. This means that they are often harder to investigate, and that recourse must commonly be had to documentation that is time-consuming to process. For this reason a premium is placed upon the pooling of effort, and it is just such teamwork that has enabled the present study. This survey of widows' assets and economic circumstances in these two market towns is based mainly on probate documents,[7] supplemented by other sources such as the Hearth Tax, court rolls and chamberlains' accounts. Two research groups have worked for over ten years on the records of these two towns and, as shown in Table 16.2, have located 349 probate documents in Woodstock and 934 in Thame, of which over one-fifth belong to women. The Thame group has developed a database which brings together the very large amount of data produced by these records; a start has been made on placing the Woodstock data in a similar database.[8] Table 16.2 shows that rather more wills have survived for Thame than for Woodstock but fewer administration bonds.[9] The figures for Thame include the rural hamlets which formed part of the parish, but the numbers living there were very few.

Wills and inventories have, of course, long been known to social and economic historians, but their systematic exploitation, for towns in

---

[6] Patten, *English towns*, p.267; Corfield, 'Small towns'.

[7] Probate documents for Woodstock are in the series MS Wills Oxon in Oxfordshire Archives, those for Thame are in the series PEC in Oxfordshire Archives. Probate documents have also been found in PROB4 and PROB11 in the Public Record Office and in miscellaneous documents in Oxfordshire Archives.

[8] The group has used a number of database systems over the years: data is now held in Microsoft Access. The database has been deposited at The Data Archive, University of Essex.

[9] Thame probate was dealt with by the Peculiar Court which met in the Court House at Thame presided over by a canon of Lincoln Cathedral or his representative on behalf of the Bishop of Lincoln. The local nature of the court may account for the greater survival of the documents.

Table 16.2 Probate documents in Thame and Woodstock

Thame	All	% of total	Women	% of total of women
Will	485	51.9	111	47.6
Inventory	337	36.1	104	44.6
Account	24	2.6	4	1.7
Admon/Bond	88	9.4	14	6.0
Total	934	100.0	233	100.0

Woodstock	All	% of total	Women	% of total of women
Will	132	37.8	27	38.0
Inventory	123	35.2	26	36.6
Account	11	3.1	1	1.4
Admon/Bond	83	23.7	17	23.9
Total	349	99.8	71	100.0

general but for small towns in particular, remains relatively rare. Rarer still are studies of particular social and economic categories, and our knowledge of the place of women in early modern urban society remains very limited. Unfortunately, probate evidence is of relatively little use for gaining insight into the affairs of either single or married women, few of whom left a will. In our two towns only some 10 per cent of women making wills or leaving sufficient property to be inventoried were either unmarried or had husbands living. Women are, however, also found in the probate documents acting as executors, administrators and in other roles. Nearly three in five of the executors in a sample of 484 wills were female. The prevalence of women as executors seems to indicate that most men were willing to leave this important and demanding task to women. Perhaps it reflects the role of women in managing the household and its assets in partnership with men and, where literacy was not common for either men or women, it was not seen as a problem that most women involved probably could not write.

Widows, however, are a different matter: if only 10 per cent of probate documents relate to single or married women, then 90 per cent pertain to widows. As Evans discovered, 'The great majority of men whose wives survived them left them either all their moveable property or the unbequeathed residue thereof. These bequests of household goods and livestock were generally unconditional, and this freedom to do what they wished with moveables may explain the large number of widows' wills'.[10] In Thame the probate documents also make it possible

[10] Evans, 'Inheritance', p.67.

to link 46 couples where both husband and widow have left a document
of some kind, and there are 17 such couples in Woodstock. In Thame
there are 25 couples where both have left an inventory and in
Woodstock 14 couples. Obviously these couples have a particular
importance for this study since this evidence gives the opportunity to
see how far widows' lives were affected by the inheritance they had.
Unfortunately in both Thame and Woodstock, as was commonly the
case elsewhere, the 'occupations' of women as stated on probate
documents were invariably 'spinster' or 'widow'. In both towns,
however, we have information from other sources about their
occupations, as innkeepers, victuallers, in a very few cases maintaining
their late husbands' business, and in many cases lending money.
Altogether a total of 158 widows have been traced in Woodstock for
this century and 750 in Thame, though the latter falls to 412 when the
parish register evidence is discounted, making it more comparable with
the figure for Woodstock.

Apart from the fact of their prominence in surviving documentation,
widows were of considerable significance in urban society, especially
amongst the middling ranks of small towns. According to Erickson,
'Most adult women in the population at any given time were not
married—they were either widowed or they had never married'.[11]
Through detailed analysis of our data we have established the length of
widowhood for 64 widows in our two towns, and the results are
presented in Table 16.3. Their mean length of widowhood was nine
years while 60 per cent lived as widows for more than ten years. Since
it is thought that the mean length of a marriage was no more than 20
years at this time,[12] widows formed a considerable part of the
community. In Woodstock, where we have some lists of inhabitants,[13]
widows also form a significant group of householders. At Michaelmas
1619 the list contained 110 men and 39 widows, meaning that widows
constituted 27 per cent of all householders in the town. The Hearth Tax
returns for 1662 and 1665 showed smaller proportions: 14 per cent and
7 per cent for 1662 and 1665 respectively in Thame, and 10 per cent
and 9 per cent respectively in Woodstock.[14] These returns, however,
only include the taxable population, not the large numbers who were
exempt, amongst whom the proportion of widows was no doubt
significantly higher.

[11] Erickson, *Women and property*, p.9.
[12] Gottlieb, *Family in the western world*, p.108.
[13] Woodstock Borough Records (WBR) 96 f.14/15.
[14] PRO, E179/255/4; E179/164/513.

Table 16.3 Length of widowhood in Thame and Woodstock

	Thame N	Woodstock N	Both Towns N	%
1 year or less	7	3	10	16
1–10 years	9	7	16	25
11–19 years	23	6	29	45
20 years or more	7	2	9	14
Total	46	18	64	100
Mean length of widowhood in years	10	8	9	
Longest widowhood	30 years	23 years		

Widowhood was no means an isolating experience, nor was it a state without power. As Todd writes, 'Prominent widows in public life showed several generations of Abingdon women that there was a positive aspect to the freedom of widowhood, a freedom that more obscure widows experienced only in their private lives'. For example, one of the Woodstock widows, Margaret Raunson, brought a case in the Portmouth Court in 1612 against John Heath and Andrew James in her role as executrix of her husband's will. Another, Meriall Taylor, who had been widowed in 1609 was in 1613 a victualler and was still bringing cases in the Portmouth Court as administrator of her husband's will.[15] These women do not readily fit the 'official' version of how women should behave as revealed in contemporary homilies and conduct books—modest, pious, confined to the house and to housekeeping.

Widows and property

At this time widows possessed certain rights in law which almost always applied. Dower was a portion which a widow had of the lands of her husband. This came to mean a third part of the freehold lands and tenements which were part of the husband's estate and which might be enjoyed for the life of the widow. However, where the widow was the second or later wife of the husband, she had no right to lands which

[15] Todd, 'The remarrying widow', p.82. This study of widows in Abingdon, another market town in Oxfordshire (Berkshire before 1974), includes a very useful resumé of the reasons why widows did not more often remarry. WBR, 77/1, 78/1–3.

would have been inherited by the children of the first wife. A special writ of right of dower enabled a widow to claim part of her dower where this had been taken by another. Dower is not to be confused with dowry—that is, the property brought to her husband on marriage. However, where the children were under-age it seems common for the wife to be left the whole estate or a major part of it with the responsibility for bringing up the children so that widows were 'guardians of inheritance'.[16] As Erickson points out, widows were often in the position of bringing up a young family alone and of ensuring that the inheritance of land and possessions followed custom and the desires of the deceased husband. When John Williams, gentleman of Woodstock, died in 1663 his wife Amy was left with five children, four of whom were minors; the inventory value was £184. She received the house until her death when it went to the eldest son Thomas. The children all received bequests from their father but Amy received the residue of the estate. By the time Amy died in 1680 her daughter Anne had married Thomas Greene and she received from her mother a debt of £9 owing to Amy together with household goods. By now the eldest son Thomas was dead, the second son John was the executor and received the house and most of the contents. Another son Michael was also dead but Oliver received 20 shillings to buy a ring. All the grandchildren received five shillings each. The value of Amy's inventory was £57: she had succeeded in bringing up the four younger children within the family home while maintaining most of the goods left by her husband.

The widow with property either absolutely—at least for her lifetime—or as dower was a person of importance in her community, and this is borne out by the evidence from Thame and Woodstock. Where the children were of age they had to be provided for, but nevertheless the widow had to be properly provided for both in goods and money and in land and property.[17] At the least she had the right to *bona paraphinalia*—the valuables she had brought as her dowry, jewels given to her by her husband and a suitable amount of household furniture and goods. In Woodstock, because of the existence of the chamberlains' accounts, we have some idea of how widows could hold on to the houses in which they had lived before their husband's death, and of how sometimes they could be evicted. Although in theory women were subjugated in law in reality the widows had power

---

[16] Erickson, *Women and property*, p.5.
[17] Evans, 'Inheritance', pp.61–3. Evans gives a valuable survey of land bequests in Suffolk towns and villages.

through their stewardship of property and their independence of male control. The Portmouth Court of Woodstock, which was a court of record and which met fortnightly on Mondays, dealt with cases of debt and trespass in the town. In 1613 William Rayer, an alderman of the borough, brought a case of trespass and ejectment against Alice Barnes, a widow with three children. Later in 1618 Rayer was paying quit rent of 3d. for her house to the town, so evidently he lost his case of ejectment against her. In 1618 she was also receiving 1d. worth of bread every Sunday for her children. John Phillipps, an alderman of the borough, died in 1608. On April 1, 1611 his widow Mary brought an action of dower to the Portmouth Court. Through her attorney Simon Jeames she brought a plea against Robert Symons for the third part of one messuage or tenement with appurtenances in the borough in the tenure of William Parker, the land having been given to Mary as the dower of her deceased husband. After 21 court appearances the matter was settled on December 23, 1611. A jury was called to hear what part of the tenement Mary Phillipps wanted. They visited the premises and agreed that she should have

> the kitchen and the chamber over it, with the entry on the north side, also the stable adjoining and the barn standing in the backside and part of the backside as it was bounded out by the jury. Also the plaintiff is to have ingress, egress and regress into and from the said premises so divided without interruption; she is to be at the charge of making the mound between the tenant and herself.

Copies were made of the agreement and placed in the town clerk's office.

The parish registers for Thame survive for the whole century, though imperfectly for 1611–12 and 1654–6, while those for Woodstock only start in 1657, and hence it has been difficult to discover reliably when or whether widows remarried before then. Remarriage was another option; in Woodstock the widow of a freeman of the borough could confer that freedom on a new husband. It has proved as difficult as Holderness thought to reconstruct the numbers of widows remarrying, but he is in no doubt about its importance: 'As an agency of social mobility it (remarriage) was a secondary, not a primary influence, but it is an influence which historians have often unjustifiably ignored'.[18] In Thame we can identify 28 widows who remarried out of a total of over 1,000 marriages. Of these we know that several of them had young children. This percentage of about 3 per cent matches the work done

---

[18] Oxfordshire Archives, parish register transcripts; Holderness, 'Widows in pre-industrial society', p.435.

by Sogner in Shropshire where he took only the cases where 'widow' was explicitly stated.[19]

Widows' assets

The probate documents for both towns provide a wealth of detailed evidence of which the inventories are the most obviously useful in considering the widows' assets. Tables 16.4a and 16.4b display the inventories for both towns in detail. The data has been arranged over two periods of 50 years to reveal significant changes across the century, showing the information from men's and women's probate separately. The value of the inventories has been broken down into three groups— with values of over £200, values between £50 and £199, and with values less than £50. In this table the very few inventories of £1,000 or more have been excluded so that the results are not distorted by a very few large values. The women's probate documents represent all the widows in this study; while virtually all the men with probate in Thame are included for comparative purposes, only those men in Woodstock whose wives are in the study are included.

In the period 1600–60 the mean value of men's inventories exceeds that of women except in the band £50–199 where the women have a mean of £103 and the men £80. However, in the lowest band the women are clearly much poorer with a mean of almost half that of the men. The table subdivides the items listed in the inventories into groups so that all the items included in the inventories can be placed sensibly in one of the groups. The credits are the amount of money listed as owing to the deceased person. These details are by no means always included, even when it appears from the will that credits exist.

Looking at the items grouped under household goods reveals that the mean of the widows' goods differed little from that of the men, and the percentage of this item was also very similar. This seems to point to the fact that many widows retained the family house and furnishings, and this is confirmed where it has proved possible to compare inventory details of husband and wife. For example, Robert Ayres of Woodstock died in 1624 and his inventory was appraised by John Glover, Bartholomew Love and John Tassell. They listed three rooms, the hall, the low chamber and the chamber over the hall. When Margaret Ayres, Robert's widow, died in May 1628, John Glover, Bartholomew Love and John Norman were the appraisers; they listed three rooms, the hall, the chamber and the chamber above. The kitchen equipment in the hall

---

[19] Sogner, 'Aspects of the demographic situation', p.132.

Table 16.4a Woodstock and Thame, inventory values by type, 1600–60

Inventory values	N		total ($\pounds$)	household	clothes	money	credits	leases	crops	animals	shop/trade
Males											
$\pounds$200+	12	total	4,485.89								
		mean	373.82								
		%		15.38	2.22	22.39	19.52	0.00	19.61	14.69	6.17
$\pounds$50–199	40	total	3,199.83								
		mean	80.00								
		%		28.96	3.56	15.73	9.24	0.63	14.57	13.07	14.25
$\pounds$0–49	91	total	2,423.05								
		mean	26.63								
		%		41.47	4.78	21.13	9.21	1.65	8.26	8.66	4.84
Females											
$\pounds$200+	2	total	442.58								
		mean	221.29								
		%		18.22	3.50	5.02	44.62	0.00	28.47	0.17	0.00
$\pounds$50–199	19	total	1,963.84								
		mean	103.36								
		%		24.96	4.51	26.16	25.40	3.56	11.28	2.75	1.37
$\pounds$0–49	42	total	681.46								
		mean	16.23								
		%		43.45	8.64	18.83	8.07	2.93	9.22	8.82	0.04

Table 16.4b Woodstock and Thame, inventory values by type, 1661–1700

Inventory values	N		total (£)	household	clothes	money	credits	leases	crops	animals	shop/trade
Males											
£200+	28	total	13,125.47								
		mean	468.77								
		%		12.25	1.06	21.42	32.97	1.23	12.45	6.48	12.15
£50–199	52	total	5,773.97								
		mean	111.04								
		%		24.23	2.76	14.52	23.94	1.00	11.27	6.46	15.83
£0–49	54	total	1,276.25								
		mean	23.63								
		%		37.59	5.39	9.66	17.98	0.63	7.82	11.86	9.08
Females											
£200+	5	total	1,695.21								
		mean	339.04								
		%		12.23	2.06	26.31	43.65	0.00	11.85	0.24	3.66
£50–199	17	total	1,676.17								
		mean	98.60								
		%		26.75	3.80	17.53	38.48	0.00	5.20	2.45	5.79
£0–49	19	total	622.20								
		mean	22.70								
		%		30.58	6.58	20.05	38.45	0.48	0.00	3.30	0.57

was almost the same as in 1624—an iron bar, two iron hooks, a toasting iron, pairs of pothooks and andirons, but one brass posnet and one brass pot had gone. However, Margaret had obviously maintained the farm since the value of crops and animals was almost identical to her husband's inventory, while the bees had increased in value. So where Robert's inventory value was £52 3s., Margaret's was £45 8s. 4d.

Clothes show the largest variation between men and women. Throughout the century the mean for women is nearly twice that for men. Additionally there are more details about the women's clothes in the wills. The widows' clothes ranged from Sibell Alnett in Thame, whose clothes were given to the poor, to Alice Rayer of Woodstock whose clothes were worth £15 10s. Sometimes the clothes were listed as old, as in the case of Anne Coles in Woodstock but it is unusual to find any details about their condition. Sometimes items of clothing appear in the will rather than the inventory as when Elizabeth Franklin of Thame left her daughter Elizabeth 'my best hatt and my best petticote and my best aprone and the rest of my wearing lynen and all the rest of my clothes and a newe gowne that I never wore'.

Because Woodstock was so much smaller than Thame in terms of surrounding farm land we could expect the ownership of crops and animals to be very different. Woodstock, as a royal borough with a very small acreage, did not possess fields of any size, although there were water meadows beside the river Glyme. However, some people owned or rented land in other places. Margaret Ayres' inventory records nine acres each of barley and corn, corn in the barn and one acre of vetches; Joane Browne had 140 quarters of malt and barley; Jane Gibbs had hay and oats; and Dorothy Gregory had hay and straw and also 120 quarters of malt. Apart from Margaret Ayres, all of this sounds like the provisions for animals kept behind the house together with malt and barley for brewing. In Thame 15 widows' inventories have entries which seem to describe farm produce—for example Margaret Green had corn in the barn, hay, wheat and maslin in the field and bacon in the Hall; Eleanor Pitman had wheat, rye, barley, beans and straw. In Thame the court rolls give details of the copyholders of land so that we have examples of widows who held land in the fields. Margaret Green held one messuage and one half-yardland by copyhold; the term was for herself, her son John and his wife Anne, rent was 12s. 5d. per annum and the value was £14. Animals listed in Woodstock inventories included sheep, lambs, pigs, cows and horses. In Thame cows, pigs, horses and sheep all appear. Grace Andrews, for example, had one bacon hog, two beasts (as cows are still called in Thame today), two heifers, and 44 sheep in their sheep fold. Maude Weathered had seven cows, two yearlings, two weaners, seven hogs and poultry: surprisingly, poultry are mentioned in only two other inventories. Bees appear in both towns and one favourite cow, Elinor Messenger's 'little doe cow' in Thame. Certainly from the total figures men had significantly more animals than women but in crops the women had a comparable percentage of their wealth in these items.

A very clear difference between men and women shows up in the column 'shops and trade'. Here it seems to have been very rare for widows to inherit the actual business conducted by their deceased husband. In the period before 1660 there is almost no trace of women doing this, although after 1660 there are a few examples. William Tripp was a tallow chandler in Thame who died in 1677 making his wife Elizabeth executrix. He had £20 out on loan and when Elizabeth died in 1687 it seems that she had continued to run the business, since the contents of the shop valued at £60 are identical to the shop goods left by William. The value of William's inventory was £148 14s. and of Elizabeth's £234 9s. Elizabeth had £130 in ready money and debts owed to her and she bequeathed to her son Joseph one guinea requiring him to pay £20, which he owed to his mother, to her daughter Elizabeth. Her son William received the residue which included the shop, but most of the furniture went to her daughter. Innkeeping businesses also seem to have been inherited in a few cases. In Woodstock Amy Williams, who died in 1680 and was the widow of John Williams who died in 1663, continued as innkeeper in the same house which was left to her by John. The rooms have the same names in both inventories—The Blue, Flower de Luce, the Middle and the Hall, but The Greene does not appear in Amy's inventory. Her inventory includes the 'signe post and board' valued at £1. Both inventories have a well-equipped brewhouse and a cellar containing hogsheads, barrels and stands, some containing beer.

Money-lending

Holderness writes that, 'The most prominent economic function of the widow in English rural society between 1500 and 1900 was money-lending . . . supplying part at least of the credit which peasant and small-town societies needed so extensively in seventeenth century England'.[20] Tables 16.4a and 16.4b make clear the prominent role played by women in the two towns in money-lending: across the whole range of wealth credits were roughly twice as important as a proportion of total wealth to women than they were to men. In the period 1600–60, among the

---

[20] Holderness, 'Widows in pre-industrial society', pp.428, 435.

wealthiest widows 44 per cent of the value of their estate was in credits, and even the least affluent had 8 per cent in credits. By the second half of the century the less affluent widows had 38 per cent of their wealth out in credits, and by now the widows were lending more than the men as a proportion at every level. This picture is confirmed by a study of the couples with linked probates, for while 33 of the widows had lent money only nine of the husbands had done so. In general it is only the probate documents with inventories that give details of money-lending. However, some accounts—of which there are few—and a few wills also have these details. It is not uncommon for outstanding debts to be left to legatees in wills so that they had to collect the money owed.

The detail of those to whom money was lent is important as it demonstrates a difference between the two towns. Woodstock men fairly often lent to notable people at court—no doubt when the court visited Woodstock courtiers called on the local shopkeepers, especially the mercers, to borrow money and also to buy goods 'on tick'. Woodstock women, however, seem very often to lend to others of their own status in the town, and widows lent to other widows. Not all Woodstock citizens lent money within the town; Anne Coles, who died in 1687, had lent £75 10s. to Richard Walker, a tailor of Oxford. In Thame much money-lending is to members of the immediate family as well as to the more extended branches. Again, as in Woodstock, money-lending seems to be done chiefly by shopkeepers rather than by the significant group in Thame calling itself yeomen or husbandmen. The widows, as important members of the group lending money, were doing this in order to improve their income. Earlier in the century borrowed money would in general fetch about 10 per cent interest per annum but it had fallen to 6 per cent by the reign of Charles II. 'The taking of interest at an equitable rate had become well established, and may indeed have been normal by 1630–50 within English rural society.'[21] For pawned goods, up to 30 per cent per annum could be charged. We have two examples of widows acting as pawnbrokers, one in each town. Margery Nurse of Woodstock, who died in 1620, left to Mary Rylye the daughter of John Rylye her kinsman 'One little cofer withe the things therein whiche was pawned unto me by the sayde John Rylye for fortye shillings'. In Thame the pawned object was a satin cushion.

The debts listed in accounts and inventories are often divided as sperate—likely to be recovered easily—and desperate—unlikely to be repaid. Where, rarely, the actual debts are listed in detail it is possible to

---

[21] Holderness, 'Widows in pre-industrial society', p.442; see also Chapter 11, above.

see how widely the credit circle spread. In Woodstock Joane Browne
was the widow of Thomas Browne who died in 1620. She died in 1624
and her executor was her son Thomas. He died shortly afterwards and
the administration of the will passed from his widow Susan to Joane's
daughter Joan Marriatt. Therefore we have among the probate
documents a will, account, inventory and administration bond and also
a codicil to the will. The value of the inventory was £222 13s. and
although the will declared 'she is not indebted to any boddy', the
accountant paid £20 owed to Thomas Miller of Woodstock on bond
by Joane Browne. The will contained a complete list of the debts
'owing unto me'. Here were debts owed by five widows of Woodstock
including Margaret Ayres who owed 28 shillings, and Ann Carden who
owed 10 shillings. Otherwise sums of three and four pounds were owed
to her, the total being £40 11s. 11d. Of this her administrator was not
able to recover £11 14s. Unfortunately, her husband Thomas Browne's
inventory does not survive, so we cannot tell whether he was also a
money-lender.

When Joan Johnson died in Woodstock in 1695 the £100 of debts
owed to her were all sperate and probably represented the £100 in gold
left by her husband; she also had £30 in her purse, perhaps accrued from
interest on the loans. Alice Rayer of Woodstock, who died in 1626,
provides another instructive example. Thomas Woodward owed her
£157 10s. on two bonds. Her husband William, who had been mayor
of the borough several times, was innkeeper of the Bear and had died in
1619. Alice's inventory was taken by, among others, Thomas
Woodward who was a mercer and innkeeper in the town and a freeman
of the borough, eventually becoming mayor himself in 1638, 1644 and
1651. This debt illustrates well the way in which prosperous families
helped one another by advancing money. The bonds Thomas
Woodward had would have provided cash for him as he acquired
freeman status. A third example is provided by Elizabeth Sparrow,
widow of Thomas who was described as a gentleman when he died in
1678. He was a mercer in Woodstock and had been mayor three times.
His inventory lists the contents of his shop in detail and the workshop
where candles were made, the total value being £666 11s. 7d. of which
£308 18s. 9d. were debts owed to him, all apparently sperate. His will
shows that he left his freehold estates and also the messuages and
tenements he held in Woodstock to his wife Elizabeth. Thomas and
Elizabeth had only one child, Grace, who by the time Elizabeth died in
1690 had married Benjamin Johnson. Elizabeth seems to have been
living in the same house; her inventory was worth £314 and sperate
debts were worth £230 with £10 desperate. Elizabeth left £200 to her

daughter Grace with the express condition that she use the money to provide £5 a year to Elizabeth's sister Sarah Keeble. If Grace had invested the money at 6 per cent she would have had more than enough to pay this pension.

It is worth noting the large sums of ready money held by widows. After 1660 the widows held more money in the house than the men did, for the least affluent an average of £12 for the widows and £2 for the men. The other source of wealth, leases, were far less evenly distributed, the men having a far larger share. Overall the widows whose probate records we have give an impression of business-like competence in managing their inheritance and making it work to their advantage by supplying an income for life. A widow with £10 a year, which many seem to have achieved, could live very comfortably.

Bequests

There was considerable variation in the manner in which widows distributed their estates, as their wills demonstrate. Juliana Druce of Thame left her son 12 pence and all the rest to the grandchildren. The son had, of course, inherited from his father, so the 12 pence was a token only. It was, in fact, very common for the grandchildren to receive legacies; Elizabeth Browne left all her valuables, which were considerable, to the children and grandchildren of her first marriage to John Pettie. Similarly Ann Minchard left most of her estate to the children of her first marriage. Elizabeth Bartlett divided her house in Thame between her son and daughter, while Ann Jacob left 12 pence to each of her children, except for her daughter Eleanor who received the residue which was again considerable. But other considerations occupied the minds of some widows. As Erickson has suggested, '. . . ordinary women took different decisions about their property than ordinary men, according to their perceptions of self-interest. Women had different ideas about moral desert, about who was in need and about what was important'.[22] For example, Alice Wray of Woodstock left her son 12 pence and all the rest of her estate to her daughter Elizabeth Sherley 'to relieve her want'. Dorothy Hoord left £5 to the poor of Woodstock, £2 to the parish church, and all the rest to her bailiff Coxeter. Elizabeth Coles of Thame left money to pay her son's debts and five shillings to buy her godson a lamb. Joane Flaxman of Thame left most of her estate to 'the poor women who looked after me when sicke'. Margaret Greene of Thame left most of her estate to her son John

---

[22] Erickson *Women and Property*, p.235.

but wanted her trees protected: 'if there be any trees yt by law may be remooved my will is yt they shall not be cutt downe rooted up or in any maner of way defaced wilfully but to remain to him ye said John entirely'. Ann Powell also of Thame made her grandchild Pharaoh Larrimore her executor and wrote in her will 'allso my will and meaninge is that mine executor shall not cutt nor lopp nor deminish any of the apple trees nor any other treese or under woods growing in or about the orchard'. Bequests to the poor were at least as commonly given by widows as by any other group. In a study by Motla (a member of the Thame research group) of 345 wills for Thame, 102 of them included bequests to the poor. Of these 28 were widows' wills and their contribution over the century was 12 per cent of the total sum of charitable bequests.[23] In Woodstock the money given was sometimes in the form of doles of bread and cake. Bequests to the church also occur often and include in Woodstock and Thame money for sermons to be preached. Elizabeth Nicholls of Woodstock wanted 20 dozen loaves and 10 dozen cakes to be distributed to the poor 'as I am carried out'.

Poor widows

By definition probate documents do not yield information about poor widows, who almost certainly outnumbered those with property or savings.[24] However, Joane Godfrye of Woodstock owed more in unpaid rent than her estate was worth when she died in 1636, and Thomas Rayer took all that there was to meet the debt. It is worthwhile to try to gain some picture of the widows as a whole and how far even those who did not leave wills—or at least whose wills have not survived— managed to live. It was held by people at that time that there was an absolute duty to care for widows and orphans as a Christian obligation and widows were seen to be 'deserving' of charity. Both towns had almshouses and charities were established by townspeople in their wills. In Thame, Nicholas Almond bequeathed a deed of property, from which one-third of the proceeds were to be paid to poor widows, lame and old people, whilst numerous other charities provided bread or clothing for the poor, often mentioning poor women if not widows as such. Here poor rate records exist only for a brief period at the beginning of the century, and these show some widows paying the poor rate—Margaret Greene, Cecilie Benson, Ann Minchard, all of whom left wills and paid four pence a month. Not surprisingly, the widows

[23] Motla, 'Changing attitudes', pp.120–138.
[24] Holderness, 'Widows in pre-industrial society', p.428.

listed as receiving poor relief do not feature in any probate document. They received either twelve pence, six pence or four pence each per week, and on one occasion one was given two shillings for shoes.

In Woodstock the wealth of town records allows a much clearer view of how the poor widows were helped. In 1615 Sir Thomas Spencer had left a charity for the town and the chamberlains' accounts show this frequently being paid to widows in the form of bread for themselves and their children. Alice Barnes received one penny every Sunday for bread for each of her three children, William, Edward and Judith. She was paying rent to the town for her house from which Thomas Rayer had tried to eject her in 1613 by a process in the Portmouth Court. Alice declared she was not guilty and asked for a jury trial, but the case petered out without a decision, and she was still in her house paying rent in 1618. Widows appeared in the town accounts for non-payment of rent and were fined for such offences as cutting down the willows by the river. Widow Aspoole, whom we have already met, was accused of stealing wood from the Park, but Widow Elizabeth Nicholls provided faggots and hardwood worth eight shillings for the soldiers building bulwarks round the town in 1642. In both towns the almshouses and doles from charities, so regularly recorded in the Woodstock chamberlains' accounts, may have provided for those poor widows who do not figure in the probate documents. Their numbers are impossible to quantify. But whilst McIntosh takes a gloomy view of women's lives as widows, most living a life of poverty, the evidence for Thame and Woodstock shows that there was another side to the story.[25]

Conclusion

The records of both of these towns have proved to be a very rich source of information about widows and their lives. The details they contain have provided a rounded picture of the lives of these women, and it seems clear that some of them were considerable figures in their towns, providing a vital service in their money-lending activities and distributing their wealth to a wide range of family members and others at their death. Nor were they unable to defend their interests. Woodstock widows had the Portmouth Court to help them in their claims, and the manor court at Thame clearly maintained widows' interests in land for their lives and the lives of their children. Widows formed a considerable section of the community. The lists of inhabitants

[25] McIntosh, *Community transformed*, p.295. Maslen, M., ed., *Woodstock Chamberlains' Accounts 1609–50.*

maintained in Woodstock make it clear that many widows were householders in their own right, and that at any one time there were at least 15–20 households headed by widows out of the hundred or so listed. Remarriage, though difficult to trace, seems to have been far less popular than keeping the independence that widowhood provided, and this independence is in itself a reflection of the financial security that many widows enjoyed.

17

Beyond the Probate Line: Probate Evidence and Related Sources in Early Modern Yorkshire

BERNARD JENNINGS

Introduction

The theme of this chapter is the value of using, in parallel, probate records and other documentation for research into industrial and social history. In studying local industrial history, the relative importance of probate evidence and other records varies considerably. In fishing and seafaring, in the seventeenth century vessels were commonly held in fractional shares: one-eighth, one-sixteenth, and so on.[1] Because of the dangers of their calling, seamen did not follow the common practice of waiting until they were old or ill before making a will. As a result the will and inventory could be many years apart, the will bequeathing shares in one or more ships, the inventory frequently noting which of the vessels had been lost. In other words, a good deal of light is thrown on the organisation and fortunes of the industry from probate records alone.[2]

Inventories also shed considerable light on another industry: leather working. Hides made up about 10 per cent of the value of cattle. When a beast was killed, or died from disease, the hide was taken to the local tannery and then put into store, to be used as required. If a process was beyond the skill of the household, perhaps saddle-making, a specialist would be brought in to work on the material of the household, the counterpart of the 'customer weaver' discussed below.

By contrast, the few tools listed in the inventories of those lead miners who were brought above the probate line by engaging also in

---

[1] See also Chapter 3, above, p.62.
[2] Borthwick Institute of Historical Research, University of York: seventeenth-century wills and inventories for the Cleveland area.

farming tell us little about the organisation of the industry. Until about 1700 the initiative in Yorkshire lead mining lay mainly with partnerships of independent working miners. They prospected for ore and if they were successful worked a given stretch of vein in return for giving the lord of the minerals a 'duty', that is, a share of the output fixed either by custom or by prior agreement. Lead mining was a speculative occupation in which success could be spectacular but short-lived. Mine workings were of little value if no payable ore was in sight, and until the development of companies holding mines on leases of 21 years, interests in a mine were usually too transient to be left in a will.[3]

The textile industries

The industry, perhaps better described as a group of industries, for which probate records are proportionately the most valuable is textiles. There are few surviving inventories for the Halifax area before the 1680s, but the wills themselves are very informative. For example, Gilbert Waterhouse (1541) left to each of his two sons, besides considerable landholdings, 'one half of all my lomes, walker sheres, cloth presses and sherbordes [and of] all other necessaries and instrumentes to them belonginge'.[4] The Waterhouse family were master clothiers and finishers. 'Walker shears' were so called because they were used to crop cloth which had been fulled, a process originally done by trampling or 'walking'. Other sixteenth-century wills from the district bequeath the ownership of booths in Blackwell Hall and St Batholomew's Cloth Fair in London.[5]

The people who made such wills were engaged in cloth production for the market, as were those with looms recorded in inventories from the 1680s. Earlier inventories from other probate jurisdictions, of which Yorkshire has a considerable number, show a different picture. John Hill of Harrogate, who died in 1589, left, in addition to the stock, crops and equipment of mixed farming, the following materials of a mixed textiles economy: wool cards, a combstock and wool combs, two heckles, a spinning wheel, a loom, two pairs of cloth shears, six stones of wool, 10lbs of coverlet yarn, five and a half yards of samoran cloth, four yards of harden, and one piece of black cloth.[6] William Lightfoot (1606), of the same township, had two spinning wheels, cards, combs, wool,

---

[3] Raistrick and Jennings, *History of lead mining*, Chapter 8.
[4] Sherbordes, a table or board on which a shearman placed cloth to be sheared.
[5] Clay and Crossley, *Halifax wills*, 1, pp.147–8; Jennings, *Pennine valley*, pp.44–5.
[6] Combstock, a post or lump of wood to which combs are attached.

hempen yarn, and a 'woolen loom, with four pairs of woollen gears, one pair for harden, and two pairs for linen thereto belonging'.[7] The loom of John Scaife, clothier, of Kettlesing in lower Nidderdale (1594), had 'three kersey gears, three plain gears, one happing gear and one broad gear'.[8]

Some exegesis is required. Loom gears were healds and slays.[9] Coverlets (vernacular term, happing) were made from long-staple wool, which was combed. Kersey was the commonest woollen cloth of the West Riding, woven in pieces about a yard wide from short-staple wool, which was carded. After weaving, the cloth was taken to the fulling mill and then cropped with shears. A heckle was a heavy comb, with several rows of long metal teeth, through which flax and hemp were drawn in the preparatory process. Cloth made from hempen yarn was widely used for sheets, shifts and shirts. In the area of the above inventories, samoran was a cloth midway in texture between linen and cloth made from hemp; it may have been made from coarse linen, finer hemp, or a mixture. In other parts of Yorkshire we find, instead of the sequence linen—samoran—harden, linen—harden—hempen.

Some households with a diverse farming-textile economy had no loom. For example, John Keighley of Scriven near Knaresborough (1558) had cattle, sheep, pigs, poultry, bees and five different arable crops, together with a spinning wheel, a pair of woollen combs, three stones of hemp, 60 leas of linen yarn, some harden yarn, 21.5 stones of wool and some kersey cloth.[10] The missing element is revealed in the inventory of Miles Waite of Birstwith (1606), which included cattle, horses, sheep, a pig, and poultry; wheat, rye, barley, and oats sown in the field; a stone of line (dressed flax), 80 lea of linen yarn, 120 lea of hemp yarn, 18 yards of 'hemp harden' valued at 18s., linen and hemp

---

[7] Harden, a course fabric made from hards or flax or hemp.
[8] The probate information for Knaresborough and Nidderdale is in Jennings, *History of Nidderdale*, Chapter 9, and Jennings, *History of Harrogate*, Chapter 9.
[9] Heald or heddle, the small cords or wires through which the warp threads are passed on a loom after going through the reed or slay, which separates the warp threads into two sets to allow the passing of the shuttle between them. Slays or reeds, a weaver's slay or reed consists of two parallel strips of wood about five inches apart with the space between them filled with pieces of metal about one-sixteenth of an inch wide and the thickness of a pen. Originally reed or cane was used instead of metal. The purpose of the slay is to keep the warp threads straight, to act as a guide for the shuttle and to push the woven weft close to the previously woven threads.
[10] A lea was a measure of length, 300 yards, used for linen and hempen yarn. Later it was also used to indicate the thickness of the yarn, a 30-lea being 30 times 300 yards to the pound weight.

cloth valued at 40s., woollen cloth valued at 33s. 4d., and cloth at
Thomas Parker's valued at 7s. Parker was a 'customer weaver', a figure
represented in literature by Silas Marner in George Eliot's novel. Other
inventories contain such entries as 'one woollen web at the webster's,
8s.' and 'one linen web at the webster's, 12s.'.

It is clear that the primary purpose of these textile operations was to
meet domestic needs. The looms in such households were probably
busy during slack periods of the farming year, providing a useful 'cash
crop' in the form of cloth surplus to domestic requirements which was
sold locally or in one of the established cloth markets. The City of York,
in 1551, relaxed its rules about the sale of woollen cloth for the benefit
of 'any husbandman or other poor creatures of the country being
unfranchised that maketh a piece or 2 of woollen cloth in a year within
his own house and bringeth to this city to sell . . . by retail'. What is
remarkable is the range of textile processes, dealing with worsted (long-
staple), woollens (short-staple), flax and hemp, all in the same
household.

Even the market-oriented weavers resisted specialisation. William
Bramley of Winsley in lower Nidderdale (1602) left three looms, one to
each of three men who were apparently his journeymen weavers.[11]
They were a broad loom, a kersey loom and a linen loom. This pattern
could be found even in the leading urban centres. Robert Dacres of
Beverley, weaver, bequeathed to a relative in 1498 'unum wollen-lome
et unum bastard-lome cum iiii heyldes et slayes pro panno lato
[broadcloth] et iiii heyldes et slais pro carsey'. His apprentice received
another bastard loom, this time with four healds and slays each for linen
and 'panno canabeo', hempen cloth.[12]

Hemp as a textile fibre has received relatively little attention from
economic historians.[13] In the standard works 'hemp' in the index usually
leads to a reference to the making of rope or twine. Evidence of hemp
cultivation can be found in two sources other than inventories: manorial
records, where the court issued regulations about the steeping of
vegetable fibres in running streams or ponds which formed part of the
public water supply and prohibited the drying of flax and hemp indoors
because of the risk of fire; and tithe records. In an early example of the
latter, from 1252, the archbishop of York instituted perpetual vicarages
in the parishes of Kilham, Pickering and Pocklington, which had been
given to the dean of York in the twelfth century. In the allocation of

---

[11] Journeyman, an artisan who worked for another.
[12] Raine, *Testamenta Eboracensia*, IV, p.136.
[13] But see Lowe, *Lancashire textile industry* and Evans, *East Anglian linen industry*.

resources, the archbishop gave the tithes of flax and hemp to the vicars of Pickering and Pocklington, but not to the vicar of Kilham, 'to whom we intend that the tithes of flax and hemp will never belong'.[14]

Flax was a field crop, normally sown at long intervals on any patch of ground because it was regarded as an exhausting crop. Hemp could be grown year after year on well-manured plots in the farm croft (or garth, or yard, according to the local terminology). In the early inventories of the Forest of Knaresborough and lower Nidderdale, when it was still the practice to list bedding and some articles of clothing in detail, linen sheets and the like accounted for only a quarter of the material woven from vegetable fibres. The remainder were described as hempen, harden or samoran. Many people must have worn, or used, shirts, shifts and sheets made from hemp which had been grown on the farm, heckled and spun in the house, and woven there or at the customer weaver's.

As the textile side of the dual economy expanded under the pressure of forces described below, each district began to specialise in the branches of production most favoured by local systems of finishing and marketing. The standards acceptable for domestic and local use had to be raised considerably to pass the scrutiny of a discerning market. As a result, the woollen-worsted producers of west Yorkshire tended to concentrate in an area centred upon Halifax, Leeds and Wakefield. To the south and north of this were two linen zones, centred upon Barnsley-Doncaster and Knaresborough-Pateley Bridge respectively; and north of the latter, in Wensleydale, Swaledale and the Sedbergh area, people turned to woollen hand-knitting. At the same time, different farming-textile balances developed. In the Knaresborough-Nidderdale area, linen weavers with three looms were usually farming on a smaller scale than those with one loom. In upper Calderdale, between Halifax and Todmorden, it was the practice to divide the farming and textile sides of the family economy between surviving sons (not necessarily in equal proportions), with the result that the scale of the two operations tended to match—a three-loom household having a much larger farm than a one-loom household—until the ranks of the wealthy master clothiers and/or merchant finishers were reached. Before the development of powered machinery from about 1770, nearly all of the capital was circulating, not fixed, consisting of materials at different stages of processing. These show up well in inventories.[15]

[14] Raine, *Register of Walter Gray*, pp.211–14.
[15] Jennings, *Pennine valley*, pp.76–85; Heywood and Jennings, *Todmorden*, pp.49–62.

The urban textile gilds were already in decline in the sixteenth century, and so the most important supplementary records in the late-seventeenth and early-eighteenth centuries, at regional level, are the letter books and accounts of cloth merchants. Heaton made good use of these in his *Yorkshire woollen and worsted industries* (1920), and concluded that the woollen and worsted branches were organised on quite different lines. In woollens the small independent clothier was dominant, but the worsted branch was controlled by capitalist merchants employing combers, weavers and finishers. He went so far as to say 'the small independent producer never existed in the worsted industry'.[16]

Heaton's researches, most of which were carried out before 1914, have stood the test of time remarkably well, but it would be surprising if a few of his judgements did not need revision in the light of new evidence, particularly the investigation of probate records. In fact there were men in the woollen branch operating on a similar scale to that of the worsted masters, employing large numbers of outworkers, often with substantial finishing equipment, and holding large stocks of wool and materials in production. On the other side of the picture, there were 'small independent clothiers' with one to three looms, owning their own equipment and materials, in the worsted branch. Some households engaged in both branches of the trade, having a woollen loom and a worsted loom, a sensible arrangement as the market for one type of cloth could be brisk while the other was slack.[17]

In the study of Yorkshire textiles before the Industrial Revolution probate documents are therefore a key source, not an optional extra. They contain a great deal of recondite technical information, as well as guiding scholars around possible pitfalls. An example of the latter is the use of the word 'pair'. We have no problems with a 'pair of scissors' or 'pair of trousers', but how many musical instruments are found in a sixteenth-century church with a 'pair of organs'? The answer, of course, is one; similarly, a 'pair of looms' is one loom.

Settlement patterns

Every weaver, working full-time, used the output of five or six spinners, who in turn had to be served by carders, combers or hecklers. Most of these ancillary workers lived in cottages which had been built on the

---

[16] Heaton, *Yorkshire woollen and worsted industries*, pp.264–71.
[17] Jennings, *Pennine valley*, pp.82–4; Heywood and Jennings, *Todmorden*, pp.60–2.

commons. Where such encroachments were prevented, the rural textile industry could not develop. In the Yorkshire Wolds, together with the North York Moors the principal sheep-rearing area of the county, there were, except around the edges, no all-season surface streams. The villages in the valleys relied upon springs, wells and ponds. A stray cottage on the hillside would have no water supply. Furthermore, it was the practice to plough and cultivate the 'common waste' nearest the villages at intervals of three to ten years as 'outfields', so encroachment would not be tolerated by the local community. By contrast, water was bubbling down the hillsides in upper Calderdale where, out of a sample of 70 farming inventories of the late-seventeenth and early-eighteenth centuries, only nine contained sheep. In a poor farming area, the loss of a quarter or half an acre of coarse grazing provoked less hostility. The availability of water power for fulling mills was therefore not the only consideration.[18]

In search of the cottagers, very few of whom left probate documents, it is logical to turn to the parish registers, particularly those which record occupations. The economic role of the majority who died below the probate line can be related to that of the minority who made wills. The relationship can normally be predicted, with the poorer section consisting of smallholders, farm labourers, large numbers of journeymen weavers in a textile district, widows and paupers. Wool combers and hecklers, who were men, may be identified, but the spinners and carders, women and children, are usually left in obscurity. In one area, however, the analysis of parish registers together with taxation returns and manorial court rolls, has revealed economic and settlement patterns which certainly could not have been deduced from probate evidence. The area is the Forest of Knaresborough, and the research was undertaken by Dr Maurice Turner and his WEA students. 'Forest' is an administrative and not a botanical term, and denotes an area subject to special rules for the preservation of beasts of the chase and their environment. By the early-fourteenth century the deer were confined to three Forest parks, totalling 3,500 acres, and licensed assarting was expanding on the existing settlements.[19] Because of the continuity of the administrative system of the Forest, the common pasture was not divided between the townships, but remained as a continuous open space of over 20 miles across. The process of assarting was brought to an abrupt halt by the Black Death of 1348–9; about 45 per cent of the land was vacated by death during the plague. When the population began to

---

[18] Jennings, *Pennine valley*, pp.79–80; Fox and Jennings, 'Wolds'.
[19] Assarting, clearing of forest or wasteland for cultivation.

recover after about 1480, the need for extra land was met mainly by unauthorised nibbling at the common. Periodic surveys by the officers of the Forest added these encroachments to the rent roll.[20]

By the middle of the sixteenth century the number of 'squatter' cottages was causing concern, but the problem proved to be intractable. The enormous size of the Forest made it difficult to police the common effectively, and some of the officers concerned were themselves offenders. Lists of encroachers presented at the Forest courts included not only landless cottagers, and other cottagers filching a little land from the common, but also men of substance who were fined for building cottages for their employees or members of their families. In fact the squatter cottage served a social purpose as accommodation for the widows of yeomen, younger sons lacking inherited land, spinster daughters, labourers and—not least—paupers supported by the parish.[21]

The wills and inventories of the sixteenth and seventeenth centuries belonged mainly to people in the long-established settlements, and trace the evolution—described above—from a farming community with textile sidelines in woollens into a dual economy concentrating upon linen. When, however, the whole population was analysed by adding those individuals who paid no taxes and left no wills or inventories, individuals who were often single and appeared in parish registers only at baptism or burial, a different picture emerged. Several squatter hamlets had developed by the seventeenth century, housing a disproportionate number of widows and spinsters, and with a different economy. There were probably many outworkers for the textile industry amongst the women and children, but many of the men were metal workers, making bridle-bits, spurs and similar products. Their market centre was not Knaresborough, as was the case with linen, but Ripon.[22]

The squatter hamlets, consisting of cottages with small plots of land and surrounded by commons, were located at a considerable distance from the older settlements. This was no doubt deliberate. One man's cottage and encroachment represented another man's lost pasture. Cottages built two or three miles away provoked less hostility. Did men take to metal working because they were too far away from the textile-farming villages to work as journeymen weavers in a master's workshop? Or did the metal workers gravitate to the squatter hamlets because land

[20] Jennings, *History of Nidderdale*, pp.46–7, 86–94, 483–5; Jennings, *History of Harrogate*, Chapter 3.

[21] Turner, 'Post-medieval colonisation', pp.72–6.

[22] Turner, 'Post-medieval colonisation', pp.81–91; Turner, *Kith and kin*, pp. 66–9.

was cheap, and some of the residual woodlands of the Forest nearby provided them with dead wood for fuel? The regular annual fine for an illegal cottage, of four old pence, became in practice a rent which remained unchanged long enough to be protected by custom.[23]

On the subject of metal working, the Hearth Tax returns sometimes list smithies, both the smelting and the blacksmith's kind. The returns show that at Dacre Banks, in Nidderdale township next to the Forest of Knaresborough, iron smelting was still going on in an area well known for its earlier ironworking industry, operated by Fountains Abbey from the twelfth to the sixteenth centuries.[24]

Tenure and inheritance

Perhaps the most important topic for which students of wills need recourse to other records is tenure and inheritance, the relevant source being manorial court rolls or books. For the first of three case studies we go to the manors of Healaugh and Muker in Swaledale.[25] The court records survive from 1642. In that year a copyholder with five sons died. Before the next meeting of the manor court one of these sons died, leaving two grandsons of the copyholder. The latter's holding was divided into six parts, four of them one-fifth of the holding, and two of them one-tenth. Most of the land in the two manors was held on customary tenure, known alternatively as copyhold because the title deeds consisted of copies of entries in the court books. By manorial rules, holdings were divided equally between sons. Daughters received no share unless there were no sons, in which case equal division applied to daughters too.

When an eldest son inherited an intact holding, any younger sons who stayed on the farm had to remain unmarried. Divisible inheritance gave all sons an equal chance to marry, thus accelerating population growth. Some farms were divided over the space of three generations into as many as 30 parts, although there was some re-consolidation through purchase and inheritance from childless relatives. Men inheriting a holding too small to support a household had to develop other occupations. Many took to lead mining, and whole families became involved in a third sector of the economy, the knitting of woollen stockings, caps and jerseys. The area had no natural advantages for this trade—the wool was brought in, the markets were distant—only fewer disadvantages than for other branches of cloth manufacture.

[23] Turner, *Kith and kin*, passim; Jennings, *History of Nidderdale*, pp.133–5.
[24] Turner, *Kith and kin*, p.64; Jennings, *History of Nidderdale*, p.61.
[25] Fieldhouse and Jennings, *History of Richmond*, pp.46–51, 135–9, 177–83.

The important point about this system in relation to the study of probate records is that customary land could not be devised by will. Freehold land elsewhere in Swaledale was often shared by will between sons (not necessarily equally), perhaps under the influence of copyhold practice, but the copyhold testator had no discretion. This system did not originate, as has sometimes been suggested, with the Norse settlement of the area. In the thirteenth century what was to become the manor of Muker was held by Rievaulx Abbey, which developed a series of large granges. At the same period a large part of the manor of Healaugh consisted of a group of seigneurial vaccaries similar to the monastic granges. During the later middle ages the granges and vaccaries were let off to rent-paying tenants. When the population began to recover from the effects of the plagues, in the late-fifteenth century, it became the practice to divide these units, most of which were very large, when a tenant was succeeded by more than one son. Practice developed into custom, and custom hardened into rule. There must have been an element of chance in this. A similar process of sub-division during the last monastic century can be traced on the Byland Abbey estates in upper Nidderdale—one grange evolving into a village of ten farms—but there the custom of partible inheritance did not develop.[26]

The second case study is the Forest of Knaresborough, already mentioned in another context. Here all the land was customary, originally bondhold,[27] and the manorial rule was primogeniture. This could be circumvented if a customary tenant surrendered the title to part of his land to a younger son or sons, receiving back a life interest. 'Surrender' was the term used for any lifetime transfer of the title to copyhold land, as the formal procedure involved the surrender of the property to the lord of the manor 'to the use of' the beneficiary. In the course of time the process became streamlined so that the customary tenant could, in a single transaction, transfer to his son or sons the 'reversion' of the title, that is the right to enjoy it after the death of the father. Any land not covered by the surrender of title or reversion passed automatically to the eldest son. It could not be directed otherwise by the will alone.[28]

In both the Forest of Knaresborough and the upper Calderdale, for lands held directly of the manor of Wakefield, the sub-letting of copyhold land became a widespread practice. Its economic basis was the difference between the level of the copyhold rents paid to the lord and

---

[26] Jennings, *History of Nidderdale*, pp.104–5.
[27] Bondhold, tenure of land in bond service, a type of copyhold.
[28] Jennings, *History of Harrogate*, p.60.

the real annual value of the land. As a result of inflation, rents charged to sub-tenants by the middle of the seventeenth century ranged between 30 and 100 times the level of the lord's rent. The customary tenants (copyholders) of the Forest of Knaresborough benefited greatly from a crown decree of 1562 which fixed rents at the medieval level and set fees for inheritance, sale, transfer or sub-letting at modest and secure rates. The copyholders of the upper Calderdale land of the manor of Wakefield bought similar privileges in 1607. At that time the 300 copyholders had a total of 700 sub-tenants, most of them holding by leases of up to 21 years. The unexpired term of a lease was the only interest that could be bequeathed by will.[29]

The significance of these tenurial arrangements to the student of wills and inventories is twofold. First, in such areas the will is usually an incomplete record of the disposal of land by a testator. Second, divisible inheritance was an important engine of industrial growth, especially in areas with limited agricultural potential. The latter process was reinforced in both upper Calderdale and the Forest of Knaresborough by the existence of extensive commons on which many cottagers established themselves, providing the essential labour force, as carders, spinners and so forth for the textile industry.[30]

There was, however, a major difference between the Swaledale system of compulsory division, and what might be called 'discretionary divisible inheritance' as practised in upper Calderdale and the Forest of Knaresborough. First, in the latter the eldest son was often given a larger share of the land, not necessarily of the industrial interests, than the younger sons, although not infrequently charged with payments to daughters. Second, the process was not allowed to proceed to the extreme fragmentation found in Swaledale. In the 'discretionary' areas sub-division and industrial growth could be interactive processes, the possibilities of industrial expansion, and to some extent of taking in extra land from the common, encouraging copyholders and those freeholders who adopted the same policies to think in terms of provision for more than one son. We can imagine families planning a strategy, possibly involving purchase and intaking,[31] which would provide for two or more sons, while keeping them on an acceptable socio-economic level. In the two Swaledale manors most of the land by the late-eighteenth century was held by smallholders, who depended for

[29] Jennings, *History of Harrogate*, pp.127–34; Jennings, *Pennine valley*, pp.25–6, 53–4.
[30] Jennings, *Pennine valley*, p.76; Jennings, *History of Harrogate*, p.213.
[31] Intaking, an intake is a temporary enclosure of the waste.

their survival on the uncertain fortunes of lead mining and the meagre rewards of knitting.[32]

As a postscript, an analogy with Sherlock Holmes' 'dog that did not bark' can be offered. In the middle of the Knaresborough-Nidderdale linen manufacturing area lay the village of Ripley. It was equally affected by considerations of raw material supply and marketing. However, the Ingilby family, lords of the manor since the fourteenth century, controlled tenure, with the land let on lease from year to year. They did not allow holdings to be sub-divided, and no one would dare encroach on the common or erect a squatter cottage. In consequence, there was no textile industry, apart from the occasional Silas Marner weaving cloth from yarn supplied by customers.[33]

---

[32] Jennings, 'Study of local history', pp.23–8.
[33] Jennings, *History of Nidderdale*, p.174.

Appendix 1

Edited Selections from Ecclesiastical Canons Concerning Probate

Canons derived their authority from the approval of each province's convocation and subsequent ratification by the crown. Until 1603 they lapsed on the death of each sovereign, but from then onwards they were made permanent. This gave particular importance to the Canterbury Canons of 1604, which were accepted by the Convocation of York in 1606, and remained unaltered until 1865.[1]

Note: Some words, phrases and sentences have been omitted without indication from the extracts below.

1329 Canon of Archbishop Simon Mepham of Canterbury

Because the ordinaries have been hitherto very heavy and costly unto the executors of testaments, about the insinuation of testaments and committing of the administration, to the intent they might the rather milk them of their money, we ordain that for the insinuation of a poor man's testament whose inventory passeth not £5 sterling, nothing in the world shall be required.[2]

1342 Canon of Archbishop John Stratford of Canterbury

Calling to mind the statute made by Boniface, Archbishop of Canterbury, concerning the goods of them that die intestate and the last wills of men of servile condition [1261], which of late is called into doubt by many men, we therefore do ordain the same firmly hereafter to be observed and kept. Other there be that let the free making of testaments and their executions and the last wills of persons of servile condition and of women also both married and unmarried, which things they do as well against the laws as against the customs of the Church hitherto approved, therefore we decree all that hereafter offend in these things, to be wrapped in the sentence of the great excommunication.

---

[1] Bray, *Anglican canons*, pp.liv–lxi.
[2] Lyndwood, *Provinciale* (1679) pp.170–1, (1929) p.65.

We forbid also any executor of testaments to be suffered to minister the goods of any testator, except a true inventory be first made of the said goods, the funeral expenses and such as shall be spent about the making of such inventory only excepted. And we will this inventory to be delivered to the ordinaries within the time appointed, and after that the testament be proved before the ordinaries, the administration of such goods shall not be committed unto any but such as can give sufficient and faithful promise to make a due reckoning of their administration.[3]

1342 Canon of Archbishop John Stratford of Canterbury

We ordain that, for the proving, allowing or insinuation of any manner of testaments, there shall nothing be received by the bishops or other ordinaries: notwithstanding, we grant the clerks that write such insinuations to receive for their labour only 6d., but if the inventory of any dead's goods pass the sum of 30s., and yet cometh not to £5, the bishops, ordinaries or other ministers may not presume to take above 12d. for the account, hearing and all things to be done about the same, or for letters of acquaintance or any other, but if the said inventories contain the sum of £5 or more yet under £20, they that intend the counts and other ministers aforesaid shall be contented with 3s. for their labour for the letters of acquaintance and other things above rehearsed. And if they contain £20 or more and yet less than £60 [sic], they shall not take above 5s. for their labours, letters and other writings: but if such inventories come to the sum of £40 [sic] or more and yet not to £100, they may receive 10s. and not above. And if the said inventories contain the sum of £100 or more and yet not £150, they shall not presume to take above 20s. and so ascending for every [£]50 rising they may receive 10s. over and beside the said 20s. and not above: notwithstanding we permit to the clerks to take for every letter of acquaintance that they write above the letters beforesaid 6d. for their labour.[4]

Canons of 1604

92. None to be cited into divers courts for probate of the same Will

We constitute and appoint that all officials exercising ecclesiastical jurisdiction whatsoever shall at the first charge with an oath all persons called, or voluntarily appearing before them, for the probate of any will

---

[3] Lyndwood, *Provinciale* (1679) pp.171–7, (1929) pp.65–7.
[4] Lyndwood, *Provinciale* (1679) pp.181–2, (1929) pp.68–9.

or the administration of any goods, whether they know, or do firmly believe, that the party deceased had at the time of his or her death any goods, or good debts, in any other diocese or peculiar jurisdiction within the said province, to the value aforesaid, and particularly specify and declare the same. Then shall he presently dismiss him, not presuming to intermeddle with the probate of the said will, or to grant administration of the goods of the party so dying intestate; but shall openly declare that the said cause belongeth to the prerogative of the archbishop of that province; willing the party to prove the said will, or require administration of the said goods, in the court of the said prerogative, within forty days next following.

Provided that if any man die while travelling, the goods that he hath about him at that present shall not cause his testament or administration to be liable unto the prerogative court.

93. *The rate of bona notabilia liable to the prerogative court*

We decree and ordain that no judge of the archbishop's prerogative shall henceforward cite any person whatsoever to any of the aforesaid intents, unless he have knowledge that the party deceased was at the time of his death possessed of goods and chattels in some other diocese, or peculiar jurisdiction within that province, than in that wherein he died, amounting to the value of £5 at the least; decreeing and declaring that whoso hath not goods in divers dioceses to the said sum or value shall not be accounted to have *bona notabilia*. Always provided that this clause, here and in the former constitution mentioned, shall not prejudice those dioceses where by composition or custom *bona notabilia* are rated at a greater sum.

125. *Convenient places to be chosen for the keeping of courts*

All officials exercising ecclesiastical jurisdiction shall appoint such meet places for the keeping of their courts, by the assignment or approbation of the bishop of the diocese, as shall be convenient for entertainment of those that are to make their appearance there, and most indifferent for their travel. And likewise they shall keep and end their courts in such convenient time as every man may return homewards in as due season as may be.

126. *Peculiar and inferior courts to exhibit the original copies of Wills into the Bishop's Registry*

Whereas deans, archdeacons, prebendaries, parsons, vicars and others, exercising ecclesiastical jurisdiction, claim liberty to prove the last wills and testaments of persons deceased within their several jurisdictions, having no known nor certain registrars nor public place to keep their records in; by reason whereof many wills, rights and legacies, upon the death or change of such persons, miscarry and cannot be found, to the great prejudice of his majesty's subjects; we therefore order and enjoin that all such possessors and exercisers of peculiar jurisdiction shall once in every year exhibit into the public registry of the bishop of the diocese, or of the dean and chapter under whose jurisdiction the said peculiars are, every original testament of every person in that time deceased, and by them proved in their several jurisdictions, or a true copy of every such testament, examined, subscribed and sealed by the peculiar judge and his notary.[5]

Glossary to Appendix 1

Insinuation: The production or delivery of a will for official registration, as a step towards procuring probate. (*OED*)
Ordinary: One who has, of his own right and not by special dispensation, immediate jurisdiction in ecclesiastical cases, for example archbishop, bishop or bishop's deputy. (*OED*)

---

[5] These 1604 Canons were reprinted on numerous occasions, most recently in Bray, *Anglican canons*, pp.389–93, 425–7.

Appendix 2

The Main Acts of Parliament Concerning Probate before 1760

Note: The dates record when the parliamentary session which approved the particular act began and are not necessarily the years when the acts were passed into law. Acts of Parliament were not given contemporary titles before the sixteenth century.

9 Hen. III, c.18	The King's debtor dying, the King shall be first paid (1225)
20 Hen. III, c.2	Widows may bequeath the crop on their lands (1235)
13 Ed. I, st.1, c.19	The ordinary chargeable to pay the debts of an intestate (1285)
13 Ed. I, st.1, c.23	Executors may have a Writ of Account (1285)
4 Ed. III, c.7	Executors shall have an action of trespass for a Wrong done to their testator (1330)
25 Ed. III, st.5, c.5	Executors of executors shall have the same rights and duties as the first executors (1350)
31 Ed. III, st.1, c.4[+]	Redressing of extortion in bishops' officers in proving of Wills (1357)
31 Ed. III, st.1, c.11[*]	To whom the ordinary may commit Administration, where a man dieth intestate, and the administrators to have actions, as executors should (1357)
3 Hen. V, c.8 [+]	Ordinaries shall take no more for proving of Testaments, with their Inventories, than was taken in the time of King Edward III (1415)
21 Hen. VIII, c.4	An Act concerning the sale of lands by executors (1529)

[*] Selections from this act are included in the extracts below.
[+] This act is paraphrased in the selected extracts from 21 Hen. VIII, c.5, below.

21 Hen. VIII, c.5*	An Act concerning fines and sums of money to be taken by the ministers of bishops and other ordinaries of Holy Church for the probate of Testaments (1529)
21 Hen. VIII, c.6	An Act concerning the taking of Mortuaries (1529)
24 Hen. VIII, c.12	An Act that appeals to the see of Rome shall not from henceforth be had nor used, but within this Realm (1532)
25 Hen. VIII, c.19	An Act showing the submission of the clergy to the King, and to give power to certain persons to make Canons and Constitutions (1533)
26 Hen. VIII, c.15	An Act for taking away certain exactions taken within the Archdeaconry of Richmond by spiritual men (1534)
27 Hen. VIII, c.10*	An Act concerning Uses and Wills (The Statute of Uses)[1] (1535)
27 Hen. VIII, c.26	An Act for laws and justice to be ministered in Wales in like form as it is in this Realm (1535)
31 Hen. VIII, c.3	An Act changing the custom of Gavelkind (1539)
32 Hen. VIII, c.1*	An Act how lands, tenements etc may be by Will, Testament or otherwise disposed (The Statute of Wills) (1540)
32 Hen. VIII, c.37	An Act for the recovery of arrearages of rents by executors and administrators (1540)
34 & 35 Hen. VIII, c.5*	An Act for the explanation of the Statute of Wills (1542–3)
13 Eliz. I, c.5	An Act against fraudulent deeds, gifts, alienations etc (1571)
43 Eliz. I, c.8	An Act against fraudulent administration of intestates' goods (1601)
7 Ja. I, c.12	An Act to avoid the double payment of debts (1609)

---

[1] Readers of the otherwise excellent account of ecclesiastical probate courts in Erickson, *Women and property*, should note that on p.37 there is a misleading reference to the Statute of Uses in 1540 (31 Hen. VIII, c.5): the author actually intended to refer to the Probate of Testaments Act of 1529 (21 Hen. VIII, c.5).

22 & 23 Ch. II, c.10*	An Act for the better settling of intestates' estates (1670)
29 Ch. II, c.3*	An Act for prevention of frauds and perjuries (1676)
30 Ch. II, st.1, c.7*	An Act to enable creditors to recover their debts of the executors and administrators of executors in their own Wrong (1677)
1 Ja. II, c.17, ss 5–8*	An Act for reviving and continuance of several Acts of Parliament therein mentioned (1685)
3 Wm. & M., c.14	An Act for relief of creditors against fraudulent devises (1691)
4 Wm. & M., c.2	An Act that the inhabitants of the Province of York may dispose of their personal estates by their Wills, notwithstanding the custom of that Province (1692)
7 & 8 Wm III, c.38	An Act to take away the custom of Wales, which hinders persons from disposing their personal estates by their Wills (1696)
10 & 11 Wm. III, c.16	An Act to enable posthumous children to take estates as if born in their father's lifetime (1699)
2 & 3 An., c.5	An Act to repeal a proviso in an Act of 4 Wm. & M., c.2 which prevents the citizens of the city of York from disposing of their personal estates by their Wills, as others inhabiting within the Province of York by that Act may do (1703)
7 An., c.19	An Act to enable infants who are possessed of estates in fee, in trust, or by way of mortgage, to make Conveyances of such estates (1708)

[Four Acts] for the public registering of all Deeds, Conveyances, Wills, and other Incumbrances, that shall be made of, or that may affect, any honours, manors, lands, tenements or hereditaments within:

2 & 3 An., c.4	the West Riding of the county of York, after 29 September 1704 (1703)
6 An., c.35	the East Riding of the county of York or the town and county of the town of Kingston upon Hull, after 29 September 1708 (1707)

7 An., c.20	the county of Middlesex, after 29 September 1709 (1708)
8 Geo. II, c.6	the North Riding of the county of York, after 29th September 1736 (1735)
11 Geo. I, c.18, ss 17–18	An Act for regulating elections within the city of London, and for preserving the peace, good order and government of the city (1724)
9 Geo. II, c.36	An Act to restrain the dispositions of land, whereby the same become unalienable (1736)
14 Geo. II, c.20, s.9*	An Act to explain and amend *An Act for prevention of frauds and perjuries* [29 Ch. II, c.3], so far as the same relates to estates *pur autre vie* (1741)
25 Geo. II, c.6, s.5	An Act for avoiding and putting an end to certain doubts and questions relating to the attestation of Wills and Codicils concerning real estates (1752)

Selected edited extracts

Note: Words, phrases and sentences have been omitted without indication from many extracts below. Most numerals, some spelling and some punctuation have been modernised and many capital letters altered also without indication. Other editorial additions or paraphrasing are indicated with square brackets.

31 Ed. III, st.1, c.11: To whom the ordinary may commit Administration, where a man dieth intestate, and the administrators to have actions, as executors should (1357)

It is assented that in case where a man dieth intestate, the ordinaries shall depute the next and most lawful friends of the dead person intestate to administer his goods; which deputies shall have an action to demand and recover as executors the debts due to the said person intestate in the King's court, for to administer and dispend for the soul of the dead.

21 Hen. VIII, c.5: An Act concerning fines and sums of money to be taken by the ministers of bishops and other ordinaries of Holy Church for the probate of Testaments (1529)

[31 Ed. III, st.1, c.4, 1357] Wherein the Parliament holden at Westminster, in the 31st year of the reign of the noble King of famous memory, Edward III, upon complaint of his people for the outrageous and grievous fines and sums of money taken by the ministers of bishops, and of other ordinaries of Holy Church, for the probate of Testaments, and for the Acquittances by the said ordinaries to be made concerning the same, the said noble King in the same Parliament, openly charged and commanded the Archbishop of Canterbury, and the other bishops for the time being, that amendment thereof should be had; and if none amendment were thereof had, it was by the authority of the same Parliament accorded, that the King should thereof make inquiry by his justices, of such oppression and extortions; and that the same justices should hear and determine them as well at the suit of the King, as of the party, as of old time hath been used, as by the same statute plainly appeareth.

[3 Hen. V, c.8, 1415] And whereat the Parliament holden at Westminster, in the 3rd year of the reign of King Henry V, it was recited, that the Commons of the Realm had oftentimes complained of them in divers Parliaments, for that divers ordinaries do take for the probation of Testaments, and other things thereunto belonging, sometime 40s. sometime 60s. and sometimes more, against right and justice, wherein the time of King Edward III, men were wont to pay for such causes but 2s.6d. or 5s. at most, by which unlawful exactions the Testaments of the testators might not be executed according to their last Wills; it was then enacted, for the avoiding of such oppressions, that no ordinary from thenceforth should take for the probation of any Testament or Inventory, or for any other thing to the same belonging, any more than was accustomed and used in the time of the said noble King Edward III, upon pain to yield to the party so grieved, three times as much as the said ordinaries did so receive; which Act did endure but to the next Parliament following, by reason that the ordinaries did then promise to reform and amend the said oppressions and exactions.

And for that the said unlawful exactions of the said ordinaries, and their ministers, be nothing reformed nor amended, but greatly augmented and increased, against right and justice, and to the great impoverishing of the King's subjects:

2. The King our Sovereign Lord, by the assent of the Lords Spiritual and Temporal, and the Commons, in this present Parliament assembled, and by the authority of the same, hath ordained and enacted, That from 1st April 1530 nothing shall be demanded, received, nor taken by any bishop, ordinary or any other manner of person whatsoever, which at any time shall have authority to take probation, insinuation, or approbation of Testaments, making of Inventories, and giving of

Acquittances, where the goods of the testator of the said Testament, or person so dying, do not amount clearly over and above the value of 100s., except only to the scribe to have for writing of the probate of the Testament of him deceased, whose goods shall not be above the same clear value of 100s., 6d. and for the commission of Administration of the goods of any man deceasing intestate, not being above like value of 100s., 6d. clear; and that nevertheless, the bishop, ordinary, or any other person having authority to take the probation of Testaments, refuse not to approve any such Testament, being lawfully tendered or offered to them to be approved, whereof the goods of the testator, or person so dying, amount not above the value of 100s., so that the said Testament be exhibited to him or them in writing, with wax thereunto affixed ready to be sealed, and that the same Testament be lawfully proved before the same ordinary (before the sealing) to be true, whole, and the last Testament of the same testator, in such form as hath been commonly accustomed in that behalf.

3. And when the goods of the testator do amount over and above the clear value of 100s. and do not exceed the sum of £40; that then no bishop, ordinary, nor other manner of person whatsoever having authority to take probation of any Testament, making of Inventories [or] giving of Acquittances, shall take but only 3s. 6d. and not above, whereof to be to the said bishop or ordinary, or other person, for him, and his ministers 2s. 6d. and not above, and 12d. residue of the said 3s. 6d. to be to the scribe for the registering of the same; and where the goods of the testator, or person so dying, do amount over and above the clear value of £40, that then the bishop nor ordinary, nor other person, shall from the 1st April, take but only 5s. and not above, whereof to be to the said bishop, ordinary, or other person having power to take the probation of such Testament, for him and his ministers 2s. 6d. and not above, and 2s. 6d. residue of the said 5s. to be to the scribe for registering of the same; or else the same scribe to be at his liberty to refuse those 2s. 6d. and have for writing of every ten lines of the same Testament, whereof every line to contain in length ten inches, 1d.

And in case any person die intestate, or that the executors named in any such Testament refuse to prove the said Testament, then the said ordinary, or other person having authority to take probate of Testament, shall grant the Administration of the goods of the testator, or person deceased, to the widow of the same person deceased, or to the next of his kin, or to both, as by the discretion of the same ordinary shall be thought good, taking surety of him or them, to whom shall be made such commission, for the true Administration of the goods, chattels, and debts, which he or they shall be authorised to minister; and in case where divers persons claim the Administration as next of kin, which be equal in degree of kindred to the testator or person deceased, that in every such case the ordinary to be at his liberty to accept any one or more making request, where divers do require the Administration.

4. Or where but one or more of them, and not all being in equality of degree, do make request, then the ordinary to admit the widow. And that the executor(s) named by the testator, or person so deceased, or such other persons to whom such Administration shall be committed, where any person dieth intestate, or by way of intestate, calling, or taking to him or them such persons, two at the least, to whom the said person so dying was indebted, or made any legacy, and upon their refusal or absence, two other honest persons, being next of kin to the person so dying, and in their default and absence, two other honest persons, and in their presence, and by their discretions, shall make, or cause to be made, a true and perfect Inventory of all the goods, chattels, wares, merchandises, as well moveable as not moveable, whatsoever that were of the said person so deceased.

6. Provided alway, that where any person having authority to take probate of Testaments, have used to take less sums of money than is above said, shall receive such sums of money for the probate of Testaments and commissions of the Administrations, as they before the making of this Act have used to take, and not above.

27 Hen. VIII, c.10: An Act concerning Uses and Wills (The Statute of Uses) (1535)

Where by the common laws of this realm, lands, tenements and hereditaments be not devisable by Testament, nor ought to be transferred from one to another, but by solemn livery and seisin, matter of record, writing made sufficient *bona fide*, but without covin or fraud; yet nevertheless, divers imaginations, subtle inventions and practices have been used, whereby the hereditaments of this realm have been conveyed from one to another by fraudulent feoffments, fines, recoveries and other assurances craftily made to secret uses, intents and trusts; and also by Wills and Testaments, sometime made by *nude parolx* and words, sometime by signs and tokens, and sometime by writing, and for the most part made by such persons as be visited with sickness, in their extreme agonies and pains, or at such time as they have scantly had any good memory or remembrance; at which times they, being provoked by greedy and covetous persons lying in wait about them, do many times dispose indiscreetly and unadvisedly their lands and inheritances; by reason whereof many heirs have been unjustly disinherited and scantly any person can be certainly assured of any lands by them purchased; also men married have lost their tenancies, women their dowers, manifest perjuries by trial of such secret Wills and Uses have been committed; the King's Highness hath lost the profits of the lands of persons attainted and many other inconveniences have happened, and daily do increase among the King's subjects, to their great trouble, and to the utter subversion of the ancient common laws of this realm.

   To the intent that the King's Highness, or any other of his subjects, shall not in any wise hereafter, by any means be deceived, damaged or hurt, by reason of such trusts or uses, that it may be enacted by this present Parliament assembled, That where any person or persons stand, or be seized, or at any time hereafter shall happen to be seized of and in any honours, castles, manors, lands, tenements, rents, services, reversions, remainders or other hereditaments to the use, confidence or trust of any other person, or of any body politic, by reason of any bargain, sale, feoffment, fine, recovery, covenant, contract, agreement, Will, or otherwise, by any means whatsoever it be; that in every such case, all and every such person and bodies politic, that have, or hereafter shall have any such use, confidence or trust, in fee-simple, fee-tail, for term of life or of years, or otherwise; or any use, confidence or trust, in remainder or reverter, shall from henceforth stand and be seized, deemed and adjudged in lawful seisin, estate and possession of and in the same honours, castles, manors, lands, tenements, rents, services, reversions, remainders and hereditaments.

32 Hen. VIII, c.1: An Act how lands, tenements etc may be by Will, Testament or otherwise disposed (The Statute of Wills) (1540)

Be it ordained and enacted by authority of this present Parliament that all and every person, having any manors, lands, tenements or hereditaments, holden in Soccage, or of the nature of Soccage Tenure, and not having any manors, lands, tenements or hereditaments holden of the King our Sovereign Lord by Knights Service, by Soccage Tenure in chief, or of the nature of Soccage Tenure in chief, nor of any other person or persons by Knights Service, from 20th July 1540, shall have full and free liberty, power and authority to give, dispose, will and devise, as well by his last Will and Testament in writing, or otherwise by any act or acts lawfully executed in his life, all his said manors, lands, tenements or hereditaments, or any of them, at his free will and pleasure; any law, statute, or other thing heretofore had, made, or used to the contrary notwithstanding.

4. And it is further enacted that all and singular persons having any manors, lands, tenements or hereditaments of Estate of Inheritance holden of the king's Highness in chief by Knights Service, from the said 20th July, shall have full power and authority, by his last Will, by writing, or otherwise by any acts lawfully executed in his life, to give, dispose, will, or assign two parts of the same manors, lands, tenements, or hereditaments in three parts to be divided, or else as much of the said manors, lands, tenements or hereditaments as shall amount to the yearly value of two parts of the same, in three parts to be divided in certainty, and by special divisions, to and for the advancement of his wife, preferment of his children and payment of his debts, or otherwise at his will and pleasure.

5. Saving and reserving to the King our Sovereign Lord, the custody, wardship and *Primer Seisin* of as much of the same manors, lands, tenements or hereditaments, as shall amount to the full and clear yearly value of the third part thereof.

34 & 35 Hen. VIII, c.5: An Act for the explanation of the Statute of Wills (1542–3)

Wherein the last Parliament holden at Westminster [in 1539–40], it was ordained and enacted how and in what manner lands, tenements and other hereditaments might by Will or Testament in writing, or otherwise by any act lawfully executed in the life of every person, be given, disposed, willed, or devised, since the making of which statute, divers doubts, questions and ambiguities have risen.

2. For a plain explanation whereof, the Lords Spiritual and Temporal, and the Commons, in this present Parliament assembled, most humbly beseech the King's Majesty, that the meaning of the letter of the same statute may be by the authority of this present Parliament enacted, declared and explained in manner and form following:

4. That all persons having a sole estate or interest in Fee-simple of and in any manors, lands, tenements, rents or other hereditaments, in possession, reversion or remainder, and having no manors, lands,

tenements or hereditaments holden of the King, his heirs or successors, or of any other person by Knights Service, shall have full and free liberty, power and authority to give, dispose, will, or devise to any person (except bodies politic and corporate) by his last Will and Testament in writing, or otherwise by any acts lawfully executed in his life by himself solely, or by himself and other jointly, all his said manors, lands, tenements, rents and hereditaments, or any of them, or any rents, commons, or other profits or commodities out of any parcel thereof, at his own free will and pleasure.

14. And it is further declared and enacted that Wills and Testaments made of any manors, lands, tenements or other hereditaments, by any woman couvert, or person within the age of 21 years, idiot, or any person *de non sane* memory, shall not be taken to be good or effectual in the law.

22 & 23 Ch. II, c.10: An Act for the better settling of intestates' estates (1670)

Be it enacted that all ordinaries and ecclesiastical judges, having power to commit Administration of the goods of persons dying intestate, shall upon their respective granting and committing of Administrations of the goods of persons dying intestate, after 1st June 1671, of the respective persons to whom any Administration is to be committed, take sufficient Bonds with two or more able sureties, respect being had to the value of the estate, in the name of the ordinary, with the condition in form and manner following:

2. *The Condition of this Obligation is such, That if the within bounden A.B. Administrator of all and singular the Goods, Chattels and Credits of C.D. deceased, do make, or cause to be made, a true and perfect Inventory of all and singular the Goods, Chattels and Credits of the said deceased, which have or shall come to the Hands, Possession or Knowledge of him the said A.B. or into the Hands and Possession of any other Person or Persons for him, and the same so made, do exhibit, or cause to be exhibited into the Registry of _____ Court, at or before the _____ Day of _____ next ensuing; and the same Goods, Chattels and Credits, and all other the Goods, Chattels and Credits of the said Deceased at the Time of his Death, which at any Time after shall come to the Hands or Possession of the said A.B. or into the Hands and Possession of any other Person or Persons for him, do well and truly Administer according to Law; And further do make, or cause to be made, a true and just Account of his said Administration, at or before the _____ Day of*

_____ *And all the Rest and Residue of the said Goods, Chattels and Credits which shall be found remaining upon the said Administrator's Account, the same being first examined and allowed of by the Judge or Judges, for the Time being, of the said Court, shall deliver and pay unto such Person or Persons respectively, as the said Judge or Judges, by his or their Decree or Sentence pursuant to the true Intent and Meaning of this Act, shall limit and appoint.*

And if it shall hereafter appear, That any last Will and Testament was made by the said Deceased, and the Executor or Executors therein named do exhibit the same into the said Court, making Request to have it allowed and approved accordingly, if the said A.B. within-bounden being thereunto required, do render and deliver the said Letters of Administration (Approbation of such Testament being first had and made) in the said Court; then this Obligation to be void and of none Effect, or else to remain in full Force and Virtue.

3. Which Bonds are hereby declared and enacted to be good to all intents and purposes, and pleadable in any courts of justice. And also that the said ordinaries, and judges respectively, are enabled to proceed and call such administrators to account, for and touching the goods of any person dying intestate; and upon hearing and due consideration thereof, to order and make just and equal distribution of what remaineth clear (after all debts, funerals, and just expenses of every sort first allowed and deducted) amongst the wife and children, or childrens' children, if any such be, or otherwise to the next of kindred to the dead person in equal degree.

4. Provided that this Act shall not any ways prejudice or hinder the customs observed within the City of London, or within the Province of York, or other places, having known and received customs peculiar to them, but that the same customs may be observed as formerly.

5. Provided always that all ordinaries, and every other person who by this Act is enabled to make distribution of the surplusage of the estate of any person dying intestate, shall distribute the surplusage of such estate in manner and form following: One third part of the said surplusage to the wife of the intestate, and all the residue by equal portions amongst the children of such persons dying intestate, other than such child or children (not being heir at law) who shall have any estate by the settlement of the intestate, or shall be advanced by the intestate in his lifetime, by portions equal to the share which shall by such distribution be allotted to the other children to whom such distribution is to be made.

And in case any child, other than the heir at law, who shall have any estate by settlement from the said intestate by portion not equal to the share which will be due to the other children by such distribution, then so much of the surplusage of the estate of such intestate, to be distributed to such child or children as shall have any land by settlement from the intestate as shall make the estate of all the said children to be equal as near as can be estimated. But the heir at law notwithstanding any land that he shall have by descent or otherwise from the intestate, is to have an equal part in the distribution with the rest of the children, without any consideration of the value of the land which he hath by descent, or otherwise from the intestate.

6. And in case there be no children, then one moiety of the said estate to be allotted to the wife of the intestate, the residue of the said estate to be distributed equally to every of the next of kindred of the intestate, who are in equal degree.

7. And in case there be no wife, then all the said estate to be distributed equally amongst the children.

8. Provided also, to the end that a due regard be had to creditors, that no such distribution of the goods of any person dying intestate be made, till after one year be fully expired after the intestate's death; and that such and every one to whom any such distribution shall be allotted, shall give bond with sufficient sureties in the said courts, that if any debt or debts truly owing to the intestate shall be afterwards recovered, that then he or she shall respectively refund to the Administrator his or her rateable part of that debt.

29 Ch. II, c.3: An Act for prevention of frauds and perjuries (1676)

For prevention of many fraudulent practices, which are commonly endeavoured to be upheld by perjury; Be it enacted that from 24th June 1677, all leases, estates, interests of freehold, or terms of years, or any uncertain interest in any manors, lands, tenements or hereditaments made by Livery or Seisin only, or by Parol, and not put in writing, and signed by the parties so making or creating the same, shall have the force and effect of leases or estates at will only, and shall not either in Law or Equity be deemed to have any greater force or effect.

5. And be it further enacted that from the said 24th June, all bequests of any lands or tenements, devisable either by force of the Statute of

Wills, or by this Statute, or by force of the custom of Kent, or any other particular custom, shall be in writing, and signed by the party so devising the same, or by some other person in his presence, and by his express directions, attested and subscribed in the presence of the said devisor, by three or four credible witnesses, or else they shall be utterly void.

12. And be it further enacted that from henceforth any estate *pur autre vie* shall be devisable by a Will in writing, signed by the party so devising the same, or by some other person in his presence, and by his express directions, attested and subscribed in the presence of the devisor by three or more witnesses; and if no such devise thereof be made, the same shall be chargeable in the hands of the heir, if it shall come to him by reason of a special occupancy, as assets by descent; and in case there be no special occupant thereof, it shall go to the executors or administrators of the party that had the estate thereof by virtue of the grant, and shall be assets in their hands.

19. And for prevention of fraudulent practices in setting up Nuncupative Wills, which have been the occasion of much perjury; Be it enacted that from 24th June 1677, no Nuncupative Will shall be good, where the estate thereby bequeathed shall exceed the value of £30, that is not proved by the oaths of three witnesses (at the least) that were present at the making thereof; nor unless it be proved that the testator at the time of pronouncing the same, did bid the persons present, or some of them, bear witness, that such was his Will, or to that effect; nor unless such Nuncupative Will were made in the time of the last sickness of the deceased, and in the house of his or her habitation or dwelling, or where he or she hath been resident for the space of ten days or more next before the making of such Will, except where such person was taken sick, being from his own home and died before he returned to the place of his dwelling.

20. And be it further enacted that after six months passed after the speaking of the pretended testamentary words, no testimony shall be received to prove any Will Nuncupative, except the said testimony, or the substance thereof, were committed to writing within six days after the making of the said Will.

21. And be it further enacted that no letters testamentary or probate of any Nuncupative Will, shall pass the seal of any court, till fourteen days at the least after the decease of the testator be fully expired; nor shall any

Nuncupative Will be at any time received to be proved, unless process have first issued to call in the widow, or next of kindred to the deceased, to the end they may contest the same, if they please.

22. And be it further enacted that no Will in writing concerning any goods or chattels, or personal estate, shall be repealed, nor shall any clause or bequest therein, be altered by any words, or Will by word of mouth only, except the same be in the life of the testator committed to writing, and after the writing thereof read unto the testator, and allowed by him, and proved to be so done by three witnesses at the least.

23. Provided always that any soldier being in actual military service, or any mariner being at sea, may dispose of his moveables, wages and personal estate, as he might have done before the making of this Act.

24. And it is hereby declared that nothing in this Act shall extend to alter the jurisdiction of probate of Wills concerning personal estates, but that the Prerogative Court of the Archbishop of Canterbury, and other ecclesiastical courts, and other courts having right to the probate of such Wills, shall retain the same right as they had before, in every respect; subject nevertheless to the rules and directions of this Act.

25. And for the explaining one Act of this present Parliament, entitled, *An Act for the better settling of Intestates' Estates*; Be it declared that neither the said Act, nor anything therein contained, shall be construed to extend to the estates of Femme Couverts that shall die intestate, but that their husbands may demand and have Administration of their rights, credits, and other personal estates, and recover and enjoy the same, as they might have done before the making of the said Act.

30 Ch. II, st.1, c.7: An Act to enable creditors to recover their debts of the executors and administrators of executors in their own Wrong (1677)

Whereas the executors and administrators of such persons who have possessed themselves of considerable personal estates of other dead persons, and converted the same to their own use, have no remedy by the rules of the Common Law, as it now stands, to pay the debts of those persons whose estate hath been so converted by their testator or intestate, which hath been found very mischievous, and many creditors defeated of their just debts, although their debtors left behind them sufficient to satisfy the same, with a great overplus:

2. For remedy whereof, be it enacted that all and every the executors and administrators of any person, who as executor or executors in his or their own Wrong, or administrators, shall from 1st August next ensuing, waste or convert any goods, chattels, estate or assets of any person deceased, to their own use, shall be liable in the same manner as their testator or intestate would have been if they had been living.

1 Ja. II, c.17: An Act for reviving and continuance of several Acts of Parliament therein mentioned

5. [Be it enacted that *An Act for the better settling Intestates' Estates* (22 & 23 Ch. II, c.10), *An Act for prevention of Frauds and Perjuries* (29 Ch. II, c.3) and *An Act for reviving both the said former Acts* (30 Ch. II, st.1, c.6, 1677) shall be in force and made perpetual.]

6. Provided always that no administrator shall, from 24th July 1677, be cited to any the courts in the said last Act mentioned, to render an Account of the personal estate of his intestate (otherwise than by an Inventory) unless it be at the instance or prosecution of some person in behalf of a minor, or having a demand out of such personal estate as a creditor or next of kin, nor be compellable to account before any the ordinaries or judges by the said last Act empowered and appointed to take the same, otherwise than as is aforesaid.

7. Provided also that if after the death of a father, any of his children shall die intestate without wife or children, in the lifetime of the mother, every brother and sister, and the representatives of them, shall have an equal share with her.

14 Geo. II, c.20, s.9: An Act to explain and amend *An Act for prevention of frauds and perjuries* [29 Ch. II, c.3], so far as the same relates to estates *pur autre vie* (1741)

9. Be it enacted that such estates *pur autre vie*, in case there be no special occupant thereof, of which no devise shall have been made, or so much thereof as shall not have been devised, shall be distributed in the same manner as the personal estate of the testator or intestate.

Glossary to Appendix 2

Covin: Conspiracy
Fee-simple: Estate in land in absolute possession of the owner and his heirs without limitation

Fee-tail: Estate of inheritance entailed or limited to a particular class of heirs

Feoff, e.g. To feoff a person to the use of another: To invest a person with the legal estate, subject to an obligation to allow the use to the other person

Honour: Seigniory of several manors held under one baron or lord paramount

Livery and/of seisin: The delivery of property into the corporal possession of a person

Seisin: Possession

Seize: To take possession

Soccage: The tenure of land by certain determinate services other than by knight-service

Appendix 3

List of Courts Covered by The British Record Society Index Library Series used in Chapter 3

Figure 3.1: Provincial courts 1401–1646

  1 Northamptonshire and Rutland wills, 1510–1652
  7 Lichfield wills and administrations, 1515–1652
  8 Berkshire wills and administrations, 1508–1652
 12 Gloucestershire wills, vol. I, 1451–1650
 17 Bristol consistory wills, 1572–1792, with wills in the Great Orphan Books, 1379–1674
 22 Dorset wills and administrations, 1568–1799
 24 Sussex wills at Lewes, 1541–1652.
 27 Leicester wills, 1495–1649
 28 Wills and administrations at Lincoln, vol. I, Wills, 1320–1600
 31 Worcester wills, vol. I, 1451–1600
 34 Gloucestershire wills, vol. II, 1600–1800
 35 Wills and administrations Exeter registry, 1559–1799
 39 Worcester wills, vol. II, 1601–1652
 41 Wills and administrations at Lincoln, vol. II, Wills, 1601–1652
 42 Huntingdonshire wills, 1479–1652
 45 Taunton archdeaconry wills, 1537–1799
 46 Exeter consistory wills and administrations, 1532–1800
 49 Chichester consistory wills, 1482–1800
 53 Dorset wills and administrations, vol. II
 56 Cornwall archdeaconry wills and administrations, vol. I, 1569–1699
 57 Wills and administrations at Lincoln, vol. IV, Archdeaconry of Stow
 78 Wills at Chelmsford, vol. I, 1400–1619
 79 Wills at Chelmsford, vol. II, 1620–1720
 82 Commissary court of London wills, vol. I, 1374–1488
 86 Testamentary records in the commissary court of London, vol. II, 1489–1570
 89 Archdeaconry court of London probate records, vol. I, 1363–1649

90 Archdeaconry court of Suffolk probate records at Ipswich, 1444–1700, vol. I
91 Archdeaconry court of Suffolk probate records at Ipswich, 1444–1700, vol. II
93 Probate records of bishop and archdeacon of Oxford, 1516–1732, vol. I
94 Probate records of bishop and archdeacon of Oxford,1516–1732, vol. II
95 Probate records of bishop and archdeacon of Sudbury, 1354–1700, vol. I
96 Probate records of bishop and archdeacon of Sudbury, 1354–1700, vol. II
97 Testamentary records in the commissary court of London, vol. III, 1571–1625
99 Archdeaconry court of Surrey probate records, 1480–1649
102 Commisary court of London probate records, vol. IV, 1626–1700
103 Consistory court of Ely probate records, 1449–1858, vol. I
104 Bedfordshire probate records 1480–1858, vol. I
105 Bedfordshire probate records 1480–1858, vol. II
106 Consistory court of Ely probate records, 1449–1858, vol. II
107 Consistory court of Ely probate records, 1449–1858, vol. III

Figure 3.2: PCC wills 1401–1629

10 Prerogative court of Canterbury wills, vol. I, 1383–1558
11 Prerogative court of Canterbury wills, vol. II, 1383–1558
18 Prerogative court of Canterbury wills, vol. III, 1558–1583
25 Prerogative court of Canterbury wills, vol. IV, 1584–1604
43 Prerogative court of Canterbury wills, vol. V, 1605–1619
44 Prerogative court of Canterbury wills, vol. VI, 1620–1629

Figure 3.3: Court for Probate wills 1653–1660

51 Prerogative court of Canterbury wills, vol. VII, 1653–1656
61 Prerogative court of Canterbury wills, vol. VIII, 1657–1660

Appendix 4

Transcripts of Sample Probate Documents

The following transcripts aim to demonstrate important aspects of the form and content of various probate documents, but not their full diversity. Limitations of space have also led to a selection of mainly shorter examples. Definitions of many less familiar words in these transcripts are given in the select glossary at the end of this appendix. Translations from the Latin are provided in square brackets together with other editorial additions, apart from the extension of abbreviations, occasional punctuation, paragraphs and minor alterations.

Note: The year before March 25th is recorded in Old Style, not New.

Wills

Introduction

Few testators wrote their own wills. Scribes converted most of their wishes concerning the fate of their property after death into legal documents with mainly conventional phrases. Normally the date was followed by a statement of their Christian faith and any instructions for burying their corpse. Because most statements of religious belief were expressed in words chosen by the scribe, it is uncertain how closely they reflected their testators' views. Nonetheless, these preambles show that the widow in No.1 died a Roman Catholic, while the Suffolk labourer (No.3A) was clearly Protestant. Occasionally, we encounter apparently very positive statements of religious conviction, such as No.7, but even this is somewhat problematic because it was based on the 1531 will of a Gloucestershire gentleman, who was convicted posthumously of heresy.

Valid wills required the testators' signatures to be dated and witnessed, assurances of their mental capacity and the appointment of one or more executors who were responsible for settling their debts and carrying out their wishes. Sometimes charitable bequests preceded those to family and friends, as in No.2, but by no means always. The larger the family, the younger the children and the wealthier the testator, the longer the will tended to be. Naturally, many fathers sought to exert from beyond the grave continuing influence on the upbringing, education or apprenticeship of their children, to prevent disputes among them (see No.3A) or to provide contingency plans for the early deaths of one or more, as in No.5. Such hypothetical arrangements increased greatly the length and complexity of many wills, especially when trying to cater for as many as six children. Future arrangements for widows were even more diverse, probably reflecting their undetectable ages and/or state of health. Often younger wives were considered to need little or no support after they remarried, see No.6, while those who had brought a dowry to the marriage could expect much better treatment. Different arrangements were sometimes made for the widow before and after her children came of age, as in No.3A.

When the widow was made the residual legatee, as in Nos.2 and 6, it was rarely clear how much she stood to inherit. Attempts to discover the relative equality of bequests to all children, as in Nos.1 and 5, can prove just as elusive because wills rarely referred to previous gifts and, since the jurisdiction of probate courts covered only personal estates, the inclusion of real estate in wills (such as Nos.3A and 5) was voluntary and often inconsistent, depending sometimes on local custom. Testators also differed greatly over the extent to which they bequeathed individual possessions, with women tending to itemise them more, as in No.1. Family history research sometimes warns against assuming that wills always mention all surviving children. In No.6, only the children of Thomas Arkill's first family were named in his will, while the unnamed ones from his second marriage had to wait for their mother to remarry to receive a legacy. Other sources reveal that five of hers were still alive when their father died at the age of 75, but their mother who was 30 years younger lived on as a widow for another 40 years.

Many wills survive as copies rather than in the original draft because the executors and the court had one each, but transcripts disguise which is which as well as those composed in haste. Small mistakes and omissions often crept into both, including Jone Stanley's will, which appears to be an immaculate copy with all signatures written by the same hand, but omits the testator's. Because most published wills do not transcribe the text in full, but just in abstract, No.3B has been included to show how little a good abstract may exclude of the essential data.

Nuncupative wills, such as No.4, were written for deceased persons who had made their wishes clear by speaking them before sufficient disinterested witnesses, but had died before they could be written out and signed. To be acceptable to most courts a nuncupative will had to contain the basic requirements of a written one, including assurances that the testator knew that he or she was making a will.

1. A widow's will, 1557.

In the name of god amen. In the forthe day of Apprell and in the yere of owre lord god Mccccclvii, I Jone Stanley weddo in parishe of Aldermaston [Alderminster] with yn dyossys of Worster beyng sycke of body [but] neverthelese holl of memory and mynd makyth my testament and laste wyll as herafter folowythe: First I bequethe my soll unto almyty god my maker to owre lady sanyt Mary and to all the hooly company of hevyn: and my body to be buryde with yn church yarde of saynt Adborogt yn Aldermaston also I bequeth to Wylliam my son a lond of whet that [lyeth] nexte Roger Broyll also I bequethe to Rychard my son a lond of whet uppon Barden and a land of barley by yond the broke: also I bequeth to Thomas my son ii platters a candylstyke and a borde clothe: also I bequethe to Jone my dowghtter a grene coverled a payre of shetts a towell a bord clothe iii platters a sawser a candylstyke and a salte seller a lytyll pan a kever a loome a payll my beste gowne a cappe and my gyrdyll: also I bequethe to Alys my dowghter yn lawe my rede coote and a payre of slevys: the rest of my goods unbequethyd my detts payd and my fewnerall kepte I geve and bequeth to Geferey my son homem I make my executur to dyspose them as he thynkyth beste for the welth of my sooll thes beryng wytnes   Rychard Myller Wylliam Myller Roger Breyll Thomas Phypps and Rychard Venton

[Jone Stanley]

[proved 17 August 1557]

[source: Worcester Record Office: 1558 IV No.478]

2. A haberdasher's will, 1624.

In the name of god Amen. The thirteenth daye of December in the yere of our Lord god 1624 and in the yere of the Reigne of our Soveraigne Lord James by the grace of god kinge of England Scotland Fraunce and Ireland Defender of the faith etc that is to say of England Fraunce and Ireland the xxiith and of Scotland the lvii, I Willyam Stanlye of the parish of Saint Lawrence of the Cittie of Winchester in the countie of South[ampton] haberdasher sicke in bodye but whole in mynde and of good remembrance I thanke god for the same make and ordayne this my Laste Will and Testament in manner and forme followinge that is to say First I bequeth my soule into the hands of almyghtie god my maker redeemer and savior.

Item I give unto the poore of this Cittie v s.
Item I give unto the church of Saint Lawrence xii d.
Item I give unto Jhoane Kilbere the Daughter of John Kilbere xl s.

The rest of all my goods unbequethed my debts and my funerall
discharged I give wholy to Jhoane Stanlye my wife whome I make my
sole Executor of this my Last Will and Testament.
In witnesse wereof I setto my hand the daye and yere above written
In the presents of John More
and Christian Hopgood

Willyam Stanlye his marke

[source: Hampshire Record Office: 1624 A75/1]

3A. A labourer's will, 1638.

In the name of God Amen. The five and twentieth day of the month
of March, in the yeare of our lord God, one thousand six hundred
thirty and eight, and in the thirteenth yeare of the reigne of our
Sovereigne lord Charles, by the grace of God, of England, Scotland,
France and Ireland King defender of the fayth etc. I John Cater of
Kennett in the county of Cambridge, and within the diocesse of
Norwich labourer although sicke and disquieted in body, yet of whole
mind and perfect remembrance (praysed be God) doe ordaine and
make this my present last will and testament in manner and forme
following: First, and before all things I doe commend my soule into the
hands of almighty God my heavenly Father hoping by the meritts,
death and passion of his deare Son Jesus Christ to have free remission
and pardon of all my sinnes, and to inherit the kingdome of heaven,
and my body to be buryed decently with Christian buryall within the
parish church yard of Kennett, and next concerning my lands and
goods, the which it hath pleased God to give mee in this life, I doe
dispose them, as hereafter followeth:

First I doe will and bequeath unto John Cater, my eldest son, my
house and tenement in Swaffham Prior, in the county of Cambridge,
with a dovehouse and all and singuler the appurtenances thereunto
belonging, the sayd John my son truely paying unto my daughters,
Susan and Philip, each of them five pounds, of good and lawfull English
mony, as soone as, and when hee shall atteine unto the age of one and
twenty yeares, that is to say fifty shillings to my daughter Susan at his
age of two and twenty yeares, and fifty shillings to my daughter Philip
at his age of three and twenty, and fifty shillings againe to my daughter
Susan at his age of foure and twenty, and fifty shillings also to my
daughter Philip at his age of five and twenty years, otherwise upon
default of these or any of these payments, at the time or times by mee
sett and appointed, my will and meaning is that my said daughters, Susan

and Philip, shall enter upon that part, which I added and purchased upon the division.

Item my will and meaning is that the towne of Kennett shall have and enjoy all and whatsoever benefitt shall arise of my sayd messuage or tenement, dovehouse and other appurtenances from the five and twentieth day of this present March, until hee shall atteine unto the age of fourteene yeares, hee, my said son John.

Item I will and bequeath unto James my son my tenement in Kennett, commonly called Tillets, with all the appurtenances thereunto belonging, reserving unto Christian my wife, her dwelling and abode in the sayd house, with the benefitt of all the appurtenances untill hee my sayd son James shall atteine unto the age of one and twenty yeares.

Item my will and meaning is, that the sayd Christian my wife shall (if she please) build her selfe one roume at the back of the chimney belonging to the said tenement, for her to enjoy during the terme of her naturall life, with halfe the commodities that shall arise from the sayd tenement.

Item I will and bequeath unto Susan my daughter, one kersie gowne, one ruffe, one fine hempen sheete, and my Bible, to be delivered unto her by my Executrix at or upon the feast of St Michael next ensuing the date of hereof.

Item I will and bequeath unto Philip my daughter, one ruffe, on paire of my best hempen sheetes, and one small hutch.

Item I will and bequeath unto the sayd towne of Kennett all my sheepe and lambes whatsoever, for and towards the putting out as apprentises my two sons, James and Richard. Further my will and full meaning is, that my sayd son James, as soone as hee shall atteine unto the age of two and twenty yeares, shall yeeld and pay unto my said son Richard the full summe of five pounds of lawfull English mony that is to say five and twenty shillings at his age of two and twenty, and five and twenty shillings at his age of three and twenty, and five and twenty shillings at his age of foure and twenty, and five and twenty shillings at his age of five and twenty years, otherwise upon default of these, or any of these payments, at the time or times by me sett and appointed, my will and meaning is, that my sayd son Richard shall enter upon the sayd tenement called Tillets, with all the appurtenances thereof.

Item my will and meaning is, that my cupbord and greatest hutch shall goe with the house or tenement called Tillets and as for the rest of my goods unbequeathed, I give them unto Christian, my wife, whom I make and ordeine the sole executrix of this my last will and testament, paying my debts, discharging my legacies, and bringing my body

decently to the grave. In witnesse whereof, I have hereunto putt my hand and seale the day and yeare above written.
Sealed and delivered in the presence of us
Oliver Bryant   John Cater
John Chenery
the mark of John Fysson

[source: Suffolk Record Office, Bury St Edmunds: IC500/1/93/77]

3B. Abstract of the same will.

John Cater of Kennett, Cambridgeshire, labourer, made 25 March 1638. Commends soul to God hoping through merits of Jesus Christ to have remission of sins and inherit kingdom of heaven. To be buried in Kennett churchyard. I bequeath to my eldest son John my house and tenement in Swaffham Prior with a dovehouse. He must start paying my daughters Susan and Philippa £5 each as soon as he is 21 at 50s. p.a. Power to distrain. The town of Kennett shall have the benefits of my messuage and dovehouse from today until my son is 14. To son James my tenement in Kennett commonly called Tillets, reserving to Christian my wife her dwelling in this house until James is 21. If she pleases, my wife may build herself a room at the back of the chimney belonging to this tenement for her use during her life, and she is to have half the commodities that shall arise from the tenement. To my daughter Susan a kersey gown, a ruff, a fine hempen sheet and my bible to be delivered to her by my executrix on Michaelmas Day next. To daughter Philippa a ruff, a pair of my best hempen sheets and a small hutch. To the town of Kennett all my sheep and lambs towards putting out my sons James and Richard as apprentices. As soon as James is 22, he is to pay Richard £5 at 20s. p.a. Power to distrain on Tillets tenement. My cupboard and greatest hutch are to go with the house called Tillets. The rest of my unbequeathed goods I give to my wife, whom I make sole executrix.

Witnesses: Oliver Bryant, John Chenery, John Fysson (mark)

[source: N. Evans (ed.), *Wills of the archdeaconry of Sudbury, 1636–38*, Suffolk Record Society, 35 (1993), p.173.]

4. A labourer's nuncupative will, 1608.

In the name of god Amen. The five and twentieth daie of March and the yere of Our Lord God one thousand Sixe hundred and eighte and in the sixthe yere of the raigne of Our soveregne lord James Kinge of

England and Scotland the xlith. Jeffrey Fincham of Mildenhall in the countie of Suffolk within the diocese of Norwich Labourer although sicke in body yet of whole mynde and perfecte remembrance did before his death openly publish and declare this his present Will Nuncupative by word of mouthe not beinge able to tarry the Wrightinge of the same by reason of the ympetuosity of deathe in manner and forme as foloweth: viz First he did commend his soule to Almightie God and his body to the earthe. Item he did will and give his house in Mildenhall aforesaid scituate in the streete there called Hallywell or elles Tenne poundes of lawfull english mony at the elecion and choise of Thomas Pechey to Thomas Kydde his Kynsman which tenne poundes was paid to the said Thomas Pechey as parcell of the purchase for the said house. Item he did give and bequeathe to the said Thomas Kidde a paire of Qwernes and Too pitche forkes and the residewe of his goodes he lefte to the use of his wife. And he named and appoynted the said Thomas Pechey to be his factor or Executor to perform this his Laste Will in the presence and testimony of Thomas Constable and Phillipp Constable his Wyfe And Alles Hoddy.

the mark of Thomas Constable
the mark of Phillipp Constable
the mark of Alles Hoddy

[source: Suffolk Record Office, Bury St Edmunds: IC500/1/95/109]

5. A cooper's will, 1671.

In the name of God Amen; the Eight Day of August 1671 in the three and twentieth yeare of the raigne of our soveraigne Lord Charles the Second King of England Scottland France and Ireland defender of the faith etc. I William Steevens the elder of the Towne of St Albans in the County of Hertford Cooper being sicke in body but of good and perfect memory praised bee God doe make and ordaine this my last Will and Testament in manner and forme following revoakeing and makeing null and voide by these presents all former Wills heretofore by me made either in word or writting and this to bee taken onely for my last Will. First I committ my soule to Allmighty God my Creator hopeing and assuredly beleiveing to receive full pardon and remission of all my sinns and to bee saved by the merritt of Jesus Christ my Redeemer and my body to the earth from whence it was taken to bee buried in such decent manner as to my Executor hereafter named shall bee thought meete and convenient and as touching such worldly Estate as the Lord in mercy hath lent mee I order and dispose of as followeth.

First I give and bequeath unto my Eldest sonne William Steevens all
that my dwelling house wherein I now live called or knowne by the
name of the Chequer situate in St Albans aforesaid with all out houses
and shopps yards backsides gardens orchards with all and singuler the
appurtenances whatsoever thereunto belonging to him and his heires
forever.

Item I give and bequeath unto my said sonne William all that my
close of pasture or meadow with the appurtenances commonly called or
knowne by the name of Wallclose lyeing and being in the parrish of St
Peters in the County of Hertford aforesaid adioyning to the brick wall
belonging to Mr Robotham and lyeing by the lane called Cock Lane to
him and his heires forever provided allways and it is my Will that hee
my said sonne William shall pay unto my second sonne Henry Steevens
the full summe of two hundred pounds of Lawfull money of England
within six monthes next after my decease and in case hee my said sonne
William shall neglect or refuse to pay unto my said sonne Henry the
aforesaid summe of two hundred pounds at or within the tyme
appointed for payment thereof then my Will and pleasure is that my said
sonne Henry shall enter upon possess and enioy all the aforesaid close
with the appurtenances and receive all the profitts thereof to himselfe
and his heires forever and that my said sonne William shall quietly leave
and yeild up the same unto him my said sonne Henry and if hee my said
sonne William shall happen to dye without Issue by him lawfully
begotten then my Will and pleasure is that my aforesaid house and close
with their appurtenances as afore bequeathed shall discend and come to
the use and behoofe of my said sonne Henry to possess and enjoy for
himselfe and his heires forever hee my said sonne Henry upon such
possession and enjoyment shall pay unto my fower daughters Mary
Elizabeth Martha and Hannah the severall and respective summes of
thirty pounds apeice of Currant money within three full yeares next
after the decease of him my said sonne William.

Item I give and bequeath unto my aforesaid sonne Henry Steevens all
that my house and land with outhouses yeards orchards and all
appurtenances whatsoever called or knowne by the name of
Pepperstock being in the parrish of Flampsteed in the County of
Hertford aforesaid now in the tenure and occupacon of Widdow
Turpin to him and his heires forever and in case he my said sonne
Henry shall happen to dye without Issue by him lawfully begotten then
my Will and pleasure is that my aforesaid house and land called
Pepperstoke with the appurtenances shall come unto my aforesaid sonne
William Steevens to enioy and possess to him and his heires forever and
then my Will is that hee my said sonne William uppon such possession

and enjoyment shall pay unto my aforesaid four daughters Mary Elizabeth Martha and Hannah the severall respective summes of thirty pounds apeice of Currant money within three yeares next after such decease of my sonne Henry aforesaid. Furthermore if it shall happen that both of my said sonnes William and Henry shall dye and neither of them have any Issue Lawfully by them begotten then my Will and pleasure is that my Houses and Lands with all their appurtenances before bequeathed unto my two sonnes aforesaid shall bee equally divided betweene my aforesaid four daughters namely Mary Elizabeth Martha and Hannah to bee to the onely uses and behoofes of them and their heires forever.

Item I give and bequeath unto my daughter Mary aforenamed wife to Edward Deareman the summe of twenty pounds of Currant English money to bee paid unto her by my said sonne William within three full yeares next after my decease.

Item I give and bequeath unto my daughter Elizabeth aforemencioned wife to Edward Stanton lately deceased the summe of forty pounds of Lawfull English money to bee paid unto her by my said sonne William within one full yeare next after my decease.

Item I give and bequeath unto my daughter Martha aforenamed wife to William Millard the summe of five pounds of Currant money to bee paid unto her by my said sonne William within three moneths next after my decease.

Item I give and bequeath unto my aforesaid sonne Henry Steevens the standing bedd with all the bedding coverlidds blancketts and curtaines thereunto belonging standing in the gate house Chamber alsoe the table and frame one forme foure chaires and a paire of Andirons all standing in the same gatehouse Chamber also the trundle bedd and bedding and all belonging to itt standing in the Chamber over the shopp alsoe the cubbord in the parlour and the chest that stands by the beddside in the Chamber over the hall alsoe the middle brasse pott the biggest of the three kettles that is in the Buttery a paire of candlestickes that stands in the parlour six pewter dishes a pewter chamber pott a pewter flaggon and a cupp.

Item I give and bequeath unto my daughter Hannah beforementioned the summe of threescore pounds of Lawfull money of England to bee paid unto her by my aforesaid sonne William within six moneths next after my decease and if it shall happen that she my said daughter Hannah shall dye without Issue Lawfully begotten of her owne body before the tyme appointed for payment of her portion of three score pounds as aforesaid then my Will is that the said portion of threescore pounds shallbee equally divided betweene my other five

Children then liveing or to soe many of them as shall bee then liveing to bee equally divided betweene them at such tyme as it should have been paid unto her in case shee had lived thereunto by my aforesaid sonne William.

Item I give and bequeath unto my said daughter Hannah the standing bed and trunble bedd standing in the Hall Chamber with all the bedding covering and curtaines belonging unto them alsoe halfe a dozen stooles foure covered chaires a box and the best chest two brasse candlestickes and a pair of Andirons all standing in the same Hall Chamber alsoe the cubbord standing in the Chamber over the parlour and the five pewter dishes and a salt standing thereon alsoe the third brasse pott and the two lesser kettles a pewter chamber pott a flaggon and a cupp being in the buttery alsoe one paire of Virginals standing in the Chamber over the gate house.

Item I give and bequeath unto my sonne Henry and my daughter Hannah aforesaid the one halfe of all my linnen in my house that is to say of sheets table cloths napkins towells and of all other kind of linnen whatsoever to bee equally divided betweene my said sonne and daughter Henry and Hannah.

Item I give and bequeath unto my two sonnes aforesaid William and Henry all my working tooles and suchlike implements belonging to my Trade to bee equally divided betweene them.

All the rest of my goods and chattells bonds and bills whatsoever unbequeathed my debts legacies and funerall discharged I leave unto my said sonne William Steevens whome I make and ordaine full and whole Executor of this my last Will and Testament. In witnesse whereof I have hereunto sett my hand and seale declareing this to bee my last Will and Testament the day and yeare first abovewritten.

the marke of William Steevens

sealed signed accknowledged and declared
the day and yeare abovewritten to bee the
last Will and Testament of the abovenamed
William Steevens in the presence of Us
John Ransford Peter Fullwood Thomas Clarke

[source: Hertfordshire Archives and Local Studies: 107/AW/20]

6. A farmer's will, 1714/5.

In the name of God Amen; I Thomas Arkill [farmer] of Seavenhampton [Gloucestershire], being of weak body, but of sound and perfect memory, doe make my Will and bequeath as followeth. Imprimis I bequeath my soul to Almighty God and my blessed Lord and Redeemer Jesus Christ my Saviour by whose meritts and intercession I hope to be saved. And as to my worldly concerns and to the satisfaction of my conscience, I make this my last Will and Testament, viz. Imprimis I make my wife Hannah my whole Executrix and to enjoy all my wealth, goods and chattels, excepting what by my will I bequeath as underwritten, but in case my wife should marry, It is my intent that the goods I leave behind me should be equally divided between her children and her my said wife, otherwise provided that my daughters Sarah and Mary may have Ten pound apeice, and Five pound in houshould stuffe, and my 3 boys Thomas James and Henry I give 1 shilling each. This I own to be my last Will to which I sett my hand this Eleventh day of February Anno Domini 1714.

Witnesses to this will are underwritten

Sealed and delivred in the presence of the witnesses following:

Mary Lawrence

Mary Mason

Thomas Arkill his mark

[source: Gloucestershire Record Office: GDR will 1715/31]

7. Extract from a will, 1537.

In Dei nomine [the name of god] Amen. The xiith day of December in the yere of our Lord God Mcccccxxxvii, the xxixth yere of the reigne of our soveraign lord Henry the viii protector of the feyth and the supreme hed immediatly under God of thys catholyke Churche of England, I William Shepard of Mendelysham in the countie of Suffolk holl of mynde and good remembrance make my testament and last wyll as hereafter foloyth:

Fyrst and before all other thynges accordyng to the perfeccion of my baptysm I forsake synne and agreying to the othe that I promysyd to God and to my prynce which ys your supreme hed of thys church of Englond immediatly under God I also forsake the Bysshoppe of Romes usurpt pouer wherin he caused me to trust and commytte me unto God and to hys marcy trustyng withoute any dowte our mystrust that by hys grace and the meretes of Jesu Cryst and by the verteu of the holy passyon and of his resurreccion I have and shall have remyssyon of my synnes and resurreccion of body and sowle. (Here I wold not that men shuld say that I dyspyset other holsome sacramentes or good seremonys. But because I am rude and unlernyd and know not the scriptur and therfor loke what Gods Word sayth of theym, that saym do I beleve without any dowt or mystrust.) As touchyng the whelth of my sowle

my grond and beleve ys that their ys but one God and one Mediator
betweene God and man which ys Ihesu Cryst so that I do excepte none
in hevyn nor in erth to be my medeator betwene me and God but only
Ihesu Cryst. (Here in thys poynte I wolde not that men shuld thynk that
I regard not the preyer of my Crysten bretheryn bot that I desyre all
good Crysten bretheryn to pray with me that Gods wyll myght be done
in me and in all men; For herin I trust to the promyse of God, he that
belevyth and ys baptysed shalbe savyd and he that belevyth not shalbe
damnyd.) . . .

[source: S. Tymms (ed.), *Wills and inventories from the registers of the
commissary of Bury St Edmunds*, Camden Society, 49 (1850),
pp.130–1.]

Inventories

Introduction

Most probate inventories followed a common pattern, like wills, but
with considerable variation in the amount and type of their detail. More
often than not they recorded the dead person's status or occupation,
although this sample's ratio of six to one was far from typical. Some
inventories' contents suggest the missing occupation, but not in No.10.
Most preambles claimed to have listed all the personal estate of these
individuals when they died or when their goods were appraised, with
the names of those who did so either here or at the end. Well-organised
inventories normally listed and valued the household goods next after
the preamble, followed by the farming and/or occupational goods, as in
Nos.9 and 11, and finally any credits and leases. Some more detailed
ones no doubt derived from lists drafted by a household's more literate
members, although they cannot now be identified. When unusual trades
or goods were involved, specialist appraisers often valued all or part of
the inventory, as with the books in No.12, which were valued nearly
seven weeks after the rest.

Household goods were appraised room by room in larger houses,
indicating the number and names of their main rooms, with good
clues to their uses. The parlour of No.11, for instance, had two
bedsteads and three feather mattresses, but the contents in No.12
show that its parlour was no longer used for sleeping. The separate
room valuations for No.13 tell us nothing about its various contents,
but the total for all its household goods (£117) suggests much more
comfort here than in No.11 (£21) or even No.12 (£68). The much
greater detail in the latter and No.14 provide insights of a different

order into these households' furnishings and lifestyles and encourage more detailed analyses. No.14 priced many more individual goods separately, while No.13 commented on the worn state of some and itemised various new consumer goods, such as a clock, looking glasses, coffee pots and curtains for windows as well as for beds. Clothes were recorded with almost as much diversity. Nos.9 and 10 just valued the wearing apparel on its own, but more frustratingly Nos.11, 12 and 13 also included the dead man's ready money in his purse. No.14 is quite different, with descriptions and separate valuations of the man's best clothes and, most unusually, of his wife's wardrobe also. No.8 alone mentions no clothes, but this widow's will (No.1) had disposed already of her best gown, red coat, cap, girdle and a pair of sleeves.

Some contents of the farming inventories naturally reflected seasonal variations. Here both No.11 in January and No.13 in September had grain stored in their barns and corn growing in their fields as well as some cows and horses, but very different-sized flocks of sheep, worth on average three shillings in 1686 and five shillings in 1718. Somewhat surprisingly the husbandman appears to have had no farm equipment. No.9's stable was used for storage and his shop contents show that he was a haberdasher who specialised in hats, with the relatively limited debts aggregated from his shop books suggesting his efficiency and, like No.12, he also enjoyed some income from rent. Nos.11 and 13 also had outstanding credits in bonds or specialty, but we cannot tell how dubious those without specialty were, although their prominent place in Mr Johnson's inventory implies their probable importance to his appraisers.

It is always tempting to assume that inventories provide 'true and perfect' valuations of each personal estate, but many were only approximate at best. Jone Stanley's will shows that No.8 excluded most of her bequests, while No.10 was drawn up four years after Christopher James's death merely to establish his heir's right to the lease for Rosemoddros. Tradesmen often owed at least as much money as was owing to them, but, like No.9, this was rarely indicated by their inventories, but merely by accounts (see No.22). Seven months before the date of his inventory (No.11), Ralph Cox died in May 1685, aged 65; his eldest son, who lived next door (aged 37), was also a husbandman who doubtless took over at least his father's farm implements between his death and the listing of his possessions. The discovery of such extra information often provides an illuminating context for some inventories and so exposes the limitations of studying them in isolation.

8. A widow's inventory, 1557.

The inventory of all the goods moveable and unmoveable of Jone Stanley wedoo of the parish of Aldermaston [Alderminster] dyssessyd the iiiith day of May in the yere of owr lord god Mccccclvii and praysyd by Wylliam Bolton Rychard Myller John Grene and Thomas Hewyns

Item Inprimis for the corne of a yard londe
  and a halfe ————————— praise   vi li xiii s iiii d
Item ii brase pannys ——— prais   iiii s
Item a coverled ———   ii s
Item a fat and kever ———   ii s
Item a towe and her part of a plowgh and plowgh geres — vii s
           Summa ——————— vii li viiii s iiii d

[source: Worcester Record Office: 1558 IV No.478]

9. A haberdasher's inventory, 1624/5.

The 14th January 1624
An Inventory of all such goodes and Chattels that William Standly of the Cittie of Winchester haberdasher died seassed of

	In the hall	[£	s	d]
Item	i Joyn table & forme	0	10	00
Item	i Joyned cubbard & side cubbard	1	6	0
Item	ii Carpettes & side boord clothes	0	16	0
Item	Winscott Benches Joyn stooles & i chaire	2	10	0
Item	his wearing aparell	£1	15	0
Item	i Silver boull & ii silver spoones	£1	12	0
	In the kitchen			
Item	iii Brasse pottes	1	0	0
Item	Kittles & other small peces of Bras	2	2	0
Item	pewter	2	0	0
Item	i Table stooles & chayres	0	9	0
Item	Drippinge pans & Broches & other Lumber	0	9	0
Item	i saffe Barelles & kivar	0	12	6
	In the Best chamber			
Item	ii Bedsteads cords & mattes & curtens	£1	14	0
Item	Bedding & Kiverledes	4	6	8
Item	i Table Coffers & a side table	0	13	0
Item	Sheetes Table clothes & napkins	2	16	0

	In the other Chamber			
Item	ii Bedsteades	0	7	0
Item	Beddinge Kiverledes blankets & other things	3	10	0
	In the stable			
	Stanning stuff wood & cole	£1	10	0
	In the shopp			
Item	Smale hatt bandes sipers & Taffate	5	1	0
	Black hattes: 19 hatts	3	16	0
	16 hattes	3	12	0
	14 hattes	1	12	0
	9 hattes	1	9	0
	12 hattes	1	14	4
	12 hattes	1	7	4
	27 hattes	2	1	0
	31 hattes	1	17	2
	36 hattes	1	18	0
	16 hattes	1	5	4
		(25	13	2)
Item	25 hattes	3	12	4
Item	33 hattes	3	1	4
Item	52 hattes	2	8	4
Item	i Coslett	1	0	0
Item	presses Cheestes & other Lumber in the shopp	3	10	0
		(£13	12	0)
Item	more dew for rent	£5	15	4
Item	mony owing uppon the books	3	18	6
		(9	13	0)
Item	mony for ware taken since his desease	£3	6	0
	Suma totalis 92 3 2			

Praisers to his Inventory whoose names are heere under written
> Mathew Carr
> Raphe Moore
> William Gilbert

[source: Hampshire Record Office: 1624 A75/2]

10. A delayed inventory, 1656.

An Inventory of all and singular the goods and Chattles of Christopher James late of the parish of Burian in the County of Cornwall deceased prysed by John Penwarthen Thomas Huggens Anno Domini 1656

Imprimis for his halfe of the tenement in
Rosemoddros   £12   00   00
Item for one cloake and the rest of his wearing close   £03   00   00
                                        Summe is   £15   00   00

[Probate granted 11 March 1660/1]

[source: Cornwall Record Office: DSB 17]

11. A husbandman's inventory, 1685/6.

January 4 Anno Domini 1685
A true and perfect Inventory had and taken of all the Goods and
Chattells of Ralph Cox of Chilverscoton in the County of Warwick
Husbandman late deceased which he was possest of att the time of his
death, praisd and prizd by us whose names are hereunto subscribed

	[£	s	d]
Inprimis money in his purse & his wearing Apparell	3	10	0
In the House			
One Table & Two forms	1	16	8
Brass & pewter	3	10	0
Land Iron fire shovel & Tongs with other Lumber	0	10	0
In the Parlour			
Two Joynd beds & Three Feather beds & all things belonging	10	0	0
A small Chest of Linnen	2	0	0
One Table two Chests 2 Coffers & one press	1	4	0
In the Chamber			
One half headed Bed, one Trunk & some Cheese	1	10	0
In the Buttery			
One Cheesepress 2 barrells with other Lumber	0	10	0
Winter Corn in the Barn	11	5	0
Oats in the Barn	3	0	0
Corn upon the Ground	16	0	0
Four Cowes & 2 heifers	10	0	0
Three Mares	8	0	0
Eight Sheep	1	4	0
One Bond	5	0	0
	78	09	08

    Praisd & prisd by us
       John Hurst the marke of Richard Clark

[source: Lichfield Record Office: B/C/11 1686 March 26]

12. A clergyman's inventory, 1691.

October 29th 1691
A true and perfect Inventory had and taken of all the Goods and
Chattells of John Perkins of Chilvers Coton in the County of Warwick
Clerk late deceased which he was possessed of at the time of his death
praised and prizd by us whose names are hereunto subscribed.

	[£	s	d]
Inprimis Money in his purse & his wearing Apparrell	3	0	0
Item in the Kitchin			
Six pewter dishes & half a dozen plates, Two pewter basins, Two small Tankards, 1 Gun, one salt, Two pewter porringers, 2 pewter Candlesticks, Thirteen spoons, 1 pewter dish & 1 little sawcer, 1 close stool pan & pewter chamber pott	1	10	0
An Irongrate in the Fornace	0	2	0
One middling Kettle, 5 lesser Kettles, 1 fornace-Kettle, Two brass potts, 1 little Flanders Kettle, 4 brass Candlesticks, 1 warming pan, 1 scummer, 1 Ladle Two brass pans, 1 bigger, 1 lesser	3	14	0
Three spitts & a pair of Cobberds, a sorry pair of pothooks, 1 chopping knife, 1 beef fork a little rosting Iron, & small fire shovell	0	5	0
A Tinn Cullender Candlebox dripping pan, Two Coffee potts, one pudding pan	0	2	6
Two dozen of Trenchers with other Lumber	0	2	6
In the Dary			
One Cheespress & Churn & 5 little shelves & other Implements	0	7	0
In the Kitchin Chamber			
Two Bed-steads 2 Feather beds, 2 Feather Bolsters, 3 blanketts 2 Coverlets, a pair of old Curtains	3	1	0
Two Coffers 1 Joynd Box, 2 other boxes, & 1 more joynd Box	0	9	0
One shelf one Flaskett & one old Coffer	0	3	0
In the Cock-loft			
one Truckle Bed, one flock bed, Blanket & coverlet, 1 sorry pillow one old Tubb with some Feathers	0	12	0
& Ashballs	0	2	6

In the Hall

Two Tables, 1 Joynd form	0	17	0
5 Chairs & an old stool, 1 little Chair	0	4	0
one salt box, 2 Cupboards, one Gunn	0	9	6
A brass morter & Iron pestill, 1 Iron dripping pan, one Land Iron, 2 pair of Tongs, 1 chafing dish, a rosting Iron, a fendal, 2 potthangers	1	0	0
One Jack & 2 shelves & pair of bellows 2 frying pans	0	9	6

In the Chamber over the Hall

One joynd Bedstead, 1 Doun bed, 1 Feather bolster & Curtains, Two blanketts & pillow & coverlett and vallance with a Truckle Bedstead	6	3	0
One hanging press, 3 green Cloth Chairs, six stools, 3 bigger 3 lesser, 1 little Table, 1 Chest, 1 Charger 1 little Trunk	1	6	0

In the Parlour

Two Tables, 2 Carpetts, 1 Court Cupboard	1	10	0
Seaven Chairs 4 Cushions, a glass case, 2 joynd stools, a Grate, fire shovell & tongs with brass knobbs	1	0	0
A Clock	1	16	0
A Looking Glass	0	1	6
six shelves	0	2	6

In the Chamber over the Parlour

One joynd bedstead, 1 Feather bed, bolster & Two pillows, Curtains & vallance, Two Blanketts, 1 red Coverlet, 1 red Rugg	5	5	6
One other joynd bedstead, 1 Feather bed, 1 good Feather bolster, Two pillows one green blankett, 1 green Rugg, curtains & vallans	2	12	0
with Two window Curtains & Rods	0	3	0
One Court Cupboard	0	3	0
One Trunk, 1 Chest, 2 Coffers, 3 Buffett stools covered with Red, 2 little joynd Boxes, 2 Carpetts	1	2	0

In the Study

Six stools, 4 covered with Red & 2 with green Two desks, 1 side cupboard, little Table & 4 shelves, some Ticknel ware with some cheese	1	10	0
1 pair of small scales with 6 weights & other Implements	0	2	0
One Twiggen Chair & looking glass	0	5	0

Linnens			
Eight pair of Fine sheets	3	0	0
Three pair of sheets & one pair more	1	10	0
Five pair of course sheets with two course Table Cloths	1	5	0
Seaventeen Diaper napkins & 2 little Diaper Table Cloths	0	15	0
One dozen & half of ordnary napkins	0	6	0
One dozen & half of other napkins	0	6	0
One large Table Cloth & 8 lesser	0	10	0
Six pair of pillow drawers	0	10	0
7 Towells	0	2	4
Three pair of sheets, 1 dozen of Flaxen napkins	1	5	0
4 pillow drawers & 2 Table cloths	0	6	0
8 napkins & a Diaper Table Cloth	0	10	0
A Chest of Drawers & a Box	0	3	0
A Trunk	0	2	0
One Silver Salt & 2 spoons	3	10	0
2 yards of Sarge	0	4	0
One peice of stuff	1	12	0
In the Buttery			
Four Barrels	0	10	0
Five shelves 2 stools little Form 1 sorry Table, 2 dozen of glass Bottells a Twiggen Costrill	0	12	0
In the Cellar			
Three Tubbs 2 Kimnells, 1 paile 2 gallons, 2 little Barrels, a Dough Tubb, 2 sives a Tunning dish, Cheesladder a little Table 3 shelves 2 grist baggs	1	5	0
In the Barn			
Winter Corn	3	0	4
Oats	0	16	0
Hay	2	10	0
One load of Coles	0	6	0
One Mare	3	10	0
Two Cows	5	10	0
Corn in the Feild	1	10	0
One Hogg	1	2	0
Mr Perkins Feather bed, one Chest of Drawers, Two Trunks, one Box with some Linens	3	10	0
Poultry	0	3	0
with other Lumber	0	3	0

Rents due

William Aropotts Rent	9	0	0
John Pingles Rent	0	10	0
Jonathan Vales Rent	3	17	6
Goodman Betts Rent	3	0	6
The viccers dues desperate	9	16	8
	106	0	4

Praised & prized by us
   John Parker   Henry Clay

The Study of Books of Mr John Perkins of Chilverscoton
   aforesaid lately deceased was December the 15th 1691
   valued & priz'd at   9   4   0
By us   Michael Armstead—Rector of Weddington
           Thomas Fraser—Minister of Woolvey

	£	s	d
The Totall Summe of this Inventory is	115	4	4

[source: Lichfield Record Office: B/C/11 1691 November 2]

13. A gentleman's inventory, 1718.

September the 5th 1718
A true and perfect Inventory of the Goods Chattles and Cattles of
Christopher Johnson of Clayworth in the County of Nottingham
Gentleman late deceased: Appraised by us whose names are subscribed

	lib	s	d
Imprimis Purse and Apparel	150	00	00
Debts upon Specialty	026	00	00
Debts without Specialty	108	06	00
Item without Specialty	026	00	00
Furniture in the Hall Room	006	10	00
Item in the great Parlour	004	00	00
Item in the little Parlour	002	10	00
Furniture in the Kitchen with the Peuter and Brass	010	00	00
Item in the Brew-house	011	10	00
Item in the Hall-Chamber	022	00	00
Item in the Chamber over the great Parlour	012	10	00
Item in the Chamber over the little Parlour	007	10	00
Plate in the same Room	025	00	00
Item Linnings	016	00	00
Twenty Acres of White Corn and Six Acres of Peas	040	06	00
Fifty Quarters of Malt	052	10	00
Eight Quarters of Wheat	008	00	00

Hay	012	00	00
Four Score and ten Sheep	022	10	00
Five Cows	018	00	00
Eight Horses	046	00	00
Nine Swine	004	00	00
One Waggon two Carts two Plows and four Harrows	020	10	00
Harness, halters and collars	005	05	00
Three Bays of Hovels with all the other Wood	014	10	00
Hold-bars and three Standhecks	001	10	00
Utensils in the Kiln-house with all other Hushelments	003	00	00
	675	17	00

Appraisers Denis Copeland
         William Gamson
         John Otter

[source: Nottinghamshire Archives: PRNW 1718]

14. Extracts from a butcher's inventory, 1588/9.

The Inventorie of all and singuler the goodes Cattelles and Chattelles of Phyllppe Freake one of the Comburgises of the towne of Leycester in the Countye of Leicester Butcher latelye deceased Indented made the xxiiiith daye of Februarye in the yeare of our Lorde God One thousande fyve hundred foure score and Eighte . . .

    In the Hall
First the Longe Table wyth the frame, one longe forme, one square table & the frame thereof, ii Cuberdes, i bason and ewre of pewterr, viii pewter flower pottes, ii turned cheires, iiii Joyned stooles, xii Cusshins, one grene Carpette, one Lawnedyron, ii hooks, i fyar yron, one peyre of tongs, i spattorne, paynted cloathes there, and one Lytle Cofer, all praysed att   v li vii s.
. . .

    In the parler
Item one square Table, frame and forme—viii s, i other Lessor square table and frame—vi s, i Joyned stoole—viii d, i cheyre—vi d, i Cubbarde and cubbarde clothe—vi s viii d, i pewter Bason & ewre, and iii pewter flower potts—v s, one Joyned Bedsteede—iii li x s, The Curtyns, vallens & curtyne Roddes—xx s, i feytherbedd—xx s, i Mattryes—v s, i Bolster—vi s viii d, iiii Whyte blanckytts—x s, i Coveringe of yarne—vi s viii d, i Coveringe of Tapstrye—L s, viii olde Cusshins—iiii s, i Launde yron, i fyer yron and i hooke—iiii s, i

Truncke—vi s, i greate Cofer—viii s, iii Lessor cofers—xii s, the
paynted clothes there—v s   xii li xiiii s ii d.
. . .

His Apparel

Item one Skarlett Gowne—vii li and a velvytt Tippitt—x s, i Blacke
Gowne—l s, i other blacke gowne—xiii s iiii d, ii olde Russet
gownes—x s, one Blacke Cote garded with velvyt—xl s, a satten
doblett—x s, one Cloke—xl s. All the Rest of his Apparell—xxvi s
viii d   xvii li.

His Wyves Apparell

Item her best Gowne—vii li, a frentche hoode—xx s, a velvytt hatt—
xxx s, a taffeta hatt lyned with velvyt—xiii s iiii d, one sylcke kertell
garded with velvytt—xx s, ii Chaneytt kertylls—xx s   xii li ii s iiii d.
. . .

In Lynnyns

Item xvii peyre of hardin sheets att iiii s a peire, vii other peyre of course
harden sheets at ii s vi d a peyre, xi peyre of flaxen sheetes att vi s viii d
a peyre, i dyaper table clothe—xiii s iiii d, i pece of Lynnyn cloth of viii
yards—viii s, i dossen of dieper napkyns—xvi s, viii yards of mydlinge—
v s iiii d, iiii Shorte table clothes—vi s viii d, iii longe table clothes—
x s, iii other table clothes—vi s, xii pillowe beares—xii s And iiii dossen
of other Napkyns—xxiiii s   xiii li ii d.

[source: W.G. Hoskins, 'An Elizabethan butcher of Leicester', in
Hoskins, *Essays in Leicestershire history* (Liverpool, 1950), pp.117–20.]

Administration

Introduction

Apart from during the Interregnum of the 1650s, the probate courts
operated in Latin until 1733, with standard abbreviations for some
common words making many of their administrative decisions even
more difficult to unravel for non-Latin specialists. The grant of probate
to the executor(s) named in an undisputed will was the most
straightforward probate activity and No.15 shows that it was already
well established by the later fourteenth century in London, with a
wording that remained familiar for over three centuries, although often
in a shortened form. Normally written as endorsements on the relevant
wills, as well as being repeated in the courts' act books, these grants
empowered executors to complete their business. An extended version

of the same approach was used in English during the seven years of the Court for Probate (see No.16).

More complex situations arose from intestacy or disputed wills or when an executor refused or could not act or the deceased had so many debts that all could not be paid from their estate. Various separate administrative documents surviving from the seventeenth century show how some courts handled these sensitive issues. The executor named in the nuncupative will (No.4) refused and so No.17 replaced him as administrator with the more usual widow; it also discloses the value of her husband's missing inventory. When no will was presented, the courts attempted to forestall future disputes by requiring close relatives to swear to the deceased's intestacy. In No.18 authority was delegated to the local vicar to administer this oath and appoint the eldest son as his father's administrator. Without such grants or letters of administration, which required them to 'swear in form' that they would 'faithfully and truely' undertake their task, administrators could not begin to act.

In certain circumstances, especially after the Restoration, administrators had to take out a bond with one or more sureties, such as No.19A, before receiving their letters of administration. This was caused by the executor being a minor so that until he came of age his administrator undertook (in No.19B) to educate and maintain him 'according to his degree and calling' and to administer his inheritance. Very similar letters of administration were prescribed for intestates' estates by parliament from 1671 onwards in 22 & 23 Charles II c.10 and appear above in Appendix 2. Refusals by next of kin to administer an estate, perhaps because it was encumbered by debt or was to be undertaken by another relative, needed recognition. No.20 shows Sybilla Carah renouncing all her claim to her daughter's goods in favour of her two sons, after which the elder one was appointed administrator.

Even after an administrator was appointed, things did not always proceed smoothly, as No.21A reveals. There the administrator's decision appears to have been challenged by his younger brother so that the probate court intervened to impose on both an agreed settlement, which included a portion for the deceased's granddaughter, who had to sign an official receipt for it (No.21B). Many of the relatively few surviving probate accounts have some potential for countering future conflict, such as Nos.21C and 22, with the latter, apparently for an innkeeper or wine retailer, leaving the administratrix with insufficient funds to settle all his debts. Both these accounts record the cost of the probate process and the funerals and also warn against assuming that the balance between their charge and discharge alone reflects accurately the deceaseds' economic circumstances.

15. Grant of probate for a will, Commissary Court of London, 1389/90.

Probatum fuit presens testamentum coram nobis, Presidente consistorii londonie, una cum codicillo eidem annexo, ii Idus Marcii Anno domini MCCClxxxix. Et commissa est administracio omnium bonorum, dictum defunctum & ipsius testamentum concernencium, Waltero Corn, executori in dicto testamento nominato, in forma iuris, & per eundem admissa, Bartholomeo Neue, coexecutore interius in eodem testamento nominato, onus administracionis huiusmodi coram nobis expresse admittere recusante. In cuius rei testimonium, sigillum officialitatis londonie, presentibus duximus apponendum. Datum Londonie, Die & anno Domini supradictis.

[This present will was proved before us, President of the consistory court of London, with one codicil annexed to it, on the day before the Ides (that is, 14th) of March in the year of our Lord 1389. And administration of all the goods of the said deceased and matters concerning his will was granted to Walter Corn, executor named in the said will who, in form of law, was admitted to the same; Bartholomew Neve, coexecutor named in the said will, has refused expressly before us to accept the burden of administration. In witness of which matter we have affixed to these presents the official seal of London. Dated at London, the day and year above written.]

[source: F.J. Furnivall, *The fifty earliest English wills* (London, 1882), p.2.]

16. Grant of probate for a will, Court for Probate, 1659.

The keeper of the Liberties of England by authority of parliament To all parsons to whome these presents shale com greetinge. Know ye that uppon the thirteenth daye of September one thousand six hundred fiftie nine before the Judges for Probate of Wills and grauntinge Administrations lawfully Authorised the last Will and testament of Richard Shutford late of Burian in the Countie of Cornwall deceased was at London in common forme proved which will is to these presents annexed and administration of all and singuler the goods Chattles and debts of the said deceased which any manner of way concerne him or his said will was graunted and commited to Katherine Shutford his Relict sole Executrix named in the said Will she havinge first taken her Oath well and truly to administer the said goods Chattles and debts accordinge to the tenor and efect of the same Will and to make or cause to be made a true and perfect Inventorie of all and singuler the goods Chattles and debts of the said deceased which have shale or may com to her hands possession or knowledge and alsoe a true and just accoumpt in and concerninge the said Administration when she shale be assigned or lawfully Caled soe to doe which tuching an Inventorie she was presently assigned to performe att or before the first daye of the moneth caled October next ensuinge. Given att London under the seale of the Court For Probate of Wills and grauntinge Administrations lawfully authorized the daye and yeare aforesaid

Math. Cotth. Keeper

Tho. Forster

R. Sankeye

[source: Cornwall Record Office: DSB/22/1]

17. Grant of Administration after executor's refusal to act, 1608.

Septimus die mensis Junii Anno domini 1608 emanavit Comissio ad administrandum bona Galfridi Fincham nuper dum vixit de Mildenhall defunct directe Elizabethe eius relicte de bone et fideliter administrandum bona etc de solvendum debita et de reddendum compotu in debita iuris forma iurat Salvo etc.

Exhibitum est Inventarium ad summam £29 9s 4d.

[On the seventh day of June 1608 a commission was issued to administer the goods of Jeffery Fincham deceased, lately of Mildenhall while he lived, to his widow Elizabeth who is directed to well and faithfully administer his goods, pay his debts and render an account of what is owed. Sworn in form.

This inventory is exhibited in the sum of £29 9s 4d.]

[source: Suffolk Record Office, Bury St Edmunds: A5/3/43]

18. Oath of Intestacy for grant of Administration, 1672.

[John Holmes eldest son of Peter Holmes late of Chilverscoton in the county of Warwick deceased]

Forma Juramenti [Form of Oath]

You shall sweare that Peter Holmes your late Father deceased dyed intestate not makeing any will soe farre as you know or beleeve, and that you will faithfully and truely administer his Goods by paying his Debts soe farre as you are bound by Law and the Inventory of his Goods will thereunto extend; you shall also make or cause to bee made a true and perfect Inventory thereof and a iust Accompt thereupon and exhibitt the same into the Registry of this Court; Soe helpe you God etc. Jurat: vicesimo septimo die Augusti 1672. domi mea coram me [Sworn 27th August 1672 before me at my home] Edvardo Abbott [vicar of Chilverscoton]

[source: Lichfield Record Office: B/C/11 1672 August]

19A. Administration bond, 1664

Noverint universi per presentes nos Josephum Noye parochie de Burian in comitatu Cornubia generosum et Johannem Perrow teneri et firmiter obligari magistro Johanni Carpenter Clerico Artium Magistro peculiaris Jurisdictionis Regie de Burian Officiali principali in ducentis libris bone et legalis monete Anglie, solvendis eidem magistro Johanni Carpenter, Executoribus Administratoribus vel Assignatis suis, Ad quam quidem solucionem bene et fideliter faciendam obligamus Nos et utrumque nostrum per se pro toto et insolido heredes Executores et Administratores Nostros firmiter per presentes, Sigillis nostris Sigillat. Datum vicessimo septimo die mensis Maii Anno Regni domini nostri Caroli Secundi dei gratia, Anglie etc., Regis etc., decimo sexto Annoque domini christi 1664.

[Know all men by these presents that we Joseph Noye of the parish of Burian in the county of Cornwall gentleman and John Perrow are held and firmly bound to Master John Carpenter, clerk, Master of Arts, principal Official of the Royal Peculiar jurisdiction of Burian, in two hundred pounds of good and lawful money of England, to be paid to the same Master John Carpenter, his executors, administrators and assigns, for making which payment we bind ourselves well and faithfully, both and each of us by himself for the whole, and our heirs, executors and administrators are firmly bound in the whole sum by these presents. Sealed with our seals. Dated 27th May in the sixteenth year of the reign of our lord Charles II by the grace of God King etc. of England etc., and in the year of our lord Christ 1664.]

19B. Letters of Administration, 1664.

The condition of this present obligation is such that whereas John Adams late of the parish of Burian deceased dyed and made his will wherein he nominated constituted and ordained Francis Adams his sole Executor, the said Executor being in his minority and not able to dispose the goods chattailes and debts of the said deceased according to lawe, therefore the Administration of all and singuler the said goods

chattailes and debts is graunted and comitted under the Seale of Office unto Joseph Noye gent during his minority, yfe there fore the said Joseph Noye doe well and truely Administer the said goods chattailes and debts according to lawe and according to the tenure of the said will, and alsoe doe make and passe over or cause to be passed, a true iust and perfect Accompt of and uppon the said Administration at all tyme and tymes when he shalbe thereunto lawfully required and all such goods chattailes and debts as shall remaine and be found due uppon the said Accompt being examined and allowed, doe well and truely deliver over unto the said Executor when he shalbe of lawfull age to receave the same. In the meane tyme doe educate and maintaine the said Executor with competent meate drinke and apparrell and other necessaries according to his degree and calling, and especially doe defend keepe and save harmelesse the said Master John Carpenter his successors officers and ministers against all persons whatsoever, for graunting and comitting the said Administration and that without fraude or delaye that then this present obligation to be voide or else to stand and be in force.
Sealed and delivered in the presence of
William Noye   Joseph Noye
Tobias Cowling   John Pearowe

[source: Cornwall Record Office: DSB/27/2]

20. Renunciation by next of kin of claim on goods, 1668/9.

February the 15th 1668
These presents shall witnesse that I Sybilla Carah of the parish of St Leaven in the county of Cornwall widdow for diverse good causes and considerations me thereunto moving and more especially out of my naturall Affection unto John Carah and Penticost Carah my sons doe therefore remitt transfer and passe over all my Right and Claime which I have or ought to have unto the goods and chattels of Mary Carah my desceased daughter unto them the sayd John Carah and Penticost Carah Irrevoclely by these presents. In witnesse wherof I have heerunto set my hande and seale the day and yeare first abovesayde.
Signed sealed and delivered in presence of us
John Smith   The signe of
John Bosustowe   Sybilla Carah

[source: Cornwall Record Office: DSB 313/3]

21A. Acceptance of division of intestate's goods, 1661.

These presents shall wittnes that Wee Martyn Martyn the naturall
sonne and Administrator of all and singuler the goods chattailes and
debts of Richard Martyn late of the parish of Gulvall and County of
Cornwall deceased, And Roger Martyn the naturall sonne likewise of
the said Richard Martyn deceased are finally agreed on concearning
the partition and devision of soe much of the said goods and chattailes
as belongeth unto us or either of us, And doe hereby freely and
cleerely exonerate acquite and discharge each other, for and
concearning the same for evermore by these presents, wittnes our
hands and seales, dated the twentieth day of May in the yeare of our
lord god 1661.
Signed sealed and acknowledged in presence of us

William Noye   The signe of Martyn Martyn
The signe of Margaret Noye   The signe of Roger Martyn

21B. Receipt for a legacy, 1661.

These presents shall wittnes that I Joane Harvey wife unto William
Harvey of the parish of Gulvall and County of Cornwall, in the absence
of the said William Harvey my husband being out of this County of
Cornwall have receaved and had by the hands of Martyn Martyn the
Administrator, of all and singuler the goods chattailes and debts of
Richard Martyn, late of the said parish of Gulvall and County of
Cornwall Fuller, deceased, and grandfather of me the said Joane Harvey
soe much goods and money as amount unto the value of nine pounds
ten shillings of good and lawfull monyes of England being in full
satisfaction of all dues and demands whatsoever payable or becoming
due unto me or the said William Harvey my husband in my right, out
of the said goods and chattailes of the said Richard Martyn my
grandfather deceased, And uppon the receipt hereof I doe exonerate
acquite and discharge the said Martyn Martyn, the Administrator
aforesaid, his Executors Administrators and Assignes and every of them
for evermore by these presents. In wittnes whereof I the said Joane
Harvey have hereunto sett my signe and seale, dated the Twentieth day
of May in the thirteenth yeare of the raigne of our soveraigne lord
Charles the second by the grace of god, of England Scotland Fraunce

and Ireland, King defender of the faith etc. Annoque Domini Christi 1661.

Sined Sealed and delevered in the presence of us

Isaac Nuton   Joane Harve
Thomas Paule

21C. A fuller's probate account, 1661.

Computus Calculum sive ratiocinium Martin Martyn filii et administratoris omnium et singulorum bonorum Jurium, Creditorum at Chattallorum Richardi Martyn nuper dum vixit parochie de Gulvall, Archidiacanatus Cornubie defuncto.

[The account, calculation or reckoning of Martin Martyn son and administrator of all and singular the goods, rights, credits and chattels of Richard Martyn, lately while he lived of the parish of Gulval in the Archdeaconry of Cornwall, deceased.]

Onus [The charge]

	£	s	d
Inprimis huiusmodi Administrator recepit de bonis Juribus Creditis et Chattallis defuncti predicti prout ex particularibus in Inventario inde confecto plenius liquet et apparet summa	25	15	4

[First this Administrator received of the goods, rights, credits and chattels of the aforesaid deceased as appears more fully from the particulars in the completed inventory the sum of]

Exposita necessaria per eundem Administratorem sequuntur [The necessary expenses by the same administrator are as follows:]

	£	s	d
Inprimis paid for the funerall expences of the deceased	1	10	0
Item paid for the letters of Administration and charges incident thereunto	0	06	0
Item paid Joane the wife of William Harvey the grandaughter of the deceased for her portion out of the said goods and Chattailes the sume of	9	10	0
Item paid for drawing hearing and Registring of this Accompt	0	13	0
Summa expositorum [total spent]	11	19	4

Sicque remanet in manibus huiusmodi Administratoris
    summam   £13   16   0
[So there remains in this administrator's hands the sum of]

[source: Cornwall Record Office AP/M 821/2, 3 & 4]

22. A probate account, 1678/9.

The Accompt of Sarah Mersher Widdow the Relict and Administratrix
of all and Singular the goodes chattles and credits of Henry Mersher late
of the Parish of Midhurst in the county of Sussex within the Diocese
and Archdeaconry of Chichester deceased made as well of and upon all
such goodes chattles and credits of the said deceased which have come
to the hands of this Accomptant as also of all such payments and
disbursements which this Accomptant hath paid and expended in and
about the Administration of the same goodes. Exhibited this tenth day
of January Anno domini 1678.

    The charge
Imprimis this Accomptant chargeth her self with all and singular the
goodes chattles and credits of the said deceased mentioned and
comprized in an Inventory thereof made and exhibited into the
Registry of this Court amounting to the summe of   £157   13s   6d

    The discharge
Imprimis this Accomptant craveth allowance for the
    Funerall expenses of the said deceased   £10
Item paid for the fees of the Letters of Administration
    ingrossing & exhibiting of the Inventory the Kings
    duty for the same with the Proctors fee & Bond for
    withdrawing of the Caveat with other charges &
    expenses for her self & sureties at the time of
    taking the letters of Administration   35s   2d
Item paid to Mr Cobden Mercer due from the
    deceased   £4   19s
Item paid to Mr Peryham Minister due from the
    deceased   £4
Item paid to Mr Pearson Mercer due from the
    deceased   23s
Item paid to Goodman Lobden Shoomaker due from
    the said deceased   10s
Item paid to Mrs Payne Sempstress due from the said
    deceased   10s

Item paid to John Budd for faggots due from the said
    deceased   £9   18s

Item paid to Thomas Mersher due from the said
    deceased upon Bond   £9

Item paid to Goodman Crowcher for Malt due from
    the deceased   £4

Item paid for License to sell wine due from the said
    deceased   £4

Item paid to Mr William Young Esq for Rent due
    from the said deceased   £10   15s

Item paid to Mr Houghton for Wine due from the
    deceased   £33

Item due to Mr Coward for Wine from the deceased
    and paid to Mr Jackson by this Accomptant   £40   3s

Item paid to Mr Hannam for Malt due fron the said
    deceased   £32   10s

Item paid to John Hughes for carriage of Wine due
    from the deceased   £4

Item paid to Mr Hayes of London for Sugar due
    from the deceased   £3   11s

Item paid to Mr Goble of Farnham for Tobacco due
    from the deceased   £3

Item paid to Mr Bowes for Physick used in the time
    of the deceaseds sickness   £2

Item paid to Mr Meale for Physick used in the time
    of the deceaseds sickness   20s

                 Summa   £179   14s   2d

Ordinary Charges

Imprimis for drawing this Accompt & counsell about
    the same   5s   4d

Item for examining this Accompt   3s   4d

Item for the admission thereof   8d

Item for the Apparitors fee   12d

Item for double ingrossing this Accompt in
    Parchment   6s   8d

Item for the *Quietus est* [it is quit] under the Seale   17s

              Summa   34s

Summa totalis expositorum et exponendorum   £181   8s   2d
[Total sum laid out and spent]

Sic restat in manibus huius Computant nil sed in
    Surplusagio est et exposuit ultra vires inventarii
    summam   £23   14s   8d

[Thus there rests in the hands of this Accountant
  nothing, but she is overspent beyond the inventory total]

            Jan: 10 1678 iuxta [next to] etc.
Sara Mersher vidua relicta dicti defuncti ac Administratrix etc. super
veritate Composito jurat per me Thomas Briggs
[SM widow and relict of the said deceased and administratrix etc.
was sworn by me to the truth of the above account. TB]

[source: West Sussex Record Office: Ep I/33/1678]

Select glossary

andiron: iron plates or bars for holding a fire in the grate
apparitor: court official
ashballs: balls of wood or fern ashes, used in washing clothes
behoofe: advantage
broches, broaches: spits
buffet stool: low stool or foot stool
carpet: covering for table or bench
chafing dish: dish for keeping food hot
chaneytt: material, possibly camlet
chees ladder: shelves for storing cheese
close stool: commode
cockloft: attic or space under roof
cords and mattes: cords laced across a bedstead to support a mat on
    which the mattress was placed
coslett: not identified, most unlikely to be corslett
costrill: large wooden bottle or small keg
diaper: linen fabric with a patterned weave
fat: vat
feather/feyther bed: mattress filled with feathers
flaskett: basket, usually used for carrying linen
fornace: boiler
gun: when made of pewter, normally a large ladle
half headed bed: bedstead without a canopy
hardin, harden: coarse linen cloth, usually made from hemp
hovel: outhouse
hushelments, lumber: small household goods of little value
hutch: chest or small cupboard
kersie: coarse, narrow woollen cloth
kertell, kirtle: gown or outer petticoat
kettle, kittle: open cooking pot

kever, kivar: shallow wooden tub, often used for cooling liquids
kimnell: wooden tub
kiverledes: coverlets
lawnedyron, landiron: large type of cobiron
linnings, lynnys: linen
lond, land: ridge or strip in an open field
loome: bucket or tub, but not a weaver's loom here
mydlinge: cloth, probably linen
ordinary: bishop or archdeacon
paynted clothes: coarse linen cloth hangings, imitation tapestry
pillowe beare/drawer: pillow case
plowgh geres: harness for ploughing
porringer: bowl, used especially for porridge
press: large cupboard
rude: rough, unlettered
russet: coarse cloth, reddish brown in colour
saffe, safe: ventilated food cupboard
sarge, serge: durable twilled worsted cloth
sipers, cypers: crepe-like material, usually black and tied round hats
scummer: skimming ladle
spattorne: spit iron
specialty: written bond or bill
standheck: rack on four posts for holding fodder or straw
stuff: goods, furniture
taffate, taffeta: silk ribbons for adorning hats
Ticknel ware: coarse earthenware from Ticknall in Derbyshire
tippit: cape or short cloak
towe: chain or rope used in pulling a plough
tunning dish: dish used as funnel in brewing
twiggen: wicker work
vallens: drapery hanging from a bed's canopy or mattress
winscott, wainscote: wooden pannelling
yard londe/land: a holding of 16 to 36 acres, depending on the manor

Consolidated Bibliography

Victoria County History of Oxfordshire, VII (London, 1953).

Victoria County History of Oxfordshire, XII (London, 1990).

Adams, B., ed., *Lifestyle and culture in Hertford. Wills and inventories for the parishes of All Saints and St. Andrew, 1660–1725* (Hertford, 1997). Hertfordshire Record Publications, 13.

Addy, J., *Death, money and the vultures: inheritance and avarice, 1660–1750* (London, 1992).

Alcock, N. W., ed., *People at home. Living in a Warwickshire village, 1500–1800* (Chichester, 1993).

Alldridge, N. J., 'House and household in Restoration Chester', *Urban History Yearbook*, 10 (1983).

Allen, R. C., 'Inferring yields from probate inventories', *Journal of Economic History*, 48 (1988).

Alsop, J. D., 'Religious preambles in early modern English wills as formulae', *Journal of Ecclesiastical History*, 40 (1989).

Ambler, R. W., B. Watkinson and L. Watkinson, eds, *Farmers and Fishermen. The probate inventories of the ancient parish of Clee, South Humberside, 1536–1742* (Hull, 1987).

Amussen, S. D., *An ordered society* (Oxford, 1988).

Appleby, A. B., *Famine in Tudor and Stuart England* (Stanford, 1978).

Arkell, T., 'The incidence of poverty in England in the later seventeenth century', *Social History*, 12 (1987).

Arkell, T., 'Household goods from probate inventories', in H. Beaufort-Murphy, ed., *West Penwith at the time of Charles II* (Penzance, 1998).

Atkinson, J. A. *et al.*, eds, *Darlington wills and inventories, 1600–1625* (Durham, 1993). Publications of the Surtees Society, 201.

Barley, M. W., 'Rural building in England', in J. Thirsk, ed., *The agrarian history of England and Wales, V, ii, 1640–1750* (Cambridge, 1985).

Beaufort-Murphy, H., ed., *West Penwith at the time of Charles II* (Penzance, 1998).

Becon, T., *The sicke mans salve* (London, *c*.1558–9).

Beier, A. L., 'The social problems of an Elizabethan country town: Warwick, 1580–90', in P. Clark, ed., *Country towns in pre-industrial England* (Leicester, 1981).

Beveridge, W., *Prices and wages in England* (London, 1939).

Bittle, W. G. and R. T. Lane, 'Inflation and philanthropy in England: a re-assessment of W. K. Jordan's data', *Economic History Review*, 29 (1976).

Blackstone, W., *Commentaries on the laws of England* (Oxford, continued by R. L. Burn, 9th ed., 1783).

Bowden, P. J., 'Statistical appendix', in J. Thirsk, ed., *The agrarian history of England and Wales, IV, 1500–1640* (Cambridge, 1967).

Bowden, P. J., 'Statistical appendix', in J. Thirsk, ed., *The agrarian history of England and Wales, V, ii, 1640–1750* (Cambridge, 1985).

Bower, J., 'The congregation of the Dover General Baptist church' (unpublished M.A. thesis, Leicester University, 1983).

Bower, J., 'Probate accounts as a source for Kentish early modern economic and social history', *Archaeologia Cantiana*, 109 (1991).

Bower, J., 'The Kent yeoman in the seventeenth century', *Archaeologia Cantiana*, 114 (1994).

Bray, G., ed., *The Anglican canons, 1529–1947* (Woodbridge, 1998). Church of England Record Society, 6.

Brears, P. C. D., ed., *Yorkshire probate inventories, 1542–1689* (Leeds, 1972).

Brewer, J. and R. Porter, eds, *Consumption and the world of goods* (London, 1993).

Brinkworth, E. R., 'The study and use of archdeacons' court records: illustrated from the Oxford records, 1566–1759', *Transactions of the Royal Historical Society, 4th series*, 25 (1943).

Brundage, J. A., *Mediaeval canon law* (London, 1995).

Burn, R., *Ecclesiastical law* (London, 1763, 3rd ed., 1775).

C[onsett], H., *The practice of the spiritual or ecclesiastical courts* (London, 1685).

Camp, A. J., *Wills and their whereabouts* (London, 4th ed., 1974).

Campbell, B. M. S. and M. Overton, 'A new perspective on medieval and early modern agriculture: six centuries of Norfolk farming *c*.1250–*c*.1850', *Past and Present*, 141 (1993).

Capp, B., 'Will formularies', *Local Population Studies*, 14 (1975).

Carew, R., *Survey of Cornwall* (1602). Reprinted in F. E. Halliday, ed., *Richard Carew: the survey of Cornwall, etc.* (London, 1953).

Carlson, E. J., 'The historical value of the Ely Consistory probate records', in E. Leedham-Green and R. Rodd, eds, *Index of the probate records of the Consistory Court of Ely, 1449–1858* (London, 1994). British Record Society, 103.

Carlson, E. J., *Marriage and the English Reformation* (Oxford, 1994).

Cash, M., ed., *Devon inventories of the sixteenth and seventeenth centuries* (1966). Devon and Cornwall Record Society, NS, 11.

Chambers, J. D., *The Vale of Trent 1670–1800: a regional study of economic change* (Cambridge, 1957). *Economic History Review*, supplement no. 3.

Charles, L. and L. Duffin, eds, *Women and work in pre-industrial England* (Beckenham, 1985).

Chartres, J. and D. Hey, eds, *English rural society, 1500–1800: essays in honour of Joan Thirsk* (Cambridge, 1990).

Chesher, V. M. and F. J. Chesher, *The Cornishman's house* (Truro, 1968).

Churches, C., 'Women and property in early modern England: a case study', *Social History*, 23 (1998).

Clark, P., ed., *Country towns in pre-industrial England* (Leicester, 1981).

Clark, P., ed., *The transformation of English provincial towns* (London, 1984).

Clark, P., ed., *Small towns in early modern Europe* (Cambridge, 1995).

Clark, P. and J. Hosking, *Population estimates of English small towns* (Leicester, 2nd ed., 1993).

Clarkson, L. A., 'The organisation of the English leather industry in the late sixteenth and seventeenth centuries', *Economic History Review*, 13 (1960).

Clarkson, L. A., 'The leather crafts in Tudor and Stuart England', *Agricultural History Review*, 14 (1966).

Clay, C., 'Lifeleasehold in the western counties of England, 1650–1750', *Agricultural History Review*, 29 (1981).

Clay, C. G. A., *Economic expansion and social change: England, 1500–1700* (Cambridge, 1984).

Clay, J. W. and E. Crossley, eds, *Halifax wills*, vol. 1 (Halifax, n.d.).

Cooper, C. H., *Annals of Cambridge* (Cambridge, 1842–1852).

Cooper, J. P., 'Patterns of inheritance and settlement by great landowners from the fifteenth to the eighteenth centuries', in J. Goody, J. Thirsk and E. P. Thompson, eds, *Family and inheritance. Rural society in western Europe, 1200–1800* (Cambridge, 1976).

Coppel, S., 'Wills and the community: a case study of Grantham', in P. Riden, ed., *Probate records and the local community* (Gloucester, 1985).

Coppel, S., 'Will-making on the deathbed', *Local Population Studies*, 40 (1988).

Corfield, P., 'Small towns, large implications: social and cultural roles of small towns in 18th century England and Wales', *British Journal for Eighteenth-Century Studies*, 10 (1987).

Cornwall Record Office, *Index to Cornish probate records* (Truro, 1984–8).

Cox, N. C. and J. J. Cox, 'Probate inventories: the legal background', *The Local Historian*, 16 (1984).

Cox, N. C. and J. J. Cox, 'Valuations in probate inventories', *The Local Historian*, 16, 17 (1985, 1986).

Craig, J. and C. Litzenberger, 'Wills as religious propaganda: the testament of William Tracy', *Journal of Ecclesiastical History*, 44 (1993).

Cressy, D., *Literacy and the social order: reading and writing in Tudor and Stuart England* (Cambridge, 1980).

Cressy, D., 'Kinship and kin interaction in early modern England', *Past and Present*, 113 (1986).

Cross, C., 'Wills as evidence of popular piety in the Reformation period. Leeds and Hull, 1540–1640', in D. Loades, ed., *The end of strife* (Edinburgh, 1984).

Cross, C., 'Northern women in the early modern period: the female testators of Hull and Leeds, 1520–1650', *Yorkshire Archaeological Journal*, 59 (1987).

Cullum, D. and P. Wardley, 'The diffusion of the Hindu-Arabic numeral system: numeracy, literacy and historical analysis of writing skills in seventeenth-century west Cornwall', *Cornish Studies*, 2 (1994).

Dannatt, G. H., 'Introduction: Banbury from 1590 to 1650, seen through wills and inventories', in J. S. W. Gibson, ed., *Banbury wills and inventories, part 1, 1591–1620* (Banbury, 1985). Banbury Historical Society, 13.

Defoe, D., *Tour through the eastern counties* (reprinted Ipswich, 1984).

Dickens, A. G., *Lollards and Protestants in the diocese of York* (London, 1959, 2nd ed., London, 1982).

Doughty, R. A., 'Industrial prices and inflation in southern England, 1401–1640', *Explorations in Economic History*, 12 (1975).

Duffin, A., *Faction and faith: politics and religion of the Cornish gentry before the Civil War* (Exeter, 1996).

Duffy, E., *The stripping of the altars: traditional religion in England, c.1400–1580* (London, 1992).

Dyer, A., 'Probate inventories of Worcester tradesmen, 1545–1614', in *Worcester Historical Society, Miscellany II* (Worcester, 1967). Worcestershire Historical Society, 5.

Dyer, A., *The city of Worcester in the sixteenth century* (Leicester, 1973).

Dyer, A., 'Urban housing: a documentary study of four Midland towns, 1530–1700', *Post-Medieval Archaeology*, 15 (1981).

Dyer, A., 'The Bishops' census of 1563: its significance and accuracy', *Local Population Studies*, 49 (1992).

Dyer, A., 'The English sweating sickness of 1551: an epidemic anatomized', *Medical History*, 41 (1997).

Dyer, C., 'Changes in the size of peasant holdings in some west Midland villages, 1400–1540', in R. M. Smith, ed., *Land, kinship and life-cycle* (Cambridge, 1984).

Dyer, C., *Standards of living in the later middle ages: social change in England c.1200–1520* (Cambridge, 1989).

Earle, P., *The making of the English middle class: business, society and family life in London, 1660–1730* (London, 1989).

Edwards, P. R., 'The development of dairy farming on the North Shropshire plain in the seventeenth century', *Midland History*, 4 (1978).

Emmison, F. G., ed., *Jacobean household inventories* (Apsley, 1938). Bedfordshire Record Society, 20.

Emmison, F. G., *Elizabethan life: morals and the church courts* (Chelmsford, 1973).

Erickson, A. L., 'An introduction to probate accounts', in G. H. Martin and P. Spufford, eds, *The records of the nation* (Woodbridge, 1990).

Erickson, A. L., *Women and property in early modern England* (London, 1993, ppb. 1995).

Erickson, A. L., 'Using Probate Accounts', in S. Sogner, ed., *Fact, fiction and forensic evidence: the potential of judicial sources for historical research in the early modern period* (Oslo, 1997). *Tid og Tanke*, 2.

Evans, N., 'Testators, literacy, education and religious belief', *Local Population Studies*, 25 (1980).

Evans, N., 'Occupations in parish registers: a note', *The Local Historian*, 15 (1983).

Evans, N., *The East Anglian linen industry: rural industry and local economy, 1500–1800* (Aldershot, 1985).

Evans, N., 'Inheritance, women, religion and education in early modern society as revealed by wills', in P. Riden, ed., *Probate records and the local community* (Gloucester, 1985).

Evans, N., ed., *Wills of the archdeaconry of Sudbury, 1630–1635* (Woodbridge, 1987). Suffolk Records Society, 29.

Evans, N., ed., *Wills of the archdeaconry of Sudbury, 1636–1638* (Woodbridge, 1993). Suffolk Records Society, 35.

Everitt, A., 'Farm labourers', in J. Thirsk, ed., *The agrarian history of England and Wales, IV, 1500–1640* (Cambridge, 1967).

Everitt, A., 'The marketing of agricultural produce', in J. Thirsk, ed., *The Agrarian History of England and Wales, IV, 1500–1640* (Cambridge, 1967).

Everitt, A., *Change in the provinces: the seventeenth century* (Leicester, 1970). Occasional Papers of the Department of English Local History, 2nd series, 1.

Eversley, D. E. C., 'A survey of population in an area of Worcestershire from 1660 to 1850 on the basis of parish registers', in D. V. Glass and D. E. C. Eversley, eds, *Population in history. Essays in historical demography* (London, 1965, ppb ed. 1974).

Faraday, M. A. and E. J. L. Cole, eds, *Calendar of probate and administrative acts 1407–1541 and abstracts of wills 1541–1581 in the court books of the Bishop of Hereford* (London, 1989). British Record Society, microfiche series 2.

Fieldhouse, R., 'The hearth tax and social structure in the borough of Richmond in 1673', *Cleveland and Teeside Local History Bulletin*, 14 (1971).

Fieldhouse, R., 'The hearth tax and other records', in A. Rogers, ed., *Group projects in local history* (Folkestone, 1977).

Fieldhouse, R. and B. Jennings, *A history of Richmond and Swaledale* (Chichester, 1978).

Finlay, R. A. P., *Population and metropolis: the demography of London, 1580–1650* (Cambridge, 1981).

Firth, C. H. and R. S. Rait, eds, *Acts and ordinances of the interregnum, 1642–1660* (London, 1911).

Fisher, H. E. S., *Ports and shipping in the South West* (Exeter, 1971). Exeter Papers in Economic History, 4.

Fisher, J., 'Influenza and inflation in Tudor England', *Economic History Review*, 18 (1965).

Fletcher, A., *A county community in peace and war: Sussex, 1600–1660* (London, 1975).

Flinn, M. W., *The European demographic system, 1500–1820* (Brighton, 1981).

Flood, S., ed., *St Albans wills, 1471–1500* (Hertford, 1993). Hertfordshire Record Publications, 9.

Flower-Smith, M., 'Arms and the men', in P. Wyatt and R. Stanes, eds, *Uffculme a peculiar parish: a Devon town from Tudor times* (Uffculme, 1997).

Fox, H. and B. Jennings, 'The Wolds', in J. Thirsk, ed., *The Oxford illustrated history of the English rural landscape* (Oxford, 1999).

Fraser, M., 'Costume in the wills and inventories', in P. Wyatt and R. Stanes, eds, *Uffculme a peculiar parish: a Devon town from Tudor times* (Uffculme, 1997).

Galley, C., *The demography of early modern towns: York in the sixteenth and seventeenth centuries* (Liverpool, 1998).

Garrard, R. P., 'English probate inventories and their use in studying the significance of the domestic interior 1570–1700', in A. van der Woude and A. Schuurman, eds, *Probate inventories: a new source for the historical study of wealth, material culture and agricultural development* (Utrecht, 1980). *Afdeling Agrarische Geschiedenis Bijdragen*, 23.

Gibson, J. S. W., *Probate jurisdictions: where to look for wills* (Plymouth, 1980 and subs. 1982, 1985, 1994).

Gibson, J. S. W., *Wills and where to find them* (Banbury, 4th ed., 1997).

Gittings, C., *Death, burial and the individual in early modern England* (London, 1984).

Gittings, C., 'Probate accounts: a neglected source', *The Local Historian*, 21 (1991).

Glass, D. V., 'Two papers on Gregory King', in D. V. Glass and D. E. C. Eversley, eds, *Population in history. Essays in historical demography* (London, 1965, ppb ed. 1974).

Glass, D. V. and D. E. C. Eversley, eds, *Population in history. Essays in historical demography* (London, 1965, 1974).

Glennie, P., 'Measuring crop yields in early modern England', in B. M. S. Campbell and M. Overton, eds, *Land, labour and livestock: historical studies in European agricultural productivity* (Manchester, 1991).

Goldberg, P. J. P., 'Women in fifteenth-century town life', in J. A. F. Thompson, ed., *Towns and townspeople in the fifteenth century* (Gloucester, 1988).

Gollanz, I., ed., *Winner and waster* (Oxford, 1921).

Goodacre, J., *The transformation of a peasant economy: townspeople and villagers in the Lutterworth area, 1500–1700* (Aldershot, 1994).

Goody, J., J. Thirsk and E. P. Thompson, eds, *Family and inheritance. Rural society in western Europe, 1200–1800* (Cambridge, 1976).

Goose, N., 'Household size and structure in early-Stuart Cambridge', *Social History*, 5 (1980).

Goose, N., 'The "Dutch" in Colchester: the economic influence of an immigrant community in the sixteenth and seventeenth centuries', *Immigrants and Minorities*, 1 (1982).

Goose, N., 'English pre-industrial urban economies', *Urban History Yearbook 1982*. Reprinted in J. Barry, ed., *The Tudor and Stuart town: a reader in English urban history, 1530–1688* (London, 1990).

Goose, N., 'Decay and regeneration in seventeenth-century Reading: a study in a changing economy', *Southern History*, 6 (1984).

Goose, N., 'Economic and social aspects of provincial towns: a comparative study of Cambridge, Colchester and Reading, c.1500–1700' (unpublished Ph.D. thesis, University of Cambridge, 1984).

Goose, N., 'The ecclesiastical returns of 1563: a cautionary note', *Local Population Studies*, 34 (1985).

Goose, N., 'In search of the urban variable: towns and the English economy, c.1500–1650', *Economic History Review*, 39 (1986).

Goose, N., 'Urban demography in pre-industrial England: what is to be done?', *Urban History*, 21 (1994).

Goose, N., 'The Bishops' census of 1563: a re-examination of its reliability', *Local Population Studies*, 56 (1996).

Goose, N. and J. Cooper, *Tudor and Stuart Colchester* (Chelmsford, 1998).

Goring, J., 'Reformation and reaction in Sussex, 1534–1559', *Sussex Archaeological Collections*, 134 (1996).

Görlach, M., *Introduction to early modern English* (Cambridge, 1991).

Gottfried, R. S., *Epidemic disease in fifteenth century England: the medical response and the demographic consequences* (Leicester, 1978).

Gottlieb, B., *The family in the western world from the Black Death to the industrial age* (Oxford, 1993).

Gough, R., *The history of Myddle* (Harmondsworth, 1981).

Green, I., 'Some one-hearth homes in west Penwith', in H. Beaufort-Murphy, ed., *West Penwith at the time of Charles II* (Penzance, 1998).

Hadwin, J. F., 'Deflating philanthropy', *Economic History Review*, 31 (1978).

Hair, P., ed., *Before the bawdy court* (London, 1972).

Hamilton, C., 'The Bridgewater debts', *Huntington Library Quarterly*, 42 (1979).

Hatcher, J. and T. C. Barker, *A history of British pewter* (London, 1974).

Havinden, M. A., 'Agricultural progress in open-field Oxfordshire', *Agricultural History Review*, 9 (1961). Reprinted in E. L. Jones, ed., *Agriculture and economic growth in England, 1650–1815* (London, 1967).

Havinden, M. A., ed., *Household and farm inventories in Oxfordshire, 1550–1590* (London, 1965).

Haward, B., 'Medieval masons', in D. Dymond and E. Martin, eds, *An historical atlas of Suffolk* (Ipswich, 1999).

Heaton, H., *The Yorkshire woollen and worsted industries* (Oxford, 1920).

Helmholz, R. H., 'Debt claims and probate jurisdiction in historical perspective', *American Journal of Legal History*, 23 (1979).

Helmholz, R. H., *Roman canon law in reformation England* (Cambridge, 1990).

Hey, D., *Rural metalworkers of Sheffield* (Leicester, 1972).

Hey, D., *An English rural community: Myddle under the Tudors and Stuarts* (Leicester, 1974).

Hey, D., *Packmen, carriers and packhorse roads* (Leicester, 1980).

Hey, D., 'The origins and early growth of the Hallamshire cutlery and allied trades', in J. Chartres and D. Hey, eds, *English rural society, 1500–1800: essays in honour of Joan Thirsk* (Cambridge, 1990).

Heywood, F. and B. Jennings, *A history of Todmorton* (Otley, 1996).

Hodson, J. H., *Cheshire, 1660–1780: restoration to industrial revolution* (Chester, 1978).

Holderness, B. A., 'Credit in a rural community, 1600–1800: some neglected aspects of probate inventories', *Midland History*, 3 (1975).

Holderness, B. A., 'Credit in English rural society before the nineteenth century; with special reference to the period 1650–1720', *Agricultural History Review*, 24 (1976).

Holderness, B. A., 'The clergy as money lenders', in R. O'Day and F. Heal, eds, *Princes and paupers in the English church, 1500–1800* (Leicester, 1981).

Holderness, B. A., 'East Anglia and the Fens', in J. Thirsk, ed., *The agrarian history of England and Wales, V, i* (Cambridge, 1984).

Holderness, B. A., 'Widows in pre-industrial society: an essay upon their economic functions', in R. M. Smith, ed., *Land, kinship and life-cycle* (Cambridge, 1984).

Holdsworth, W., *A history of English law* (London, 1903–25; reprint 1966–71).

Holme, R., *The academy of armory* (Chester, 1688).

Hoskins, W. G., 'The Leicestershire farmer in the sixteenth century', *Transactions of the Leicestershire Archaeological Society*, 22 (1944–5). Revised version in W. G. Hoskins, *Essays in Leicestershire history* (Liverpool, 1950).

Hoskins, W. G., 'The Leicestershire farmer in the seventeenth century', *Agricultural History*, 25 (1951). Reprinted in W. G. Hoskins, *Provincial England* (London, 1965).

Hoskins, W. G., 'The rebuilding of rural England, 1570–1640', *Past and Present*, 4 (1953). Reprinted in W. G. Hoskins, *Provincial England* (London, 1965).

Hoskins, W. G., 'An Elizabethan provincial town: Leicester', in J. H. Plumb, ed., *Studies in social history* (London, 1955). Reprinted in W. G. Hoskins, *Provincial England* (London, 1965).

Hoskins, W. G., *The Midland peasant* (London, 1957).

Hoskins, W. G., 'The Elizabethan merchants of Exeter', in S. Bindoff and J. Hurstfield, eds, *Elizabeth government and society* (London, 1961). Reprinted in W. G. Hoskins, *Old Devon* (Newton Abbot, 1966) and in P. Clark, ed., *The early modern town: a reader* (London, 1976).

Hoskins, W. G., *Old Devon* (Newton Abbot, 1966).

Hoskins, W. G., *The age of plunder: the England of Henry VIII, 1500–1547* (London, 1976).

Houlbrooke, R., *Church courts and the people during the English Reformation, 1520–1570* (Oxford, 1979).

Houlbrooke, R., *The English family, 1450–1700* (London, 1984).

Houlbrooke, R., *Death, religion and the family in England, 1480–1750* (London, 1988).

Howell, C., 'Peasant inheritance customs in the Midlands, 1280–1700', in J. Goody, J. Thirsk and E. P. Thompson, eds, *Family and inheritance. Rural society in western Europe, 1200–1800* (Cambridge, 1976).

Hudson, P., 'Land, the social structure and industry in two Yorkshire townships *c.*1660–1800', in P. Swan and D. Foster, eds, *Essays in regional and local history* (Beverley, 1992).

Hufton, O., *The prospect before her* (London, 1995).

Humphery-Smith, C. R., ed., *The Phillimore atlas and index of parish registers* (Chichester, 1984).

Jack, S., *Towns in Tudor and Stuart Britain* (London, 1985).

Jackson, G. F., *Shropshire word-book* (London, 1879).

Jennings, B., *A history of Harrogate and Knaresborough* (Huddersfield, 1970).

Jennings, B., ed., *A history of Nidderdale* (York, 3rd ed., 1992).

Jennings, B., ed., *Pennine valley: a history of Upper Calderdale* (Otley, 1992).

Jennings, B., 'The study of local history in the Pennines: the comparative dimension', *Transactions of the Halifax Antiquarian Society*, 3 (1995).

Johnson, S., *A dictionary of the English language* (London, 1775).

Johnston, J. A., 'The probate inventories and wills of a Worcestershire parish, 1676–1775', *Midland History*, 1 (1971).

Johnston, J. A., ed., *Probate inventories of Lincoln citizens, 1661–1714* (Woodbridge, 1991). Lincoln Record Society, 80.

Johnston, J. A., 'Family, kin and community in eight Lincolnshire parishes, 1567–1800', *Rural History*, 6 (1995).

Jones, J., *Family life in Shakespeare's England: Stratford-upon-Avon, 1570–1630* (Stroud, 1996).

Jordan, W. K., *Philanthropy in England, 1480–1640. A study of the changing pattern of English social aspirations* (London, 1959).

Jordan, W. K., *The charities of London, 1480–1660* (abridged ed., Connecticut, 1974, 1st ed. 1960).

Jordan, W. K., *The charities of rural England, 1480–1660* (London, 1961).

Kenyon, G. H., 'Petworth town and trades 1610–1760, part 1', *Sussex Archaeological Collections*, 96 (1958).

Kitching, C., 'Probate during the Civil War and Interregnum', *Journal of the Society of Archivists*, 5 (1976).

Kussmaul, A., *A general view of the rural economy of England, 1538–1840* (Cambridge, 1990).

Lacey, K. E., 'Women and work in fourteenth and fifteenth century London', in L. Charles and L. Duffin, eds, *Women and work in pre-industrial England* (Beckenham, 1985).

Lander, S., 'Church courts and the Reformation in the diocese of Chichester, 1500–1558', in R. O'Day and F. Heal, eds, *Continuity and change: personnel and administration of the church in England, 1500–1642* (Leicester, 1976).

Lansberry, H. C. F., ed., *Sevenoaks wills and inventories in the reign of Charles II* (Maidstone, 1988). Kent Archaeological Society, 25.

Large, P., 'Urban growth and agricultural change in the West Midlands during the seventeenth and eighteenth centuries', in P. Clark, ed., *The transformation of English provincial towns* (London, 1984).

Large, P., 'Rural society and agricultural change: Ombersley, 1580–1700', in J. Chartres and D. Hey, eds, *English rural society, 1500–1800: essays in honour of Joan Thirsk* (Cambridge, 1990).

Leedham-Green, E. and R. Rodd, eds, *Index of the probate records of the Consistory Court of Ely, 1449–1858* (London, 1994–6). British Record Society, 104, 106, 107.

Lemire, B., 'Peddling fashion; salesmen, pawnbrokers, tailors, thieves and the second-hand clothes trade in England, *c.*1770–1800', *Textile History*, 22 (1991).

Levine, D. and K. Wrightson, *The making of an industrial society. Whickham, 1560–1725* (Oxford, 1991).

Litzenberger, C., 'Local responses to changes in religious policy based on evidence from Gloucestershire wills (1540–1580)', *Continuity and Change*, 8 (1993).

Litzenberger, C., 'Responses of the laity to changes in official religious policy in Gloucestershire (1541–1580)' (unpublished Ph.D. thesis, University of Cambridge, 1993).

Lowe, N., *The Lancashire textile industry in the sixteenth century* (Manchester, 1972). Chetham Society, 20.

Lyndwood, W., *Provinciale* (1st ed. 1433, Oxford, 1679; 1st English translation, 1534). Also edited by J. V. Bullard and H. C. Bell (London, 1929).

Lyon-Turner, G., *Original records of early nonconformity under persecution and indulgence* (London, 1911).

MacCaffrey, W. T., *Exeter, 1540–1640: the growth of an English county town* (London, 1958, 2nd ed., Cambridge, Massachusetts, 1975).

Macfarlane, A., ed., *The family life of Ralph Josselin, a seventeenth century clergyman* (Cambridge, 1970).

Macfarlane, A., ed., *The diary of Ralph Josselin, 1616–1683* (London, 1976).

Macfarlane, A., *Reconstructing historical communities* (Cambridge, 1977).

Macfarlane, A., *The origins of English individualism* (Oxford, 1978).

Machin, R., ed., *Probate inventories and manorial excepts of Chetnole, Leigh and Yetminster* (Bristol, 1976).

Maitland, F. W. and M. Bateson, eds, *Cambridge borough charters* (Cambridge, 1901).

Marchant, R. A., *The puritans and the church courts in the diocese of York, 1560–1642* (London, 1960).

Marchant, R. A., *The church under the law: justice, administration and discipline in the diocese of York 1560–1640* (Cambridge, 1969).

Marcombe, D., *English small town life: Retford 1562–1642* (Nottingham, 1993).

Marsh, C., 'In the name of God? Will-making and faith in early modern England', in G. H. Martin and P. Spufford, eds, *The records of the nation* (Woodbridge, 1990).

Marsh, C., *The family of love in English society, 1550–1630* (Cambridge, 1994).

Marshall, J. D., 'Agrarian wealth and social structure in pre-industrial Cumbria', *Economic History Review*, 33 (1980).

Martin, G. H. and P. Spufford, eds, *The records of the nation* (Woodbridge, 1990).

Maslen, M., ed., *Woodstock Chamberlains' Accounts 1609–50* (Oxford, 1993), Oxfordshire Record Society, 58.

Mathews, J. and G. F. Mathews, eds, *Years books of probate, 1630–1653* (6 vols, London, 1902–1913).

Matlock Population Studies Group, 'Wills and their scribes', *Local Population Studies*, 8 (1972).

Mayhew, G. J., 'The progress of the Reformation in east Sussex 1530–1559: the evidence from wills', *Southern History*, 5 (1983).

McDonald, M., 'The brewhouse in the Ironbridge Gorge and further afield' (unpublished MA dissertation, University of Birmingham, Ironbridge Institute, 1987–88).

McIntosh, M. K., *A community transformed: Havering, 1580–1620* (Cambridge, 1991).

McKenna, S. and C. M. Nunn, eds, *Stockport in the mid-seventeenth century, 1660–1669* (Stockport, 1992).

Melton, F. T., *Sir Robert Clayton and the origins of English deposit banking, 1658–1685* (Cambridge, 1986).

Milward, R., *A glossary of household, farming and trade terms from probate inventories* (Chesterfield, 3rd ed., 1986).

Mitchell, I., 'The development of urban retailing, 1700–1815', in P. Clark, ed., *The transformation of English provincial towns* (London, 1984).

Mitson, A., 'The significance of kinship networks in the seventeenth century: south-west Nottinghamshire', in C. Phythian-Adams, ed., *Societies, cultures and kinships, 1580–1850* (Leicester, 1993).

Moore, J. S., ed., *The goods and chattels of our forefathers: Frampton Cotterell and district probate inventories, 1539–1804* (Chichester, 1976).

Moore, J. S., ed., *Clifton and Westbury probate inventories, 1609–1761* (Bristol, 1981).

Moore, J. S., 'Probate inventories: problems and prospects', in P. Riden, ed., *Probate records and the local community* (Gloucester, 1985).

Moore, J. S., ' "Jack Fisher's 'flu": a virus revisited', *Economic History Review*, 46 (1993).

Moore, J. S., ' "Jack Fisher's 'flu": a virus still virulent', *Economic History Review*, 47 (1994).

Motla, P., 'Changing attitudes to poverty in Thame, *c*.1600–*c*.1700', *Oxfordshire Local History*, 4 (1994).

Moyse, M., 'Helpston in the seventeenth and early eighteenth centuries: a study based on wills', *Northamptonshire Past and Present*, 9 (1997/8).

Muldrew, C., 'Credit and the courts: debt litigation in a seventeenth century urban community', *Economic History Review*, 46 (1993).

Munby, L. M., ed., *Life and death in Kings Langley: wills and inventories, 1498–1659* (Kings Langley, 1981).

Nelson, W., *Lex Testamentaria* (1714).

North, C., 'Fustians, figs and frankincense: Jacobean shop inventories for Cornwall', *Journal of the Royal Institution of Cornwall*, NS, 2 (1995).

O'Brien, P. K., 'Agriculture and the home market for English industry, 1660–1820', *English Historical Review*, 50 (1985).

O'Connor, R. D., *The weights and measures of England* (London, 1987).

O'Day, R., *The debate on the English Reformation* (London, 1986).

Orton, H., *The phonology of a south Durham dialect* (London, 1933).

Overton, M., 'Estimating crop yields from probate inventories: an example from East Anglia 1585–1735', *Journal of Economic History*, 39 (1979).

Overton, M., 'English probate inventories and the measurement of agricultural change', in A. van der Woude and A. Schuurman, eds, *Probate inventories: a new source for the historical study of wealth, material culture and agricultural development* (Utrecht, 1980). *Afdeling Agrarische Geschiedenis Bijdragen*, 23.

Overton, M., *A bibliography of British probate inventories* (Newcastle-upon-Tyne, 1983).

Overton, M., 'The diffusion of agricultural innovations in early modern England: turnips and clover in Norfolk and Suffolk 1580–1740', *Transactions of the Institute of British Geographers*, NS, 10 (1985).

Overton, M., 'Re-estimating crop yields from probate inventories: a comment', *Journal of Economic History*, 50 (1990).

Overton, M., 'A computer management system for probate inventories', *History and Computing*, 8 (1995).

Overton, M., *Agricultural revolution in England: the transformation of the agrarian economy 1500–1800* (Cambridge, 1996).

Owen, D. M., ed., *The making of King's Lynn. A documentary survey* (Oxford, 1984).

Palliser, D. M., *The Reformation in York, 1534–1553* (York, 1971).

Palliser, D. M., *Tudor York* (Oxford, 1979).

Palliser, D. M., *The age of Elizabeth: England under the later Tudors, 1547–1603* (Harlow, 1983).

Patten, J., 'Urban occupations in pre-industrial England', *Transactions of the Institute of British Geographers*, 2 (1977).

Patten, J., *English towns, 1500–1700* (Folkestone, 1978).

Patten, J., 'Changing occupational structures in the East Anglian countryside, 1500–1700', in H. S. A. Fox and R. A. Butlin, eds, *Change in the countryside* (London, 1979).

Perkins, J., *A profitable booke . . . treating of the laws of England* (London, 1530).

Perkins, W., *A salve for a sicke man* (Cambridge, 1595).

Perneby, W., *A direction to death* (London, 1599).

Phelps Brown, H. and S. V. Hopkins, 'Seven centuries of the prices of consumables, compared with builders' wage-rates', *Economica*, 23 (1956). Reprinted in H. Phelps Brown and S. V. Hopkins, *A perspective on wages and prices* (London, 1981).

Phillips, C. B., 'Town and country: economic change in Kendal, c.1550–1700', in P. Clark, ed., *The transformation of English provincial towns* (London, 1984).

Phillips, C. B., 'Probate records and the Kendal shoemakers in the seventeenth century', in P. Riden, ed., *Probate records and the local community* (Gloucester, 1985).

Phythian-Adams, C., 'Urban decay in late medieval England', in P. Abrams and E. A. Wrigley, eds, *Towns in societies* (Cambridge, 1978).

Pickles, M. F., 'Agrarian society and wealth in mid-Wharfedale, 1664–1743', *Yorkshire Archaeological Journal*, 53 (1981).

Platt, C., *The great rebuildings of Tudor and Stuart England* (London, 1994).

Plumb, D., 'John Foxe and the later Lollards of the Thames Valley' (unpublished Ph.D. thesis, University of Cambridge, 1987).

Poole, E., 'Will formularies', *Local Population Studies*, 17 (1976).

Portman, D., *Exeter houses, 1400–1700* (Exeter, 1966).

Pound, J. F., 'The validity of the freemen's lists: some Norwich evidence', *Economic History Review*, 34 (1981).

Pounds, N. J. G., *Population of Cornwall before the first census* (Exeter, 1976). Exeter Papers in Economic History, 11.

Pressnell, L. S., *Country banking in the industrial revolution* (Oxford, 1956).

Priestley, U. and P. J. Corfield, 'Rooms and room use in Norwich housing, 1580–1730', *Post-Medieval Archaeology*, 16 (1982).

Prior, M., ed., *Women in English society, 1500–1800* (London, 1985).

Prior, M., 'Wives and wills, 1558–1700', in J. Chartres and D. Hey, eds, *English rural society, 1500–1800: essays in honour of Joan Thirsk* (Cambridge, 1990).

Raine, J., ed., *Testamenta Eboracensia*, vol. 4 (6 vols, Durham, 1836–1902). Publications of the Surtees Society, 53.

Raine, J., ed., *Depositions and other ecclesiastical proceedings from the courts of Durham* (Durham, 1845). Publications of the Surtees Society, 21.

Raine, J., ed., *The register, or rolls, of Walter Gray, Archbishop of York* (Durham, 1872). Publications of the Surtees Society, 56.

Raistrick, A. and B. Jennings, *A history of lead mining in the Pennines* (Littleborough, 1983).

Rappaport, S., *Worlds within worlds: structures of life in sixteenth-century London* (Cambridge, 1989).

Razzell, P., *Essays in English population history* (London, 1994).

Razzell, P., 'The conundrum of eighteenth-century English population growth', *Journal of the Social History of Medicine*, 44 (1998).

Reed, M., 'Economic structure and change in seventeenth-century Ipswich', in P. Clark, ed., *Country towns in pre-industrial England* (London, 1981).

Reed, M., ed., *Buckinghamshire probate inventories, 1661–1714* (Aylesbury, 1988). Buckinghamshire Record Society, 24.

Riden, P., ed., *Probate records and the local community* (Gloucester, 1985).

Ripley, P., 'Village and town: occupations and wealth in the hinterland of Gloucester, 1660–1700', *Agricultural History Review*, 32 (1984).

Roberts, E. and K. Parker, eds, *Southampton probate inventories, 1447–1575* (2 vols, Southampton, 1992). Southampton Records Series, XXXIV.

Rogers, J. E. T., *A history of agriculture and prices in England from the year after the Oxford parliament, 1259, to the commencement of the continental war, 1793* (Oxford, 1866–1902).

Rowlands, M., 'Society and industry in the West Midlands at the end of the seventeenth century', *Midland History*, 4 (1977).

Rowlands, M. B., *Masters and men* (Manchester, 1975).

Salisbury, J., *A glossary of words and phrases used in south-east Worcestershire* (London, 1893).

Schofield, R. S., 'Measurement of illiteracy', in J. Goody, ed., *Literacy in traditional societies* (Cambridge, 1968).

Schofield, R. S., 'Crisis mortality', *Local Population Studies*, 9 (1972).

Schofield, R. S., 'Representativeness and family reconstitution', *Annales de Demographie Historique* (1972).

Schofield, R. S., *Parish register aggregate analysis: the population history of England database and introductory guide* (Colchester, 1998). A *Local Population Studies* supplement.

Serjeant, W. R. and R. K. Serjeant, eds, *Index of the probate records of the court of the archdeacon of Sudbury 1354–1700* (London, 1984). British Record Society, 95–96.

Serjeant, W. R. and R. K. Serjeant, eds, *Index of the probate records of the court of the archdeacon of Suffolk, 1444–1700* (London, 1979–1980). British Record Society, 90–91.

Shammas, C., *The pre-industrial consumer in England and America* (Oxford, 1990).

Shammas, C., 'Changes in English and Anglo-American consumption from 1550 to 1800', in J. Brewer and R. Porter, eds, *Consumption and the world of goods* (London, 1993).

Shaw, S., *History and antiquities of Staffordshire* (London, 1801, reprinted 1976).

Sheail, J., 'The distribution of taxable population and wealth in England during the early sixteenth century', *Transactions of the Institute of British Geographers*, 55 (1972).

Sheehan, M. M., *The will in medieval England* (Toronto, 1963).

Skipp, V., *Crisis and development: an ecological case study of the Forest of Arden, 1570–1674* (Cambridge, 1978).

Skipp, V. H. T., 'Economic and social change in the Forest of Arden 1530–1649', in J. Thirsk, ed., *Land, church and people* (Reading, 1970). *Agricultural History Review* supplement.

Slack, P., 'Introduction', in *The plague reconsidered. A new look at its origins and effects in the sixteenth and seventeenth centuries* (Matlock, 1977). A *Local Population Studies* supplement.

Slack, P., 'Mortality crises and epidemic disease in England, 1485–1610', in C. Webster, ed., *Health, medicine and mortality in the sixteenth century* (Cambridge, 1979).

Slack, P., *The impact of plague in Tudor and Stuart England* (Oxford, 1985).

Slack, P., *Poverty and policy in Tudor and Stuart England* (London, 1988).

Slack, P., *The English poor law, 1531–1782* (Basingstoke, 1990).

Smith, R. M., ed., *Land, kinship and life-cycle* (Cambridge, 1984).

Sogner, S., 'Aspects of the demographic situation in seventeen parishes in Shropshire, 1711–1760', *Population Studies*, 17 (1963).

Spufford, M., 'The significance of the Cambridgeshire hearth tax', *Proceedings of the Cambridgeshire Antiquarian Society*, 55 (1962).

Spufford, M., 'The dissenting churches in Cambridgeshire from 1660 to 1700', *Proceedings of the Cambridgeshire Antiquarian Society*, 61 (1968).

Spufford, M., 'The schooling of the peasantry in Cambridgeshire, 1575–1700', in J. Thirsk, ed., *Land, church and people* (Reading, 1970). *Agricultural History Review* supplement.

Spufford, M., 'Religious preambles and the scribes of villagers' wills in Cambridgeshire, 1570–1700', *Local Population Studies*, 7 (1971).

Spufford, M., 'The social status of some seventeenth century rural dissenters', in G. J. Cuming and D. Baker, eds, *Studies in Church History* 8 (1971).

Spufford, M., *Contrasting communities: English villagers in the sixteenth and seventeenth centuries* (Cambridge, 1974, ppb. 1979).

Spufford, M., 'Peasant inheritance customs and land distribution in Cambridgeshire from the sixteenth to the eighteenth centuries', in J. Goody, J. Thirsk and E. P. Thompson, eds, *Family and inheritance. Rural society in western Europe, 1200–1800* (Cambridge, 1976).

Spufford, M., 'Will formularies', *Local Population Studies*, 19 (1977).

Spufford, M., *Small books and pleasant histories: popular fiction and its readership in seventeenth-century England* (Cambridge, 1981).

Spufford, M., 'The limitations of the probate inventory', in J. Chartres and D. Hey, eds, *English rural society, 1500–1800: essays in honour of Joan Thirsk* (Cambridge, 1990).

Spufford, M., ed., *The world of rural dissenters, 1520–1725* (Cambridge, 1995).

Spufford, M. and M. Takahashi, 'Families, will witnesses, and economic structure in the Fens and on the chalk: sixteenth and seventeenth century Chippenham and Willingham', *Albion*, 28 (1996).

Spufford, P., 'Les liens du crédit au village dans l'Angleterre du XVIIe siècle', *Annales: Histoire, Sciences Sociales*, 6 (1994).

Spufford, P., 'Access to credit and capital in the commercial centres of Europe', in K. Davids and J. Lucassen, eds, *The miracle mirrored. The Dutch republic in European perspective* (Cambridge, 1995).

Spufford, P., M. Brett and A. L. Erickson, eds, *Probate accounts of England and Wales* (2 vols, London, 1999). British Record Society, 112–3.

Stanes, A., 'The peculiar of Uffculme', in P. Wyatt and R. Stanes, eds, *Uffculme a peculiar parish: a Devon town from Tudor times* (Uffculme, 1997).

Steer, F. W., ed., *Farm and cottage inventories of mid-Essex, 1635–1749* (Chelmsford, 1950; reprinted Chichester, 1969).

Stephens, W. B., 'The foreign trade of Plymouth and the Cornish ports in the early 17th century', *Transactions of the Devonshire Association*, 101 (1969).

Stephens, W. B., *Sources for English local history* (Manchester, 1973).

Stoate, T. L., *Cornwall protestation returns, 1641* (Bristol, 1974).

Stone, L., 'Literacy and education in England, 1640–1900', *Past and Present*, 42 (1969).

Stone, L., *The family, sex and marriage in England, 1500–1800* (abridged ed., Harmondsworth, 1979).

Storey, M., ed., *Two East Anglian diaries. Isaac Archer and William Coe* (Woodbridge, 1994). Suffolk Records Society, 36.

Styles, J., 'Manufacturing, consumption and design in eighteenth-century England', in J. Brewer and R. Porter, eds, *Consumption and the world of goods* (London, 1993).

Styles, P., 'The social structure of Kineton hundred in the reign of Charles II', *Transactions of the Birmingham Archaeological Society*, 78 (1962). Reprinted in P. Styles, *Studies in seventeenth century West Midlands history* (Kineton, 1978).

Sundby, B., *Studies in the middle English dialect material of Worcestershire records* (Bergen/Oslo, 1963).

Sutton, C., *Disce mori* (1600).

Swinburne, H., *A briefe treatise of testaments and last wills* (London, 1635, 1677, 1st ed. 1590).

Takahashi, M., 'The number of wills proved in the sixteenth and seventeenth centuries. Graphs, will tables and commentary', in G. H. Martin and P. Spufford, eds, *The records of the nation* (Woodbridge, 1990).

Tarver, A., *Church court records* (Chichester, 1995).

Tawney, A. J. and R. H. Tawney, 'An occupational census of the seventeenth century', *Economic History Review*, 5 (1934–1935).

Thirsk, J., *English peasant farming* (London, 1957).

Thirsk, J., 'Industries in the countryside', in F. J. Fisher, ed., *Essays in the economic and social history of Tudor and Stuart England* (Cambridge, 1961).

Thirsk, J., *Unexplored sources in local records: sources of information on population, 1500–1760* (Chichester, 1965).

Thirsk, J., ed., *The agrarian history of England and Wales, IV, 1500–1640* (Cambridge, 1967).

Thirsk, J., 'The farming regions of England', in J. Thirsk, ed., *The agrarian history of England and Wales, IV, 1500–1640* (Cambridge, 1967).

Thirsk, J., ed., *Land, church and people* (Reading, 1970).

Thirsk, J., 'Seventeenth century agriculture and social change', in J. Thirsk, ed., *Land, church and people* (Reading, 1970). An *Agricultural History Review* supplement.

Thirsk, J., *Economic policy and projects: the development of a consumer society in early modern England* (Oxford, 1978).

Thirsk, J., ed., *The agrarian history of England and Wales, V, 1640–1750* (2 vols, Cambridge, 1984–1985).

Thompson, E. P., 'The grid of inheritance: a comment', in J. Goody, J. Thirsk and E. P. Thompson, eds, *Family and inheritance. Rural society in western Europe, 1200–1800* (Cambridge, 1976).

Thurley, C. and D. Thurley, eds, *Index of the probate records of the court of the archdeacon of Ely, 1513–1857* (London, 1970). British Record Society, 88.

Tiller, K., 'Shopkeeping in seventeenth-century Oxfordshire', *Oxoniensia*, 62 (1997).

Todd, B., 'Freebench and free enterprise: widows and their property in two Berkshire villages', in J. Chartres and D. Hey, eds, *English rural society, 1500–1800: essays in honour of Joan Thirsk* (Cambridge, 1990).

Todd, B. J., 'The remarrying widow: a stereotype reconsidered', in M. Prior, ed., *Women in English society* (London, 1985).

Trinder, B., *The industrial archaeology of Shropshire* (Chichester, 1996).

Trinder, B., *The industrial revolution in Shropshire* (Chichester, 2nd ed., 1981).

Trinder, B. and J. Cox, eds, *Yeomen and colliers in Telford: probate inventories for Dudley, Lilleshall, Wellington and Wrockwardine, 1660–1750* (Chichester, 1980).

Tucker, M., 'Houses, furnishings and household equipment', in P. Wyatt and R. Stanes, eds, *Uffculme a peculiar parish: a Devon town from Tudor times* (Uffculme, 1997).

Turner, M., 'Post-medieval colonisation in the forests of Bowland, Knaresborough and Pickering' (unpublished Ph.D. thesis, Hull University, 1987).

Turner, M., ed., *Kith and kin: Nidderdale familes, 1500–1750* (Knaresborough, 1995).

Vaisey, D. G., ed., *Probate inventories of Lichfield and district, 1568–1680* (1969). Staffordshire Record Society, 5.

Vaisey, D.G., ed., *Diary of Thomas Turner, 1754–1765* (Oxford and New York, 1984).

Vaisey, D. G., 'Probate inventories and provincial retailers in the seventeenth century', in P. Riden, ed., *Probate records and the local community* (Gloucester, 1985).

van der Woude, A. and A. Schuurman, eds, *Probate inventories: a new source for the historical study of wealth, material culture and agricultural development* (Utrecht, 1980). *Afdeling Agrarische Geschiedenis Bijdragen*, 23.

Vann, R. T., 'Wills and the family in an English town: Banbury, 1550–1800', *Journal of Family History*, 4 (1979).

Wadley, T. P., ed., *Notes on the wills in the Great Orphan Book and Book of Wills at Bristol* (Bristol, 1886). Bristol and Gloucestershire Archaeological Society, 1–5.

Wales, T., 'Poverty, poor relief and life cycle', in R. M. Smith, ed., *Land, kinship and life-cycle* (Cambridge, 1984).

Weatherill, L., 'Consumer behaviour and social status in England, 1660–1750', *Continuity and Change*, 2 (1986).

Weatherill, L., *Consumer behaviour and material culture in Britain, 1660–1760* (London, 1988).

Weatherill, L., 'The meaning of consumer behaviour', in J. Brewer and R. Porter, eds, *Consumption and the world of goods* (London, 1993).

Weiner, E. S. C., 'The use of non-literary manuscript texts for the study of dialect lexis', in E. W. Schneider, ed., *Englishes around the world* (Amsterdam/Philadelphia, 1997).

West, W., *Symbolaeographia* (London, 1590).

Whetter, J., *Cornwall in the seventeenth century* (Padstow, 1974).

Whiteman, A. and V. Russell, 'The Protestation returns, 1641–1642: Part II, Partial census or snapshot? Some evidence from Penwith Hundred, Cornwall', *Local Population Studies*, 56 (1996).

Whiting, R., *The blind devotion of the people* (Cambridge, 1989).

Whittle, J., 'Inheritance, marriage, widowhood and remarriage: a comparative perspective on women and landholding in north-east Norfolk, 1440–1580', *Continuity and Change*, 13 (1998).

Wilbraham, R., 'An attempt at a glossary of some words used in Cheshire', *Archaeologia*, 19 (1818).

Willis, A. J., *Church life in Kent being church court records of the Canterbury diocese, 1559–1565* (Chichester, 1975).

Wright, S., '"Churmaids, huswyfes and hucksters": the employment of women in Tudor and Stuart Salisbury', in L. Charles and L. Duffin, eds, *Women and work in pre-industrial England* (Beckenham, 1985).

Wrightson, K. and D. Levine, *Poverty and piety in an English village: Terling* (Oxford, 1979, 1995).

Wrigley, E. A., *Population and History* (London, 1969).

Wrigley, E. A., 'Births and baptisms: the use of Anglican baptism registers as a source of information about the number of births in England before the beginning of civil registration', *Population Studies*, 31 (1977).

Wrigley, E. A., 'How reliable is our knowledge of the demographic characteristics of the English population in the early modern period?', *Historical Journal*, 40 (1997).

Wrigley, E. A. and R. S. Schofield, *The population history of England 1541–1871: a reconstruction* (London, 1981).

Wyatt, P., ed., *The Uffculme wills and inventories* (1997). Devon and Cornwall Record Society, 40.

Wyatt, P. and R. Stanes, eds, *Uffculme a peculiar parish: a Devon town from Tudor times* (Uffculme, 1997).

Yelling, J. A., *Common field and enclosure in England 1450–1850* (London, 1977).

Zell, M., 'Wealth, trades and agriculture in the Elizabethan Weald', in A. Detsicas and N. Yates, eds, *Studies in modern Kentish history* (Maidstone, 1983).

Zell, M., 'The social parameters of probate records in the sixteenth century', *Bulletin of the Institute of Historical Research*, 57 (1984).

Zell, M., ' "Fisher's 'flu and Moore's probates": quantifying the mortality crisis of 1556–60', *Economic History Review*, 47 (1994).

Zell, M., *Industry in the countryside: Wealden society in the sixteenth century* (Cambridge, 1994).

Zupko, R. E., *British weights and measures* (Madison, Wisconsin, 1977).

Index of Subjects

accounts, probate, 10, 34–6, 103–19,
  229–52
  accountants' expenses, 110–13
  the accounting process, 110–14
  and child-rearing, 247–51
  content of, 103, 107–10, 118–19, 214,
    229, 236–8
  courts' fees, 112, 237
  debts and credits in, 108, 110–11,
    116–17, 213–28
  debts in, 113, 115, 237, 299–300
  disputed, 240, 245–51
  example of, 239
  exhibited with inventory, 251
  format of, 33, 118
  funeral costs in, 108, 237, 300
  as an historical source, 114–19, 236–52
  compared with Hearth Taxes, 105,
    107
  and inheritance, 109
  compared with inventories, 112,
    116–17, 214, 229
  landholding in, 108–9, 221–2
  and litigation, 114–15
  marriage settlements in, 109
  medical expenses in, 108
  and orphans, 108, 116–18
  outstanding obligations in, 108
  prices in, 108
  real property in, 221–2
  reluctance to produce, 234–5
  requirement for, 35–6, 114–15
  and social status, 244
  survival of, 35–6, 104–7, 115–16,
    214–15, 218, 230–2, 234–6, 238–47
  values of, 244–5
  and wealth, 116–18
  used with wills, 109
administration bonds, 20–1
administration, letters of, 9, 21, 23
administrators
  checks on, 25–34, 35–6, 112–14
  identity of, 9, 20, 29, 110
  motives of, 28
  responsibilities of, 8, 9, 11, 17–18,
    25–30, 35, 103

  widows as, 9, 20, 110
agriculture, 74–9
  in Cambridgeshire, 182
  crops, 74–9, 280–4, 317
  crop yields, 78–9
  dairying, 75–7, 273–4
  enclosure, 74, 182
  equipment, 78
  field patterns, 74
  labourers, in Cambridgeshire, 183–5
  livestock, 75–7, 317–18
  merchants and retailers in, 300
Arches, Court of, 15–16

Bacon, Francis, 263
Becon, Thomas, 169–71, 175
Blackwell Hall, 326
Bridgnorth Fair, 125
Burn, Richard, 16, 23, 25, 26, 29, 30,
  33, 124, 126

Carew, Richard, 286, 288–9, 304
charity, 50–4, 302, 321–2
  in Cornwall, 302
children
  provision for, 8, 10, 108, 117–18,
    225–6, 302
  rearing of, 247–51, 312
commerce
  see trade
consumption patterns, 89–92, 101,
  279–80, 286, 294–5
  in Cornwall, 286, 294–9
courts
  civil, 27–8, 110
  ecclesiastical, 3–7, 110, 126
  ecclesiastical, impact of Civil Wars and
    Interregnum, 4, 179, 233
  ecclesiastical, decline of, 4
  ecclesiastical, fees in, 7–9, 12, 26, 235
  ecclesiastical, jurisdiction of, 5–7, 9,
    11, 15–17, 35–6, 232–4, 247
  manorial, 233
  manorial, and landholding, 7–8, 22,
    66–8, 333–6
  of orphans, 17, 38

413

courts (*cont.*):
  peculiar, 6, 11, 15–16, 27, 230, 233
  Vice-Chancellor's, 11, 17, 178, 193
credit
  see debts and credit

debts and credit
  in Cornwall, 302, 318–21
  credit, 82–3
  debts, 7, 8, 10, 28–9, 82–3, 299–300
  debts, in inventories, 100–1
  debts, litigation over, 216
  debts, types of, 215–16
  interest rates, 219–21, 319
  lenders, 223–26
  mortgages, 221–2, 224–5
  pawnbroking, 319
  reasons for borrowing, 222–3
  relationship of borrowers and lenders,
    223–7, 319–21
  rural, 213–28
dower, 24, 311–13
dowry, 22–3, 225–6, 312
dual occupations, 61–2, 79–80, 84, 182,
    300, 325–8

entails, 24–5
estate, charges on, 8
executors
  checks on, 25–34, 35–6, 112–14
  identity of, 23, 29, 65–6, 110,
    299–300, 309
  motives of, 28
  refusal to act, 9, 20
  responsibilities of, 8, 9, 11, 17–18,
    25–30, 35, 103
  women as, 293–4, 303

family
  affective relationships, 65–6, 109
  see also children, kinship
fens
  draining of, 177, 183–4
  economy of, 184
fertility
  see population
fishing, 183, 301–2
freebench, 23
friends and neighbours, 65, 164–5,
    226–7

Great Rebuilding, the, 86

Hearth Tax, 73–4, 88–9, 105, 107, 310,
    333
  widows in, 310
Herrick, Robert, 263
Holdsworth, William, 14, 37
Holme, Randall, 277–9, 281, 282
housing
  rural, 85–9, 272–3
  urban, 87–8, 298

industry
  in Cambridgeshire, 182–3, 186
  and inheritance patterns, 333–6
  knitting, 333
  lead-mining, 325–6, 333
  leather, 81–2, 325
  malting, 177
  metalworking, 61, 62, 79–80, 332–3
  textiles, 58, 61, 80–1, 282, 326–32
  tin-mining, 301
  urban, 58–9, 61, 83–5, 87–8, 329–30
  in Yorkshire, 325–36
inheritance, 19–25, 66–9, 333–5
  disputes over, 8, 10–11, 18–19, 33
  of land, 7–8, 18, 22–3, 31–32, 44,
    48–9, 66–9, 333–6
  in towns, 68
  by women, 22–4, 62–3, 65, 69,
    311–14
intestacy, 9–10, 19, 20, 22, 109, 236–7,
    245
inventories, probate, 72–102
  compared with accounts, 299–300
  and agriculture, 74–9, 280–4, 300
  appraisers of, 293–4
  books in, 94–5
  cash in, 321
  cash and clothes in, 298–9
  clothes in, 92–3, 317
  content of, 30–1, 34, 269–72,
    291–302
  content of, in Cornwall, 291–302
  coopery ware in, 274–8
  crops in, 74–9, 317
  debts in, 31, 299–300, 314–15,
    318–21
  debts in, in Cornwall, 299–300
  fabrics in, 294

Index of Places and Ecclesiastical Jurisdictions

Places

Bedfordshire, 85
  Studham, 226
Berkshire, 107, 201
  Reading, 40, 45, 47, 49, 58, 59, 60, 62, 63, 190–212
Buckinghamshire, 53
  Fawley, 224–5
  Marlow, 216
  Winslow, 220

Cambridgeshire, 11, 60, 72, 86, 88, 95, 98, 107, 112, 114, 144–57, 166, 171, 176–88, 226
  Balsham, 146–7, 153, 166
  Cambridge, 11, 45, 46, 47, 48–9, 58, 59, 60, 61–2, 88, 172–3, 177, 178, 179, 183, 185–6, 190–212, 223
  Cambridge University, 11, 17, 131–2, 139, 178, 205, 207–8, 224
  Chesterton, 177
  Chippenham, 65, 67–8, 177, 182, 218, 224
  Cottenham, 157
  Ely, 113, 171, 177, 179, 181
  Horningsea, 166
  Ickleton, 171
  Isle of Ely, 60, 177, 183, 184
  Linton, 177, 185–6, 188
  Little Shelford, 160, 165, 166
  Little Wilbraham, 146–7
  Littleport, 177, 185–6, 188
  Meldreth, 164
  Milton, 175
  Orwell, 54, 67–8, 144, 145–6, 147–52, 154–7, 182
  Shudy Camps, 166
  Soham, 177
  Sutton, 160–1
  Swavesey, 160, 162, 163–4
  Whittlesey, 170

Willingham, 44, 54, 65, 67–8, 151–7, 162, 177, 184
Wisbech, 166
Cheshire, 77, 86, 96, 107, 279, 281
  Chester, 19, 83, 96
  Daresbury, 221
  Stockport, 87, 89, 94
Cornwall, 75, 78, 86, 89, 91, 98, 99, 100, 101, 107, 285–305
  Bodmin, 286, 287, 290, 302
  Falmouth, 289
  Fowey, 287, 289, 290, 291, 295, 299, 301
  Golant, 291
  Helston, 287, 291, 298, 299–300, 302
  Kenwyn, 301
  Launceston, 286, 287, 290, 295, 300, 302
  Liskeard, 286, 287, 288, 290, 294, 298, 299, 302
  Lostwithiel, 287, 300
  Madron, 290
  Millbrook, 287, 290
  Mitchell, 287
  Padstow, 287
  Penryn, 289
  Penzance, 287, 289, 290, 301
  Saltash, 287, 290, 294, 298
  St Columb Major, 287, 288, 298
  St Ives, 287, 289, 290, 291, 298, 301, 302
  Stratton, 287
  Tregony, 287, 288, 290, 294, 295, 304
  Truro, 287, 289, 290, 294, 298, 299–300, 302
Cumberland, 77
  Whitehaven, 68
Cumbria, 83, 89–90, 99

Derbyshire, 230, 232, 235, 245
  Allestree, 248
  Brailsford, 250
  Caldwell, 248